CREATIVE INDUSTRIES IN INDIA

As digitalization meets local traditions, there is great potential for creative industries (CI) to promote economic and social development in middle- and low-income countries. This book explores the economic and cultural relevance of these industries in India.

The book identifies key topics regarding cultural and creative industries in India, which has a rich cultural heritage and a young demographic and is undergoing swift socio-economic change. It contains the most sophisticated and comprehensive mappings of CI in India to date. It also features numerous case studies, which illuminate the growth of CI in India, its intersections with caste and gender, the central role of handloom, handicraft, and other local practices within communities, as well as the specific challenges in safeguarding and harnessing various creative industry assets to promote sustainable development and social change.

Rich with empirical data, this book will be an essential read for scholars and researchers of cultural studies, economics, history, social work, development studies, media studies, and South Asian studies.

Abdul Shaban is Professor at the School of Development Studies, Tata Institute of Social Sciences, Deonar, Mumbai, India.

Filip Vermeylen is Professor of Global Art Markets at the Department of Arts and Culture Studies at Erasmus University Rotterdam, the Netherlands.

Christian Handke is Associate Professor (tenured) of Cultural Economics at Erasmus University Rotterdam, the Netherlands.

CREATIVE INDUSTRIES IN INDIA

Edited by Abdul Shaban, Filip Vermeylen and Christian Handke

Routledge
Taylor & Francis Group
LONDON AND NEW YORK

Cover image: Bhagyalakshmi Daga

First published 2023
by Routledge
4 Park Square, Milton Park, Abingdon, Oxon OX14 4RN

and by Routledge
605 Third Avenue, New York, NY 10158

Routledge is an imprint of the Taylor & Francis Group, an informa business

British Library Cataloguing-in-Publication Data
A catalogue record for this book is available from the British Library

ISBN: 978-0-367-61503-1 (hbk)
ISBN: 978-0-367-65424-5 (pbk)
ISBN: 978-1-003-12937-0 (ebk)

DOI: 10.4324/9781003129370

Typeset in Bembo
by Apex CoVantage, LLC

CONTENTS

FIGURES

TABLES

CONTRIBUTORS

Zinat Aboli is Assistant Professor in the Department of Multimedia and Mass Communication, Mithibai College, Vile Parle (West), Mumbai. She has served as the head of the department for several years. She is a sociologist, and her research interests include gender, inequality, social media, creative industries, and women entrepreneurs.

Purushottam Bhandare is a research scholar at the School of Management and Labour Studies, Tata Institute of Social Sciences (TISS), Mumbai. He received an Executive Post Graduate Diploma in Analytics and MPhil in management and labour studies from TISS, Mumbai; an MBA in banking technology from Pondicherry University; and Master of Business Laws from the National Law School of India University, Bangalore. His broad fields of interest are financial inclusion, digital finance, financial literacy, and data analytics. He is a member of the Indian Science Congress and the Indian Association of Social Sciences and Health. He is associated with IFactor as a data and research consultant.

Philippe Cadène is Professor of Geography and Development Studies at the Université de Paris and member of the CESSMA laboratory. He has conducted various research projects on India over the past four decades and produced numerous publications on globalization, social changes, and economic development in this country. His research topics focus on metropolitan dynamics, regional development, and entrepreneurial networks. He is currently the director of the GHES School (Geography, History, Economy and Society) in his university where he also heads the master's degree 'Dynamics of Emerging and Developing Countries'.

Meghamrita Chakraborty is a doctoral researcher at the School of Development Studies, TISS. She completed her master's in geography from the Centre for the Study of Regional Development (CSRD), The Jawaharlal Nehru University, New Delhi. She has submitted and completed her MPhil dissertation on 'Street Vendors in Urban Economy: Study of Garment Selling Vendors in Mumbai' from TISS, Mumbai. She was awarded the Erasmus

Plus Fellowship by the Erasmus University Rotterdam, the Netherlands, and has been the recipient of the ICSSR Short Term Fellowship for PhD students. Her areas of interests are urban and industrial geography, creative economy, innovation, and entrepreneurism in India. She is currently working on industrial and creative entrepreneurial clusters in India.

Ujjwal Dadhich is a PhD scholar at the School of Development Studies, Tata Institute for Social Sciences. His research interests include creative communities, urban development, urban water governance, collective action, and traditional water management systems.

Bhagyalakshmi Daga is a lecturer and PhD candidate at the Erasmus School of History, Culture and Communication at the Erasmus University Rotterdam (EUR) in the Netherlands. She graduated with a master's in cultural economics and entrepreneurship at EUR. Her PhD project focuses on the impact of informality on the socio-economic development of the independent music industry in India. Her research interests include cultural and creative industries, digitalization, and the informal economy.

Aleem Faizee is a journalist, founder editor of ummid.com, and visiting lecturer at J.A.T. Arts, Science and Commerce College, Malegaon, Maharashtra. He has written extensively on Mollywood and textile industry of Malegaon in several leading English and regional newspapers of India.

Christian Handke, PhD, is Associate Professor of Cultural Economics at Erasmus University Rotterdam. From 2012 to 2018, he was programme director of the Master in Cultural Economics and Entrepreneurship programme. Christian Handke's research focuses on cultural and creative industries, cultural economics, innovation and technological change, as well as the economics of copyright, and text and data mining. He has contributed to leading specialized journals in these fields, such as the *Journal of Cultural Economics* and *Information Economics and Policy*. He has consulted for a variety of public and private organizations, including the European Commission, the National Academies of the Sciences (USA), Industry Canada, the UK Intellectual Property Office, the federal German Expert Commission on Research and Innovation (EFI), the federal German Ministry of Justice and Consumer Protection, and the Spanish Fundación Autor. Christian Handke is currently the president of the Society for Economic Research on Copyright Issues (SERCI), executive board member of the Association of Cultural Economics International (ACEI), and associate editor of the *Journal of Cultural Economics*.

Ellen Loots is Assistant Professor of Cultural Economics and Entrepreneurship in the Department of Arts and Culture Studies at Erasmus University Rotterdam, the Netherlands. She obtained a PhD in applied economics from Antwerp University (Belgium) on evaluation processes in arts and culture. In her research, Ellen investigates how the performance of organizations in the creative industries leads to organizational change and how diverse types of value are created and evaluated by various stakeholders. Her focus is on the socio-dynamic processes (including collaboration and cooperation) within organizations and the micro-foundations (including motivation, personality, behaviour) of entrepreneurship.

Gandharva Pednekar is Research Scholar and Teaching Assistant at the School of Development Studies, TISS, Mumbai, where he is currently pursuing his PhD programme in development studies. He holds postgraduate degrees in geography, population studies, and development administration, and an MPhil in development studies. He has been assistant writer for two regional films, viz. *Shree Partner* (2012) and *Judgement* (2019). His broad fields of interest are Indian cinema, population and development, urban geography, corporate social responsibility, resettlement and rehabilitation, and research methodology. He is also associated with Yusuf Meherally Centre, Utkarsh Sanstha, and the Family Welfare Agency as a social research consultant.

Rinku is currently engaged in PhD research at the School of Development Studies, TISS, Mumbai. His research interests are broadly centred on public policy, value chain analysis, creative industries, creative entrepreneurship, social entrepreneurship, urban development, and so on. Currently, he is working on the 'Value Chain Analysis of Chikankari: A Creative Industry Cluster of Lucknow'. His MPhil dissertation topic is 'Industrial Clusters at Peripheries of Mega-Cities: A Case Study of Bhiwandi's Power Loom Industry'.

Sanjukta Sattar is Professor in the Department of Geography at the University of Mumbai. She is currently working on the industrial and craft geographies of India. She has published several papers on tourism and social issues in Indian cities. Her areas of interest include urban socio-spatial segregation, social exclusion, urban infrastructure, and the role and impact of tourism.

Abdul Shaban is Professor at the School of Development Studies, Tata Institute of Social Sciences, Mumbai, India. He is an urban geographer and economist with research interests in issues related to cities, entrepreneurship, creative industries, and religious minorities. He is especially interested in research on creative clusters, creative cities, and possibilities of using creative and cultural industries for social, local, and regional development. He has been a member of various committees and commissions formed by the states and the central government, India. He has also been a visiting professor/fellow at several universities, which include LSE, UK, Muenster University, Germany, Erasmus University, the Netherlands, and Paris Diderot University, France.

S.S. Sripriya holds a master's degree in management studies from the University of Mumbai and an MPhil and PhD in rural development from TISS, Mumbai. Her main areas of interest include ageing, migration, and informal economy. She participated in the 'International Training Programme on Social Gerontology', organized by the UN International Institute on Ageing, Malta and ILC-India. She has recently worked as a programme officer in the International Institute for Population Sciences, Mumbai, in a UN-sponsored project in the area of population ageing. She has authored a book titled *Skilling Youth for India's Development* and published eight scientific papers in peer-reviewed journals/edited volumes. She has presented papers in over 15 national and international conferences/seminars on various developmental issues including population ageing in India. She is a member of the Indian Association for Social Sciences and Health and a senior research fellow (Honorary) at The International Institute of Migration and Development, Thiruvananthapuram, Kerala, India.

Filip Vermeylen (PhD, Columbia University, 2002) is Professor of Global Art Markets at the Erasmus University Rotterdam and is currently Research Director of the Department of Arts and Culture Studies. He lectures and publishes on various aspects of the economics of art and culture. He is especially interested in the history and functioning of art markets since the Renaissance, the notion of quality in the visual arts, the role of intermediaries as arbiters of taste, and emerging art markets, with a special focus on India. He is a board member of The International Art Market Association (TIAMSA) and co-founder and board member of the Rotterdam Arts & Sciences Lab (www.rasl.nu).

ACKNOWLEDGEMENTS

India is a culturally diverse country and rich in the traditional creative sector. It also has rapidly developing modern creative sectors like IT, design, cinema, TV, and creative service industries. However, there has been a lack of any detailed examination of the size, diversity, and distribution of the creative sector in India. A meeting of the three editors in 2017 at Erasmus University Rotterdam led to the firming up of the idea of bringing out a volume on the creative economy of India to fill this gap. Professor Abdul Shaban and Professor Filip Vermeylen are very thankful to the ICSSR, New Delhi and NWO, the Netherlands, for financial assistance to initiate initial work on creative industries in India. The ICSSR-NWO research and visit grants made possible to collect the needed data and have ideas on a comprehensive volume on this sector.

The Erasmus Plus and ICSSR, New Delhi, fundings during 2018–19 made it possible for the editors and some of the PhD students of both the institutions to visit India and the Netherlands respectively and to organize a joint conference at TISS in 2018 and later at Erasmus University Rotterdam, in 2019. The success of these conferences confirmed the potential for an edited volume.

We have received encouragement and support from several individuals and organizations, which led to this volume. Professor Abdul Shaban would like to thank Professor Shalini Bharat, the director of TISS, who provided institutional support and encouragement. Professor Shaban would also like to especially thank Professor S. Parasuraman, former director of Tata Institute of Social Sciences (TISS), and Professor Andy Pratt for their initial support.

The original plan had been to submit the final manuscript to the publisher in November 2020. The outbreak of COVID-19 in March 2020 affected the families of some of the editors and authors, which delayed the submission of the final manuscript. We are particularly grateful to Ms Shoma Choudhury and her colleagues at Routledge for their patience and excellent publishing support under these challenging circumstances.

Finally, we must acknowledge the inevitable limitations of our edited volume. There is a huge scope for extending the mapping and documentation of creative industries in India. The wealth and idiosyncrasies of this sector in the subcontinent are as bewildering as it is inspiring. We hope our work will help others to extend, refine, and challenge the ideas expressed in this volume.

ABBREVIATIONS

AIC	Akaike Information Criterion
AVW	Audio-Visual Workers
BAHVY	Baba Saheb Ambedkar Hastshilp Vikas Yojana
BRLP	Bihar Rural Livelihoods Promotion Society
CAGR	Compound Annual Growth Rate
CBC	Canadian Broadcasting Corporation
CCI	Cultural and Creative Industries
CD	Compact Disc
CEPC	Carpet Export Promotion Council
CHCDS	Comprehensive Handloom Cluster Development Scheme
CI	Creative Industries
CII	The Confederation of Indian Industry
CISAC	The International Confederation of Societies of Authors and Composers
CIW	Creative Industry Workers
CMC	Computer Maintenance Corporation
CMIE	Centre for Monitoring Indian Economy
CSTW	Cultural Sites Workers
CSW	Cultural Service Workers
DE	Directory Establishment
DI	Digital Industry
DIT	Department of Information Technology
DJ	Disc Jockey
DSW	Design Sector Workers
DVD	Digital Versatile Disc
EC	Economic Census
EY	Ernst & Young
FICCI	The Federation of Indian Chambers of Commerce and Industry
GVA	Gross Value Addition
HHW	Handloom and Handicraft Workers
IBEF	Indian Brand Equity Foundation
ICT	Information and Communication Technologies

IFPI	International Federation of the Phonographic Industry
ILO	International Labour Organization
IMI	Indian Music Industry
INR	Indian Rupee
IP	Intellectual Property
IPR	Intellectual Property Right
IT	Information Technology
ITES	IT-enabled Services
MAI	Mithila Art Institute
MDH	Mahashian Di Hatti
ML	Maximum Likelihood
MoSPI	Ministry of Statistics and Programme Implementation, Government of India
MSME	Micro, Small, and Medium Enterprises
NDE	Non-directory Establishment
NGO	Non-governmental Organization
NHDP	National Handicrafts Development Programme
NIC	National Industrial Classification
NMW	New Media Workers
OAE	Own Account Establishment
OBC	Other Backward Classes
ODOP	One District One Product
OLS	Ordinary Least Square
OMR	Optical Mark Recognition
OTT	Over the Top
P2P	Peer-to-Peer
PPMW	Publishing and Print Media Workers
PSBT	Public Service Broadcasting Trust
R&D	Research and Development
SC	Scheduled Caste
TV	Television
UN	United Nations
UNCTAD	United Nations Conference on Trade and Development
UNESCO	United Nations Educational, Scientific, and Cultural Organization
UNFPA	United Nations Population Fund
VAW	Visual Art Workers
VCD	Video Compact Disc
VHS	Video Home System

Section I

CONCEPTS, METHODS, AND INTRODUCTION TO THE VOLUME

Research on cultural and creative industries (CCI) in India needs to respond to diverse and idiosyncratic circumstances. Accordingly, the first section in this volume addresses some fundamental and pervasive issues: what are the most useful conceptual frameworks and definitions for CCI research in India? What adaptations are required for specific research endeavours? Why are market failures common in CCI? Considering the scope for government failure, what is the adequate ambition and extent of public cultural policy? What are the most useful sources of data to identify the size and geographies of CCI in India? The general introduction in Chapter 1, jointly authored by the volume editors, discusses the motivation behind this book in a nutshell to provide information on how better to promote and harness CCI for desirable socio-economic development in India. The chapter introduces general issues in research on CCI and related policies, and specific opportunities and challenges in the case of India. It also takes stock of some general themes that emerge across this volume regarding CCI in India, including relevant reports and sources of data, growth of Indian CCI, clustering patterns, the social embeddedness of CCI in India, informal organizations, and the peculiar coincidence and occasional linkages between traditional, pre-industrial modes of production in some Indian CCI with a wider trend of digitalization. Chapter 2 draws on general economics as well as on the sub-discipline of cultural economics. It challenges several common but misleading pre-conceived ideas and identifies overarching research questions regarding CCI in India. Chapter 3 applies the United Nations Conference on Trade and Development's (UNCTAD) sophisticated classification system of CCI and its various components to the Indian situation. It lays the foundations for the ambitious geographical mapping of Indian CCI in Section II. Section I also illustrates that research on Indian CCI has the potential to generate new insights and help improve the state of the art in generic CCI research.

DOI: 10.4324/9781003129370-1

1

INTRODUCTION

Abdul Shaban, Filip Vermeylen and Christian Handke

Over the last decades, cultural and creative industries (CCI) have received much attention in debates on economic policy and socio-economic development (UNCTAD 2018; Lee 2014; Hesmondhalgh and Pratt 2005; Potts 2009). There is sustained interest in the role of CCI in urban and regional development, employment generation, export earnings, poverty alleviation, and soft power, for instance. This volume seeks to foster the debate on how to support and harness CCI to promote desirable development, from sustainable wealth generation to civil society and social cohesion, in India.

Cultural industries today are addressed as a central piece in liberal societies and market economies, which generate wealth and attractive job opportunities in their own right, and can help promote creativity, innovation, and quality of life in other parts of society.[1] We are certain that this pragmatic perspective is useful.

At the heart of the concept of 'cultural industries' lay the arts and culture – the fine and performing arts, arts and craft (particularly important in India), music, literature, and other fictional media content, such as movies, television series, or video games – which serve broad and somewhat elusive purposes for entertainment, inspiration, and education. 'Creative industries' are a broader concept, including the cultural industries, but also other industries, where creative human labour generates highly differentiated goods and services – from advertising to architecture, from fashion to industrial design, cuisine, and even functional computer software or any type of research – which convey symbolic meaning. For influential discussions and documentations of the development of these concepts, see, for instance, Caves (2000), Cunningham (2001), Throsby (2001) Garnham (2005), Galloway and Dunlop (2007), Potts and Cunningham (2008), or UNCTAD (2010). In this volume, in particular, Chapters 2 and 3 engage with definitional issues. This volume mostly deals with a variety of cultural industries and related practices in India. In a sense, we focus on core aspects of the concept. A notable and deliberate exception are Chapters 4 to 6, which develop sophisticated mappings of CCI in India and thus yield a reasonably comprehensive overview of the core (cultural industries) and its more hybrid extensions in the rest of the creative industries, in as far as the official, quantitative data goes.

DOI: 10.4324/9781003129370-2

Three stylized facts motivate this volume. First, CCI have great potential to contribute to socio-economic development. Second, across the CCI, there is a considerable diversity and many idiosyncrasies, which should be well understood in order to better promote and harness this sector under specific circumstances. Third, much work remains to develop adequate related policies for middle-income countries such as India. Let us consider these points, and how they relate to each other, in a little more detail.

1.1 CCI and socio-economic development

With increasing prosperity, there has been a significant shift towards the consumption of creative goods and services around the world. In G-7 countries this shift is very conspicuous. While quantitative indicators remain questionable because of definitional challenges, Ryan (2003), for instance, estimates that about half of all consumer spending in G-7 countries is now on creative goods and services, broadly defined. Other, relatively modest but still rather impressive, estimates are that CCI account for about 11% of GDP in the USA and about 10% in South Korea (CISAC 2014).

These are the results of reasonably consistent trends over decades, and there may well be a rather general pattern of disproportionally strong growth in CCI in conjunction with socio-economic development. As Kebir and Crevoisier (2008: 54) observe, "During the Fordist period, economic development and cultural development were more frequently opposed than integrated. Cultural development meant creation and liberation, whereas economic development signified routine, the reproduction of standardised products". However, in the post-Fordist period, this distinction has blurred. The CCI have become more integrated with other economic sectors.

Rather than just being pushed along by increasing demand from wealthier and more educated populations (often with some leisure time), some academics and policymakers consider CCI as major drivers of the economic growth and quality of life in their own right, facilitating advances in other aspects of the economy and society (Kockel 2002; Florida 2002; Ahluwalia 2006; UNESCO 2013; UNCTAD 2018). Over a decade ago, UNCTAD (2010: xix) proposed that "adequately nurtured, creativity fuels culture, constitutes the key ingredient for job creation, innovation and trade while contributing to social inclusion, cultural diversity, and environmental sustainability".

This quote also illustrates the expectation that CCI generate benefits over and beyond conventional economic indicators. They are recognized for the 'non-monetized social benefits' (UNESCO 2013: 9) they bring about. There is a great hope that CCI can foster a sense of belonging and pride in the local culture and networks. CCI may also give rise to relatively strong multiplier effects through backward and forward linkages in the supply chain, and in particular by providing an arena for exploring and popularizing innovative technologies, norms, and ideas.

1.2 Idiosyncrasies and diversity of CCI

CCI, and specifically cultural activities, operate differently from conventional concepts of work, production, and industries – see Chapter 2. Some of these alleged idiosyncratic procedures and contributions of CCI include:

i The outputs of CCI are symbolically charged and raise 'specific and social and political questions' (UNESCO 2013: 16s)
ii CCI production is often more environmentally friendly than mass manufacturing (Kacerauskas et al. 2021)
iii CCI mostly employ highly skilled workers (Munro 2017; Newbigin 2014)
iv CCI relies on 'informal cultural systems, process and institutions' (UNESCO 2013: 16)
v CCI thrive in local communities and thus generate 'new localisms', counteracting and complementing globalization and homogenization trends (Boccella and Salerno 2016; Flew 2012)
vi CCI provide identity and respect to the places and people (OECD 2018)
vii CCI strengthen the social capital rather than disrupting it (Chuluunbaatar et al. 2014)
viii CCI empower marginalized members of society, especially women, who are often linked to the traditional arts and crafts (UNCTAD 2010)
ix CCI develop linkages between antiquated norms and traditions and current technologies, practices, and routines (UNCTAD 2010)
x CCI relies on and often celebrate diversity and multiculturalism (Palanivel 2019)
xi CCI generate "social energy, confidence, and engagement, enabling both individuals and groups to aspire to and imagine alternative futures" (UNESCO 2013: 17)
xii CCI promote 'human-centred' development, which may help bring about "sustainable, inclusive and equitable outcomes" (UNCTAD 2010: 17).

Clearly, not all aspects of the CCI will perform equally well in all these respects. After all, creative projects range from mainstream action movies to operatic performances and from video games to artful tapestries. Nonetheless, if at least some of these hopes are reasonably well-founded, there is much to gain from thriving CCI in any society.

1.3 Cultural policy

As argued in Chapter 2, CCI are not only perceived as economically and socially important, but there is also much scepticism about whether they can thrive without a substantial and adequate framework of public investments and regulation (O'Brien and Oakley 2017).

It is in this context that public support and engagement with the CCI continue to take shape. The United Nations Educational, Scientific, and Cultural

Organization (UNESCO 2013: 10) proposed that "investments in identity, innovation, and creativity can help to build new development pathways for individuals, local communities and countries" and observed that

> local decisions makers are shaping their own creative economy development pathways. They are prioritizing support for economic development by strengthening the business and managerial skills of cultural actors and for inclusive social development with a focus on women, youth and indigenous peoples . . . the creative economy is not only one of the most rapidly growing sectors of the world economy, but also a highly transformative one in terms of income-generation, job creation and export earnings.

CCI are often seen as a tool for poverty alleviation, 'social inclusion', and 'empowerment' (UNESCO 2013). The greatest need for this would be found in poorer and marginalized communities. However, the creative sectors in highly developed, relatively affluent societies have received the most attention. This volume seeks to help fill that gap.

So-called developing countries in the 'global south' account for a large and increasing share of the world's population and possess significant cultural assets. A broad range of countries have not participated in modernization, globalization, and homogenization processes to the same extent as the most affluent contemporary countries. On the one hand, that means developing countries host much of the world's unique and diverse cultural traditions. On the other hand, few resources are available to sustain and harness these assets, and they are often threatened by further marginalization in the course of economic development. In terms of employment, GDP contributions, and exports, the share of CCI in many of these countries remains relatively low (Shaban and Vermeylen 2015). Nonetheless, CCI offer important complements and alternatives in economic development, since the production of fungible primary goods and mass manufacturing often attract low prices in the international market, can cause significant environmental damage, and are often associated with social disruption. The beaten track of industrialization is hardly the most promising for latecomers. A more sustainable development strategy is to try and skip – or leapfrog – into a contemporary mixed economy, in which capital-intensive modes of production and advanced technology integrate with local communities and their cultural assets, so that there is broad participation in creative and innovative processes, and rising economies shape their own unique niches.

1.4 The specific challenge of India as we see it

First, a word of caution: this volume seeks to provide useful information to promote awareness and debates. We deem this useful because the evidence base for CCI-related policy debates in India is rudimentary. Even with the advances offered by the contributing authors to this volume, we need to remain cautious and flexible regarding policy implications. The specific policy recommendation is that more research is required, and we seek to raise useful questions and stylized facts, for broader communities to engage with and improve upon.

India, the second-largest country by population, is in a process of swift social and economic change, endowed with a broad and diverse cultural heritage, and skilful artisan communities. The liberal and syncretic traditions of India provide much scope for creativity in Indian society (Shaban and Vermeylen 2015). A growing middle class fosters demand for creative goods and services, and in the long run, there are good prospects for Indian CCI serving the domestic market. At the same time, low costs and the unique skill-base in some Indian communities entail the substantial potential for exports. We challenge anyone travelling to India from abroad not to get excited about the abundant, unique, and affordable supply of creative works in the country. Yet, in the short run, economic pressures often do not facilitate the preservation, cultivation, and gradual development of local cultural assets.

A large section of creative workers in India is engaged in arts and crafts. Chapter 4 shows that this sector constitutes about 62% of all creative workers. With the use of digital ICT for marketing and facilitated international trade, there is much potential for the Indian craft sector to reach out to affluent potential customers, who appreciate authentic, handmade, and customized or personalized goods. Digitalization may also help artisans appropriate a greater share of the retail revenues, compared to the miserly conditions some of them seem to get from traditional intermediary traders. The joint potential for poverty alleviation and promoting upward social mobility, for strengthening local and rural communities, as well as India's export earnings, seems clear enough. Arguably, these could be major aspects of a CCI policy for India.

Deliberate public policy measures may be required to foster arts and crafts, however. At present, due to poverty and the absence of public support, in India many artisans abandon CCI-related work and shift to agricultural and construction work. "In India, a majority of the artisans and artists, who otherwise would have flourished, are unemployed and form major shares of the neo-poor" (Shaban and Vermeylen 2015: 69–70). In fact:

> India is a country with over a crore [10 million] of handloom weavers and an equal, if not larger, number of crafts people engaged in diverse crafts from pottery to basket making, stone ware, glass ware, handmade paper products and multifarious other utility items made out of local available materials.
>
> (Jaitly 2005)

A particular issue in India is informality: many traditional craftspeople have tended to operate outside of the formal economy, avoiding administrative chores and taxes but also with virtually no access to specific public services. They enjoy hardly any public social security measures in case of temporary underemployment or sickness, and in places, general education services are also lacking. For instance, many skilled craftspeople seem to lack the business skills – or the effective support by unions and other representatives of their trade – to bargain effectively with wholesalers or to spot entrepreneurial opportunities.

The introduction of trade and product standards illustrates the ambiguity of formalization in this context. Appropriate standards can foster trust, promote health and safety, and thus help bring about reasonably efficient markets for creative goods and services. Furthermore, adherence to international standards is required to access most foreign markets. However, the heedless implementation of standards can be devastating for traditional craftspeople and creative workers, who have limited experience with such measures. A recent case in point is the Indian government's general introduction of the Hallmark standard[2] in gold-related craft products, via the Bureau of Indian Standards on 15 June 2021 (Pakrasi 2021). Larger corporate jewellers had already acquired the certificates or found it reasonably straightforward to do so, drawing on their standing resources and networks. Self-employed craftspeople and other more fragmented aspects of the industry found it hard to understand and comply with technical standards, and to deal with the bureaucratic processes of acquiring Hallmark certificates. It aggravated the situation that media and policymakers referred to smaller jewellers as unreliable regarding the purity of the gold. In August 2021, 350 associations and federations of jewellers in India called for a strike against uniformly hallmarking all the products. They argued that 'impractical laws' would force the industry to the brink of collapse (The Hindu 2021).

Besides the particular Indian arts and craft tradition, the Indian media and entertainment sector exhibits fundamentally different conditions but also has enormous potential. The domestic market is humongous in terms of the sheer number of customers, so Indian CCI can exploit economies of scale and scope as well as network effects. Bollywood movies are already popular in many parts of the world, in particular throughout Asia and North Africa (see Chapter 10).

Regarding other aspects of the CCI, India is gradually integrating and finding its position in regional and global markets. For instance, the India Arts fair, New Delhi, now attracted a significant number of galleries from across the world. However, compared to other large and quickly developing countries, there remains much untapped potential to establish such arenas for all the major sub-sectors of the creative economy. Furthermore, the 'Make in India' campaign was launched in 2014 to promote the manufacturing sector in the country, with vast potential to integrate Indian CCI. However, by now it seems that the campaign has largely failed. At present, little attention is paid to it, even by the Indian government (Babu 2020).

To realize the potential of its cultural and creative sector, India needs to build on existing human capital through appropriate educational and upskilling policies, and on establishing a permissive legal and regulatory framework. Given the cultural diversity and great social disparity within the country, as well as the structure of Indian CCI in strong local clusters, local levels of governance and expertise regarding specific conditions in the respective communities are required. It is important that a broad and reliable national framework is well coordinated with state/regional-level, municipal- and panchayat-level public policy measures, which should be knowledgeable about and responsive to specific communities' needs.

Overall, an important challenge in India is to ensure that the development of CCI does not keep relegating traditionally skilled workers to low-skilled labour – and thus at best relatively passive consumers of mass culture disseminated via media technology – but instead revalues and enhances the existing skills and traditions. If that were better accomplished, CCI can indeed promote upward social mobility, social cohesion, and sustainable broader development (Verbanova 2009).

The point is not to conserve current conditions, which are still marred by abject poverty for many Indians and massive social inequality. The point is to empower more and more Indians to actively participate in CCI on their own terms, to help them shape changes in and reap some of the social and economic rewards. Economic growth and the diffusion of digital information and communication technology offer vast opportunities in this respect, but also threaten to aggravate inequalities and marginalization along a digital divide.

1.5 Indian CCI policy

In India, few resources are dedicated to cultural policy, and responsibilities for policies regarding the CCI are diffused over various ministries and government agencies with little co-ordination. The national Ministry of Culture is narrowly tasked with the "protection, development, and promotion of the country's tangible heritage, intangible heritage, and knowledge heritage" (Ministry of Culture 2020: 1). The budget of the Ministry of Culture is one of the smallest of all ministries and accounts for about 0.07% of the total central government expenditure.[3] With these resources, the ministry mainly oversees the protection of selected community heritages, while cultural heritage from other groups seems to be less of a priority.

In 2006, the Government of India adopted the notion of creative industries coined by the UK's Department of Culture, Media, and Sports (DCMS). However, the government's focus was very much on crafts rather than on other cultural expressions, technological change, or the interfaces between various aspects of creative industries and between CCI and the rest of the economy (Ahluwalia 2006). Overall, India's set of CCI policies, like the apparent performance of the CCI themselves, trails way behind those of highly developed Western countries, but also behind those of, for instance, China.

Industrial associations like the Federation of Indian Chambers of Commerce & Industry (FICCI) and the Confederation of Indian Industry (CII) have been pressing the government to adopt more ambitious policies to promote different sectors of CCI (CII 2021). About a decade ago, the FICCI (2010a) already provided a series of suggestions to strengthen the sector – in its report on 'Art Industry in India: Policy Recommendations' – including advice 'to learn from China'. The report also suggested:

> World class Art Institutes/Centres for Excellence need to be established on a PPP [public private partnership] basis . . . a single-window clearance system needs to be set-up for the art industry so that one is required to approach only one authority which in turn would internally co-ordinate amongst the different forums and the import/export of artwork is done seamlessly.
>
> (FICCI 2010a: 2)

In China, an emphasis on CCI in economic policy does indeed coincide with the large and quickly increasing performance of that aspect of the economy. The Chinese Communist Party in its 17th National Congress stressed 'creation' rather than 'manufacturing' (CISAC 2014: 41). As a result, 'created in China' has become their slogan rather than 'made in China' (UNCTAD 2010: 47). Furthermore, China has also emphasized, "financial institutions to encourage financial support for . . . emerging cultural creative industries" (UNCTAD 2010: 48). The gross value added by Chinese copyright-related industries was US$1059 billion in 2019, with an annual increase of about 10% from 2018, and accounted for over 7% of the country's GDP (Beijing Forum for Performing Arts 2020). This development suggests that there is also much potential in India.

1.6 The contribution of the present volume

This volume collates 17 chapters that discuss and document the current state of CCI in India from a variety of disciplinary and empirical perspectives. We are pleased that we could engage a diverse range of Indian and international scholars, and that we benefitted from exchanging divergent views.

The contributing authors are united by the desire to better understand CCI in India and to provide useful information to stakeholders and policymakers so that they can harness CCI to promote desirable social and economic development. There is great hope for creative industries promoting economic and social development in lower-middle-income countries like India. As digitalization meets local traditions, it is of great regional and international import to exploit these opportunities in India – with its huge cultural heritage, gigantic population, and young demographic. Furthermore, various contributors question whether Western traditions of arts and culture provide useful templates for India and make suggestions for useful alternatives. The volume explores the potential of CCI to foster and sustain equitable growth and gainful employment, as well as other social benefits. It also documents good practices and valued traditions, some of which continue to be threatened.

This volume contains detailed mappings of the Indian CCI, as well as industry studies, and more specific case studies. Readers must appreciate that comprehensiveness was out of reach, as do we. The case studies provide no systematic and complete coverage but present local pockets of knowledge to be extended upon in future work. The following major themes emerge throughout this volume regarding central challenges and features of the Indian creative sector.

1.6.1 The challenges of reliable data

Unlike other countries, such as the UK, in India there is no coherent attempt to collate official data and publish separate indicators on the cultural and creative sector, for instance, based on the Census of India, Economic Census, National Sample Survey Office (NSSO). There is little information on the exact size, diversity, and distribution of creative activities in India.

There have been, however, several noteworthy reports on aspects of Indian CCI. An FICCI (2010b) report on the 'art industry' – including theatre, dance, and crafts – highlighted the growth and potential for further 'wealth creation'. It estimates nominal revenue growth in Indian performing arts from INR 236 billion in 2012 to INR 275 billion in 2017, with an average nominal growth rate per year during the period of 2.5%. It argued that the main challenges faced by these industries were 'inadequate infrastructure', the costs of 'easing out permission' from bureaucrats, as well as other costs associated with bureaucracy (FICCI 2016: 27). Concerning the 'craft industry', the major challenges the report highlighted were the lack of adequate data and lack of access to credit as well as to the latest technology and infrastructure. Among others, the report did recommend developing creative clusters and integrating those with smart cities. However, the report does not provide details on where the workers and industries were located, and which are the existing creative clusters in the country.

The Boston Consulting Group-CII (2017) report on 'Media and Entertainment' estimated that aggregate annual revenues of the Indian media and entertainment industries was about INR 4,500 billion in 2017 (2.8% of GDP), and that they directly employed about 1.0–1.2 million workers. The report predicted that the industry had the potential to almost double its revenue and create an additional 0.7–0.8 million jobs by 2022 (The Boston Consulting Group-CII 2017: 8, 24, 26). It argued that due to the digital revolution, the industry was also going through a structural change, which could come to benefit India:

> India is in a unique position to take advantage of these tectonic shifts, given both its significant long-term growth potential as well as its demographic dividend, which offers it a unique opportunity to continue the strong double-digit growth in the media industry. The right

> enabling ecosystem to identify and build the required talent pipeline will be critical to monetize this growth and create value.
>
> (The Boston Consulting Group-CII 2017: 6)

FICCI-KPMG (2018), in their report on 'Visual Arts Industry in India: Painting the Future', highlighted: "India has witnessed an increasing appetite for art amongst the public, driven by the advent of a growing number of cultural initiatives, including city-based art festivals, exhibitions in galleries and other grand events such as art biennales" (FICCI-KPMG 2018: 1). India's visual art market was estimated at around INR 14.6 billion in 2017, up from INR 13.5 billion in 2013. It also observed that the Indian Ministry of Culture did not exhaust its budget – for instance, in 2017 the allocated budget to the Ministry was INR 25.0 billion, but the Ministry's total expenditure was only INR 17.2 billion (FICCI-KPMG 2018: 28). The report lamented:

> There is an inherent lack of art awareness in the country, with limited education to help develop creativity and expression through art. Furthermore, factors such as inadequate financing, lack of upskilling and improper infrastructure have also added to the industry's woes. The art industry and its surrounding ecosystem play a vital role in improving the country's cultural value and attractiveness to visitors, while also helping to create individuality in a highly competitive and globalised market. However, to facilitate this, the government could take on a more supportive role in terms of circumventing long-standing issues.
>
> (FICCI-KPMG 2018: 2)

Furthermore, Goswami (2020) and Rampazzo (2020) recently discussed developments of 'Bollywood', albeit with limited recourse to comprehensive quantitative data.

Patnaik (2020) is among the first to more comprehensively assess the size of the creative economy in India. She draws on data from the Annual Survey of Industries (ASI) and the Centre for Monitoring Indian Economy's (CMIE) Prowess data, among others. Her work adopts the World Intellectual Property Organization's (WIPO) copyright model. She argues that the Gross Value Added (GVA) by copyright-relevant industries in 2016–17 was INR 888.89 billion with total employment of 1.1 million. A problem with the data and with the application of the WIPO copyright model is that it largely omits the substantial share of informal/unregistered enterprises and employment arrangements in Indian CCI, where intellectual property plays virtually no role (as also discussed in Chapter 3). Furthermore, the ASI does not provide data at the district or city level, so it does not support detailed assessment of geographical clustering. On the other hand, the CMIE Prowess data is pooled from companies' annual reports, and smaller enterprises, even if they are formalized, are not obliged to publish those. This may explain why Patnaik's (2020) employment figures on the CCI/copyright industries as a whole fall well below the figures reported, for instance, by The Boston Consulting Group-CII (2017) for Indian 'Media and Entertainment' estimates only.

In this volume, Chapters 2 to 4 develop another mapping of the CCI in India, which mitigates some of these problems. We use the data from Economic Census (EC), Government of India, which none of the previous studies have used (MoSPI 1998, 2016). The EC provides data for all economic establishments – formal and informal, and covering much of the smaller enterprises – on the nature of activities according to National Industrial Classification (NIC) codes and on the number of workers involved. What is more, this data is available at the district level. It helps the authors identify geographic clusters of CCI, which is essential for preparation of developing a targeted policy catering to specific local circumstances.

1.6.2 Clustering and agglomerations

This volume documents the clustering of CCI in India. Specific industries exhibit unique patterns, but there are some cities and regions where multiple CCI conglomerate. Beyond quantitative mapping, several chapters develop fascinating case studies, which illuminate reasons behind clustering over a wide range of specific CCI, as well as some of the internal operations of specific clusters.

According to UNESCO (2013: 29), "clustering is seen as a means of equipping industries or regions to exploit their natural advantages in ways that enable them to achieve higher levels of innovation and competitiveness". Clusters not only facilitate knowledge spillovers and deliberate cooperation but also foster competition between firms, promoting efficiency. Interactions between local government, firms, and workers in clusters enable information exchanges and mutual learning, as well as the development and joint use of institutions and infrastructure and matching of complementary goods and services. In our cases, for instance, denominations of origin can work as signals of quality to consumers, where individual, small enterprises lack the resources to develop brands by themselves.

Chapter 4 develops an unprecedented overview of numerous CCI clusters throughout India. It also reviews initial evidence on main drivers of CCI growth and clustering. Chapter 6 highlights cluster overlap/co-location between digital hi-tech industries and CCI. Chapter 14 zooms in on arts and crafts clusters, which play an extraordinary role in India and have been the main target of public policy measures. Other chapters zoom in on even more specific products and locations. Chapter 16 deals with a leather manufacturing cluster and emerging entrepreneurship in Dharavi. Chapter 17 discusses the emergence of the carpet industry cluster in Khairabad, Uttar Pradesh. Chapter 8 examines the Madhubani painting industry, while Chapter 15 discusses drivers behind the clustering of the jewellery industry in Jaipur.

Clusters often constitute 'creative fields', which not only result in competitive advantages of participating firms but also attract new firms and related industries. Initial clusters often tend to expand, so that they can graduate into wider, diversified creative localities and creative regions. Many of the Indian clusters are rather large in terms of the number of workers involved, so they may exploit economies of scale and scope, as well as network effects, without requiring firm-level integration.

1.6.3 Cities are important creative centres

A consistent theme across many chapters is specific cities as centres of CCI. Major cities in western and southern India host expanding CCI clusters: Mumbai (Bollywood, jewellery, and software), Jaipur (jewellery), Hyderabad (new media and audio-visual entertainment), Bangalore (software), Chennai (film industry), Delhi and Noida (for book and newspaper publishing), Kolkata (art crafts), Varanasi (saris), Surat (jewellery), Ernakulum (films), Kancheepuram (software), and Srinagar (crafts and folk art).

Several of these cities have been included in the UNECO's Creative Cities Network (Masood 2021), albeit not necessarily for the specific clusters identified by the mapping in Chapter 4: Jaipur and recently Srinagar for crafts and folk arts, Mumbai for films, Chennai and Varanasi for music, and Hyderabad for gastronomy.

Municipal, regional, and national policies should nurture these clusters and help them expand their trading relations throughout the vast domestic as well as international market. What is more, in a large and diverse country such as India, digitalization opens further scope for linkages between creative communities beyond urban centres and beyond conventional trading. Chapter 6 highlights how the CCI cluster takes advantage of digital industries. Chapter 11 highlights how non-Bollywood music creates its own market, harnessing digital ICT. Digital technologies enable new marketing methods for Madhubani paintings (Chapter 8), for the traditional carpet industry of Khairabad (Chapter 17), and even for subaltern cinema of Malegaon (Chapter 13). As highlighted in Chapter 15, jewellery craftspeople of Jaipur harnessed digital technologies to access international markets and networks. Chapter 16 shows how even artisans from a marginalized caste take advantage of digital technologies.

1.6.4 The challenges of informality and formalization

Many creative workers and CCI enterprises are informal, those not registered under the 1948 Factories Act of the Government of India. This records intrinsically motivated creative workers, as well as individuals seeking to make their livelihood in the shadow economy. Where the informal existence beyond the bureaucratic chores may have its advantage, it also entails limited access to markets and to public services for individuals, lack of state support for enterprises, as well as a lack of effective health and safety regulations and general trust on the consumer side. What is more, workers in the informal parts in Indian CCI are often subjected to exploitative conditions by more established and knowledgeable traders and firms – as documented, for instance, in Chapters 7, 8, 11, 12, 13, 16, and 17.

Some formalization of enterprises seems a virtually inevitable aspect of development, even for most of the CCI. However, the proverbial red tape of formalities, reporting duties, heedless applications of general rules, and of course obligatory tax and insurance payments can at times stifle activity (an additional concern may be corruption, but informal workers may be subjected to this as well). It remains a daring task to shape reasonably adequate statutory regulations, with respect to idiosyncratic and divergent circumstances across the Indian subcontinent and the various CCI.

Another important issue is how informal aspects of the economy interact with formalized industry. For instance, in India many craft products are produced in the informal sector and find their way to market via formalized firms, for instance wholesalers. As UNESCO (2013: 28) acknowledges, "Methods that identify the connections between the informal and formal sectors will be particularly useful for policy development and analysis". In this volume, Chapter 17 contains the most ambitious engagement with this important topic.

1.6.5 Digital technology and the creative sector

Digital technologies have profound transformative impacts on all aspects of society, which have been unfolding for decades and will continue to instigate change for the foreseeable future. The Indian government's 'Digital India' programme envisions to transform India into a digitally empowered society and knowledge economy through expansion of digital infrastructure, integrating governance and services through digital networks, and to digitally empowering the citizens by creating digital literacy (Government of India 2021a).[4] Use of advanced digital ICT is expanding quickly, albeit from a low base. Many CCI are deeply involved with digital technologies (Towse and Handke 2013).

Obviously, the level of involvement differs across the CCI. For suppliers of creative media content – from films to video games, for instance – virtually any aspects of creation, reproduction, dissemination, retailing, social valorization processes involving critics and end-users, and back-office tasks are complemented and changing. For suppliers of traditional craft goods and performances, creation processes remain much less affected, but new opportunities are developing in particular for marketing purposes. Technical restrictions to reach out to geographically distant cooperation partners or customers are becoming less important, but regulatory restrictions may become more consequential in that process. According to UNCTAD (2018: 15):

> On the one hand, the digital age is revolutionizing the marketplace and democratizing access on both commercial and consumer ends. On the other, unequal geographic balance of trade, logistical roadblocks, policy gaps, and inadequate infrastructure persist, limiting access to these goods and services.

This volume discusses some positive and some negative consequences of digitalization on various CCI. First and foremost, stakeholders, who lack access to the technical infrastructure and the required skills to effectively use for their own ends, will lose in relative terms to those equipped with those resources. For instance, larger wholesalers and internet service providers may gain market power. In this volume, Chapters 6 and 17 engage with the issue. Furthermore, some traded CCI services may become largely obsolete with digitalization. Audio-visual entertainment online displaces demand for the subaltern cinema in Malegoan, which enforces the suppliers to revise their business model (Chapter 13). Like many so-called developing countries, there is often a fascinating clash between modes of production, which precede industrialization, with the dissemination of digital ICT and clever new ways of using them to provide an array of new services. Chapter 6 reveals that creative clusters are also mainly located where the digital industries are concentrated, with notable exception of the arts and crafts. This hints at a geographical separation in Indian CCI between traditional modes of production and the high technology industries, over and beyond the notorious digital divide. Most people use digital ICT, but the savvy users may pull away from the laggards even in a literal sense.

1.6.6 India emerging as a major exporter and increasingly major importer of creative goods

India's share in the worldwide creative goods exports has risen over the years. As discussed in Chapter 5, India ranked 8th in terms of the value of creative goods exports in 2015 (its economy was the 7th largest in terms of GDP).

India's imports of creative goods are also quickly expanding. A growing middle class in India also draws on imported creative goods and services to satisfy their needs for entertainment and inspiration (Shaban 2021; Shariff 2010). A healthy development of CCI in India is not only important to sustain a desirable foreign trade balance. Perhaps even more importantly, it is crucial for social and cultural reasons that Indian cultural expressions are not drowned out by international competitors.

1.6.7 Creative communities

Creative communities – groups of people with shared norms and values, shaped through common experiences and traditions – are at the heart of CCI clusters. This concerns suppliers and their cooperation and mutual learning. It also concerns linkages and mutual understanding between suppliers and consumers. In India, various religions and the caste system shape CCI practices as well.

For instance, Madhubani painting is carried out in communities of specific locality and in a specific set of families in Madhubani, Bihar, drawing on extensive cultural heritage inherited and continuously re-enacted there (see Chapter 8). The Sonar caste is associated with Indian jewellery, but now other caste groups are entering into this business. Some Muslim communities in India are renowned for refined jewellery designs and crafts. Chapter 15 highlights the role of these communities. Chapter 17 examines the traditional skills regarding artful weaving of textiles and carpets held in Muslim communities in Khairabad. As discussed in Chapter 16, craftspeople working with leather workers in Mumbai are predominantly engaged lower castes from Hindus and Buddhists, and Muslim communities. Shared norms and values within specific communities also relate to attitudes towards entrepreneurship, innovation, and creativity. In particular, Chapter 16 highlights this issue.

Traditionally, many workers in Indian CCI are members of traditionally poorer communities with limited social status. The traded association between occupations, caste status, or other community affiliation is strong and may inhibit upward social mobility. However, with socio-economic development, disproportionate growth in some CCI, and new export opportunities, marginalized artisan communities may employ their skills to foster their economic position and eventually their social status. This may diminish problems with extensive social stratification, which the Indian government also strives to diminish with affirmative actions in government and other occupations. In this volume, in particular, Chapter 7 – on the Kalbeliyas communities engaging in traditional performing arts in Rajasthan – relates to this. With adequate government support and regulation, these communities can improve their living conditions, while drawing on their unique skills and cultural heritage.

1.7 Summary and outlook

Social and cultural diversity can be a major factor promoting creativity, innovation, and long-term economic growth, if coupled with strong institutions that ensure social cohesion and enable effective conflict resolution procedures between various aspects of society (for empirical studies, see Ager and Bruckner 2013; Rodríguez-Pose and von Berlepsch 2019). Within India, the CCI relate to this vision of positive socio-economic development in various ways.

On the one hand, Indian CCI can draw on the scale and diversity of Indian cultural heritage, syncretic traditions in the subcontinent, as well as existing and large clusters established in many parts of the country. On the other hand, thriving CCI provide opportunities for upward social mobility of current creative workers – in particular, craftspeople – and those developing new skills and making use of new opportunities associated with digitalization. Furthermore, engagement with CCI products can be a powerful tool to foster the feeling of belonging across social divides within the country and communication and respect between different social and religious groups within India. Finally, CCI are increasingly appreciated as complements to other economic sectors. They can attract skilled people of all types and counter brain drain experienced in India. CCI can also help develop and market appealing manufacturing products and functional services. Overall, CCI simultaneously thrive on diversity and socio-economic development, and they tend to promote it.

The present volume collates extensive and original evidence and insights regarding the state of CCI in India. There are encouraging signs that CCI do contribute to desirable socio-economic development in the subcontinent. As, for instance, the cultural economic literature suggests, specific CCI exhibit rather different essential characteristics, while they all tend to be subject to various and pronounced market failure; to fully harness their potential, an extensive policy framework may be required that is adequately adapted to industry-specific and local circumstances (see Chapter 2). The COVID-19 pandemic, which hit as much of this volume was reaching maturity, is a case in point. Most CCI are particularly vulnerable to economic recessions, when some consumers are forced to focus their expenditure on essential goods, and the many small enterprises and freelancers that characterize CCI face liquidity problems. However, many digital services even benefit, as restrictions on physical markets and direct social interaction do not directly concern them. A recent report by The British Council (2021) documents the divergent developments across Indian CCI. About 16% of the CCI enterprises were on the verge of closure, and 22% of them appeared to be losing more than 75% of their annual income in 2021 (The British Council 2021: 7). In the face of such strong, exogenous, and temporary shocks, governmental support seems important. Enough CCI capacities need to be sustained so that Indian CCI can quickly bounce back when the immediate crisis subsides. In any case, we hope this volume will inspire further researchers, stakeholders, and policymakers to rise to the challenge of better understanding the operations and needs of CCI in India and thoroughly engage with it.

Notes

1 The term 'culture industry' (Kulturindustrie) was coined in the 1940s by Theodor W. Adorno and Max Horkheimer (Adorno and Horkheimer 1947/1997), leading members

of the Frankfurt School of critical theory, which used the term in a pejorative manner to connote the commodification of culture. It "scathingly decried the commodification of art as providing an ideological legitimization of capitalist societies" (UNESCO 2013: 20).

2 Hallmarking is monitored by the Bureau of Indian Standard. It is a standardization of the quality of the product. As per the hallmarking standard, the jewellers across the country can only sell gold of standards of 14, 18, and 22 carats.

3 The budget of the Ministry of the Culture was INR 26.9 billion (about US$363.2 million) in 2021–22, up from INR 22.12 billion in 2020–21 (Press Information Bureau 2021). The total budgeted expenditure of the Government of India in 2021–22 is expected to be INR 34,832.4 billion, while in the budget outlay in the year 2020–21 was INR 34,503.1 billion (Government of India 2021b).

4 It is no doubt that there has been the huge spread of digital technology in India in the last two decades. However, affordability and digital literacy remain significant issues creating digital divides. The attempt to rapidly spread digital literacy through the government efforts and growth of the household income of marginalized sections to afford the cost which private service providers demand only can tackle this issue of digital divide. The NSSO 75th round data for the year 2017–18 shows that in India only 16.5% (20.0% of male and 12.8% of female) of the total population above 5 years of age was able to operate a computer, 20.1% (25% of male 14.9% of female) were able to use the internet, and only 17.6% (22.3% of male and 12.5% of female) had used the internet in the last 30 days. Further, in rural areas, only 13% (17.1% male and 18.5% female) of the population was able to use internet as against 37.1% (43.5% male and 30.1% female) in urban areas (MoSPI 2019: 47–48).

References

Adorno, T. W., and Horkheimer, M. (1947/Re-edition 1997). *Dialektik der Aufklaerung*. Berlin: Suhrkamp.

Ager, P., and Bruckner, M. (2013). Cultural diversity and economic growth: Evidence from the US during the age of mass migration. *European Economic Review*, 64(C), 76–97.

Ahluwalia, M. S. (2006). *Positioning the Big Idea-India: Creative and Cultural Industries as a Lead Sector*. New Delhi: Asian Heritage Foundation.

Babu, M. S. (2020, 20 January). Why 'Make in India' has failed. *The Hindu*. Available at: www.thehindu.com/opinion/op-ed/why-make-in-india-has-failed/article30601269.ece (last accessed on 25 March 2022).

Beijing Forum for Performing Arts (2020, 31 December). The added value of China's copyright-related industries topped RMB 7 trillion. Available at: www.beijingforum.art/eng/jjzg/xydt/202101/t20210122_225766.html (last accessed 25 March 2022).

Boccella, N., and Salerno, I. (2016). Creative economy, cultural industries and local development. *Procedia – Social and Behavioral Sciences*, 223, 291–296. https://doi.org/10.1016/j.sbspro.2016.05.370 (last accessed on 25 March 2022).

The Boston Consulting Group-CII (2017). *Media & Entertainment: The Nucleus of India's Creative Economy (Unleashing the Talent Tsunami to Drive the Growth)*. Mumbai: The Boston Consulting Group.

The British Council (2021). *Taking the Temperature Report 2: The Deepening Impact of COVID-19 on India's Creative Economy*. New Delhi: The British Council.

Caves, R. (2000). *Creative Industries: Contracts between Art and Commerce*. Cambridge, MA: Harvard University Press.

Chuluunbaatar, E., Ottavia, Luh, D. B., and Kung, S.F. (2014). The role of cluster and social capital in cultural and creative industries development. *Procedia – Social and Behavioral Sciences*, 109, 552–557. doi:10.1016/j.sbspro.2013.12.506

CII (2021, 17 November). Media & entertainment. Available at: www.cii.in/PressreleasesDetail.aspx?enc=Iv7An8BGFT4CXHjvGMYaOnDVbyIMGioWymSyLK7B/en0yXpmgSVawphw9jTOTaUSMN28fkuKKIQdfQAiHidIAQ== (last accessed on 25 March 2022).

CISAC (2014): The creative industries and the BRICS: A review of state of the creative economy in Brazil, Russia, India, China, and South Africa, International Confederation of Societies of Authors and Composers (CISAC), Communication Department. Available at: www.cisac.org/CisacPortal/cisacDownloadFile.do?docId=26900 (last accessed on 25 March 2022).

Cunningham, S. (2001). From cultural to creative industries: Theory, industry and policy implications. Culturelink, Special Issue, ed. Colin Mercer, 9–32.

FICCI (2010a). *Art Industry in India: Policy Recommendations*. New Delhi: FICCI.

FICCI (2010b). Release of report on art industry in India: Policy recommendations. Available at: https://ficci.in/spdocument/20781/Report-2010.pdf (last accessed on 25 March 2022).

FICCI (2016). *Creative Arts in India: Theatre, Dance and Craft Industry*. New Delhi: Ernst & Young.

FICCI-KPMG (2018). *Visual Industry in India: Painting the Future*. New Delhi: FICCI.

Flew, T. (2012). *Creative Industries and Urban Development. Creative Cities in the 21st Century*. Abingdon: Routledge.

Florida, R. (2002). *The Rise of the Creative Class: And How It's Transforming Work, Leisure and Everyday Life*. New York: Basic Books.

Galloway, S., and Dunlop, S. (2007). A critique of definition of the cultural and creative industries in public policy. *International Journal of Cultural Policy*, 13(1), 17–31.

Garnham, N. (2005). From cultural to creative industries. *International Journal of Cultural Policy*, 11, 15–29.

Goswami, A. (2020). 'New Bollywood' and Emergence of 'Production House' Culture. In Malik, K. and Dudrah, R. (eds.), *South Asian Creative and Cultural Industries*. London: Routledge.

Government of India (2021a). Vision of digital India. Available at: www.digitalindia.gov.in/content/vision-and-vision-areas (last accessed on 25 March 2022).

Government of India (2021b). Budget at a glance. Available at: file:///C:/Users/shaba/Downloads/budget_at_a_glance.pdf (last accessed on 25 March 2022).

Hesmondhalgh, D., and Pratt, A. C. (2005). Cultural industries and cultural policy. *International Journal of Cultural Policy*, 11(1), 1–13.

The Hindu (2021, 20 August). Jewellers plan token stir against hallmarking. Available at: www.thehindu.com/news/national/jewellers-to-go-on-token-strike-on-august-23-against-gold-hallmarking/article36014133.ece (last accessed on 25 March 2022).

Jaitly, J. (2005). Crafts as industry: Creative industries, symposium on culture based development strategies. *Seminar*, 553(September). Available at: www.india-seminar.com/2005/553/553%20jaya%20jaitly.htm (last accessed on 25 March 2022).

Kacerauskas, T., Streimikiene D., and Bartkute, R. (2021). Environmental sustainability of creative economy: Evidence from a Lithuanian case study. *Sustainability*, 13, 9730. https://doi.org/ 10.3390/su13179730

Kebir, L., and Crevoisier, O. (2008). Cultural resources and regional development: The case of cultural legacy of watchmaking. In Cooke, P. and Lazzeretti, L. (eds.), *Creative Cities,*

Cultural Clusters and Local Economic Development, pp. 48–69. Cheltenham, UK: Edward Elgar.

Kockel, U. (2002). Culture and economy: A brief introduction. In Kockel, U. (ed.), *Culture and Economy: Contemporary Perspective*, pp. 1–10. Burlington, UK: Ashgate.

Lee, N. (2014). The creative industries and urban economic growth in the UK. *Environment and Planning A: Economy and Space*, 46(2), 455–470. https://doi.org/10.1068/a4472

Masood, B. (2021, 9 November). Explained: Why UNESCO has designated Srinagar as creative city. *The Indian Express*. Available at: https://indianexpress.com/article/explained/srinagar-unesco-creative-city-explained-7614289/ (last accessed on 25 March 2022).

Ministry of Culture (2020). Annual report, 2019–20. Government of India, New Delhi. Available at: www.indiaculture.nic.in/sites/default/files/annual-reports/ENGLISH%20-%20MINISTRY%20OF%20CULTURE%20AR%202019-20.pdf (last accessed on 25 March 2022).

MoSPI (1998). All India Report of Fourth Economic Census. Government of India, New Delhi.

MoSPI (2016). All India Report of Sixth Economic Census. Government of India, New Delhi.

MoSPI (2019). *Key Indicators of Household Social Consumption on Education in India, NSS 75th Round*. New Delhi: National Statistical Office. Available at: http://mospi.nic.in/sites/default/files/publication_reports/KI_Education_75th_Final.pdf (last accessed on 25 March 2022).

Munro, E. (2017). Building soft skills in the creative economy: Creative intermediaries, business support and the 'soft skills gap'. *Poetics*, 64(64): 14–24. https://doi.org/10.1016/j.poetic.2017.07.002

Newbigin, J. (2014). New skills for a new economy. British Council. Available at: https://creativeconomy.britishcouncil.org/guide/new-skills-new-economy/ (last accessed on 25 March 2022).

O'Brien, D., and Oakley, K. (Eds.). (2017). *Cultural Policy. Series: Critical Concepts in Media and Cultural Studies*. Routledge: London.

OECD (2018, November). The value of culture and the creative industries in local development. Available at: www.oecd.org/cfe/leed/2018-SACCI-Handbook.pdf (last accessed on 25 March 2022).

Pakrasi, S. (2021, 15 June). Gold hallmarking mandatory from today: All you need to know. Available at: www.hindustantimes.com/business/gold-hallmarking-mandatory-from-today-all-you-need-to-know-101623719196086.html (last accessed on 25 March 2022).

Palanivel, T. (2019, 23 January). How cultural and creative industries can power human development in the 21st Century. UNDP. Available at: http://hdr.undp.org/en/content/how-cultural-and-creative-industries-can-power-human-development-21st-century (last accessed on 25 March 2022).

Patnaik, M. (2020). *Measuring India's Creative Economy*. New Delhi: Esya Centre.

Potts, J. (2009). Why creative industries matter to economic evolution. *Economics of Innovation and New Technology*, 18(7), 663–673. doi:10.1080/10438590802564592

Potts, J., and Cunningham, S. (2008). Four models of the creative industries. *International Journal of Cultural Policy*, 14(3), 233–247. doi:10.1080/10286630802281780

Press Information Bureau (2021). Outlay for annual budget 2021–22 of ministry of culture is rs. 2687.99 cr., outlay higher by 21.53% over revised annual outlay in FY 2020–21. Government of India, New Delhi. Available at: https://pib.gov.in/Pressreleaseshare.aspx?PRID=1694267 (last accessed on 25 March 2022).

Rampazzo, G. (2020). The production of Ek Tha Tiger: The marriage of convenience between Bollywood and the Irish film and tourist industries. In Malik, K. and Dudrah, R. (eds.), *South Asian Creative and Cultural Industries*. London: Routledge.

Rodríguez-Pose, A., and von Berlepsch, V. (2019). Does population diversity matter for economic development in the very long term? Historic migration, diversity and county wealth in the US. *European Journal of Population*, 35(4), 873–911.

Ryan, P. (2003). *The Creative Economy: Creative Clusters Key to Knowledge-based Economy*. Tokyo, Japan: Marubeni Corporation Economic Research Institute.

Shaban, A. (2021). Growth and determinants of the middle class in rural and urban India in the post-liberalisation period. In Batabyal, A. A., Higano, Y., and Nijkamp, P. (eds.), *Rural-Urban Dichotomies and Spatial Development in Asia*. Singapore: Springer.

Shaban, A., and Vermeylen, F. (2015). Trade in the creative sector: Comparing India with China, Brazil and UK. *Economic and Political Weekly*, 50(20), 68–75.

Shariff, A. (2010). Rural income and employment diversity in India during 1994 and 2005. *Journal of Developing Societies*, 25(2), 165–208.

Throsby, D. (2001). *Economics and Culture*. Cambridge: Cambridge University Press.

Towse, R., and Handke, C. (Eds.) (2013). *Handbook on the Digital Creative Economy*. Cheltenham, UK: Edward Elgar.

UNCTAD (2010). Creative economy report 2010. Viewed on 9 November 2014. Available at: http://unctad.org/en/Docs/ditctab20103_en.pdf (last accessed on 25 March 2022).

UNCTAD (2018). Creative economy outlook: Trends in international trade in creative industries. Available at: https://unctad.org/system/files/official-document/ditcted2018d3_en.pdf (last accessed on 4 July 2022).

UNESCO (2013). *Creative Economy Report 2013: Widening Local Development Pathways*. New York: United Nations.

Verbanova, L. 2009. How to better use rural resources for cultural development, and revitalize rural life through culture? Available at: www.aughty.org/pdf/revit_rural_culture.pdf (last accessed on 25 March 2022).

2

CULTURAL POLICY AND DEVELOPMENT

What are creative industries, and why do we care?

Christian Handke

2.1 Introduction

Over recent years, there are great hopes for cultural and creative industries (CCI) to promote economic and social development, also in middle-income countries such as India. As a cultural economist, one would tend to agree. However, economic reasoning often grates against the conventional rhetoric regarding cultural policy. Consider, for instance, the Indian government's headline text on its arts and culture policy website:

> India has one of the world's largest collections of songs, music, dance, theatre, folk traditions, performing arts, rites and rituals, paintings and writings that are known, as the 'Intangible Cultural Heritage' (ICH) of humanity. In order to preserve these elements, the Ministry of Culture implements a number of schemes and programmes aimed at providing financial support to individuals, groups and cultural organizations engaged in performing, visual and literary arts etc.
>
> (india.gov.in 2019)

I would immediately stress a different aspect. India has one of the youngest demographics of any major country in the world. In this context, it seems peculiar for cultural policy to emphasize cultural heritage. A country with a gigantic population and more than half of its inhabitants below the age of 25 should not just aim to preserve heritage – it should aim to shape the future. The CCI are central in the process of digitalization, and will keep on changing. There is great potential for growth through CCI, and cultural policy should set a framework for citizens to exploit these opportunities *extending* on its cultural heritage.

This chapter suggests a framework in which to structure debates on cultural policy. That framework is based on various parts of economics and many of the

DOI: 10.4324/9781003129370-3

components may even seem conventional for specialist economists. However, they are certainly unconventional in writing on cultural policy. A particular aim of this chapter is to challenge some widely held preconceived ideas regarding CCI and cultural policy. For instance, I will argue that CCI and the luxuries they supply are not negligible in developing countries that experience rapid, general economic growth but also need to cater for a large share of their population with limited access to more essential goods and services, regarding, for instance, health, nutrition, and shelter. To the contrary, in the course of socio-economic development, CCI have an increasing role to play.

2.2 What are cultural and creative industries?

2.2.1 From definitions . . .

There is some confusion about what the CCI entail. That is not just a challenge in academic debates. Without reasonably precise definitions, there is great scope for miscommunication. Without precise definitions, it is also hard to assess the role of CCI in socio-economic development. To clarify, it is helpful to consider three basic types of definitions of CCI: ostensible, enumerative, and analytical definitions (Handke 2004).

Ostensible definitions provide a couple of specific examples that illustrate parts of what constitutes the concept to be defined. For the CCI, this could be the production and consumption of music, fiction literature and films, and video games, for instance. Ostensible definitions are common in policy documents and even in academic writing on CCI, but they are inevitably rough and ready.

Enumerative definitions are more ambitious and refined. An enumerative definition proposes a list of items that, as a whole, make up all the elements of a wider concept. For instance, Throsby (2008) contains an enumerative definition of CCI that distinguishes (1) the core creative industries of literature, music, performing arts, visual arts, (2) other cultural industries of film, museums, galleries, libraries and photography, (3) wider cultural industries of heritage services, publishing and print media, sound recording, television and radio, video and computer games, and (4) related industries of advertising, architecture, design, and fashion. Other authors often include sports, crafts, cuisine, or even gambling and adult entertainment.

Enumerative definitions are essential in accounting exercises that strive to generate comprehensive quantitative indicators of the role of CCI in an economy or society. In practice, there are almost as many enumerative definitions of CCI as there are authors writing on the subject. One reason for these contested boundaries is the lack of a clear and generally accepted analytical definition of CCI.

Analytical definitions consist of a number of statements that stipulate those shared features of everything that falls within the definition that distinguish them from anything that does not. Paraphrasing Throsby (2008), for instance, CCI are (1) suppliers of symbolic goods and services, which (2) use some human creativity as an important input, and (3) the products they supply give rise to intellectual property (IP) 'at least potentially'. This is perhaps the most influential and precise analytical definition of CCI, but it is far from perfect. On the one hand, an analytical definition ideally would not be circular (would not explain one opaque term with another). However, in Throsby's (2008) definition, there is an element of circularity: it defines CCI with 'symbolic' and 'human creativity', which are also contestable concepts. Furthermore, the qualifiers – 'some human creativity' and giving rise to intellectual property 'at least potentially' – leave much scope for interpretation. Finally, intellectual property is a legal concept that changes over time and has different meanings in different territories. Clearly, there has been much creativity without anything resembling contemporary IP – think of Sangam literature or Shakespeare. Any analytical definition strives to identify *universal* characteristics, and IP is thus a problematic aspect of definitions of CCI.

The weakness of analytical definitions of CCI makes it hard to develop generally accepted enumerative definitions, which play an important role in contemporary policy. This is a central problem in devising cultural policy as a means to foster socio-economic development.

2.2.2 . . . to practical implications

Over and beyond this fundamental challenge in defining and measuring CCI, there are several practical issues that spring from any thorough discussion of the concept of CCI. Regarding cultural policy in middle-income, rapidly developing countries such as India, three issues seem particularly relevant:

First, CCI are labour-intensive, with human creativity/work being more important than in advanced agricultural and manufacturing operations, for instance. In many aspects of the economy, development means an increasing use of capital – in particular machinery, computer software, and data – relative to labour and thus the displacement of human work and employment. Agriculture becomes less important as a locus of employment. Nowadays, manufacturing and the production of routine services also become increasingly capital-intensive with automation. Thus, in terms of employment, the relative importance of labour-intensive CCI is bound to increase. What is more, creative products tend to be luxury goods in an economic sense: demand for them increases disproportionally with increasing household wealth. Thus, the absolute importance of CCI is bound to rapidly increase with economic development. Therefore, it is a misconception that CCI are negligible in development because they concern luxury goods as defined in economics and do not concern goods and services that are essential for human sustenance in the short run. To the contrary, CCI adopt an increasing role with development and can perpetuate the process of development, as I will also argue here.

Second, there may be no monotonic association between IP protection and growth in CCI. Consider the experience in highly developed economies in North America and Europe with unauthorized copying online. De facto levels of copyright protection decreased substantially and many studies suggest that unauthorized digital copying explains much of these decreases; for literature reviews, see Handke (2011), Liebowitz (2013), or Watson et al. (2015). However, the diversity and quality of supply of new music recordings and films increased over the same period – a puzzling result for economists, as it seems to contradict the law of supply. In fact, the only empirical study to this date that identifies any adverse effect of unauthorized copying on the supply of new creative works is on Indian films by Telang and Waldfogel (2018). If the observations from highly developed economies are anything to go by, it is misleading to assume that IP protection is generally and positively associated with growth in CCI. The devil seems to be in the detail. The challenge is to strike an adequate balance: on the one hand, to establish quasi-property rights for conventional markets to operate reasonably well; on the other hand, to limit the burden for consumers and small creative projects that sophisticated IP systems can entail. For instance, we cannot expect traditional craftsmen and -women in India to quickly acquire the skills to use IP systems to their advantage.

Third, various aspects of the CCI have different roles in different countries. In India, there is a rich tradition of arts and crafts, where creators/craftspeople closely adhere to long-established formats in their manual and creative work. That is distinct from the arts in Western traditions that emphasize originality, individual authorship, and the breaking of boundaries. It is also different from markets for reproducible cultural products, such as films, where technology enables mass reproduction and sales of identical copies as media content. In the arts as well as in content industries, there are strong superstar effects: attention and revenues are highly concentrated on a small minority of creators. In the crafts, there is greater scope for a large number of skilled labourers to make a living. The potential of crafts to secure reasonable employment conditions and sustainable levels of income for many craftspeople is promising regarding upward social mobility and an equitable socio-economic development in middle-income countries. However, arts and crafts are also associated with a lower social standing of successful creators. Furthermore, the labour intensity of crafts means that Baumol's cost disease (Baumol and Bowen 1993; Baumol and Towse 1997) might apply to them: with technological development, the productivity of crafts may not increase at the same rate as the productivity of more capital-intensive modes of production in the media content industry or manufacturing. In this context, a challenge for Indian cultural policy is to strike another precarious balance. On the one hand, creative works ought not to be perceived as fungible commodities that might as well be produced anywhere as long as the superficial look and feel of the final goods is reminiscent of handcrafted, traditional cultural goods – think of Saris produced in Chinese factories. On the other hand, if crafts would graduate to a level of appreciation more similar to the arts, there is the risk of very inequitable labour markets that would hardly improve the lot of the majority of mediocre craftspeople – or of craftspeople less capable to present themselves as 'proper' artists.

2.3 Why do we care about cultural and creative industries?

2.3.1 Cultural economics: a growing field of research

After these preliminaries, the rest of this chapter revolves around the question why anyone concerned with socio-economic development – and in particular policymakers and academics trying to inform policymakers – would care about CCI in India. For starters, let us document that CCI have received increasing attention in economic research, which documents an understanding that these industries have an important role to play in contemporary economies. Figure 2.1 plots data on the share of academic journal articles on CCI in academic articles in the areas of business and economics listed on the database Web of Science (WoS), which we assembled for another project at Erasmus University Rotterdam. The underlying methods are documented in **Box 2.1**.

Box 2.1 Assessing growth in economic research on CCI

WoS was the first, reasonably comprehensive database for academic publications. It covers publications in thousands of prestigious journals and as of May 2019 featured over 40 million items, including about 700,000 articles classified into the research area Business and Economics. To establish the number of articles in this research area, we ran searches on 13 expressions closely associated with CCI.[1] In total, these searches yielded 1,092 original articles. Screening by human reading identified 350 irrelevant items, leaving a corpus of 742 business and/or economics articles on 'arts and culture' in total. To control for an increasing number of academic publications on WoS over time, we then ran a search on the number of business and economics articles that feature the definite article 'the', as a proxy for the total number of articles in that research area. Finally, we divided the annual number of CCI articles published by this proxy for the total number of articles. Overall, this gives a rough indication of the trends in the share of CCI articles in the total number of articles within the Business and Economics research area on WoS.

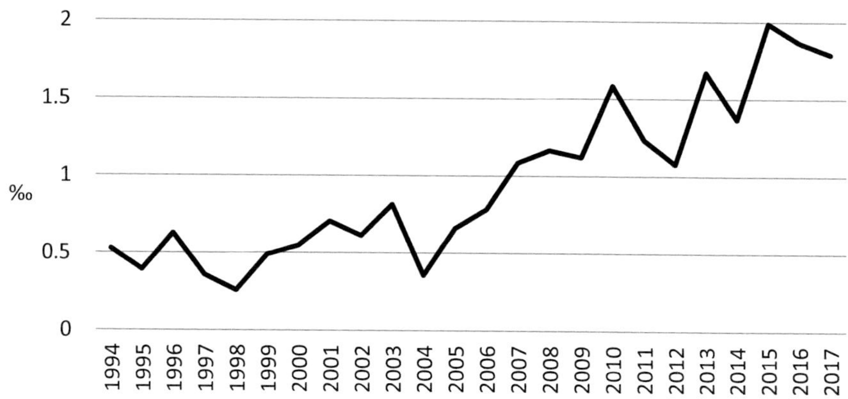

Figure 2.1 The ‰ share of articles on CCI in all business and economics articles featured on the Web of Science database

Source: Author's calculations based on data collected on the WoS-database.

According to the bibliometric exercise presented in Figure 2.1, the share of articles on CCI has increased considerably and quite consistently since 2005. In 2016 and 2017, it has been almost four times higher than the average between 1994 and 1999. Of course, we cannot exclude the possibility that data availability is driving this development at least in part, or that the interests of economics scholars are subject to fads and fashions. Nevertheless, these observations provide some indication that successful researchers in the areas of business and economics consider CCI an increasingly relevant aspect of contemporary economies.

2.3.2 Economic characteristics of CCI

In addition to the definition criteria of CCI discussed earlier, economists working on CCI have identified a range of more advanced, shared economic characteristics of these industries; see, for instance, Towse (1997, 2011), Caves (2000), Blaug (2001), or Ginsburgh and Throsby (2006).

First, creative products have public good attributes. They tend to be non-rival in consumption: use by one party often does not adversely affect the utility of the same good for others. They also tend to be non-excludable: for important aspects of creative works, it is hard to establish effective exclusive property rights, which would be required for conventional markets to efficiently operate. This applies in particular to creative works that are disseminated as media content – think of unauthorized dissemination of recorded music or films online. However, important aspects of physical creative objects are also easily observed and emulated by others. As a rule, valuable new ideas and works are costly to create but relatively easily copied. They thus usually give rise to positive externalities. Due to the positive externalities that these quasi-public goods entail, the market value of creative works (the number of units sold times price) only reflects a relatively small part of their total social value, and the provision of public goods through conventional markets is problematic.

Second, creative goods have experience good attributes. Creative goods are highly differentiated, and users care about minute differences between them. Users will have clear preferences for specific works from a range of different films, books, or craft objects available to them. What is more, there are usually so many product variants available that users cannot inform themselves about all options. Users take decisions on how to commit their time and money to specific product variants under incomplete information – for instance as they consider a sub-set of all films available to them and ultimately decide on what screenings to attend. To reduce search costs, users also tend to consider signals of quality by other parties, such as professional or user reviews, sales rankings, or prizes and awards. Demand for specific creative works thus comes about in complex social processes and gives rise to superstar effects and herd behaviour that does not necessarily faithfully reflect intrinsic quality and optimal choices.

Overall, markets for creative products tend to be complex with many different works supplied, many different suppliers, and affluent users appreciating variety. One challenge is to keep the costs of the myriad of informational exchanges and transactions as low as possible. Digitalization has the potential to lower transaction costs and thus to make CCI of any type more efficient and to foster growth in CCI.

Experience good attributes also relate to the role of education and prior experience with creative works in shaping tastes for creative products. Many creative products do not only require a sufficient level of general-purpose education to be accessible – think of language and reading skills and literature. Creative works also often require specific knowledge to be fully appreciated. Taste for sophisticated creative works tends to increase with prior engagement with similar works, which enables consumers to understand creative achievements and symbolic meaning.

Furthermore, there is extensive evidence for intrinsic motivation to create (e.g. Throsby 1994; Caves 2000; Frey and Jegen 2001): creative workers accept below-average earnings, especially when they enjoy extensive control over the types of goods they produce. Of course, for intrinsic motivation to play a strong role in practice, creative workers need to be able to sustain themselves even when they emphasize creative liberty over income maximization. This is less of a challenge in affluent societies and societies with lavish social welfare systems, but may pose restrictions on the broad participation in the CCI by workers in developing economies.

2.3.3 Expected benefits of CCI

It is widely appreciated that cultural products have public good attributes in the sense that their commercial value and contribution to national accounts only capture relatively modest part of their full social value. Table 2.1 provides an

Table 2.1 Expected benefits of cultural and creative industries (rough overview)

	Commercial	*Beyond conventional markets*
Domestic	Employment	• Social cohesion • Innovation and adaptation • Attracting other skilled labourers and wealthy connoisseurs
External	Exports	• Status and soft power

Source: Author.

overview of some CCI benefits, distinguishing between the domestic economy and in terms of external trade, as well as between commercial values and benefits that accrue beyond conventional markets and national accounts.

Regarding the commercial benefits of CCI, these industries have the potential to provide gainful employment opportunities for skilled and creative domestic workers and citizens trading with these products. Competitive economies can also benefit from external trade of CCI, especially when they can export valuable goods and services to relatively high-income countries under favourable terms; on the performance of India in external trade of creative products, see Shaban and Vermeylen (2015).

Beyond these commercial benefits that are reflected in national accounts, there are great hopes that CCI are an important arena for communication between citizens that would foster mutual understanding, civic pride, and social cohesion. Another domestic benefit of CCI concerns synergies between CCI and other industries, in particular the role that cultural and creative activities can play as in fostering opportunities for innovation and adaptation of other industries. For instance, engagement in creative and cultural activities may foster more generally applicable skills related to creative problem-solving and communication. In any case, creative media content helps foster demand for media technology and telecommunication services – if an attractive range of content is available at low prices online, the demand for computer hardware, smartphones, and broadband access will increase. Another example are creative services that are used to make other goods more appealing, say with clever industrial design, packaging, or advertising. Furthermore, there is some evidence that local hubs of CCI activities make these locations more attractive for other highly educated and skilled people – so that academics in all sorts of professions would favour living where there are strong CCI (Florida 2005). Last but not least, regarding external CCI benefits, countries that manage to export much attractive cultural and creative services may attract tourism, gain status and soft power, and ensure that the perspectives of their citizens are noticed in other territories.

2.3.4 How do CCI benefits come about?

What is more, there is a potential for growth in CCI to foster self-perpetuating processes, for instance where increasing employment in CCI fosters social cohesion and makes a location more attractive for tourists and skilled workers in other professions, generating general economic growth beyond the CCI and increasing the demand for creative goods and services. This begets the question, how best to exploit that potential – or in other words, does art follow wealth or does wealth follow art? This is of obvious relevance for cultural policy.

The predominant pattern may be that art follows wealth. Regarding the demand side of CCI, creative and cultural products tend to be luxury goods in the sense that as people get wealthier, they spend an increasing share of their disposable income on CCI products. On the supply side of CCI, intrinsic motivation to create means that if people's most imminent needs are covered, they prefer creative work over other labour, even if creative work does not yield the same level of income as more humdrum employment. If the positive externalities of CCI compensate for the subsequent reduction in conventional measures of value generation, intrinsic motivation to create means that CCI will thrive as communities get wealthier. In this line of reasoning, any economic growth begets growth in CCI and there may be little need for cultural policy to trigger this process.

The predominant pattern may also be that wealth follows art. A certain level of CCI activities and the non-commercial benefits it entails may be required to enable growth in other parts of the economy, for instance because a vibrant cultural live enables innovative other activities or the retention and attraction of highly skilled workers in other professions and other highly productive industries. In this line of reasoning, CCI has the potential to instigate and promote more general economic growth, and an adequate cultural policy appears as an important element of a broader range of policies aimed at fostering socio-economic development.

Arguably, neither of these two abstract scenarios is generally a more valid description of the role of CCI and thus cultural policy in economic development. In all probability, the underlying mechanisms are more complex and context specific.

When faced with the question of how and how much of scarce public resources to commit to specific ends, such as cultural policy, many economists instead tend to favour the market mechanism. For all the potential benefits of CCI, in functioning markets, choices of sovereign consumers reflect their preferences and needs and provide suppliers with the best information available on what should be produced at what amounts. Where this market mechanism that coordinates demand and supply fails in the short run, competition between rival suppliers ensures that firms that happen to supply the right products thrive at the expense of other firms. Thus, efficient markets and liberal economies at large should be self-correcting. Sooner or later, liberal economies converge on an optimal allocation of resources in a process that does not require any central authority – for instance a government – to understand exactly what is required or why there may be any need for change. In essence, that is the argument in liberal market economics, with Hayek (1945) being a famous proponent. In this perspective, the type of academic exercise conducted in this chapter would be of little practical value and extensive cultural policy would not be required to maximize social welfare.

So, do Hayekian markets provide the answer to cultural policy? One fundamental counter-argument is that markets can be slow to adapt to changing circumstances, so that government policy may have a role in speeding things up. Another is that governments are better equipped than private agents to establish institutional arrangements required for reasonably efficient markets. Standard welfare economics stipulates a range of conditions for 'market failure', where unregulated markets do not reliably approximate an optimal allocation of resources. Thus, to come to terms with some fundamental economic reasoning regarding the adequate scale and scope of cultural policy, it is helpful to appreciate the idiosyncratic economic characteristics of CCI.

2.3.5 Market failure

Many of the economic characteristics of CCI relate to sources of market failure such as market power, public goods and external effects, uncertainty and incomplete information, as well as transaction costs. Some of these issues have already featured in this chapter.

For instance, creative works tend to have attributes of public goods. The cost structure of CCI aggravates the issue: it is costly to create new valuable cultural works, and reproducing them is much cheaper. This also applies to physical arts or crafts objects, if to a lesser extent. Competition from copy-cats can make it hard for creators to recoup the up-front costs of creation. Basic economic reasoning implies that under these circumstances, the supply of new creative works will fall below its socially desirable level. Copyright policy is one means to mitigate that problem in the CCI.

Market power is also often rife in CCI. First, effective copyright policy by definition establishes market power for rights holders: they can charge prices in excess of marginal costs and – in the case of success – recoup their upfront costs of creation. Thus copyright policy mitigates one source of market failure by aggravating another, and requires a difficult balance. Second and more profoundly, CCI are organized in relatively small and flexible creative teams and more integrated and stable intermediary firms that trade in creative works (Caves 2000). Think of an author, who seeks a contract with a traditional publisher or uses the standard terms and conditions of an online platform to make his work available there. With great integration among intermediary firms, there is the risk that these firms acquire market power and appropriate much of the surplus value generated along the entire value chain of CCI. In conventional welfare economics, these distributional effects are not a prime concern as long as they do not adversely affect efficiency. Unquestionable problems arise when integration and market power leads to centralized control, where management of a few organizations operate under little pressure from actual or potential competition. Then it may take very long for the market mechanism to correct mistakes by large organizations and millions of customers and other stakeholders may be adversely affected.

Another source of market failure in CCI is uncertainty. As creative works have attributes of experience goods, consumers take decisions under incomplete information. The complex and interdependent processes in which users assess creative products do not reliably converge on optimal choices.

In short, due to multiple sources of market failure, we cannot trust markets to reliably bring about an optimal allocation of resources in CCI.

2.3.6 Government failure

If markets fail, it is tempting to jump to the conclusion that (cultural) policy is required. However, market failure is a necessary but not a sufficient condition to justify government interventions.

First, government agencies are subject to incentive problems: officials do not face the full consequences of their actions, say when they favour one type of cultural production over others and thus influence what types of works become available to citizens. Subjugating CCI to extensive public policy instils an element of centralized control that – similarly to private firms wielding market power – can give rise to faulty decisions that are not swiftly corrected by competition in markets. What is more, like all individuals, government officials may have their own interests in mind, as public choice analyses emphasizes (Buchanan and Tollison 1984). They may even collude with specific stakeholders in the CCI when devising cultural policy to promote partial interests to the detriment of society at large.

Second, even government agencies made up of impeccable civil servants with the best intensions are subject to informational problems: with constant innovation and extensive uncertainty in the CCI, it is hard for policymakers to anticipate the best way to satisfy the needs and cater to the preferences of a diverse range of citizens. Regarding CCI, these problems are particularly daring. On the one hand, it is hard to define and measure essential functions of creative works, and thus what types of creative works should be promoted by public policy. On the other hand, CCI are innovation intensive, as creative works are often appreciated subject to an element of uniqueness, novelty, or surprise. It is thus extremely hard for cultural policymakers to anticipate what the best decisions for society at large would be, whereas in reasonably competitive markets, suppliers either happen to manage to respond to user needs or lose market share to competitors.

In short, some of the very same economic characteristics of CCI that make government intervention desirable mean that it is hard to bring about adequate cultural policy.

2.3.7 CCI as a soft issue

The problem in shaping adequate cultural policy in developing, middle-income countries runs even deeper than that. CCI projects often yield uncertain benefits, which are hard to measure. CCI may also look like relatively trivial pursuits. In middle-income countries, many inhabitants have very limited access to health services and nutrition, for instance. CCI cater for needs that are less essential for short-term sustenance. In economic terms, creative products are luxury goods that require a reasonable level of wealth and provision of essential goods and services before they can be appreciated. Many creative products also require a sufficient level of education and knowledge to be fully appreciated. Therefore, in poor countries there will be greater emphasis on the provision of essential services and education, and cultural policy appears secondary at best. In other words, CCI are often perceived as a 'soft issues'. Promoting luxuries is hardly worthwhile in the face of absolute poverty, right?

However, in the course of ongoing processes of socio-economic development, CCI have a more prominent role to play. Let's assume that India is following a conventional, positive development trajectory. This implies increasing wealth and perhaps a more equal distribution with the establishment of a sizable middle class of skilled workers. It also implies rising levels of general-purpose education. On the supply side, this means that in increasingly affluent societies, more skilled workers will favour working in CCI, as they can afford to care about the quality of work and not just the maximization of pecuniary income. In a sense, creative work is what affluent people do. In this perspective, art follows wealth. On the demand side, increasing wealth means that households not only spend greater absolute amounts on creative products, they also dedicate a greater proportion of their disposable income to creative products. Thus, strong domestic CCI that cater for the needs of citizens within the same territory will become engines of growth at some level of socio-economic development. In this perspective, wealth follows art – that is CCI can promote or sustain economic growth.

Thus, in this conventional type of positive socio-economic development, we would predict more abundant supply, as well as increasing appreciation and demand for creative works. Promoting CCI can thus be good proactive policy, as it fosters the role of CCI as engines of growth that thrive in and contribute to economic growth and development more generally.

2.4 Conclusions and outlook

This chapter has developed a rather abstract, general assessment of the role of CCI in development. There are several fundamental messages that should provide useful guidelines for shaping adequate cultural policy in middle-income and quickly developing countries such as India. Some of these issues may even be counter-intuitive and thus particularly useful, because they have the potential to change and improve upon predominant attitudes regarding cultural policy.

2.4.1 Don't get stuck in definitional issues

For instance, one should not get stuck in definitional issues. Like most concepts in applied social sciences, the exact definition criteria and boundaries of CCI are contested and fuzzy and this is likely to remain the case for the foreseeable future. That is lamentable, for instance, because it is hard to develop quantitative indicators of the economic impact of CCI. However, since positive externalities are one of the very points why CCI are of interest, any attempt at clear delineations is bound to be problematic. In spite of this challenge, economic assessments of CCI suggest that these industries have an increasing role to play in sustaining economic growth in developing countries and economics provides a framework that helps develop practical insights on how best to benefit from this process.

2.4.2 We care about CCI because of the dual challenge of market failure and government failure – not because they are big

Furthermore, in assessing the need for public cultural policy, current metrics of the absolute size of the CCI is not the main concern. The growth potential of CCI should be decisive in forward-looking policy, also regarding their potential to promote innovation and growth in other aspects of the economy and to generate non-commercial benefits. For devising adequate cultural policy, the two central questions are: (1) how pronounced is market failure in specific CCI? And (2) can specific government policy mitigate market failure and unhinge CCI growth without excessive costs and unintended consequences?

This chapter has presented several reasons why market failure regarding CCI is probably very pronounced. It has also illustrated that it is hard to answer the question what type of cultural policy and how much of it is most likely to mitigate these problems and to help fully exploit the growth potential of CCI. This chapter also emphasized the complexity of CCI themselves as well as the variety of their commercial and wider social benefits. That makes cultural policy-making challenging. On the one hand, there is great need for careful assessments, and economic theory provides a useful framework, as long as wider social benefits are not sidelined. On the other hand, any assessment of complex social systems may yield misleading predictions that do not transpire in practice. Empirical evidence is required, for instance, to establish whether policies achieve their intended results without excessive costs and unintended consequences. The methods of applied economics use theory and empirics as complementary tools, where theory identifies challenges, policy options, and empirically testable statements, and empirics provide information to alter and improve upon the application of theory to specific circumstances. Thus economic reasoning and empirical methods, and in particular the specialized literature on cultural economics, provide a relatively sophisticated framework to structure debates on cultural policy.

Overall, because of the dual challenge of market failure and government failure, CCI and cultural policy deserve extensive attention and research. Here lays a challenge for any practically minded researcher, who seeks to develop useful policy insights. This chapter focused on fundamental aspects of theory. Cultural policy also requires empirical evidence. The other chapters in this volume offer useful information in this respect.

2.4.3 Luxuries are not negligible

Creative products are usually luxuries: while their consumption by the uneducated or destitute may be close to zero, with increasing wealth and education, household expenditure of creative products increases disproportionally. This does not mean that CCI would be negligible in public policy and development. In the course of development, the potential of CCI for gainful employment and economic growth is likely to expand quite quickly compared to many other industries. Cultural policy can help prepare and foster this structural change in the national economy, so that art can not only swiftly follow wealth but also become an engine of further economic growth and development.

2.4.4 Labour intensity of CCI is a boon

The labour intensity of CCI has often been seen as a reason why these industries are likely to experience relative decline in the course of economic development and technological change. According to Baumol's cost disease, labour-intensive industries do not keep pace with productivity increases in technology and are thus relegated to increasingly minor roles with development. This chapter has argued that for CCI, the reverse is more likely to be the case in developing countries. On the one hand, for many experience goods such as creative products, the potential of digitalization to yield productivity increases are more pronounced than in other parts of the economy. Better informed users can make better choices, for instance, and with less uncertainty, may expand their engagement with creative products. On the other hand, with increasing wealth and education, employment in the CCI is likely to grow at an even greater pace than the economy at large.

2.4.5 Beware of the artist-superstar

There is however a challenge to ensure that many individuals have the opportunity of gainful employment in the CCI. The core CCI – the arts and cultural industries – is prone to superstar effects: extremely uneven distributions of income among creative workers. A tiny handful of the most successful creators reap the bulk of the rewards, and the wealthiest creators are not necessarily the most talented or industrious. If CCI are to promote social mobility and reasonably equitable economic development, extensive superstar effects are a problem. Citizens in high-income countries may still be willing to try their luck as a creator. Beyond the most wealthy territories and social groups, people will tend to be more risk-averse, and large parts of the population will hardly participate on the supply side.

2.4.6 Further questions

Obviously, there is a general need for empirical research on specific CCI in India to spot challenges and opportunities in the diverse, specific settings found in this country. There are also some overarching questions that are likely to be central in many of these cases. Let's conclude with a couple of suggestions for future research on such central questions.

First, we ought to better understand when art follows wealth and at what levels of general socio-economic development it starts working the other way around. In very poor communities and times of crisis, the provision of essential goods and services regarding health, nutrition, and general-purpose education will often take precedence over policy directly concerned with CCI. With somewhat higher standards of living and good prospects for economic growth, cultural policy can make a strong contribution to sustain and foster positive developments. We need to explore how to alter the scale and scope of cultural policy over ongoing processes of socio-economic development.

Second, there is some hope that CCI can promote upward social mobility. We need to better understand whether and how CCI can provide marginal social groups with better opportunities to participate in general economic growth, whether that concerns women, members of poor communities, or in the Indian case, lower castes.

Third, the CCI are central participants in the process of digitalization (Towse and Handke 2013). Many creative products can be accessed and used via widely available ICT hardware and the Internet. Any creative product can be marketed and traded online, and ICT can help spread information on creative products, driving back uncertainty and inefficiency. Digitalization helps making CCI as a whole more productive and efficient. What is more, many manufactured goods and services are more attractive in combination with creative products. Exports are also facilitated in this context. As Indian expats in Silicon Valley and colleagues in Bangalore will testify, digitalization provides new opportunities and India – with its relatively low labour costs and large and relatively well-educated population of young people, as well as its rich cultural heritage – is in a promising position to harness CCI as an engine of growth and development. The interface between socio-economic development, digitalization, and CCI requires much more attention.

Finally, I am of course aware of the terrible impact of the Corona pandemic on Indians (Yadav et al. 2021). The pandemic also constitutes a substantial exogenous shock on the CCI, and provides additional impetus for digitalization in the sector. However, the impact of the Corona pandemic has its limits,[1] will almost certainly become less severe over time, and there are many other pressing needs for most Indians. It thus also seems likely that over the coming years, the expenditure on countermeasures will be limited in India. If that holds, the more long-standing and gradual sources of socio-economic change involving CCI in India, on which this chapter focuses, will continue to play the central role in related policy.

Note

1 Lewnard et al. (2021) estimate ca. 5.2 "excess deaths" per 1,000 inhabitants between 1 March and 30 June 2021 for the Chennai region, for which relatively high-quality data is available.

References

Baumol, W. J., and Bowen, W. G. (1993). *Performing Arts-the Economic Dilemma: A Study of Problems Common to Theater, Opera, Music and Dance*. Aldershot, UK: Gregg Revivals.

Baumol, W. J., and Towse, R. (Eds.) (1997). *Baumol's Cost Disease: The Arts and Other Victims*. Cheltenham: Edward Elgar Publishing.

Blaug, M. (2001). Where are we now on cultural economics? *Journal of Economic Surveys*, 15(2), 123–143.

Buchanan, J. M., and Tollison, R. D. (Eds.) (1984). *The Theory of Public Choice – II*. Ann Arbor, MI: University of Michigan Press.

Caves, R. E. (2000). *Creative Industries: Contracts between Art and Commerce* (No. 20). Cambridge, MA: Harvard University Press.

Florida, R. (2005). *Cities and the Creative Class*. Abingdon-on-Thames: Routledge.

Frey, B. S., and Jegen, R. (2001). Motivation crowding theory. *Journal of Economic Surveys*, 15(5), 589–611.

Ginsburgh, V. A., and Throsby, D. (Eds.) (2006). *Handbook of the Economics of Art and Culture* (Vol. 1). Amsterdam: Elsevier.

Handke, C. (2004). Defining creative industries by comparing the creation of novelty. Published in the reader of the *Workshop Creative Industries – A measure for Urban Development?*, 64–81.

Handke, C. (2011). Economic effect of copyright: The empirical evidence so far. Report for the National Academies of the Sciences, Washington DC, USA.

Hayek, F. A. (1945). The use of knowledge in society. *The American Economic Review*, 35(4), 519–530.

india.gov.in (2019). Art & culture. Available at: www.india.gov.in/topics/art-culture (last accessed on 12 June 2019).

Lewnard, J. A., Mahmud, A., Narayan, T., Wahl, B., Selvavinayagam, T. S., Mohan, C. B., and Laxminarayan, R. (2021, 22 December). All-cause mortality during the COVID-19 pandemic in Chennai, India: An observational study. *Lancet*. Pre-print available at: https://doi.org/10.1016/ S1473-3099(21)00746-5

Liebowitz, S. J. (2013). Internet piracy: The estimated impact on sales. In Towse, R. and Handke, C. (eds.), *Handbook on the Digital Creative Economy*, pp. 262–273. Cheltenham: Edward Elgar Publishing.

Shaban, A., and Vermeylen, F. (2015). Trade in the creative sector. *Economic & Political Weekly*, 50(20), 69–75.

Telang, R., and Waldfogel, J. (2018). Piracy and new product creation: A Bollywood story. *Information Economics and Policy*, 43, 1–11.

Throsby, D. (1994). A work-preference model of artist behaviour. In Peacock, A. and Rizzo, I. (eds.), *Cultural Economics and Cultural Policies*, pp. 69–80. Dordrecht: Springer.

Throsby, D. (2008). Modelling the cultural industries. *International Journal of Cultural Policy*, 14(3), 217–232.

Towse, R. (1997). Copyright as an economic incentive. *Hume Papers on Public Policy*, 5, 32–45.

Towse, R. (Ed.) (2011). *A Handbook of Cultural Economics*. Cheltenham: Edward Elgar Publishing.

Towse, R., and Handke, C. (Eds.) (2013). *Handbook on the Digital Creative Economy*. Cheltenham: Edward Elgar Publishing.

Watson, S. J., Zizzo, D. J., and Fleming, P. (2015). Determinants of unlawful file sharing: A scoping review. *PLoS One*, 10(6), e0127921.

Yadav, S., Yadav, P. K., and Yadav, N. (2021). Impact of COVID-19 on life expectancy at birth in India: A decomposition analysis. *BMC Public Health* 21, 1906ff.

3

CREATIVE INDUSTRIES

Definitions, methodologies, and classifications for India

Abdul Shaban

3.1 Introduction

In recent decades, academic and policy interests on cultural and creative industries (CCIs) have grown. However, there is still no universally agreed up on definition of CCIs, and they have been a subject of gripping and charged debate and discussions. There is also no consensus among scholars and practitioners on the activities to be included into CCIs. What is 'cultural' in cultural industries, and similarly, what is 'creative' is creative industries (CIs) have also been debated and remain sources of difference between various studies and organizations engaged in collection, dissemination, and promotion of these industries.

Apart from academic research, the commercial aspect and the mode of production of CCIs have also been integral part of the un-ending debate. In recent years, the commercial aspect of culture has become an important source of employment, income, and trade. The commercialization of culture has also led the emergence of terms like 'economy of culture' to denote the economic significance of the culture in the post-war economy at the global level. It was in this commercial context that, in the post-war period, the term 'culture industries' was used by Theodor Adorno and Max Horkheimer (1947) and subsequently by Herbert Marcuse (1991) for describing emerging mass entertainment. Despite the definitional confusions between the cultural and creative industries (Cunningham 2002; Galloway and Dunlop 2007), this commercial aspect of culture and creativity has evoked enormous interest of governments and organizations advocating development, multiculturalism, equality, cultural justice, and peace (UNESCO 2013). Further, it has now been largely accepted that CIs represent much larger canvas, and the cultural industries are a subset of the same. In the CCI literature, the debates have also raged about the cultural versus commercial values and 'whose' culture these industries represent (high versus popular culture). Rooted in this debate, the symbolic text model of creative industries puts at the centre the popular cultural in its definition of CIs.

 DOI: 10.4324/9781003129370-4

The term 'creative industry' originated from the report of the Department of Communications and the Arts (1994), Government of Australia, on 'Creative Nation' (UNCTAD 2010). The term got wider popularity in 1997 when United Kingdom's Department of Culture, Media and Sport (DCMS) set up the Creative Industries Task Force. Since then, the concept has got broadened and now includes many commercial activities, many of them with comparatively lower cultural contents, such as software activities, than commercial contents. The present chapter examines this raging debate on definition of CCIs, and then endeavours to identify the CIs in India based on the National Industrial Classifications (NICs) used in the Economic Censuses (ECs), as they are the best source of data to examine the size, geographies, and growth of the creative industries in India, which we take up in the next chapter.

3.2 Defining creative and cultural industries

Horkheimer and Adorno (2002) used the term 'cultural industries' to refer to "industrially produced commercial entertainment – broadcasting, film, publishing, recorded music – as distinct from the subsidised 'arts' – visual and performing arts, museums and galleries" (Galloway and Dunlop 2007: 18), which became background for further discussion and initiation of many policies by UNESCO in 1978 and Council of Europe in 1980 (Garnham 1990: 165). This also led to the development of French cultural policy since the early 1980s (Towse 2000; Flew 2002). Given the engagement of the European Council and UNESCO, the acceptance of the concept in public planning and policy grew rapidly among different countries and organizations. For instance, in Australia, it was adopted in the early 1990s (Howkins 2002: 1), while in the UK it was done around 1997 (Flew 2002; Caust 2003; Pratt 2004). Cunningham (2002) argues that where cultural industries in early 20th century arose from their concatenation with large-scale media, the CIs have emerged from technological advancement of the late 20th and early 21st centuries, in which World Wide Web (WWW) and digitalization have been main drivers of the industry. In recent years, it has also been seen that the term 'cultural industries' is being abandoned in the favour of 'creative industries' (Galloway and Dunlop 2007: 19).

The term CCIs is value loaded, and various other terms such as 'originality', 'creativity', 'intellectual property', 'symbolism', 'used value', and 'joint goods' (Galloway and Dunlop 2007) have been used to convey what creative and cultural industries constitute. Besides, other studies have also attempted to capture the essence of the creative and cultural goods and services by production methods (Garnham 1990; Hesmondhalgh 2002; Towse 2003).

The activities based on individual and/or group 'creativity' are related to CIs (Galloway and Dunlop 2007). However, many activities can be creative, or what may be 'creative' for one person may not be for others. Further, creativity can be resulting from 'individuals', as 'attribute of people', or it can be embedded and constituent of 'process' (UNCTAD 2010). There is no agreement on which source of 'creativity' is accounted for or is constituent of CIs. Additionally, if the creativity is 'innovativeness', then financial and business services may score high (Creative Skillset 2013), which we often do not find in the list of creative industries. UNCTAD (2010) cautions us that "creativity is not the same as innovation" (p. 1) and uses it more to convey the 'originality', which it defines as "creating something from nothing or reworking something that already exists" (p. 1). As such, the term creativity becomes a lose term to associate with the sector and that is why there have been many definitions, as we will see later, of CIs.

The intellectual property rights (IPRs) have also been associated with creativity and defining CIs. The activities which can be used to generate copyrights and can be protected through the copyright laws are, that is why, considered by some of the researchers as core of CCIs (Towse 2003). This copyright line of thinking and definition leads to include not only the cultural activities which are specific to communities and regions but also to 'knowledge industry' into CIs. The knowledge economy model as such leads to the argument that the definition of CI then should apply to any activities where "brain power is preponderant and where the outcome is intellectual property" (Howkins 2002: 2), and this has led many to argue that the old distinction among 'industry, science and culture' are obsolete and any such distinctions are barriers to progress (Galloway and Dunlop 2007: 20). Following this approach, as one does not have a very concise definition of creativity, a large number of activities can get included into CIs. One such example is the definition by the Task Force on Creative Industries by the DCMS, Government of UK. The Task Force defined creative industries as "those industries which have their origin in individual creativity, skill and talent and which have a potential for wealth and job creation through the generation and exploitation of intellectual property" (Government of UK 2015). Galloway and Dunlop (2007) argue that the two terms 'creativity' and 'IPR' thus lead us to very ambiguous situation about "what is 'cultural' in the 'cultural' or 'creative' in the 'industries'" (p. 20).

To have sharper ability to distinguish the activities which may fall under 'creative and cultural' categories, the concept of 'symbolic meaning' has been mobilized. Advocates of this viewpoint argue that 'symbolic meaning' is the essence of the cultural goods, and the economic value of the goods is derived from their cultural values (Galloway and Dunlop 2007: 20). The application of symbolic meaning led to the emergence of 'Symbolic Text' and 'Concentric Circle' models. In both these models, core cultural activities are those with symbolic meanings (UNCTAD 2010).

Bilton and Leary (2004) have argued that 'use value' should be the defining concept of cultural and creative industries. This leads to inclusion of symbolic goods and services which 'first use' the communication of ideas, rather than functional values (Galloway and Dunlop 2007: 21), like music, films, plays, books, while others like architecture, design, and fashion where functionalities come first rather than their symbolic contents get excluded from cultural industry.

Throsby (2001) argues that the cultural goods and services should contain all the three characteristics discussed earlier. That is, they should have (a) creativity in their production, (b) symbolic meaning, and (c) embodiment of intellectual property. Throsby's argument leads to conceptualization of cultural and creative goods and services in concentric model where at the core are the goods and services with symbolic meanings and at the periphery are those what are referred to as 'joint goods' with some cultural and other non-cultural (functional) contents. The proportion of the same may be difficult to ascertain and define, as what should be the proportion of cultural and functional contents to designate an activity as belonging to CCIs (Galloway and Dunlop 2007).

The previous discussion shows the complexity that has been involved in defining CCIs. Many studies have claimed that given the definitional ambiguity, it is very difficult to exclude many activities from CCIs, and even "design and production of Coca-Cola can be part of the cultural industry" (Flew 2002: 13). Further, given the broad sense in which 'culture' is used, "we might equally conclude that everything is cultural" (Galloway and Dunlop 2007: 23), and therefore:

> Some have argued, on the basis of the flexibility of the term culture, that it is useless to talk of the cultural activities at all. Others have also implied this by arguing that all industries are cultural, because all industries are involved in the production of goods and services which become part of the web of meaning we know as culture.
>
> (Hesmondhalgh and Pratt 2005: 6)

However, Galloway and Dunlop (2007) argue that it is not appropriate to stretch the concepts involved in defining and identifying the creative and cultural goods and services "beyond breaking point" (p. 23) but stick to the 'meaningful' use of the terms as:

> The main interest in such industries is the symbolic, aesthetic and, for want of a better term, artistic, nature of their output, because these outputs can potentially have a strong influence on the way we understand society.
>
> (Hesmondhalgh and Pratt 2005: 6)

Similarly, Creative Skillset (2013) argues that all goods may have some level of creativity, but some may have more of it. "At some point, an industry has a sufficient proportion of 'creativity, skill and talent' to be deemed to be part of the Creative Industries, with other sectors falling below this arbitrary benchmark" (Creative Skillset 2013: 6). In fact, the main challenge in the definition of creative and cultural industries lies overcoming this 'arbitrariness'.

There has been yet another debate in the literature regarding whether the goods and services produced on industrial scale or mass scale with cultural contents should be considered as cultural industry or those which are produced at individual level or at cottage scale (Garnham 1990; Hesmondhalgh 2002; Towse 2003). Adorno used the conception of cultural industry mainly for those activities which "employ industrial technologies and modes of organization to produce and distribute cultural goods and services" (Galloway and Dunlop 2007: 24) in contrast to those that are produced at cottage scale or through pre-industrial means. Hesmondhalgh (2002) argues that "the core cultural industries deal with the industrial production and circulation of texts [the production of social meaning] and are centrally reliant on the work of symbol creators" (p. 12). It needs to be understood that production method cannot define what is cultural (Galloway and Dunlop 2007), but any of these methods can be used in the production of cultural and creative goods and services. Specially, the cottage scale and one off are more common in the context of developing countries.

Production of knowledge has also been considered as creative industry. The knowledge economy today produces different kind of information which may have their functional or scientific usages. As the cultural knowledge is traditional or intergenerational knowledge, "the distinctive aspects of cultural sector have been subsumed within the wider creative industries agenda – culture is now viewed as just one more 'knowledge economy asset'" (Galloway and Dunlop 2007: 25).

Given the lack of any strict and agreed definition of CCIs, Banks and O'Connor (2009) have called it as "loosely defined set of economic activities" (p. 365). Though differences in approaches to identify the CCIs exist, it has now been accepted that (a) creative industries relate to the production or goods and services that have cultural, artistic and entertainment values (Caves 2000; Friedman and Jones 2011) or those goods and services which carry more symbolic than material worth (Hirsch 1972), and (b) the cultural industry are subset of creative industries [creative industries include also products and services like fashion and software, which are not considered part of cultural goods (UNCTAD 2010: 5)], and (c) the mode of production does not matter but creative goods and services can be produced at any scale.

3.3 International organizations and classification methods

The literature which started emerging since 1960s about the relationship between culture and economics (Myerscough 1988; UNCTAD 2019) opened up possibilities to create theoretical and empirical frameworks about CIs. Besides individual researchers, by 2010s several organizations and governments, as we will see subsequently, put forth their own efforts in this regard. The latter started constituting expert groups to create frameworks for identification of CCIs to enable the larger purpose of gathering related data and design effective cultural policies. Availability of data at various geographic scales enabled the researchers to further empirically and theoretically test the relationship between creativity/culture and economics. The purpose of these efforts was not to make the economic goals 'subservient to cultural ones' but understanding "both the cultural and economic moments" (Banks and O'Connor 2009: 367). To Bill Ryan (1992), this double emphasis on 'arts-commerce' has been interesting in this field. In fact, the major definitions of CCIs propagated by individuals, organizations, and governments attempt to balance this double emphasis. Some of these definitions and their recognition of creative goods and services are discussed here.

The DCMS, Government of UK (DCMS 2001; UNCTAD 2010) adopted its own definition in 1990s of CIs. DCMS (2001) defines CIs "as those requiring creativity, skill and talent, with potential for wealth and job creation through the exploitation of their intellectual property" (UNCTAD 2010: 6) and identified 13 industries as CIs (Table 3.1).

Symbolic Text model has emerged from critical cultural studies tradition of Europe, and specially of the UK (Hesmondhalgh 2002). Because of its ideological nature, it focuses on popular culture rather than high culture (UNCTAD 2010). It classifies goods and services in three categories – core, peripheral, and borderline. A total of 12 goods and services are recognized as creative industries under this framework.

The Work Foundations adapted David Throsby's (2001) concentric circles model. In this framework, arts are considered as purest form of creativity and as such are located at the core of this model. As one moves away from the core, the cultural contents in goods and services decline. A total of 15 goods and services are recognized as part of creative industries under this framework (see Table 3.1).

UNESCO defines creative industries as those "combine the creation, production and commercialization of contents which are intangible and cultural in nature" (UNCTAD 2010: 5). France has adopted the definition of cultural industry as "that combine the functions of conception, creation and production of culture with more industrial functions in the large-scale manufacture and commercialization of cultural products" (Département des études, de la prospective et des statistiques 2006; UNCTAD 2010: 5).

The World Intellectual Property Organization's (WIPO) copyright model recognizes those goods and services as CIs which have "intellectual property as embodiment of creativity" (UNCTAD 2010: 6). It has three broad subcategories of goods and services, and in the 'partial copyright industries', the intellectual property is considered to be playing the least role in their functions.

The UNCTAD (2010) model of creative industries is very comprehensive and has been guided by international economic development agenda. It relies on 'creativity' and 'artistic components' of goods and services, and as such defines creative industries as "any economic activity producing symbolic

Table 3.1 Creative industries models

UK DCMS model	*Symbolic texts model*	*Concentric circles model*	*WIPO copyright model*	*UNCTAD model*
1. Advertising	**I. Core cultural industries**	**I. Core creative arts**	**I. Core copyright industry**	**I. Heritage**
2. Architecture	1. Advertising	1. Literature	1. Advertising	I.a. Traditional cultural expression
3. Arts and antiques market	2. Film	2. Music	2. Collecting societies	1. Art crafts
4. Crafts	3. Internet	3. Performing arts	3. Film and video	2. Festivals and celebrations
5. Design	4. Music	4. Visual arts	4. Music	I.b. Cultural sites
6. Fashion	5. Publishing		5. Performing arts	3. Archaeological sites
7. Film and video	6. Television and radio	**II. Other core cultural industries**	6. Publishing	4. Museums
8. Music	7 Video and computer games	5. Film	7. Software	5. Libraries
9. Performing arts		6. Museum and libraries	8. Television and radio	6. Exhibitions, etc.
10. Publishing	**II. Peripheral cultural industries**		9. Visual and graphic art	
11. Software	8. Creative arts	**III. Wider cultural industries**		**II. Arts**
12. Television and radio		7. Heritage services	**II. Interdependent copyright industries**	II.a. Performing arts
13. Video and computer games	**III. Borderline cultural industries**	8. Publishing	10. Blank recording material	7. Live music
	9. Consumer electronics	9. Sound recording	11. Consumer electronics	8. Theatre
	10. Fashion	10. Television and radio	12. Musical instruments	9. Dance
	11 Software	11. Video and computer game	13. Paper	10. Opera
	12. Sports		14. Photocopiers, photographic equipment	11. Circus
		IV. Related industries		12. Puppetry, etc.
		12. Advertising	**III. Partial copyright industries**	II.b. Visual arts
		13. Architecture	15. Architecture	13. Paintings
		14. Design	16. Clothing, footwear	14. Sculptures
		15. Fashion	17. Design	15. Photography

18. Fashion	16. Antiques, etc.
19. Household goods	
20. Toys	**III. Media**
	III.a. Audio-visuals
	17. Films
	18. Television
	19. Radio
	20. Other broadcasting
	III.b. Publishing and print media
	21. Books
	22. Press and other publications
	IV. Functional creations
	IV.a. New media
	23. Software
	24. Video games
	25. Digitized creative contents
	IV.b. Design
	26. Interior
	27. Graphic
	28. Fashion
	29. Jewellery
	30. Toys
	IV. Creative services
	31. Architectural
	32. Advertising
	33. Creative R&D
	34. Cultural and recreational

Source: Compiled from UNCTAD (2010).

products with a heavy reliance on intellectual property and for as wide a market as possible" (UNCTAD 2010: 7, 2004). UNCTAD identifies five characteristics of creative goods and services,

- are the cycles of creation, production and distribution of goods and services that use creativity and intellectual capital as primary inputs;
- constitute a set of knowledge-based activities, focused on but not limited to arts, potentially generating revenues from trade and intellectual property rights;
- comprise tangible products and intangible intellectual or artistic services with creative content, economic value and market objectives;
- stand at the crossroads of the artisan, services and industrial sectors; and
- constitute a new dynamic sector in world trade.

(UNCTAD 2010: 8)

UNCTAD (2010) identifies 34 goods and services as part of CIs, under four major groups and nine sub-groups. The UNCTAD framework is based on upstream (traditional cultural activities) and downstream (more commercial in nature or closure to market) activities (UNCTAD 2010).

However, an important question here is whether some models are more important than others? It is not considered so. UNCTAD's Creative Economy Report (UNCTAD 2010) argues, "there are no 'right' or 'wrong' models of the creative industries, simply different ways of interpreting the structural characteristics of creative production" (p. 8). One can chose any of such models as per their preferences and contexts. However, each of the model will result into different size of creative industries, if one uses the same to find its size empirically. In this volume, we have largely used the UNCTAD (2010) model of creative industries. Both subjective preferences of wider range of goods and services included in this model and objective situation, as it helps in identification of activities from different NICs and thus computation of size of the workforce and industry from Economic Censuses of India, have guided us in choice of this model.

3.4 Identification, classification, and data sources for India

Given the wide variation in definitions by individuals and organizations, Banks and O'Connor argue:

> What counts as a creative industry cannot be imposed from without, according to a set of universal and objectively applied criteria, but tends to be constructed (often in *ad hoc* fashion) according to local politics, history and geography.
>
> (Banks and O'Connor 2009: 366)

This does provide the freedom to construct a definition as per the local history, geography, and culture and include and exclude the goods and services as per some objective criteria. India is one of the major cultural spaces of the world, and as such a definition of CIs can be created as per the context. Given the wide range of the models mentioned in Table 3.1, options are also available for one to choose and apply any one of those models, or modify certain models to create one best suited for the Indian context. For instance, one can remove gambling, video games, etc. from the list as they are not considered culturally acceptable by a large section of Indian families across the social groups in India. Further, even one can think of regional and community-based definition of CCIs, based on what is culturally accepted or considered culturally polluting or profane. However, to be more objective and keeping the data comparable to other countries and contexts, we have largely used the UNCTAD definition of creative industries in this volume. Once we have accepted the UNCTAD definition, the challenge for us has been to (a) locate the data and (b) align the indicators as per National Industrial Classification (NICs), which are equivalent of Standard Industrial Classification (SICs), though with enormous grouping and categorization differences.

In India, data related to occupation are collected by the National Sample Survey Office (NSSO) and Census of India, but where the NSSO has too thin samples across the states to make it meaningful for examining the share of people employed in creative industries, the Census of India (for 2001 and 2011) data has limitation of categories of occupations, only very broad categories of occupations like agriculture, agricultural labour, household industries and other industries, and service sectors can be examined from these data. The Annual Survey of Industries (ASI) data is another source of public data, but it provides information only at state and registered industry level and does not allow to assess the situation with respect to district level or informal sector. It is understood that in India, where the industrial development is still low, a large number of creative industries operate in informal sector. The other important source of industrial data is Economic Survey (EC). Periodically, economic surveys have been conducted in India, and they provide data for all the economic enterprises in the country at district level with precision of 3- or 4-digit levels of NIC. The last such survey was conducted in 2013–14, and data at district level are available for 3 digits of NIC. The Third EC, conducted in 1990 (MoSPI 1998), is the first such census which has electronically usable data, but the data are not available for most of the districts of Chhattisgarh, one of the Indian States. Thus, it makes the data less useful. The Fourth EC, conducted in 1998, has the electronic data available for all the districts and NIC of industries up to 4-digit level. Given the EC data are found most useful for identification of size and distribution of CIs in India, these have been used in many of the chapters in this volume.

The 4-digit NIC of EC 1998 and 3-digit NIC of EC 2013–14 are still very broad groups of industrial classification. The NIC 4 digits of EC 1998 offer more accurate identification of creative goods and services than NIC 3 digits available for EC 2013–14. However, if available, NIC 5 digits would be far advantageous for our purpose. The NICs in India have been modified over the time with the aim to make them coherent and equivalent to SICs. The EC 2013–14 uses NIC 2008 classification which is far more refined in categorization than that used in the EC 1998.

In India, there exists hardly any work on CIs in the aforementioned framework. This implies that one needs to create a framework of classification of NICs used in ECs to conform the categories of creative industries presented by UNCTAD. Next, we discuss the subcategory-wise concordance of the NIC used in 1998 and 2013–14 ECs. This helps in finding out the number of enterprises in India engaged in creative industries, their geographic locations, sources of finance, ownership of these industries by social groups, and the number of persons employed in those industries. With regard to occupation, the data available from ECs are on total persons employed, not on the activities they perform. Therefore, it is quite possible that some of workers do regular non-creative works. Given the limitation in the data, it is not possible to separate such workers from creative workers. However, even if the data has some impurity, it provide us information about the geographies, numbers, and other characteristics of these industries. Next, we outline the sectors and sub-sectors of CIs in India.

3.4.1 Heritage

This is considered as the cultural core of any society and related to its "historical, anthropological, ethnic, aesthetic and societal viewpoints, influences creativity and is the origin of a number of heritage goods and services as well as cultural activities" (UNCTAD 2010: 8). In fact, these social attributes and material productions are considered to be the source for particularities and distinctiveness of cultural industries of a society. The heritage is classified by UNCTAD (2010) into two sub-groups: traditional cultural expression and cultural sites.

3.4.1.1 Traditional cultural expression

This group includes art crafts, festivals, and celebrations. In fact, India is known for its art crafts, festivals, and celebration. Each region and communities have their own heritages which combine to shape regional as well as national culture. The art and crafts in India are largely grouped in handloom and handicrafts. Both the terms are synonymously used. In India:

> Handicraft describes a craft or occupation requiring skilled use of hands. Handicrafts are items made by hand, often using simple tools. These items can be functional, artistic and/ or traditional in nature.
>
> (MoSPI 2016: 202)

In India, the handloom and handicraft also include the specific food processing and products which are influenced by local cultural practices and demanded inclusion because of being representative of local or regional specialities. Therefore, the food products have also been added to the list of art crafts in this study. ECs count each of the economic establishments as standalone enterprises. That means if a company has two units of production located in two places, both get counted separately as two units. An economic establishment, for EC in India, is:

> A unit situated in a single location in which predominantly one kind of economic activity is carried out such that at least a part of the goods and/or services produced by the unit goes for sale (i.e. entire produce is not for sole consumption).
>
> (MoSPI 2016: 201)

This data as such becomes very useful for understanding the creative geographies or creativity in space. The EC 2013–14 has provided a separate data for arts and crafts; the NICs of EC 1998 best representing the arts crafts are presented in Table 3.2.

Table 3.2 Art crafts-related NICs

UNCTAD-recognized activities	*NIC of EC 1998 (NIC 4 digits)*	*NIC of EC 2013–14 (NIC 3 digits)*	*Remarks*
1. Arts and Crafts	*Food product related*: 2230, 2006, 2034, 2036, 2039, 2025, 2006, 2111, 2013, 2044, 2193 *Non-food product related:* 2403, 2411, 2412, 2413, 2431, 2461, 2621, 2625, 2631, 2633, 2634, 2635, 2637, 2671, 2672, 2911, 2913, 2915, 2917, 2931, 2991, 2992, 2993, 2793, 3084, 3861, 3893, 3895, 3896, 3898	Handloom and Handicraft industries have been put as separate category in the EC	The EC 2013–14 (MoSPI 2016) recognized art craft (handloom and handicraft) related activities are often cottage industries. These essentially represent the cultural expression and are related to food and non-food products. Based on this classification, the NIC of EC 98 has been classified by the author to identify art craft (handloom and handicraft) activities.
2. Festivals and celebrations	Not identifiable	Not identifiable	For EC98, it is clubbed with NIC 9599 (see creative service).

Note: 2230 (Production of country liquor, arrack and toddy, etc.); 2006 (Processing and canning of meat); 2034 (Processing and canning of fish); 2036 (Processing and canning of frog legs); 2039

(*Continued*)

Table 3.2 (Continued)

(Processing and preserving of fish crustacea and similar foods); 2025 (Manufacture of sauces, jams, jellies, marmalades, etc.); 2006 (Processing and canning of meat); 2111 (manufacture of vegetable oils and fats through 'ghanis' (oil expeller)); 2013 (Manufacture of butter, cream, ghee, cheese, khoya, etc.); 2044 (Processing and grinding of grain manually); 2193 (Manufacture of sweetmeats); 2403 (Preparatory operations on man-made textile fibres); 2411 (Wool spinning other than in mills); 2412 (Weaving and finishing of woollen khadi); 2413 (Wool weaving and finishing on handlooms); 2431 (Bleaching and dyeing of woollen textiles by hand); 2461 (Bleaching, dyeing, and printing of silk textiles by hand); 2621 (Embroidery work by hand); 2625 (Making of laces and fringes by hand); 2631 (Manufacture of blankets and shawls by hand); 2633 (Manufacture of cotton carpets by hand); 2634 (Manufacture of woollen carpets by hand); 2635 (Manufacture of silk carpets by hand); 2637 (Manufacture of durries, druggets, and rugs by hand); 2671 (Manufacture of curtains, bed-covers, and furnishings by hand printed); 2672 (Manufacture of curtains, bed-covers, and furnishings by hand embroidered), 2911 (Manufacture of leather shoes by/on hand/cottage scale); 2913 (Manufacture of leather-cum-rubber/plastic cloth shoes by/on hand/cottage scale); 2915 (Manufacture of leather sandals and chappals by/on hand/cottage scale); 2917 (Manufacture of leather-cum-rubber/plastic cloth sandals and chappals by/on hand/cottage scale); 2931 (Manufacture of travel goods like suitcases, bags and holdalls, etc.); 2991 (Embroidering and embossing of leather articles by hand); 2992 (Manufacture of hand-printed leather articles); 2993 (Stuffing of animals and birds hides); 2793 (Manufacture of wooden toys, decoration pieces, wooden lamp stands, etc. (including hand-carved wood articles, walking sticks, and articles made from coconut shells, etc.); 3084 (Manufacture of fireworks); 3861 (Manufacture of musical instruments by hand); 3893 (Manufacture by hand of children's play equipment including toys and toy musical instruments, not included elsewhere); 3895 (Manufacture of articles from bones, ivory and horns, etc.); 3896 (Manufacture of wigs and false beards, etc.); 3898 (Manufacture of novelties, lampshades, presentation articles, badges, etc., including artificial flowers and art works.

Source: Author.

Table 3.3 Cultural sites-related NICs

UNCTAD-recognized activities	*NIC of EC 1998 (NIC 4 digits)*	*NIC of EC 2013–14 (NIC 3 digit)*	*Remarks*
Archaeological sites, museums, and libraries	9570, 9580, 9561, 9562, 9563, 9564, 9565, 9566	910 (Libraries, archives, museums, and other cultural activities)	–
Exhibitions, etc.	–	8239 (Organization of conventions and trade shows)	For exhibition, the NICs are not available for economic census 1998.

Note: 9570 (Audio and video cassette libraries); 9580 (Video parlours, electronic games, and other amusement centres); 9561 (Libraries and information centres); 9562 (Museums); 9563 (Botanical and zoological gardens); 9564 (Zoos); 9565 (Game sanctuaries); 9566 (Game sanctuaries).

Source: Author.

3.4.1.2 Cultural sites

Cultural sites include archaeological sites, museums, and libraries. The NICs related to these are presented in Table 3.3.

3.4.2 Arts

This group of goods and service is strongly related to culture and heritage and carries significant symbolic meanings (UNCTAD 2010). Arts are divided into two groups: visual arts and performing arts.

3.4.2.1 Performing arts

This sub-group constitutes live music, theatre, dance, opera, circus, and puppetry (UNCTAD 2010). India has enormous regional richness and variations in performing arts. The NICs representing the performing arts are identified and presented in Table 3.4.

3.4.2.2 Visual arts

Sculpture, painting, antiques, and photography are included in this subgroup and the NICs representing them are given in Table 3.5.

3.4.3 Media

This groups contain the "media that produce creative contents with the purpose of communicating with large audience" (UNCTAD 2010: 8) and have two sub-groups.

Table 3.4 Performing arts–related NICs

UNCTAD-recognized activities	*NIC of EC 1998 (NIC 4 digits)*	*NIC of EC 2013–14 (NIC 3 digits)*	*Remarks*
Live music, theatre, dance, opera, circus, puppetry	9520 (Stage production and related services)	900 (Creative, arts and entertainment activities)	These are roughly performing arts related activities. NIC 900 also include painting, sculptures, and antiques. As such this category for 2013–14 is mixed of performing and visual arts

Table 3.5 Visual arts–related NICs

UNCTAD-recognized activities	*NIC of EC 1998 (NIC 4 digits)*	*NIC of EC 2013–14 (NIC 3 digits)*	*Remarks*
Paintings, sculptures, photography, and antiques	9630 (Portrait and commercial photographic studios)	742 (Photographic activities)	The NIC codes for sculpture, paintings, and antiques for EC 2013–14 included in NIC 900. For EC 1998, the same are not available.

Source: Author.

3.4.3.1. Audio-visuals

This sub-group includes "films, television, radio and other broadcasting" (UNCTAD 2010: 8). The related NICs from EC 1998 and EC 2013–14 are presented in Table 3.6.

3.4.3.2 Publishing and print media

This sub-group includes books, press, and other publications. The NICs identified for representing them are presented in Table 3.7.

Table 3.6 Audio visual–related NICs

UNCTAD-recognized activities	*NIC of EC 1998 (NIC 4 digits)*	*NIC of EC 2013–14 (NIC 3 digits)*	*Remarks*
Film, television, radio, other broadcasting	9500 (Motion picture and video film production); 9540 (Radio and television broadcasting and related services)	591 (Motion picture, video, and television programme activities); 602 (Television programming and broadcasting activities); 601 (Radio broadcasting)	–

Source: Author.

Table 3.7 Publishing and print media–related NICs

UNCTAD-recognized activities	*NIC of EC 1998 (NIC 4 digits)*	*NIC of EC 2013–14 (NIC 3 digits)*	*Remarks*
Books, press, and other publications	2840, 2860, 2870, 2880, 2851, 2852, 2853, 2891, 2892, 2899	581 (Publishing of books, periodicals, and other publishing activities); 592 (Sound recording and music publishing activities)	–

Note: 2840 (Printing and publishing of newspapers); 2860 (Printing of bank notes, currency notes, postage stamps, security passes, stamp papers, and other similar products); 2870 (Engraving, etching, block-making, etc.), 2880 (Book binding on account of others); 2851 (Printing but not publishing of periodicals, books, journals, directories, atlases, maps and sheet music, schedules and pamphlets, etc.); 2852 (Publishing but not printing of periodicals, books, journals, directories, atlases, maps and sheet music, etc.), 2853 (Printing and publishing of periodicals, books journals, directories, atlases, maps and sheet music, etc.); 2891 (Envelope printing, postcard printing, and embossing); 2892 (Manufacture of playing cards); 2899 (Printing and allied activities).

Source: Author.

3.4.4 Functional creations

UNCTAD (2010) has separated media and related activities which are "more demand-driven and service oriented" (p. 8) into a group called 'functional creations'. It is assumed that the goods and services in this group are created more for functional purposes. This group is divided into three sub-groups.

3.4.4.1 New media

This sub-group includes software, video games, and goods and services with digitized creative contents. The NICs related to this sub-group are presented in Table 3.8.

3.4.4.2 Design

Interior design, graphic, fashion, jewellery, and toys are included in this sub-group. Particularly, in gems and jewellery design and manufacturing, India has a long tradition. The NICs representing these activities are presented in Table 3.9.

3.4.4.3 Creative services

This group largely relate to commerce and knowledge creation, and include architectural activities, advertising, creative R&D, and cultural and recreational services. The NICs related to this group are presented in Table 3.10.

Table 3.8 New media related NICs

UNCTAD-recognized activities	*NIC of EC 1998 (NIC 4 digits)*	*NIC of EC 2013–14 (NIC 3 digits)*	*Remarks*
Software, video games, digitized creative content	8921 (Computer consultancy services); 8922 (Software supply services); 8923 (Data processing services); 8924 (Data bank activities); 8933 (Business and management consultancy activities)	620 (Computer programming, consultancy, and related activities); 582 (Software publishing); 324 (Manufacture of games and toys); 631 (Data processing, hosting, and related activities; web portals); 639 (Other information service activities)	In this category, we have also included business management services (for EC 1998), which are often done through digitalized creative contents. The other information activities for EC 2013–14 relates to digitalized contents and services. Given the aggregated nature of activities in these NICs, they also include some aspects of creative services. NIC 324 may include some aspects of design.

Source: Author.

Table 3.9 Design related NICs

UNCTAD-recognized activities	*NIC of EC 1998 (NIC 4 digits)*	*NIC of EC 2013–14 (NIC 3 digits)*	*Remarks*
Interior, graphic, fashion, jewellery, and toys	3831 (Manufacture of gold jewellery); 3832 (Manufacture of silver jewellery); 3833 (Manufacture of jewellery of other precious metals or metals clad with precious metals); 3834 (Manufacture of precious/semi-precious stone jewellery); 3535 (Manufacture of gold and silver articles including presentation coins of gold and silver other than jewellery); 3836 (Manufacture of gold and silver articles including presentation coins of gold and silver other than jewellery); 3837 (Other gem cutting and polishing by hand); 3838 (Manufacture of synthetic stone jewellery, costume jewellery and imitation jewellery); 3839 (Manufacture of zari and other jewellery and related articles); 8994 (Fashion designing services); 2870 (Engraving, etching, and block-making etc.)	741 (Specialized design activities, and include Fashion design related to textiles, wearing apparel, shoes, jewellery, furniture, and other fashion goods as well as other personal or household goods; Activities of interior decorators; Services of graphic designers; and Other specialized design activities)	–

Source: Author.

Table 3.10 Creative services–related NICs.

UNCTAD-recognized activities	*NIC of EC 1998 (NIC 4 digits)*	*NIC of EC 2013–14 (NIC 3 digits)*	*Remarks*
Architectural, advertising, creative R&D, cultural and recreational	8940, 8960, 3892, 8932, 9510, 9530, 9550, 9620, 9591, 9599, 8970, 8931, 9220	711; 731; 732; 932; 721; 722	–

Note: 8940 (Architectural and engineering and other technical consultancy activities); 8960 (Advertising); 3892 (Making of advertising sign-boards and displays, etc.); 8932 (Market research services); 9510 (Motion picture distribution and projection services); 9530 (Authors, music composers, singers, dancers, magicians, and other independent artistes not elsewhere classified); 9550 (Operation of circuses and race tracks); 9620 (Hair dressing such as those done by barbers, hair dressing saloons and beauty shops, etc.); 9591 (Gymnasia); 9599 (Other recreational services); 8970 (Press agency activities); 8931 (Project management activities); 9220 (Research and development); 711 (Architectural and engineering activities and related technical consultancy); 731 (Advertising); 732 (Market research and public opinion polling); 932 (Other amusement and recreation activities); 721 (Research and experimental development on natural sciences and engineering); 722 (Research and experimental development on social sciences and humanities).

Source: Author.

3.5 Conclusions

The concept of and literature on CCIs have evolved over the time. However, the definitions and classification methods of CCIs are yet to be settled. Broadly, the goods and services with symbolic meanings are recognized as part of cultural industries, and CIs are considered wider grouping of activities including both knowledge based, such as software, and cultural goods and services. Over the years, because of its commercial values, CIs have become economically strategic. As there has not been any one acceptable definition of CIs, many countries, organizations, and individual researchers have come up with their own specific definitions and criteria to classify CIs. However, none of these definitions or classifications are considered superior or inferior to others for all purposes.

In India, there has hardly been any known attempt to map the CIs at sub-sectoral and national levels. The present chapter is such an attempt to fill this gap using the UNCTAD (2010) definition and classification method. The adoption of this UNCTAD methodology can facilitate the international comparability. However, the problem has been the availability of detailed data to accomplish such a classification. In India, the EC data are the only set of data which can be used to understand the size and geography of CIs both comprehensively, and at micro-geography level. We have used the EC data for 1998 and 2013–14 for this purpose. However, these data are still rough as they provide NIC 3-digit or NIC 4-digit level details (rather than 5-digit level which provide more precision about the nature of activities), and many creative activities therefore may be lumped up with other non-creative activities. Additionally, the occupation codes for individuals employed in the industries are also not available. This again introduces impurity to the employment data in CIs as there may be individuals working in creative industries as regular office workers rather than as creative workers. However, given the limitations mentioned earlier, the ECs still represent the best data source to classify and map the CIs and related employment in India at national, state, and district levels. Even these data can be precisely organized at the ward (cities are divided in wards) or tehsil levels (Indian districts are divided in tehsils).

References

Adorno, T., and Horkheimer, M. (1947/1979). *Dialektik der Aufklärung: Philosophische Fragmente.* Amsterdam, Querido. English translation by John Cumming, *Dialectic of Enlightenment.* London: Verso.

Banks, M., and O'Connor, J. (2009). After the creative industries. *International Journal of Cultural Policy*, 15(4), 365–373. doi:10.1080/10286630902989027

Bilton, C., and Leary, R. (2004). What can managers do for creativity? Brokering creativity in the creative industries. *International Journal of Cultural Policy*, 8(1), 49–64.

Caust, J. (2003). Putting the 'art' back into arts policy making: How arts policy has been 'captured' by the economists and the marketers. *International Journal of Cultural Policy*, 9(1), 51–63.

Caves, R. E. (2000). *Creative Industries: Contracts between Art and Commerce.* Cambridge, MA: Harvard University Press.

Creative Skillset (2013). Classifying and measuring the creative industries. Available at: www.screenskills.com/media/1549/classifying_and_measuring_the_creative_industries.pdf

Cunningham, S. (2002). From cultural to creative industries, theory, industry and policy implications. *Culturelink*, Special Issue, 19–32

DCMS (2001). *The Creative Industries Mapping Document 2001*. London: HMSO.

Département des études, de la prospective et des statistiques (2006, January). *Aperçu statistique des industries culturelles*, No. 16. Paris: Ministry of Culture and Communication, Government of France.

Department of Communications and the Arts (1994). Creative nation. Available at: https://apo.org.au/node/29704

Flew, T. (2002). Beyond ad hocery: Defining the creative industries. Paper presented at Cultural Sites, Cultural Theory, Cultural Policy, the second international conference on cultural policy research, Te Papa, Wellington, New Zealand, 23–26 January. Available at https://eprints.qut.edu.au/256/

Friedman, W. A., and Jones, G. (2011). Creative industries in history. *The Business History Review*, 85(2), 237–244.

Galloway, S., and Dunlop, S. (2007). A critique of definitions of the cultural and creative industries in public policy. *International Journal of Cultural Policy*, 13(1), 17–31. doi:10.1080/10286630701201657.

Garnham, N. (1990). *Capitalism and Communication: Global Culture and the Economics of Information*. London: The Sage Publications.

Government of UK (2015, 13 January). Official statistics: Creative industries economic estimates January 2015–key findings. Available at: www.gov.uk/government/statistics/creative-industries-economic-estimates-january-2015/creative-industries-economic-estimates-january-2015-key-findings (last accessed on 25 March 2022).

Hesmondhalgh, D. (2002). *The Cultural Industries*. London: Sage Publications.

Hesmondhalgh, D., and Pratt, A. C. (2005). Cultural industries and cultural policy. *International Journal of Cultural Policy*, 11(1), 1–13.

Hirsch, P. M. (1972). Processing fads and fashions: An organization-set analysis of cultural industry systems. *American Journal of Sociology*, 77(4), 639–659.

Horkheimer, M., and Adorno, T. (2002). *Dialectic of Enlightenment*. Stanford: Stanford University Press.

Howkins, J. (2002, 12 December). Speech to the Inception Session, The Mayor's Commission on the Creative Industries, London.

Marcuse, H. (1991). *One Dimensional Man: Studies in the Ideology of Advanced Industrial Society*. Boston: Beacon.

MoSPI (1998). All India Report of Fourth Economic Census. Government of India, New Delhi.

MoSPI (2016). All India Report of Sixth Economic Census. Government of India, New Delhi.

Myerscough, J. (1988). *The Economic Importance of the Arts in Britain*. London: Policy Studies Institute.

Pratt, A. C. (2004). The cultural economy, a call for spatialised 'production of culture' perspectives. *International Journal of Cultural Studies*, 7(1), 117–128.

Ryan, B. (1992). *Making Capital from Culture: The Corporate Form of Capitalist Cultural Production*. New York: Walter de Gruyter.

Throsby, D. (2001). *Economics and Culture*. Cambridge: Cambridge University Press.

Towse, R. (2000). Cultural economics, copyright, and the cultural industries. Paper presented at The Long Run conference, Erasmus University, Rotterdam, February.

Towse, R. (2003). Cultural industries. In Towse, R. (ed.), *A Handbook of Cultural Economics*, pp. 170–182. Cheltenham: Edward Elgar.

UNCTAD (2004). UNCTAD XI high-level panel on creative industries and development agenda. Available at: www.unctad.org/en/docs/tdximisc1_en.pdf (last accessed on 25 March 2022).

UNCTAD (2010). *Creative Economy Report 2010*. Geneva: UNCTAD.

UNCTAD (2019). How the creative economy can help power development. Available at: https://unctad.org/news/how-creative-economy-can-help-power-development (last accessed on 25 March 2022).

UNESCO (2013). *Creative Economy Report 2013: Widening Local Development Pathways*. New York: UNDP.

Section II

ENGAGING WITH OFFICIAL STATISTICS

Section II contains pioneering work on documenting and analysing official Indian Government statistics regarding CCI. At an unprecedented level of comprehensiveness, detail, and precision, Section II illustrates the size of CCI in India, regional patterns of distribution, and how those relate to regional variations in wealth, education, urbanization, and the location of digital industries, as well as the export performance of Indian CCI. What is more, by employing the UNCTAD classification framework, results are relatively compatible and comparable to statistics from other territories. Chapter 4 maps the CCI across Indian states and districts according to the number of enterprises and the number of workers engaged, identifying multiple clusters that can provide springboards for further development. Chapter 5 documents exports of creative goods from India and India's position in the global trade of creative goods and services. Chapter 6 focuses on the co-location of CCI and digital industries, and thus documents locational relations and the apparent complementarities in India. Overall, this section provides essential reading for anyone interested in the bigger picture of the current location and strengths of Indian CCI and the scope for further development.

DOI: 10.4324/9781003129370-5

4

SIZE, GROWTH, AND GEOGRAPHIES OF CREATIVE INDUSTRIES IN INDIA

Abdul Shaban and Filip Vermeylen

4.1 Introduction

India is endowed with enormous cultural diversity, which can make it a global leader in the creative sector. The development of knowledge and related industries can have a multiplier effect in the promotion and branding of cultural products. However, India has not strategized its policies and administrative frameworks to promote and develop the creative industries (CIs) (Shaban and Vermeylen 2015). There has been a lack of coherent policy framework and definition in the country in this regard. As mentioned in the previous chapter, there is no coherent set of data available which can help to assess the size, diversity, distribution, and growth of this sector. There are a few studies (Patnaik 2020a, 2020b; Matthew n.d.) that have come up with their estimates based on different data sets. However, such data cannot be taken as consistent evidence for a complete understanding of the creative sector in the country. As mentioned in the previous chapter, another major problem concerning the creative industries has been the definitional ambiguity. Many organizations and researchers have propounded their own definitions rather than developing a common framework. Studies on the size of creative industries in India are, therefore, caught in these two issues of data quality and definitional ambiguity.

To illustrate this, we cite two recent estimates. Megha Patnaik (2020a, 2020b) following the WIPO copyright definition of creative industries, and data from Annual Survey of Industries (ASI), Centre for Monitoring Indian Economy's (CMIE) Prowess data, and various industry reports, assesses that gross value addition (GVA) in Indian copyright industries was INR 890 billion (about US$13.2 billion) in 2016–17, which was about 0.58% of the total value added in the economy in comparison to 5.5% at the global level. That means that India's creative sector in terms of its size in monetary terms is still very small. Patnaik argues that printing press, literature, dramatic arts, music, and film constitute about 45% of this value addition while creative works through television

DOI: 10.4324/9781003129370-6

and radio contribute about 40% of the gross value added. Patnaik argues that employment size in the creative sector based on the WIPO definition is about 1.1 million persons. However, there are issues with the data set used. The ASI data is only for registered firms, and, in India, there are a number of informal creative enterprises which are not registered under the Factories Act, 1948. Such enterprises are mainly run by households or are seasonal. In 2013–14, the own account establishments (OAE) run by households, which are not registered, constituted 72.4% of the total creative establishments (see Appendix Tables 4A.1 and 4A.2). About 52.4% of the GVA in the Indian economy arose from the informal sector in 2017–18, and the informal sector employed 86.8% of the total workers in 2019. These indicate the significance of the informal sector in the Indian economy (Murthy 2019). Even though the informal sector's contribution in the total value added is relatively small, in terms of share in total CI employment it is large. The CMIE Prowess data are further problematic in the estimation of the size of the creative sector as they are based on the annual reports of sampled companies, which do not guarantee that all the firms have been included in the Prowess database. Matthew (n.d.) estimates that India has 40 million workers in CIs. However, the number computed by us and presented here are almost 10 times lower than those estimated by Mathew.

Given these limitations, we opted to use the Economic Census (EC) data, which includes both the registered and non-registered (informal sector) industries and provide us possibilities to assess the distribution at the state and district levels. EC data has its advantages. In EC all the industries are included, and data is available for industrial enterprises and the number of workers, along with other useful information. The main limitation of EC data is that it does not contain GVA, and NIC is up to 3 digits (for 2013–14) for some rounds and 4 for others (for 1998). We have used this EC data for capturing the distribution of workers and CIs in the country. Further, we have used the UNCTAD (2010) definition of creative industries which is relatively wider in conception and easier to relate to the NICs.

We have classified the CIs in sub-sectors (as discussed in Chapter 3) and presented the number of enterprises and workers by state and districts. We have mapped the number of workers by the district to access the geographical concentration of workers by the district to identify the clustering patterns. The mapping of the absolute size of workers may have the limitation that the bigger districts with large populations may have a larger number of workers than smaller districts, but the advantage of this is that it helps to capture the number in space at microspatial scale as opposed to states, which are larger spatial units and some of the states are even larger in area and population than many European countries. Further, as our aim is not to assess the share of CI workers and enterprises within respective districts but to find out where workers are located, the plotting of numbers of workers fairly serves our purpose. A high concentration of (number of) workers in a district and its surrounding districts is called 'clustering' (alternatively, clustering can also be defined as ratio of creative workers to the total workers or population). We have not used any threshold number of population to define a cluster, but it has been based on a relatively higher number of workers located in a district and/or its surrounding districts. While plotting the absolute numbers on a map, we have used Jenks' natural break classification method (Jenks 1977; Rey et al. 2016), which helps us in finding out structural breaks in the data as it minimizes the within-group variance and maximizes the between-group variance. Therefore, the data may look oddly classed on maps, but it shows natural breaks in distribution over space. We have also attempted to study the impact of per capita income, higher education, and urbanization rate on creative sector workers at the state level in India. We assume that these factors positively impact the distribution of workers.

The rest of this chapter is divided as follows. Section 4.2 presents the size and growth of CIs at the all-India level, while Section 4.3 deals with the geographies of creative industries (all creative enterprises and workers) at the regional or state level. Section 4.4 studies the sectoral (UNCTAD grouping) distribution and clustering of CIs in India, while Section 4.5 examines the determinants of the distribution of creative sector workers at the state level. Section 4.6 concludes the chapter.

4.2 Size and growth

The data related to CIs at the all-India level are presented in Tables 4.1 and 4.2. From these tables, the following major observations with regard to growth and sectoral shares can be made. First, CIs have experienced significant growth between 1998 and 2013–14. The number of creative enterprises has increased from about 1.52 million to about 2.54 million in the 15 years period, experiencing a compound growth rate of 3.5% per annum, while the number of workers has also grown at roughly the same rate (3.4% per annum) during this period, which has led to the expansion of the size of CI workers from about 4.08 million to 6.76 million. Second, there are some discernible patterns in growth by sector both in terms of the number of creative enterprises and workers engaged therein. Performing arts has experienced the highest growth rate, followed by new media, art crafts (handloom and handicrafts), visual arts, and audio-visuals. The higher growth rates of these sectors are not surprising, as they experienced higher demand within (and also outside) the country since the liberalization. The liberalization-led economic growth has resulted in the rise of the Indian middle class (Shaban 2021) who are the major consumers of these goods and services. The design, creative services, and publishing and print media have experienced negative growth rates and the reasons may be the impact of digitalization on these sectors. The online content and even imports from other countries obviate the needs of workers and specialized design studios. The creative service sector also seems to be affected by digitalization as online availability of information diminishes the demand of this sector. For instance, information being available on the internet obviates the hiring of

Table 4.1 Growth of creative industries by sectors in India

S. no.	*Creative industries by sectors*	*1998*			*2013–14*			*CAGR (%), 1998 and 2013–14*	
		Enterprises (000)	*Mean no. of workers*	*Total workers (000)*	*Enterprises (000)*	*Mean no. of workers*	*Total workers (000)*	*Enterprises*	*Workers*
1	Art crafts	341.8	3.0	1015.5	1873.6	2.2	4204.8	12.0	9.9
2	Cultural sites	60.2	2.3	141.3	79.7	2.2	175.1	1.9	1.4
3	Performing arts	3.2	4.1	13.0	114.9	2.5	291.5	26.9	23.0
4	Visual arts	93.1	1.8	164.6	197.9	1.7	337.9	5.2	4.9
5	Audio-visuals	19.8	3.5	69.4	32.3	3.7	120.4	3.3	3.7
6	Publishing and print media	93.4	5.0	465.5	39.6	3.6	141.3	−5.5	−7.6
7	New media	16.8	5.7	96.0	116.0	9.9	1143.6	13.8	18.0
8	Design	212.5	3.3	700.8	21.8	3.0	64.5	−14.1	−14.7
9	Creative services	679.8	2.1	1410.3	66.0	4.3	285.5	−14.4	−10.1
	Total	1520.6	2.7	4076.5	2541.7	2.7	6764.6	3.5	3.4

Note: CAGR = compound annual growth rate (%).

Source: Computed using data from MoSPI (1998, 2016).

Table 4.2 Share (%) of enterprises and workers by sectors in India

S. no.	*Creative industries by sectors*	*1998*		*2013–14*	
		Enterprises (%)	*Total workers (%)*	*Enterprises (%)*	*Total workers (%)*
1	Art crafts	22.5	24.9	73.7	62.2
2	Cultural sites	4.0	3.5	3.1	2.6
3	Performing arts and visual arts	0.2	0.3	4.5	4.3
4	Visual arts	6.1	4.0	7.8	5.0
5	Audio-visuals	1.3	1.7	1.3	1.8
6	Publishing and print media	6.1	11.4	1.6	2.1
7	New media	1.1	2.4	4.6	16.9
8	Design	14.0	17.2	0.9	1.0
9	Creative services	44.7	34.6	2.6	4.2
	Total	100.0	100.0	100.0	100.0

Source: Computed using data from MoSPI (1998, 2016).

guides by visitors. Similarly, information on design can be provided from other countries through the internet, as we see in the gems and jewellery industries.

Third, with regard to the constitution of CIs in terms of share of different sub-sectors, creative services constituted the largest share in 1998, but the share of art craft (handloom and handicraft) has massively increased in 2013–14 (Table 4.2). New media has experienced a significant increase in its share, from 1.1% of total creative enterprises and 2.4% of the total CI workers in 1998 to 4.6% of the enterprises and 16.9% of the workers in 2013–14. In fact, India has had an edge over other countries like China in information and communication technologies (ICT) as it has a large base of English educated population. Hyderabad and Bengaluru rapidly rose in the last decade of 20th century and thereafter due to the location and growth of ICT industries in these cities. The decline of the share of creative services (the category includes architectural services, advertisements, creative R&D, and cultural and recreational services) has been very significant. We understand that this may also result from a less than exact match of the National Industrial Classification (NIC) in both the years (see Chapter 3), but this rate of decline obviously shows that the decline is real and substantial. However, growth in art crafts (handloom and handicraft) has more than compensated for the decline in creative services in terms of employment generation and the number of enterprises. Lastly, the average number of workers in creative sector enterprises in India is very small. It is interesting to note that it has been the same, i.e. 2.7 workers per enterprise, in 1998 as well as in 2013–14. New media and creative services saw significant consolidation, in terms of the increase of workers per industry during the period, but the art crafts and performing arts experienced a comparatively large decline in workers per enterprise.

Fourth, about 6% of creative enterprises in 1998 and 10% in 2013–14 were seasonal in nature (operating only for a few months in a year), and the shares of the total workers engaged in these enterprises were 5.3% and 8.1%, respectively, in the same years. As expected, art crafts related enterprises are more seasonal in nature than any other type of enterprises. Substantial share of performing arts and creative services has also emerged as seasonal in comparison to those in the year 1998 (see Appendix Table 4A.1).

Fifth, most of the CIs in India are informal in nature. In 1998, about 97% of creative enterprises were unregistered, and a substantial share of the same was from Own Account Enterprises (OAEs). OAEs are that category of enterprises which do not employ any hired workers on fairly regular basis and are largely run by households. For 2013–14, the data related to registered and unregistered enterprises is not available but the share of OAE was substantially higher, 72.4% of the total enterprises, in comparison to that in (69.9%) 1998 (see Table 4A.2). More than 90% of the workers were working in non-registered or informal creative enterprises in 1998. The share of informal enterprises we cannot accurately measure as data on registered and unregistered enterprises are not available, but it may be still around 90%, as the share workers in OAEs has risen in 2013–14 while those in NDEs has remained almost the same.

Sixth, as most of industries are informal in nature, they lack formal finance. About 87% of enterprises (employing about 81% of the workers) in 1998 and 83% (employing about 80% of the total workers) in 2013–14 were self-financed (Table 4A.3). Available data show that considerable share (%) of enterprises from cultural sites and performing arts had donations from civil society groups and non-profit organizations, while substantial share of cultural sites had received funding from the government.

Seventh, In India, the share of proprietary (private) creative enterprises is very large. It was about 97% in 1998, while the same was about 93% in 2013–14 (Table 4A.4). However, the workers employed in non-proprietary enterprises have increased substantially from 6.8% to 21.2% in 2013–14. This shows that trust- and government-owned larger enterprises are emerging in the country.

Eighth, given that India is largely a patriarchal society, the ownership of creative enterprises by females are quite low (Table 4A.5). However, the share of female-owned enterprises has also risen substantially, i.e. from 4.1% (employing 3.8% of the total workers) in 1998 to 18.5% (employing 14.0% of the total workers) in 2013–14. Sectorally, noticeable presence of female-owned enterprises is only in art crafts (about 21.9% of the total art craft enterprises) and cultural site (20.6% of the total enterprises related to cultural sites) sectors.

4.3 Geographies of creative industries

What are the regional growth patterns and clustering of CIs? The data presented in Table 4.3 reveals that at the state level, the southern and western states of the country have a higher concentration of enterprises as well workers in the country. Gujarat, Maharashtra, Karnataka, Andhra Pradesh, Tamil Nadu, and Kerala stand out in terms of relatively higher concentrations of both the enterprises and workers in comparison to other states. Outside these

Table 4.3 Growth of total creative enterprises, workers, and mean workers by states, 1998 and 2013–14

States	*Creative enterprises (000)*		*CI workers (000)*		*CAGR (%)*		*Mean workers / enterprise*	
	1998	*2013–14*	*1998*	*2013–14*	*Enterprises*	*Workers*	*1998*	*2013–14*
Andaman and Nicobar Islands	0.4	0.5	1.6	1.5	0.4	−0.1	3.6	3.3
Andhra Pradesh	96.7	172.4	181.3	326.3	3.9	4.0	1.9	1.9
Arunachal Pradesh	0.8	0.8	2.3	2.1	−0.2	−0.8	2.9	2.6
Assam	20.7	105.9	68.2	225.9	11.5	8.3	3.3	2.1
Bihar	48.1	56.8	88.0	106.9	1.1	1.3	1.8	1.9
Chandigarh	1.8	1.7	10.7	22.8	−0.5	5.2	5.9	13.5
Chhattisgarh	23.0	28.8	42.6	59.5	1.5	2.3	1.9	2.1
Dadra and Nagar Haveli	0.1	0.3	0.6	0.7	6.7	1.4	5.5	2.6
Daman and Diu	0.2	0.2	0.6	0.6	1.9	0.3	3.5	2.7
Delhi	53.7	23.4	259.7	100.8	−5.4	−6.1	4.8	4.3
Goa	4.8	2.6	11.6	7.1	−4.0	−3.2	2.4	2.7
Gujarat	84.6	105.8	417.2	348.6	1.5	−1.2	4.9	3.3
Haryana	31.6	32.6	64.5	86.0	0.2	1.9	2.0	2.6
Himachal Pradesh	11.2	17.7	23.8	27.3	3.1	0.9	2.1	1.5
Jammu and Kashmir	17.3	60.3	37.8	112.7	8.7	7.6	2.2	1.9
Jharkhand	13.4	27.6	27.6	59.2	4.9	5.2	2.1	2.1
Karnataka	71.4	95.9	186.9	308.2	2.0	3.4	2.6	3.2
Kerala	81.4	77.4	191.2	238.6	−0.3	1.5	2.3	3.1
Lakshadweep	0.1	0.1	0.4	0.4	3.4	0.7	5.0	3.4
Madhya Pradesh	83.1	74.7	164.8	157.3	−0.7	−0.3	2.0	2.1
Maharashtra	152.6	170.3	420.9	664.2	0.7	3.1	2.8	3.9
Manipur	5.0	59.0	10.9	79.5	17.9	14.1	2.2	1.3
Meghalaya	1.2	4.6	4.1	10.3	9.7	6.3	3.6	2.2
Mizoram	0.8	2.9	2.1	7.1	8.9	8.6	2.6	2.4
Nagaland	0.7	5.4	2.2	14.8	14.0	13.6	2.9	2.8
Odisha	51.7	171.0	99.7	368.5	8.3	9.1	1.9	2.2
Puducherry	2.3	2.2	11.2	12.6	−0.4	0.8	4.9	5.9
Punjab	37.0	41.7	78.6	92.2	0.8	1.1	2.1	2.2
Rajasthan	83.1	161.8	170.7	353.2	4.5	5.0	2.1	2.2
Sikkim	0.4	1.1	1.2	2.5	6.7	5.2	2.9	2.4
Tamil Nadu	111.4	190.4	323.3	621.8	3.6	4.5	2.9	3.3
Telangana	81.9	71.0	228.0	437.0	−1.0	4.4	2.8	6.2
Tripura	4.9	13.7	8.9	22.9	7.2	6.5	1.8	1.7
Uttar Pradesh	154.2	363.0	405.7	949.2	5.9	5.8	2.6	2.6
Uttarakhand	9.9	14.7	19.3	31.9	2.6	3.4	1.9	2.2
West Bengal	178.8	383.5	508.5	904.1	5.2	3.9	2.8	2.4
Total	1520.6	2541.7	4076.5	6764.6	3.5	3.4	2.7	2.7

Note: CAGR (compound annual growth rate (%).

Source: Computed using data from MoSPI (1998, 2016).

states, Bengal is another state of higher concentration of CIs. Bengal is known for its handloom and handicraft and so are the southern and western states of India. There are many handloom and handicraft clusters which are further discussed in Chapters 6 and 14. There are also isolated pockets of concentration within some of the states like Uttar Pradesh, Rajasthan, and Jammu and Kashmir. This concentration also becomes very visible when one maps the concentration ratio (that is computed as CI workers in a district divided by total CI workers at all-India level multiplied by 1000) of workers in 1998 and 2013–14. Figure 4.1 shows that there are prominent clusters of concentrations of CI workers in (a) the Kolkata region, (b) Mumbai-Pune region, (c) Surat, (d) Hyderabad region, (e) Bengaluru, and (f) Kanchipuram. Bareilly in Uttar Pradesh is the only major cluster in northern India. There are several secondary clusters of workers and prominent of them are Jaipur, Noida, Varanasi, Coimbatore, Ernakulam, and Thiruvananthapuram. The tertiary clusters are again more prominent in southern India (Tamil Nadu, Karnataka, Kerala, and Andhra Pradesh) and in Agra-Jaipur-Bareilly-Amritsar belt. Lucknow-Kanpur in Uttar Pradesh and Berpeta, Kamrup, and Nagaon are other tertiary concentrations of the CI workers in India. As such, we find that the geography of creative industries in India is very uneven, and the geography of 1998 of CI workers also persists in 2013–14 without much changes (Figures 4.1 and 4.2).

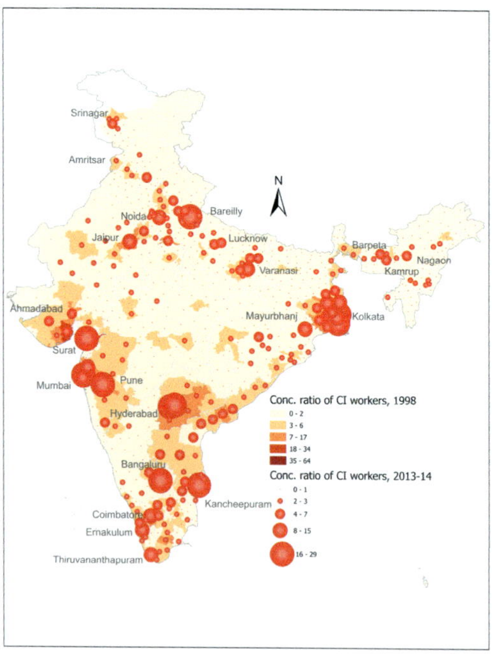

Figure 4.1 Concentration ratios of CI workers by districts in India, 1998 and 2013–14

Source: Computed using data from MoSPI (1998, 2016).

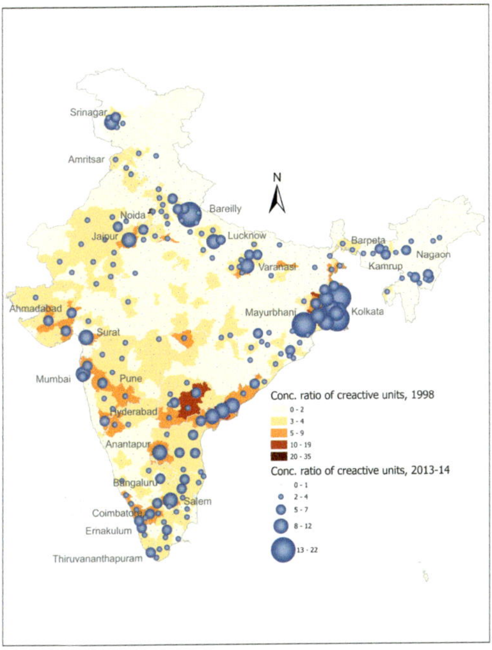

Figure 4.2 Concentration ratios of CI establishments by districts in India, 1998 and 2013–14

Source: Computed using data from MoSPI (1998, 2016).

It also needs to be noted that the mapping of number of creative enterprises has limited significance as the enterprises differ in terms of size of workers. The disconnect between the spatial importance due to enterprises and workers can be seen comparing both Figures 4.1 and 4.2. The concentration ratio of creative enterprises is much lower in southern India than the concentration ratio of workers. That shows that the number of workers per enterprise in southern India is higher than those in northern India (see Table 4.1). Further, the growth of creative enterprises and workers is higher in northern and north-eastern Indian states as compared to the southern states. As most of the northern and north-eastern states of the country are economically undeveloped but now growing (Sanga and Shaban 2017), it shows that as the development is trickling down, the disposable income is growing, the demand-driven growth of CIs is picking up.

In terms of concentration of industries, in 1998, Delhi (combined all the districts of Delhi, as data are not available at district level for Delhi) ranked first with a concentration ratio of CI workers of 63.7 (concentration ratio is computed as CI workers in a district divided by total CI workers at all-India level multiplied by 1000). Delhi was followed by Greater Mumbai (with a concentration ratio of CI workers 33.7), Kolkata (27.8), Surat (26.0), Bhavnagar (18.2), Nalgonda (16.7), Bengaluru (15.4), Hugli (13.8), North 24 Parganas (13.4), Ahmedabad (12.1), and Chennai (11.8). Thus, in 1998, we had all the top metropolitan districts among the top 10 districts in terms of the concentration of CI workers. However, West Bengal had three districts in the top 10, i.e. Kolkata, Hugli, and North 24 Parganas. This was mainly because of the high concentration of art craft (handloom and handicrafts) workers in Hugli and North 24 Parganas.

We have more fine-grained data in 2013–14, as Delhi data is available by districts (that was only available at the state level in 1998) which is more comparable to other districts of India. In 2013–14, the top 10 districts in descending order, in terms of concentration ratio of workers, were Rangareddy (concentration ratio 29.0), the extension and neighbouring district of Hyderabad, Kanchipuram (24.9), Mumbai Suburban (24.7), Hyderabad (22.0), North 24 Parganas (21.7), Pune (19.6), Surat (19.1), Bengaluru (19.0), Bareilly (18.7), and Haora (18.1). Thus, for most of the districts, the order did not change. Delhi and Mumbai lost their positions because of the division of workers data in several districts for Delhi, and for Mumbai in Mumbai and Mumbai Sub-urban districts. However, Hyderabad and Rangareddy emerge in 2013–14 as a new cluster of concentration of CI workers.

4.4 Sectoral clustering and patterns in the distribution

In this section, we examine the growth and distribution of enterprises and workers at state level, and clustering patterns of workers at district level of nine major sectors of CIs.

4.4.1 Art crafts

In India, art crafts (handloom and handicraft) constitutes the largest sector of CIs (see Chapters 14 to 17 for detailed discussion on India's art crafts). State-wise distribution, growth rates, and relative concentration of workers and art craft establishments are presented in Table 4.4. The major observations which can be drawn from the table and the district-wise distribution presented in Figure 4.3 are as follows. First, West Bengal has a major concentration of art craft workers and industries and is followed by Uttar Pradesh, Odisha, Andhra Pradesh, Gujarat, and Assam. However, it also needs to be noted that the eastern states of India have more particularities of culture, and this has given rise to region-specific crafts, for instance in West Bengal, Orissa, and Assam. These states are still economically and educationally underdeveloped and as such traditional craft industries employ a large share of the total workers. In this globalization phase, where the demand for crafts is rising with development, these states stand to benefit much by promoting their crafts and integrating the same with national and international markets. Cultural marketing is the approach they can adopt with an open policy of welcoming foreign and domestic tourists and

Table 4.4 Growth of art craft enterprises, workers, and location quotient by states, 1998 and 2013–14

States	*Enterprises (000)*		*Workers (000)*		*CAGR (%)*		*LQ for workers*	
	1998	*2013–14*	*1998*	*2013–14*	*Enterprises*	*workers*	*1998*	*2013–14*
Andaman and Nicobar Islands	0.0	0.2	0.2	0.4	12.5	4.8	0.5	0.4
Andhra Pradesh	27.4	141.3	46.7	254.0	11.6	12.0	1.0	1.3
Arunachal Pradesh	0.1	0.2	0.4	0.6	7.4	3.2	0.7	0.5
Assam	2.3	91.1	10.3	189.9	28.0	21.5	0.6	1.4
Bihar	13.9	31.8	24.3	60.8	5.7	6.3	1.1	0.9
Chandigarh	0.2	0.3	0.9	0.6	3.2	−2.9	0.3	0.0
Chhattisgarh	3.1	21.4	6.6	42.1	13.6	13.2	0.6	1.1
Dadra and Nagar Haveli	0.0	0.1	0.1	0.1	15.8	4.4	0.5	0.3
Daman and Diu	0.0	0.0	0.1	0.0	5.2	−6.2	0.9	0.1
Delhi	4.3	9.3	32.8	35.6	5.2	0.5	0.5	0.6
Goa	2.1	0.9	4.3	1.5	−5.4	−6.8	1.4	0.3
Gujarat	7.0	67.9	31.6	245.8	16.4	14.6	0.3	1.1
Haryana	5.0	16.7	15.9	41.8	8.4	6.6	1.0	0.8
Himachal Pradesh	4.4	12.2	8.8	17.2	7.1	4.6	1.5	1.0
Jammu and Kashmir	12.3	54.4	29.7	100.6	10.4	8.5	3.1	1.4
Jharkhand	1.3	15.0	3.2	30.8	17.4	16.2	0.5	0.8
Karnataka	10.9	62.9	36.9	149.4	12.4	9.8	0.8	0.8
Kerala	9.2	30.3	36.4	66.9	8.3	4.2	0.8	0.5
Lakshadweep	0.0	0.0	0.0	0.1	13.1	0.4	0.5	0.2
Madhya Pradesh	13.9	50.6	32.2	98.8	9.0	7.8	0.8	1.0
Maharashtra	18.2	84.7	59.1	215.4	10.8	9.0	0.6	0.5
Manipur	2.3	57.0	3.6	75.1	23.7	22.4	1.3	1.5
Meghalaya	0.2	3.8	0.6	7.7	22.6	18.4	0.6	1.2
Mizoram	0.0	2.4	0.1	5.9	34.7	29.7	0.2	1.3
Nagaland	0.0	4.8	0.1	13.6	53.2	44.2	0.1	1.5
Odisha	7.3	146.1	13.7	305.5	22.2	23.0	0.5	1.3
Puducherry	0.1	0.4	1.3	2.7	7.0	4.9	0.5	0.3
Punjab	6.4	15.2	22.0	39.9	5.9	4.0	1.2	0.7
Rajasthan	25.1	123.9	55.6	263.3	11.2	10.9	1.3	1.2
Sikkim	0.1	0.8	0.4	1.6	14.1	10.4	1.2	1.0
Tamil Nadu	10.7	127.4	64.6	310.2	18.0	11.0	0.8	0.8
Telangana	43.3	40.4	119.1	74.5	−0.5	−3.1	2.1	0.3
Tripura	1.0	10.9	1.7	18.2	17.6	17.2	0.8	1.3
Uttar Pradesh	50.2	310.0	186.1	769.6	12.9	9.9	1.8	1.3
Uttarakhand	2.9	9.4	5.5	18.4	8.1	8.4	1.2	0.9
West Bengal	56.8	330.1	160.8	746.2	12.4	10.8	1.2	1.3
Total	341.8	1873.6	1015.5	4204.8	12.0	9.9	1.0	1.0

Note: CAGR = Compound annual growth rate; LQ = Location quotient.

Source: Computed using data from MoSPI (1998, 2016).

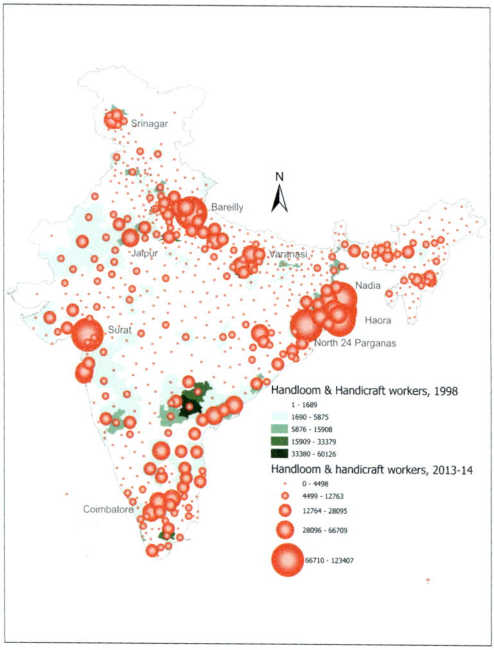

Figure 4.3 Concentration of art craft workers by districts in India, 1998 and 2013–14

Source: Computed using data from MoSPI (1998, 2016).

training the workers to bring creative changes in the products to align them with tastes and the needs of the consumers.

Second, the growth rate of enterprises in many states has been higher than workers, except in Andhra Pradesh; this shows the growth of small enterprises. At the all-India level as well, the growth rate of workers has been lower than CI enterprises. Third, the relative concentration of art craft workers as shown by the location quotients have changed over time among Indian states. The relative concentrations have strengthened in the eastern and in most of the north-eastern states of the country. But it has declined in major states like Uttar Pradesh, Bihar, Telangana, and Jammu and Kashmir.

Fourth, there are four primary, i.e. major (recognized in terms of size of concentration of workers based on four group classification by Jenks' method), and secondary clusters of art craft workers. The primary clusters in order of their size are (a) Kolkata and its neighbouring districts, (b) western Uttar Pradesh (with Bareilly as the major hub), (c) a contiguous area of northern Tamil Nadu, southern Karnataka, and coastal Andhra Pradesh, and (d) Surat-Mumbai region. The secondary clusters are (a) south-eastern Uttar Pradesh, with Varanasi as the major hub, (b) Srinagar region, (c) Brahmaputra valley of Assam, and (4) Manipur. Besides these primary and secondary clusters, we have several districts with sizeable shares of art craft workers (see also Chapter 6 and 14). Fifth, there has been a relative decline in the position of some of the districts in terms of the number of art craft workers in western Rajasthan, western Maharashtra, and Telangana in 2013–14 in comparison to 1998 (compare the shaded colour and size of the spheres in Figure 4.3). One of the reasons for this may be that they have experienced a shift from this traditional sector to better paying works, as art crafts (handloom and handicrafts) are mainly of subsistence nature in many districts. This is very plausible as Telangana, Maharashtra, and also Rajasthan have experienced better economic growth, especially after 1998 (Sanga and Shaban 2017). In 1998, Nalgonda district of Telangana, known for its Pochampally *saris*, ranked first in terms of art craft workers in the country (with 60,126 workers) and was followed by Bhadohi (known for its carpet industry), Delhi, Kolkata, Warangal, Agra (known for marble craft), and Hugli (known for *dhotis* and *saris*). However, in 2013, Bareilly emerged as the district with the highest number of art craft workers (123,407) and was followed by Haora, Surat, North 24 Parganas, Nadia, South 24 Parganas, Mayurbhanj, Varanasi, Bardhaman, and Jaipur districts, in descending order.

4.4.2 Cultural sites

India is an old civilization. It has historical continuity in growth of its culture. It needs to be noted that what we call India geographically is a space of cultural conglomeration in which several cultural streams have taken birth, persisted, and grown. The newer cultures by new rulers were planted but the older ones continued to grow, and the older ones did impact the evolution of the newer cultures and made them more composite (Khilnani 1997). For instance, Taj Mahal of Agra is a blend of Islamic, Indian, and Persian style of Architecture (Britannica 2021). The cultural styles of different regions and communities coexist together and enhance the beauty of Taj Mahal, and several other tangible and intangible heritages, including languages, dresses, foods, and celebrations.

Several of the communities, sects, and saints created their own temples, mosques, churches, etc., at regional and local levels, as were the monuments created by the rulers at the supra-regional level. Many of these cultural sites have been identified by Archaeological Survey of India, which also plays very important role in their conservation and protection. There are currently "more than 3,650 ancient monuments and archaeological sites and remains of national importance" (Archaeological Survey of India 2011a). India has total 981 world heritage. "These include 759 cultural, 193 natural and 29 mixed properties in 137 state parties" (Archaeological Survey of India 2011b). These cultural sites are visited by millions of tourists annually and play important role in the economic development of the regions they are located in.

The cultural sites in India are located in clusters. There are three primary clusters of workers of cultural sites in India, (a) Tamil Nadu-Kerala-southern Karnataka, (b) Southern West Bengal, and (c) Jharkhand-Southern

Bihar (Figure 4.4 and Table 4.5). The secondary clusters are (a) Mumbai-Pune region, (b) Vadodara-Ahmedabad region, and (c) Brahmaputra valley of Assam. It is interesting to note that in many states the numbers of creative enterprises and workers have experienced negative growth rates between 1998 and 2013–14. Jharkhand, Orissa, Gujarat, and Goa are the only states with significant positive growth rates of workers. The rise of digital technologies may have impacted the workers in this sector, and there may also have been declines of many religious places and traditional places of fairs. The lack of preservation may be leading to the lack of conservations, which in turn may be negatively affecting the employment in the sector. This is why Verma (2021) laments the state neglect of cultural sites and heritage in India and importantly points out that this ignorance of the national culture and history only leads to cultural conservativeness among people. Verma's argument implies that better awareness of national cultural heritage, many of which arose from a mixed traditions, will lead to better appreciations of all the heritages and their preservations and conservations.

In terms of the number of workers, Delhi state ranked first in 1998 with 9,301 cultural site workers, but none of its districts finds a place in the top 10 districts in 2013–14. In 1998, Delhi was followed by Mumbai and Bengaluru.

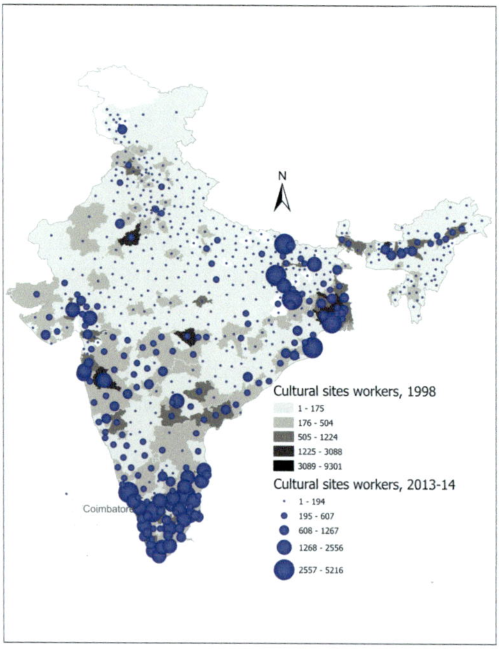

Figure 4.4 Distribution of workers employed at cultural sites, 1998 and 2013–14

Source: Computed using data from MoSPI (1998, 2016).

Table 4.5 Growth of cultural sites, workers, and location quotient by states, 1998 and 2013–14

States	*Enterprises (000)*		*Workers (000)*		*CAGR (%)*		*LQ enterprises*		*LQ for workers*	
	1998	*2013–14*	*1998*	*2013–14*	*Enterprises*	*workers*	*1998*	*2013–14*	*1998*	*2013–14*
Andaman and Nicobar Islands	0.1	0.0	0.2	0.2	−5.2	−1.1	3.4	1.7	3.7	4.1
Andhra Pradesh	2.8	1.8	4.8	4.0	−2.7	−1.2	0.7	0.3	0.8	0.5
Arunachal Pradesh	0.2	0.0	0.4	0.1	−11.6	−10.1	5.4	1.0	5.2	1.5
Assam	2.2	2.5	8.7	7.0	1.0	−1.5	2.7	0.8	3.7	1.2
Bihar	1.0	9.0	1.8	14.6	15.8	14.8	0.5	5.0	0.6	5.3
Chandigarh	0.1	0.0	0.7	0.1	−11.1	−14.0	1.7	0.4	2.0	0.1
Chhattisgarh	0.7	0.9	1.3	1.5	1.5	1.0	0.8	1.0	0.9	1.0
Dadra and Nagar Haveli	0.0	0.0	0.0	0.0	−1.7	−6.9	2.2	0.8	2.3	0.9
Daman and Diu	0.0	0.0	0.0	0.0	1.5	2.7	1.2	1.4	0.6	1.1
Delhi	3.7	0.2	9.3	1.1	−17.2	−13.2	2.1	0.3	1.1	0.4
Goa	0.2	0.2	0.4	0.7	0.5	4.3	0.8	2.2	0.9	3.8
Gujarat	2.1	3.5	4.6	9.9	3.6	5.3	0.6	1.1	0.3	1.1
Haryana	1.3	0.3	2.1	0.9	−8.4	−5.3	1.1	0.3	0.9	0.4
Himachal Pradesh	0.4	0.1	0.9	0.3	−10.7	−6.8	1.1	0.1	1.1	0.4
Jammu and Kashmir	0.2	0.8	0.4	1.4	10.0	9.3	0.3	0.4	0.3	0.5
Jharkhand	0.4	4.5	1.2	8.7	18.4	13.9	0.7	5.2	1.3	5.7
Karnataka	3.0	3.5	8.9	6.4	1.0	−2.2	1.0	1.2	1.4	0.8
Kerala	11.3	9.4	16.6	17.2	−1.2	0.2	3.5	3.9	2.5	2.8
Lakshadweep	0.0	0.0	0.1	0.1	0.4	−1.2	6.1	4.8	5.1	5.2
Madhya Pradesh	2.3	0.5	5.0	1.5	−9.7	−7.7	0.7	0.2	0.9	0.4
Maharashtra	5.6	10.3	15.9	20.2	4.1	1.6	0.9	1.9	1.1	1.2
Manipur	0.2	0.1	0.7	0.2	−6.4	−7.0	1.2	0.0	1.9	0.1
Meghalaya	0.2	0.0	0.5	0.1	−14.0	−9.2	3.6	0.1	3.2	0.4
Mizoram	0.3	0.1	0.4	0.2	−7.1	−5.1	9.6	1.1	5.6	1.0
Nagaland	0.1	0.1	0.2	0.1	−2.7	−3.7	3.3	0.3	3.4	0.3
Odisha	1.2	2.3	3.5	9.7	4.7	6.9	0.6	0.4	1.0	1.0
Puducherry	0.2	0.1	0.6	0.3	−4.6	−5.1	2.7	1.8	1.5	0.8
Punjab	2.4	0.4	3.8	1.4	−11.2	−6.3	1.8	0.3	1.5	0.6
Rajasthan	2.2	1.4	4.6	3.2	−3.0	−2.5	0.7	0.3	0.8	0.3
Sikkim	0.0	0.0	0.1	0.0	−7.1	−2.8	2.4	0.4	1.7	0.7
Tamil Nadu	6.4	18.7	14.0	43.5	7.4	7.9	1.4	3.1	1.2	2.7
Telangana	1.7	1.0	4.3	3.4	−3.7	−1.5	0.5	0.4	0.5	0.3
Tripura	0.1	0.1	0.5	0.2	−2.8	−5.0	0.7	0.2	1.5	0.4
Uttar Pradesh	1.7	1.7	3.4	4.1	−0.2	1.2	0.3	0.1	0.2	0.2
Uttarakhand	0.3	0.1	0.6	0.2	−10.3	−5.4	0.8	0.1	0.9	0.3
West Bengal	5.6	5.9	20.8	12.7	0.4	−3.3	0.8	0.5	1.2	0.5
Total	60.2	79.7	141.3	175.1	1.9	1.4	1.0	1.0	1.0	1.0

Note: CAGR = Compound annual growth rate; LQ = Location quotient.

Source: Computed using data from MoSPI (1998, 2016).

In 1998, among the top 10 districts (including Delhi as a state), Kerala and West Bengal had three districts each. From Kerala, Ernakulum, Kannur, and Thiruvananthapuram ranked 6th, 8th, and 9th, respectively, while from West Bengal, Kolkata, Hugli, and Medinipur ranked 4th, 5th, and 7th, respectively. The 10th position was occupied by Chennai. However, in 2013–14, Purbi Champaran, Aurangabad, and Kendrapara ranked 1st, 2nd, and 3rd, respectively. From Kerala, we had Kannur and Thiruvananthapuram ranking as 8th and 9th, but none of the districts from West Bengal could find a place in the top 10 districts. This shows that in recent years the emphasis on cultural sites has changed in West Bengal. Purbi Champaran and Aurangabad have been known for Buddhist cultural sites, and the demand for these places grew in early 2000s which has pulled upward the ranking of these districts.

4.4.3 Performing arts

The tradition of performing arts in India is very old (Wade 1983). The Indian *raga* system is known for its coherence and melodies (see Bandoypadhyaya 1970). Performing arts are also mixed up with religion (Massey and Massey 1996) and regional cultural systems. Deity and gods have been prayed to in songs, music, dance, etc. The regional cultural festivals have also been associated with various performing arts like circus, theatre, drama, nautanki (a type of musical drama), etc. *Bhajan* (devotional songs, solo or duet), *Kirtan* (a group song to deity or chant), and dances have been an integral part of Hindu religious places, whereas Muslim shrines are known for Sufi music and *qawwalis* (is sung in group and narrates a legend or spiritual idea). Music and dance are considered as one of the methods of salvation. Bharat Natyam and Kathakali (Wade 1983) are religious for Hindus as is whirling dance of Sufis for Muslims.

Music is not only performed and played at religious places, but they are an integral part of everyday life and celebrations. India has also produced eminent musicians in various traditions of songs and music and some of them are Amjad Ali Khan (Sarod Player), Subbulakshmi (vocalist), Vinay Bharat Ram (singer), Vilayat Khan (sitar player), Bismillah Khan (shehnai player), Vishwanathan (flute player), Zakir Hussein (table player), Balachender (veena player), Nazakat Ali Khan (vocalist), Pandit Ravi Shankar (sitar player), and Begum Parveen Sultana (classical singer).

Bollywood is known for its music and songs, and it had luminaries like Mukesh Kumar (singer), Mohammad Rafi (singer), Talat Mahmood (singer), Lata Mangeshkar (singer), Asha Bhosle (singer), Suraiya (singer), Kishore Kumar (singer), Mahendra Kapoor (singer), again to name a few. The regional varieties emerging from folk songs and tradition are also amazing. Peculiarities of music and songs in India are that they not only have several streams or traditions but are also syncretized through of mixing of various religious and cultural traditions (Wade 1983).

Each region of India has its own specific music, theatre, circus, and dance. There are specific *gharanas* (houses or families which continue the tradition of performing arts in those regions). Distinguished individuals have emerged in performing arts from those *gharanas*. For instance, Kirana Gharana of north India produced prominent classical musicians like Abdul Karim Khan and Abdul Wahid Khan, while Agra gharana produced Vilayat Ali Khan, Faiyaz Ali Khan, Nathan Khan, and M.R. Gautam (Wade 1983). The regional specific dances in India are Bharat Natyam from Tamil Nadu, Kuchipudi from Andhra Pradesh, Kathakali and Mohiniyattam from Kerala, Kathak from Uttar Pradesh, Odissi from Odisha, Bhangra and Jhumar from Punjab, Manipuri from Manipur, Garba from Gujarat, Rouf from Kashmir, Ghoomar from Rajasthan, Chhau from Mayurbhanj of Orissa, Bihu and Sattriya from Assam, Lavani from Maharashtra, to mention a few. There are many other forms of dances and music in most of the states of India, but due to lack of spaces we are not able to mention them here.

The data relating to workers, establishments, growth rate, and location quotients of workers related to performing arts are produced in Table 4.6. The prominent states in terms of size of workers in India in 2013–14 were Uttar Pradesh, West Bengal, Telangana, Tamil Nadu, Rajasthan Maharashtra, Odisha, and Andhra Pradesh. Most of these states have also experienced a very high growth rate of workers in performing arts, and in most of the cases, the growth rate has been above 30% per annum. At the all-India level, the growth rate of workers in this sector was 23% while the increase in establishments was about 27%. This shows that the number of small enterprises (with lower number of workers) is growing faster. However, in 2013–14, in terms of relative concentration of workers, Lakshadweep, Goa, and Daman and Diu stand out with location coefficients of 11.2, 6.0, and 5.2, respectively. This shows that in this sector they specialize. However, district-level analysis shows that there is only one primary cluster of performing art in India, that is, the Mumbai-Pune region (Figure 4.5). Pune had the highest number of workers (total 8,748) in performing art in 2013–14 and was followed by Mumbai Suburban (7,764 workers), and Thane (5,477). There are several secondary clusters, which include the south and central Gujarat (from Surat to Ahmedabad), Delhi and its neighbouring districts, central and western Punjab, Kolkata region, Hyderabad region, and Kerala.

4.4.4 Visual arts

Given its varied culture, India is also very rich in painting traditions, sculptures, antiques, and added to this are the technology-enabled photography. Each of regions of the country are having their own types of painting traditions and sculptures. The visual arts market in India was estimated to be INR 13.5 billion in 2013 and INR 14.6 billion in 2017 (KPMG-FICCI 2018: 1). However, India still in general lacks the appreciation of visual arts: the art and artists are not given

Table 4.6 Growth of performing arts enterprises, worker, and location quotient by states, 1998 and 2013–14

States	*Enterprises (000)*		*Workers (000)*		*CAGR (%)*		*LQ for workers*	
	1998	*2013–14*	*1998*	*2013–14*	*Enterprises*	*Workers*	*1998*	*2013–14*
Andaman and Nicobar Islands	0.0	0.0	0.0	0.0	–	–	0	0.5
Andhra Pradesh	0.2	6.4	0.3	13.9	28.4	28.9	0.5	1.0
Arunachal Pradesh	0.0	0.1	0.0	0.2	35.5	44.3	0.1	2.8
Assam	0.0	5.1	0.3	10.9	37.1	28.2	1.2	1.1
Bihar	0.1	3.9	0.1	7.4	31.1	32.2	0.4	1.6
Chandigarh	0.0	0.3	0.0	0.6	45.1	45.8	0.1	0.6
Chhattisgarh	0.0	1.5	0.0	3.2	33.6	36.6	0.2	1.3
Dadra and Nagar Haveli	0.0	0.0	0.0	0.1	–	–	0.0	2.5
Daman and Diu	0.0	0.0	0.0	0.1	–	–	0.0	5.3
Delhi	0.5	2.6	2.4	9.0	11.4	9.2	2.9	2.1
Goa	0.0	0.7	0.0	1.8	26.3	28.4	1.2	6.0
Gujarat	0.1	7.3	0.1	19.4	38.9	39.1	0.1	1.3
Haryana	0.0	2.3	0.0	4.7	33.1	37.5	0.2	1.3
Himachal Pradesh	0.0	0.8	0.0	1.3	33.5	29.8	0.3	1.1
Jammu and Kashmir	0.0	0.8	0.0	1.6	32.5	34.2	0.2	0.3
Jharkhand	0.0	0.8	0.1	2.0	26.8	26.0	0.7	0.8
Karnataka	0.3	0.9	0.8	2.8	7.8	8.4	1.4	0.2
Kerala	0.1	5.6	0.2	13.0	31.9	30.2	0.4	1.3
Lakshadweep	0.0	0.0	0.0	0.2	–	–	0.0	11.2
Madhya Pradesh	0.1	5.6	0.3	14.0	29.7	29.1	0.6	2.1
Maharashtra	0.4	16.4	1.5	46.8	28.7	25.7	1.1	1.6
Manipur	0.0	0.7	0.3	1.3	24.7	9.4	9.6	0.4
Meghalaya	0.0	0.1	0.0	0.2	35.7	32.2	0.2	0.4
Mizoram	0.0	0.0	0.0	0.1	16.4	13.1	2.0	0.3
Nagaland	0.0	0.1	0.0	0.1	18.2	19.3	1.4	0.2
Odisha	0.1	4.9	0.3	13.7	29.2	28.1	1.0	0.9
Puducherry	0.0	0.2	0.0	0.6	32.1	29.3	0.3	1.0
Punjab	0.1	6.2	0.2	11.9	31.2	29.7	1.0	3.0
Rajasthan	0.1	7.6	0.2	20.8	34.5	37.0	0.3	1.4
Sikkim	0.0	0.0	0.0	0.1	–	–	0.0	0.5
Tamil Nadu	0.2	8.2	0.8	20.1	26.7	24.3	0.7	0.8
Telangana	0.1	5.1	2.3	18.9	28.1	14.9	3.2	1.0
Tripura	0.0	0.5	0.0	0.7	23.6	22.2	1.1	0.7
Uttar Pradesh	0.2	10.6	0.4	27.2	31.1	33.4	0.3	0.7
Uttarakhand	0.0	0.6	0.1	1.7	27.8	24.8	1.0	1.2
West Bengal	0.5	9.0	2.0	20.9	21.2	17.1	1.2	0.5
Total	3.2	114.9	13.0	291.5	26.9	23.0	1.0	1.0

Note: CAGR = Compound annual growth rate; LQ = Location quotient.

Source: Computed using data from MoSPI (1998, 2016).

the importance as we find in the Western countries, Japan, China, Brazil, and wealthier Arab States. However, in recent years, its importance in the middle class is growing. There are several art galleries which attempt to exhibit the

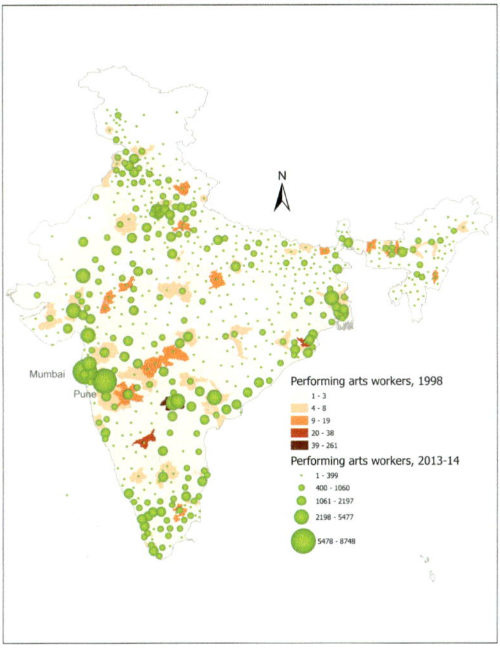

Figure 4.5 Distribution of workers in performing arts by district, 1998 and 2013–14

Source: Computed using data from MoSPI (1998, 2016).

creations of the artists at national and international levels. Some of such galleries are "Vadehra Art Gallery (New Delhi), Nature Morte (New Delhi), Gallery Chemould (Mumbai), Chatterjee & Lal (Mumbai), DAG Modern (New Delhi), Espace Gallery (New Delhi), Experimenter (Kolkata), Lakeeren Art Gallery (Mumbai) amongst others" (KPMG-FICCI 2018: 4). In European countries (such as France), most of the cities have developed their own museum to showcase their heritages. However, India despite being culturally rich, lacks this tradition. The museums are located mainly in metropolitan areas while medium and smaller cities almost have none. Some of the major museums in India which attempt to showcase regional fine arts or national heritage are the "National Gallery of Modern Art (New Delhi, Mumbai, and Bengaluru), Dr. Bhau Daji Lad Museum (Mumbai), and Chhatrapati Shivaji Maharaj Vastu Sangrahalaya (Mumbai)" (KPMG-FICCI 2018: 4). Commercialization of visual arts are also very limited and confined to largely higher class. A majority of the painters, sculptures, and photographers, and so in other related activities of visual arts, live mainly at subsistence level as the market of these arts are not developed. Only a few companies or houses of auctions exist and some of these are Saffronart, Sotheby's, Pundole's, AstaGuru, and Bonhams (KPMG-FICCI 2018: 5). Some non-commercial platforms have also emerged to support artists and popularize visual arts. KHOJ, an international artist association, and Foundation for Indian Contemporary Art (FICA) are such non-commercial platforms.

The visual art is mainly represented by photographic activities for both the reference years while painting and other aspects of it are merged with other NICs of creative sectors (see Chapter 3 for details). However, photographic activities are the major sub-sector in this sector. We can draw the following observations from the data presented in Table 4.7 and Figure 4.6. First, the visual art workers in almost all the states and union territories, except in Delhi, Nagaland, and Arunachal Pradesh, have shown significant growth between

Table 4.7 Growth of visual arts enterprises, workers, and location quotient by states, 1998 and 2013–14

States	*Enterprises (000)*		*Workers (000)*		*CAGR (%)*		*LQ for workers*	
	1998	*2013–14*	*1998*	*2013–14*	*Enterprises*	*Workers*	*1998*	*2013–14*
Andaman and Nicobar Islands	0.0	0.1	0.1	0.2	4.8	3.3	1.8	2.4
Andhra Pradesh	4.5	11.2	7.9	20.6	6.3	6.6	1.1	1.3
Arunachal Pradesh	0.1	0.1	0.2	0.1	−2.5	−3.8	1.9	1.0
Assam	1.5	3.4	2.8	5.1	5.8	4.0	1.0	0.5
Bihar	2.0	3.8	3.8	5.9	4.4	3.1	1.1	1.1
Chandigarh	0.3	0.4	0.6	0.8	2.6	1.9	1.4	0.7
Chhattisgarh	1.3	2.3	2.1	3.6	4.0	3.7	1.2	1.2
Dadra and Nagar Haveli	0.0	0.0	0.0	0.1	12.4	11.6	0.5	1.9
Daman and Diu	0.0	0.1	0.0	0.1	12.9	13.8	0.6	3.2
Delhi	10.8	3.7	16.8	7.9	−6.9	−5.0	1.6	1.6
Goa	0.1	0.3	0.2	0.6	6.3	5.8	0.5	1.6
Gujarat	4.2	11.0	6.9	19.0	6.6	6.9	0.4	1.1
Haryana	3.3	6.8	4.4	10.4	5.0	5.9	1.7	2.4
Himachal Pradesh	1.2	3.0	1.6	3.5	6.0	5.4	1.7	2.6
Jammu and Kashmir	0.5	2.1	0.8	3.0	9.5	9.2	0.5	0.5
Jharkhand	0.8	2.3	1.4	4.0	7.3	7.3	1.2	1.3
Karnataka	3.6	12.3	7.3	22.1	8.4	7.6	1.0	1.4
Kerala	5.2	11.9	10.0	21.9	5.7	5.4	1.3	1.8
Lakshadweep	0.0	0.0	0.0	0.0	7.6	11.8	0.4	1.6
Madhya Pradesh	4.5	7.7	6.7	12.4	3.7	4.1	1.0	1.6
Maharashtra	9.1	22.9	16.9	36.6	6.3	5.3	1.0	1.1
Manipur	0.3	0.2	0.5	0.5	0.0	−0.5	1.2	0.1
Meghalaya	0.1	0.2	0.3	0.4	4.0	2.8	1.6	0.8
Mizoram	0.1	0.1	0.1	0.2	2.7	4.7	1.0	0.5
Nagaland	0.2	0.2	0.5	0.3	−0.4	−3.6	5.1	0.4
Odisha	2.0	5.9	3.4	9.0	7.4	6.6	0.9	0.5
Puducherry	0.2	0.5	0.3	0.9	7.7	6.7	0.7	1.4
Punjab	5.7	11.5	8.8	17.7	4.8	4.8	2.8	3.8
Rajasthan	5.7	13.3	8.6	19.8	5.8	5.7	1.2	1.1
Sikkim	0.0	0.0	0.1	0.1	3.3	2.1	1.2	0.6
Tamil Nadu	4.7	15.5	11.3	31.4	8.4	7.0	0.9	1.0
Telangana	3.5	10.2	9.2	24.8	7.4	6.8	1.0	1.1

Tripura	0.3	0.7	0.5	0.9	5.4	3.7	1.4	0.8
Uttar Pradesh	10.5	20.1	16.5	30.4	4.5	4.2	1.0	0.6
Uttarakhand	1.3	2.7	1.8	3.8	5.3	5.0	2.4	2.4
West Bengal	5.9	11.5	12.1	20.2	4.6	3.5	0.6	0.4
Total	93.1	197.9	164.6	337.9	5.2	4.9	1.0	1.0

Note: CAGR = Compound annual growth rate; LQ = Location quotient.

Source: Computed using data from MoSPI (1998, 2016).

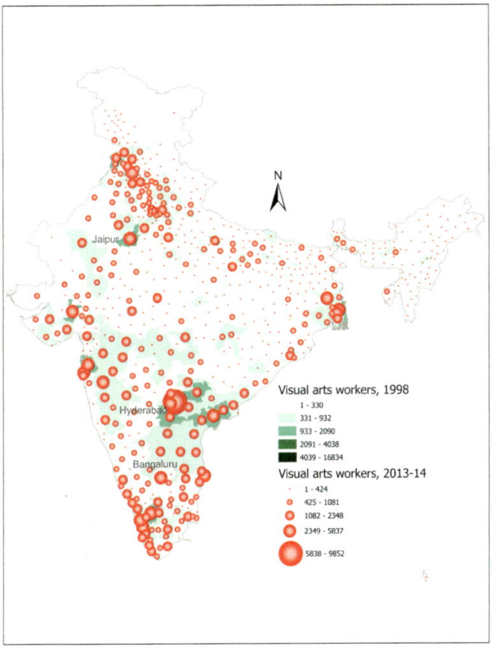

Figure 4.6 Distribution of workers engaged in visual arts by district, 1998 and 2013–14

Source: Computed using data from MoSPI (1998, 2016).

1998 and 2013–14. However, the highest growth rate is seen in smaller states like Dadra and Nagar Haveli and Daman and Diu. Southern states like Karnataka, Tamil Nadu, Telangana, and Andhra Pradesh have also shown relatively higher growth in comparison to other major states in the country. Second, the southern (Karnataka, Kerala, Telangana, Andhra Pradesh, and Tamil Nadu) and western states of India (Maharashtra and Gujarat) and northern-western states (Punjab, Haryana and Rajasthan) have a relatively higher concentration of visual art workers, which makes their location quotient also higher. Third, one finds five major broad regional clusters of visual art workers in 2013–14 and these are (a) Kerala, Tamil Nadu, and Southern Karnataka, (b) Hyderabad region, (c) Mumbai-Ahmedabad belt, (d) Agra-Jaipur-Amritsar region, and

(e) southern Bengal. However, Hyderabad in 2013–14 ranked first in terms of number of workers (9,852 workers) and was followed by Bengaluru (5,837), North 24 Parganas (4,922), Chennai (4,187), Rangareddy (3,918), Mumbai Suburban (3,887), and Pune (3,480).

4.4.5 Audio-visual

Film, television, radio, and other broadcasting constitute the audio-visual sector. This is one of the very potential creative sectors of India and has also shown very high growth rate in recent years. As per the KPMG (2013a), the year-on-year growth rate in 2013 of films was 11.5% (with total value of INR 125.3 billion in 2013), television 12.7% (INR 417.2 billion), animation, visual effects (VFX), and gaming 16.4% (INR 58.9 billion), radio 15.0% (INR 14.6 billion), and music showing downward trend −9.6% (INR 9.6 billion). KPMG (2013a) also estimated the employment in each of the sectors in 2013 as 0.14 million in television (likely to rise to 0.28 in 2017 and 0.64 in 2022), 0.02 million in radio (likely to rise to 0.07 in 2017 and 0.13 in 2022), 0.02 million in animation, VFX, and games (likely to rise to 0.03 in 2017 and 0.04 in 2022), and 0.16 million in films (likely to rise to 0.24 in 2017 and 0.44 in 2022). KPMG (2020) estimated the compound annual growth rate of the monetary size of television sector between the financial year (1 April to 31 March) 2016–2020 as 9% (with total value of INR 778 billion in 2020), films 0% (INR 183 billion in 2020), animation, VFX, and gaming 15% (INR 101 billion in 2020), radio −11% (INR 25 billion in 2020), and music 15% (INR 19 billion in 2020). In 2020 report, KPMG (2020) also included digital and OTT platform which showed annual growth rate between the same years of 26% (with total size of INR 218 billion in 2020). However, some of these gross estimates, especially of employment, do not correspond with the Economic Census 2013–14 data used in this chapter.

India is one of the major producers of films in the world (see Chapter 10) and what we call Bollywood is mainly the Hindi cinema industry located in Mumbai and Mumbai Suburban districts. In 2013–14, Mumbai Suburban (with 8,183 workers) ranked first in terms of the number of workers in this sector in the country, while Mumbai district ranked 5th with 3,956 workers (Greater Mumbai was bifurcated in Mumbai and Mumbai-Suburban districts and for 2013–14 the data are available for both the districts separately).

The Telugu cinema is another major film industry located in Hyderabad (the district ranked 2nd in terms of the number of audio-visual workers in the country), while Kolkata (ranked third in terms of the number of workers) is known for the production of Bengali cinema. Ernakulam (ranked 6th with 2,544 workers in this sector) is a centre of the Malayalam film industry, while Chennai is the centre of Tamil cinema. This is why we find that these districts are the centres of concentrations of audio-visual industry workers (Figure 4.7). These are also the districts where television industries and radio, broadcasting

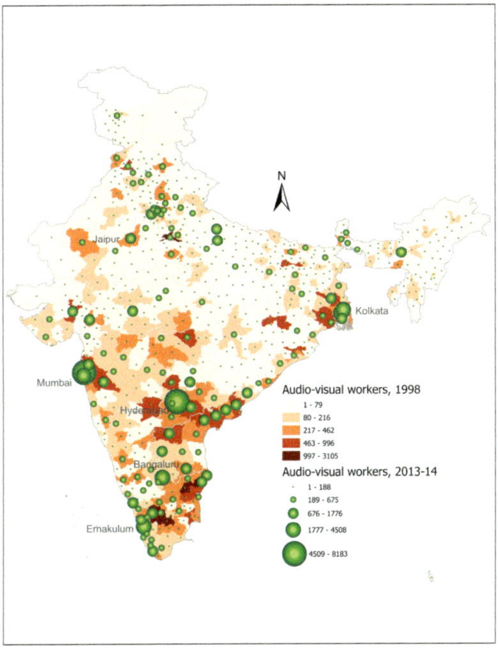

Figure 4.7 Distribution of workers engaged in audio-visual industries by district, 1998 and 2013–14

Source: Computed using data from MoSPI (1998, 2016).

regional and national news and entertainment programmes, are located. Besides these, other major centres of the television industry are Noida and New Delhi, Jaipur, Guwahati, and Lucknow. Overall, the southern and western states of India have the major share of total workers in this sector (Table 4.8).

4.4.6 Publishing and print media

Books, press, and other publications constitute publishing and other print media. As one can imagine, the rise of ICT has severely impacted this sector. The sector has become more online and paper publishing has diminished (see KPMG 2020). Additionally, the publishing activities are shifted to other countries as the contents can be sent online easily to other destinations. For instance, many books publishing companies in India, including Routledge and Springer, publish the majority of books and contents from other countries rather than India. Springer largely publishes Indian-authored books from Singapore or European countries while Routledge does it from London and New York. However, Chennai has emerged as major centre for content editing and typesetting for several publishers including Springer.

Table 4.8 Growth of audio-visual enterprises, worker, and location quotient by states, 1998 and 2013–14

States	*Enterprises (000)*		*Workers (000)*		*CAGR (%)*		*LQ for workers*	
	1998	*2013–14*	*1998*	*2013–14*	*Enterprises*	*Workers*	*1998*	*2013–14*
Andaman and Nicobar Islands	0.0	0.0	0.0	0.2	11.3	16.4	0.6	5.7
Andhra Pradesh	1.6	3.7	4.1	10.7	5.8	6.6	1.3	1.8
Arunachal Pradesh	0.0	0.0	0.3	0.2	1.5	−4.7	8.6	4.5
Assam	0.3	0.4	1.0	2.4	2.8	5.7	0.9	0.6
Bihar	0.4	1.4	2.2	3.4	9.2	2.8	1.5	1.8
Chandigarh	0.0	0.0	0.2	0.6	3.5	8.7	0.9	1.5
Chhattisgarh	0.2	0.4	0.6	1.3	5.8	5.6	0.8	1.2
Dadra and Nagar Haveli	0.0	0.0	0.1	0.1	−1.6	−6.4	14.1	4.1
Daman and Diu	0.0	0.0	0.0	0.0	7.6	7.8	1.1	3.2
Delhi	0.2	1.1	3.1	3.4	12.9	0.6	0.7	1.9
Goa	0.1	0.0	0.2	0.0	−11.8	−10.8	0.8	0.2
Gujarat	0.7	1.4	2.4	4.0	4.7	3.4	0.3	0.6
Haryana	0.6	0.6	1.2	2.0	0.7	3.3	1.1	1.3
Himachal Pradesh	0.1	0.1	0.6	0.4	0.9	−2.3	1.6	0.9
Jammu and Kashmir	0.2	0.3	0.4	0.7	4.6	4.1	0.6	0.4
Jharkhand	0.2	0.8	0.8	1.6	10.0	4.7	1.7	1.5
Karnataka	1.3	1.1	4.5	6.6	−1.2	2.5	1.4	1.2
Kerala	1.1	1.9	3.3	8.8	3.4	6.8	1.0	2.1
Lakshadweep	0.0	0.0	0.0	0.0	0.0	−0.3	4.2	3.5
Madhya Pradesh	1.1	1.6	2.7	4.2	2.8	3.1	0.9	1.5
Maharashtra	1.7	3.0	7.9	18.4	3.7	5.8	1.1	1.6
Manipur	0.0	0.1	0.2	0.3	10.8	2.4	1.3	0.2
Meghalaya	0.0	0.0	0.3	0.1	0.7	−6.5	4.9	0.7
Mizoram	0.0	0.1	0.2	0.2	7.0	1.5	5.5	1.9
Nagaland	0.0	0.0	0.0	0.1	13.9	9.7	0.5	0.3
Odisha	0.7	0.9	2.8	2.4	1.7	−0.9	1.6	0.4
Puducherry	0.1	0.2	0.3	0.7	2.0	6.1	1.5	3.2
Punjab	0.6	0.9	1.8	2.2	3.2	1.4	1.3	1.3
Rajasthan	0.6	1.2	1.9	3.2	4.4	3.6	0.6	0.5
Sikkim	0.0	0.0	0.1	0.3	6.8	6.9	4.9	6.0
Tamil Nadu	5.1	2.0	12.5	8.0	−5.9	−2.9	2.3	0.7
Telangana	0.8	2.0	3.3	12.0	6.0	9.0	0.8	1.5
Tripura	0.0	0.0	0.3	0.2	−3.2	−2.3	1.7	0.4
Uttar Pradesh	1.1	3.4	5.0	8.9	7.9	3.9	0.7	0.5
Uttarakhand	0.1	0.2	0.5	0.7	3.3	2.3	1.6	1.3
West Bengal	0.9	3.4	4.5	12.0	9.2	6.7	0.5	0.7
Total	19.8	32.3	69.4	120.4	3.3	3.7	1.0	1.0

Note: CAGR = Compound annual growth rate; LQ = Location quotient.

Source: Computed using data from MoSPI (1998, 2016).

Additionally, the usual pamphlet printing often used for intimation, celebration, and in festivals have shifted to online where individuals themselves are designing and publishing the same. This again negatively impacts this sector in terms of its organized growth. As per KPMG (2020), the revenue of print subsector at current prices was of INR 288 billion which increased to INR

333 billion, with a compound annual growth rate of 2%. In fact, during the financial year 2019–2020, the growth has been negative, −8%.

There is a decline in the publishing and print media sector across the states in the country (Table 4.9). The most substantial decline of this sector between 1998 and 2013–13 has been in Delhi, which was major hub for publishing and printing. The sector also declined in southern states like Telangana, Karnataka, Kerala, Tamil Nadu, and Andhra Pradesh.

Second, in terms of the concentration of industry, the district-level mapping shows that the industry is very much clustered. The primary clusters of the publishing and print media are (a) Jaipur and (b) Hyderabad, while there are several secondary clusters, and some of them are (a) Noida (including adjoining districts of Delhi), (b) Mumbai, Mumbai Suburban, and Thane, (c) Kolkata, (d) Patna, (e) Bengaluru, (f) Puducherry, (g) Coimbatore, (h) Amritsar, and (i) Chennai (see Figure 4.8). There are also tertiary nodes of concentration of workers of these sectors more visible in Tamil Nadu and Southern Karnataka, and in western Uttar Pradesh, Haryana, and Punjab. In 1998, the first ranked district in terms of the number of workers in this sector was Mumbai (26,173 workers) and was followed by Kolkata (20,657), Bengaluru (12,038), and Chennai (10,798). In 2013–14,

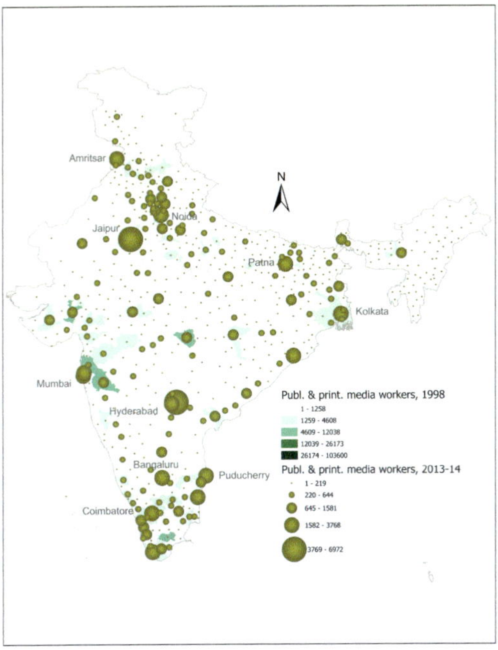

Figure 4.8 Distribution of workers engaged in publishing and print media by district, 1998 and 2013–14

Source: Computed using data from MoSPI (1998, 2016).

Table 4.9 Growth of publishing and printing enterprises, worker, and location quotient by states, 1998 and 2013–14

States	*Enterprises (000)*		*Workers (000)*		*CAGR (%)*		*LQ enterprises*		*LQ for workers*	
	1998	*2013–14*	*1998*	*2013–14*	*Enterprises*	*Workers*	*1998*	*2013–14*	*1998*	*2013–14*
Andaman and Nicobar Islands	0.0	0.0	0.2	0.1	−4.5	−7.5	1.4	2.5	1.1	1.9
Andhra Pradesh	3.2	1.6	11.6	5.7	−4.6	−4.6	0.5	0.6	0.6	0.8
Arunachal Pradesh	0.0	0.0	0.1	0.1	3.5	−0.8	0.5	3.7	0.5	2.8
Assam	1.5	0.5	8.2	2.3	−7.4	−8.2	1.2	0.3	1.1	0.5
Bihar	1.4	2.8	4.9	6.6	4.6	2.0	0.5	3.2	0.5	3.0
Chandigarh	0.3	0.1	3.8	0.6	−10.4	−11.6	2.4	2.0	3.1	1.3
Chhattisgarh	1.1	0.7	5.2	2.8	−3.2	−4.0	0.8	1.5	1.1	2.2
Dadra and Nagar Haveli	0.0	0.0	0.2	0.0	1.3	−12.1	1.4	2.5	2.9	1.9
Daman and Diu	0.0	0.0	0.2	0.0	−11.3	−15.5	1.7	0.9	2.7	1.1
Delhi	10.9	0.3	103.6	2.2	−21.0	−22.5	3.3	0.9	3.5	1.1
Goa	0.3	0.0	1.7	0.2	−16.0	−13.6	1.0	0.5	1.3	1.3
Gujarat	5.2	1.8	22.3	5.8	−6.7	−8.6	1.0	1.1	0.5	0.8
Haryana	1.4	2.1	6.5	4.4	2.8	−2.6	0.7	4.1	0.9	2.5
Himachal Pradesh	0.3	0.1	3.7	0.6	−5.7	−11.8	0.5	0.5	1.4	1.0
Jammu and Kashmir	0.2	0.3	0.5	1.3	2.9	6.8	0.2	0.4	0.1	0.6
Jharkhand	0.3	1.3	1.2	3.2	10.2	6.6	0.4	2.9	0.4	2.6
Karnataka	6.4	1.4	23.6	6.6	−9.4	−8.2	1.5	1.0	1.1	1.0
Kerala	6.6	1.6	28.4	7.7	−9.1	−8.4	1.3	1.3	1.3	1.5
Lakshadweep	0.0	0.0	0.1	0.0	−11.3	−26.7	1.4	0.5	2.6	0.1
Madhya Pradesh	4.0	1.7	17.2	5.0	−5.6	−7.9	0.8	1.5	0.9	1.5
Maharashtra	11.9	3.0	60.1	13.9	−8.8	−9.3	1.3	1.1	1.3	1.0

Manipur	0.2	0.1	1.2	0.3	−6.7	−8.2	0.7	0.1	1.0	0.2
Meghalaya	0.1	0.0	0.6	0.2	−1.8	−8.7	0.9	0.7	1.3	0.7
Mizoram	0.1	0.1	0.7	0.2	−4.8	−7.6	2.6	1.4	3.0	1.5
Nagaland	0.1	0.0	0.3	0.1	−5.0	−8.8	1.2	0.3	1.2	0.2
Odisha	1.4	1.4	5.2	4.2	−0.3	−1.4	0.4	0.5	0.5	0.5
Puducherry	0.3	0.1	1.8	2.5	−7.9	2.3	2.5	3.0	1.4	9.6
Punjab	2.2	1.3	6.7	4.2	−3.5	−3.2	1.0	2.0	0.8	2.2
Rajasthan	2.7	4.1	8.2	11.8	2.9	2.5	0.5	1.6	0.4	1.6
Sikkim	0.0	0.0	0.0	0.2	–	–	0.0	1.7	0.0	3.3
Tamil Nadu	9.7	3.9	44.5	13.1	−6.0	−7.8	1.4	1.3	1.2	1.0
Telangana	2.7	2.1	13.4	11.4	−1.7	−1.1	0.5	1.9	0.5	1.2
Tripura	0.2	0.0	1.1	0.0	−20.2	−25.3	0.7	0.0	1.1	0.0
Uttar Pradesh	7.1	4.4	32.6	15.2	−3.1	−5.0	0.8	0.8	0.7	0.8
Uttarakhand	0.5	0.4	1.8	1.7	−1.4	−0.3	0.8	1.8	0.8	2.6
West Bengal	10.9	2.4	43.9	7.1	−9.6	−11.4	1.0	0.4	0.8	0.4
Total	93.4	39.6	465.5	141.3	−5.5	−7.6	1.0	1.0	1.0	1.0

Note: CAGR = Compound annual growth rate; LQ = Location quotient.

Source: Computed using data from MoSPI (1998, 2016).

Hyderabad ranked first but with only 6,972 workers in this sector. Hyderabad was followed by Jaipur (4,972 workers), Mumbai (3,768), Noida, that is Gautam Buddha Nagar, (3,022), and Rangareddy (2,918).

4.4.7 New media

Constituents of new media are software, video games, and digitized creative content. In the new media sector, India has made significant progress since the 1990s. Because of its large share of English-speaking technical manpower, next to the USA, India in the 1990s and 2010s got bulk of the global subcontracting in IT and IT-enabled services (ITES) (Hung 2009). Some of its cities alike Bengaluru, Hyderabad, Kancheepuram, Pune, and Noida are known for the clustering of software and ITES, while many other cities like Mumbai, Delhi, Kolkata, Ahmedabad, and Jaipur have their new initiatives to attract the software industry and related knowledge industries. Bengaluru (formerly known as Bangalore) was one of the first Indian cities to get prominence of the location of software industries in the city in the 1990s and now it has several of its competitors such as Hyderabad, Noida, and Pune. "The ITES/BPO industry has taken root in most of India's leading cities, including NCR, Mumbai, Bengaluru, Chennai, Kolkata, Hyderabad, Kochi, Ahmedabad, and Pune" (Hung 2009: 32). Naidu (2003) argues that research investment carried out over time in industries and defence was the prime reason for Bengaluru emerging as an IT hub in India. In a similar vein, D'Costa argues:

> Through a series of interrelated investments, the government of India unwittingly created the modern technological hub of Bangalore. For example, since 1954 Bangalore has been the headquarters for the Indian Air Force, while the Ministry of Defense established Bharat Electronics Limited in the city. Other technology-related public sector enterprises were established such as the Indian Telephone Industries, Hindustan Aeronautics, and various R&D centers. The establishment of the Department of Electronics in 1970, rechristened the Department of Information Technology (DIT), has been instrumental in providing a state-supported technical infrastructure supporting the Indian IT industry. For example, the National Informatics Center, Computer Maintenance Corporation (CMC), the National Center for Software Development and Computing Technology, and regional computer centers were established.
>
> (D'Costa 2009: 633–635)

Another reason for the location of the software and knowledge industry mainly in the southern and western states of the country has been the growth of technological education institutions in these states initially in the 1950s and 1960s. The southern states of India like Karnataka, Andhra Pradesh, and Tamil Nadu had an advantage over other states. By 1961, out of 2,428 technological institutions in the country, about half were in these southern states (D'Costa 2009), in which Bengaluru, Hyderabad, Chennai, and other neighbouring cities had major concentrations.

Hyderabad started growing in the early 1990s when then Chief Minister of undivided Andhra Pradesh, Chandrababu Naidu, imagined making Hyderabad *Cyberabad (a digital city)*, and as a result of his initiatives and investments, there was a rapid growth of software industries in the city and export revenue rose from less than the US$1 million in 1992 to the US$250 million in 1999–2000, and employment in the industry during the same period grew from 12,000 to 23,000 (Biswas 2004: 824). However, in relation to Bengaluru, Hyderabad is considered having industries lower in value chain (i.e., the products are not as higher in value added term as in Bangalore).

Kancheepuram, though not recognized commonly in literature on software industry, has made rapid progress in terms of number of workers in this sector. Introducing the district of Kancheepuram, the Government of India (2013) writes:

> The district is also known for the numerous electronic and software enterprises in the IT corridor, giant car manufactures like Ford, Hyundai, BMW and Nissan, telecommunication multinationals like Nokia and Flextronics and the famous glass manufacturer Saint Gobain Glass.
>
> (p. 1)

Kancheepuram has several industrial estates hosting a number of software companies and some of these estates in 2013 were Dr Vikram Sarabhai Industrial Estate, SIPCOT IT Complex, and Mahindra Industrial Park (Special Economic Zone). The district also had 245 large firms, and one of the major export items was software (Government of India 2013: 26). The Chennai OMR software cluster in 2012–13 itself had 1,000 enterprises, 75,000 employees, and export of products and processes of about INR 7.5 billion (Government of India 2013). This shows that Kancheepuram, though with a low-value chain industry in the IT sector, is one of the rising districts in the software industry.

Pune has emerged as another hub of software and ITES. Almost all the major industries are located in the city. The city has several IT parks. The Rajeev Gandhi IT Park (special economic zone) was built by a government investment of INR 1.55 billion, and in the year 2011–12 employed about 0.15 million persons, and export was of about the US$10 billion, 60% of Maharashtra's total IT export (Kulkarni 2012). This initial financial stimulus by the Government led to the investment by other major companies in the city of about INR 60 billion in this sector till that year (Kulkarni 2012).

Mumbai is the financial capital of India and is known for locations of major national and foreign banks (Mohan 2005). Therefore, IT companies have been attracted to the city. However, higher manpower and infrastructure cost does create diseconomies of agglomeration in the city. Jaipur, Ahmedabad, Noida, and Kolkata are other new towns that have the substantial number of workers in these industries (Figure 4.9). In fact, the new town or Rajarhat of Kolkata has attracted such industries.

Because of the reasons mentioned earlier, the southern and western states of the country have a higher number of workers engaged in the new media industry (Table 4.10), and they also have a significantly higher annual growth rate of the sector. In 1998, Hyderabad district ranked first (total workers in the new media sector, 11,838) and was followed by Bengaluru (10,406), Mumbai (6,931), Chennai (4,832), Kolkata (3,779), Pune (3,285), and Vadodara (2,111). The figures of workers are lower in the economic census reported here as they are more refined than what is reported elsewhere and cited above from other studies. The 2013–14, the top rank district in the number of new media workers was Rangareddy (a neighbouring district and extension of Hyderabad) with 174,859 workers and was followed by Kancheepuram (total workers 147,196), Pune (101,380), Hyderabad (93,986), Mumbai Suburban (77,161), and Noida (56,364). Rangareddy, Kancheepuram, and Pune had a location quotient of 5.2, 5.2, and 4.7, respectively, in 2013–14, indicating that as a district they specialize in this sector in India.

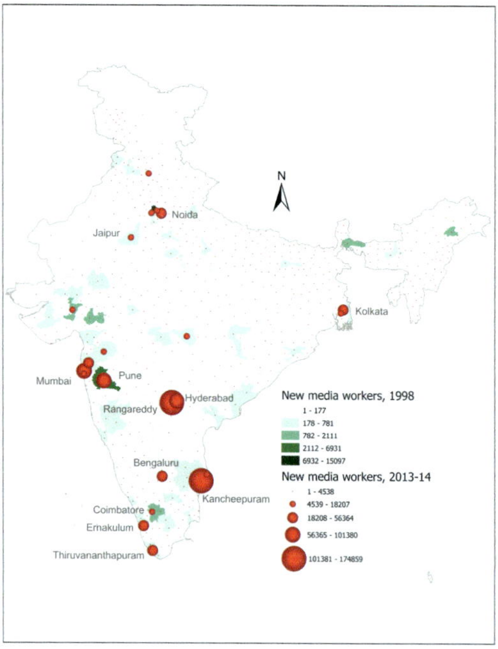

Figure 4.9 Location of workers of new media sector by districts, 1998 and 2013–14

Source: Computed using data from MoSPI (1998, 2016).

Table 4.10 Growth of new media enterprises, worker, and location quotient by states, 1998 and 2013–14

States	*Enterprises (000)*		*Workers (000)*		*CAGR (%)*		*LQ for workers*	
	1998	*2013–14*	*1998*	*2013–14*	*Enterprises*	*Workers*	*1998*	*2013–14*
Andaman and Nicobar Islands	0.0	0.0	0.0	0.1	19.8	20.9	0.2	0.5
Andhra Pradesh	0.4	3.9	1.6	10.2	16.4	13.1	0.4	0.2
Arunachal Pradesh	0.0	0.2	0.0	0.4	30.9	20.1	0.5	1.1
Assam	0.1	2.1	1.8	4.7	21.5	6.5	1.1	0.1
Bihar	0.2	3.1	0.6	5.8	18.5	16.4	0.3	0.3
Chandigarh	0.1	0.4	0.9	18.2	9.6	22.3	3.5	4.7
Chhattisgarh	0.2	1.3	0.5	3.6	13.8	14.1	0.5	0.4
Dadra and Nagar Haveli	0.0	0.0	0.0	0.1	14.9	18.7	0.6	0.9
Daman and Diu	0.0	0.0	0.0	0.2	19.4	25.9	0.4	1.5
Delhi	1.0	4.2	15.1	26.2	10.0	3.8	2.5	1.5
Goa	0.1	0.1	0.6	0.5	−1.9	−0.3	2.1	0.5
Gujarat	2.0	5.7	6.6	22.9	7.4	8.6	0.7	0.4
Haryana	0.3	2.1	0.7	16.2	14.0	23.7	0.4	1.1
Himachal Pradesh	0.1	1.0	0.2	2.3	20.7	19.8	0.3	0.5
Jammu and Kashmir	0.0	1.0	0.1	2.9	24.2	24.7	0.1	0.2
Jharkhand	0.1	1.9	0.4	6.1	23.1	20.2	0.6	0.6
Karnataka	1.5	8.0	11.5	63.3	12.0	12.1	2.6	1.2
Kerala	0.9	8.9	3.1	78.6	16.8	24.0	0.7	1.9
Lakshadweep	0.0	0.0	0.0	0.0	–	–	0.0	0.6
Madhya Pradesh	0.6	5.3	1.5	15.4	15.7	16.6	0.4	0.6
Maharashtra	2.6	17.4	13.5	242.3	13.5	21.2	1.4	2.2
Manipur	0.0	0.3	0.1	0.6	24.6	14.5	0.3	0.0
Meghalaya	0.0	0.2	0.1	0.9	21.5	17.2	0.9	0.5
Mizoram	0.0	0.0	0.1	0.1	11.1	2.8	1.0	0.1
Nagaland	0.0	0.1	0.0	0.4	–	–	0.0	0.1
Odisha	0.2	3.0	1.0	7.1	19.7	13.9	0.4	0.1
Puducherry	0.1	0.6	0.4	3.9	12.9	15.9	1.6	1.8
Punjab	0.6	2.0	1.2	6.8	8.9	12.0	0.7	0.4
Rajasthan	0.6	6.8	1.6	22.3	17.5	19.3	0.4	0.4
Sikkim	0.0	0.1	0.0	0.2	–	–	0.0	0.4
Tamil Nadu	2.4	9.8	11.3	178.4	9.8	20.2	1.5	1.7
Telangana	1.2	5.9	12.7	272.3	11.3	22.7	2.4	3.7
Tripura	0.0	0.4	0.0	0.6	31.2	21.5	0.1	0.1
Uttar Pradesh	0.7	9.0	2.8	74.4	18.4	24.4	0.3	0.5
Uttarakhand	0.1	0.8	0.3	3.4	16.7	18.5	0.6	0.6
West Bengal	0.7	10.2	5.8	52.3	19.1	15.8	0.5	0.3
Total	16.8	116.0	96.0	1143.6	13.8	18.0	1.0	1.0

Note: CAGR = Compound annual growth rate; LQ = Location quotient.

Source: Computed using data from MoSPI (1998, 2016).

4.4.8 Design

Interior, graphic, fashion, jewellery, and toys constitute the design sector of creative industries. The major constituent of the industry is gems and jewellery for which India is well known. This is one of the major export earners for India (see Chapter 5). The gem and jewellery industry had been scattered and almost every town had its own local enterprises catering for the local population. However, since the liberalization, this sub-sector of design has gone through a transformation in terms of consolidation, market orientation, and shift towards higher value-added products which includes even diamond cutting and designing. The emergence of many national and global brands has wreaked havoc on local designers and manufacturers and many are out of business as the bigger manufacturers ensure purity of products (like of gold, silver, titanium, diamond, etc.), and also have uniform price base. However, the guarantee of purity of materials has been one aspect which has attracted the customers to the brand products. Some of such brands are Tanishq (by Tata Group), Reliance Jewels (by Reliance), and Kalyan Jewellers India Ltd. However, today, India is more known not for only domestic consumption of gems and jewellery but also intermediate and final processing. Many industrial enterprises in Gujarat, Maharashtra, and Rajasthan are engaged in this. They import diamonds, precious stones, gold, and other materials from South Africa and other European countries and then process and export back the same (Choudhary and Julka 2018). Jaipur, which has been known since medieval times for its gems and jewellery industry has become capital of this industry. Interior design and fashion industries are also mainly located in the major urban centres of India and seems to have also gone through consolidation like gems and jewellery industry after the liberalization.

As per KPMG (2013b), the market size of the gems and jewellery in 2012–13 was about INR 4,541 billion, and that constituted about 5.9% of India's GDP, while the total employment in the sector was about 464,000. This employment figure is marginally higher than what we find from Economic Census 2013–14 data, as they are estimates by the KPMG.

The data relating to the design sector is presented in Table 4.11 and through Figure 4.10. The following major observations can be drawn from the same. First, Maharashtra and Gujarat are the major hubs of this sector. Though they have experienced a significant decline in the number of workers engaged in this sector, in 2013–14 they rank first and second. Southern states like Karnataka, Kerala, Tamil Nadu, Andhra Pradesh, and Telangana rank comparatively better than other states after the western states. Outside the western and southern regions of the country, West Bengal is also known for its gems and jewellery sector. Second, almost all the states have experienced a decline in the growth rates of workers in this sector. Third, the location quotient of workers in this sector shows that Tripura, Dadra and Nagar Haveli, Daman and Diu, and Gujarat remain the states of specialization in this sector.

Table 4.11 Growth of design enterprises, worker, and location quotient by states, 1998 and 2013–14

States	*Enterprises (000)*		*Workers (000)*		*CAGR (%)*		*LQ for workers*	
	1998	*2013–14*	*1998*	*2013–14*	*Enterprises*	*Workers*	*1998*	*2013–14*
Andaman and Nicobar Islands	0.0	0.0	0.2	0.1	−4.7	−9.8	0.9	3.5
Andhra Pradesh	13.4	0.9	28.0	1.8	−16.8	−16.6	0.9	0.6
Arunachal Pradesh	0.0	0.0	0.1	0.0	−12.0	−14.4	0.2	0.4
Assam	3.1	0.1	7.3	0.3	−19.1	−19.5	0.6	0.1
Bihar	2.0	0.2	3.2	0.3	−15.5	−15.5	0.2	0.3
Chandigarh	0.0	0.1	0.1	0.2	6.8	4.0	0.1	0.9
Chhattisgarh	2.5	0.1	4.3	0.3	−18.4	−17.2	0.6	0.4
Dadra and Nagar Haveli	0.0	0.0	0.0	0.0	–	–	0.0	5.4
Daman and Diu	0.0	0.0	0.0	0.0	−3.3	0.0	0.1	2.3
Delhi	0.9	0.5	6.0	2.4	−4.1	−5.9	0.1	2.5
Goa	0.6	0.0	0.9	0.0	−27.6	−26.4	0.4	0.1
Gujarat	25.3	2.6	269.1	8.9	−14.2	−20.3	3.8	2.7
Haryana	3.9	0.2	6.2	0.5	−19.3	−15.6	0.6	0.6
Himachal Pradesh	0.9	0.1	1.3	0.1	−16.7	−15.8	0.3	0.4
Jammu and Kashmir	0.3	0.2	0.4	0.3	−3.7	−3.2	0.1	0.2
Jharkhand	1.0	0.3	1.5	0.9	−7.7	−3.8	0.3	1.5
Karnataka	10.3	1.7	18.8	7.5	−11.2	−5.9	0.6	2.6
Kerala	14.0	1.5	29.3	4.2	−14.0	−12.2	0.9	1.8
Lakshadweep	0.0	0.0	0.0	0.0	−7.1	−7.1	0.1	0.5
Madhya Pradesh	10.4	0.5	17.4	0.9	−18.6	−17.7	0.6	0.6
Maharashtra	20.4	3.2	64.8	10.5	−11.6	−11.4	0.9	1.7
Manipur	0.9	0.0	2.4	0.0	−30.5	−32.9	1.3	0.0
Meghalaya	0.1	0.0	0.3	0.1	−12.7	−12.1	0.5	0.5
Mizoram	0.0	0.1	0.0	0.2	21.6	13.5	0.1	2.5
Nagaland	0.0	0.1	0.0	0.1	6.4	4.3	0.1	0.6
Odisha	5.5	0.4	9.3	0.8	−15.6	−15.2	0.5	0.2
Puducherry	0.4	0.0	0.7	0.1	−13.0	−11.1	0.4	1.0
Punjab	5.2	0.2	9.9	0.3	−20.8	−20.5	0.7	0.4
Rajasthan	13.6	0.5	26.6	1.0	−20.1	−19.8	0.9	0.3
Sikkim	0.0	0.0	0.1	0.0	−19.3	−24.4	0.3	0.0
Tamil Nadu	24.9	1.4	70.0	4.4	−17.6	−16.8	1.3	0.7
Telangana	5.6	2.7	11.6	8.1	−4.7	−2.4	0.3	1.9
Tripura	0.6	0.9	1.0	1.7	2.8	3.4	0.7	7.8
Uttar Pradesh	14.2	0.6	24.8	1.8	−19.3	−16.2	0.4	0.2
Uttarakhand	0.4	0.1	0.6	0.2	−11.0	−7.7	0.2	0.6
West Bengal	31.8	2.8	84.2	6.7	−15.0	−15.5	1.0	0.8
Total	212.5	21.8	700.8	64.5	−14.1	−14.7	1.0	1.0

Note: CAGR = Compound annual growth rate; LQ = Location quotient.

Source: Computed using data from MoSPI (1998, 2016).

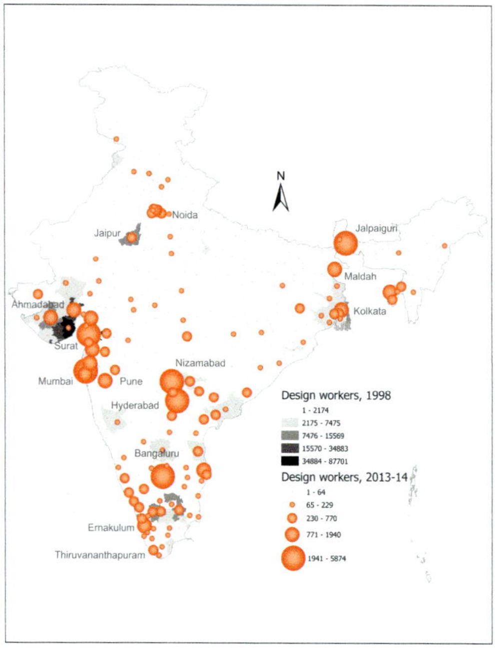

Figure 4.10 Distribution of design workers by district, 1998 and 2013–14

Source: Computed using data from MoSPI (1998, 2016).

Fourth, when we plot district-level workers data of this sector, we find four primary clusters. The first primary cluster is the Pune-Mumbai-Surat-Ahmedabad belt, while the second major cluster is the Hyderabad-Nizamabad region. The third major cluster spreads across several districts of Kerala-Tamil Nadu-South Karnataka region. This third cluster has Bengaluru as the major centre of this activity. Kolkata region also has several districts with a relatively higher concentration of workers in this sector, and this region together with Maldah and Jalpaiguri can be considered constituting the fourth largest cluster of the design sector. Manipur, Delhi (centred at Noida), and coastal Andhra Pradesh are seen as tertiary clusters. In terms of the number of workers, Surat district in 1998 has ranked first (with 87,701 workers) and was followed by Bhavnagar (67,639), Mumbai (34,883), Amreli (26,639), Ahmedabad (22,050), and Kolkata (155,050). However, in 2013–14, Bhavnagar has lost its position (which also had a location quotient of 5.3 and ranked first in 1998 in this regard), and Bengaluru has the highest number of workers in this sector (total workers 5,874). Bengaluru was followed by Mumbai Suburban (3,559), Surat (3,351), Nizamabad (3,271), Hyderabad (3,105), and Jalpaiguri (2,603). The KPMG (2013b) has identified Surat and Ahmedabad as centres of diamond processing, Bhavnagar and Jaipur for gemstone processing, and Kolkata, Thrissur, and Coimbatore for handmade jewelleries.

4.4.9 Creative services

Creative services is a group of several activities including architecture, advertising, research, and development (R&D), and cultural and recreational services. This sector has also seen massive decline between the years 1998 and 2013–14. The reasons for the decline again can be located in digitalization, consolidation, and demand for quality services available online. The local architectural services which people used to avail themselves are now brought from major professional enterprises located in major cities and even outside the country. Further, the availability of digital messaging has made it possible to have real-time consultancy and services. Advertising has faced similar challenges. Online contents from YouTube, Google Maps, Wikipedia, Quora.com, etc. have massively impacted the need for creative services. The research and development activities have also grown as the number of institutions have increased but that has not compensated for the decline in other sectors.

From the data presented in Table 4.12 and Figure 4.11, we can make the following major observations related to distribution and growth of creative services in India. First, the sector has experienced significant declines in almost all the states during 1998 and 2013–14. The decline of workers in this sector has been of more than 10% per annum. Second, the regional divide in the

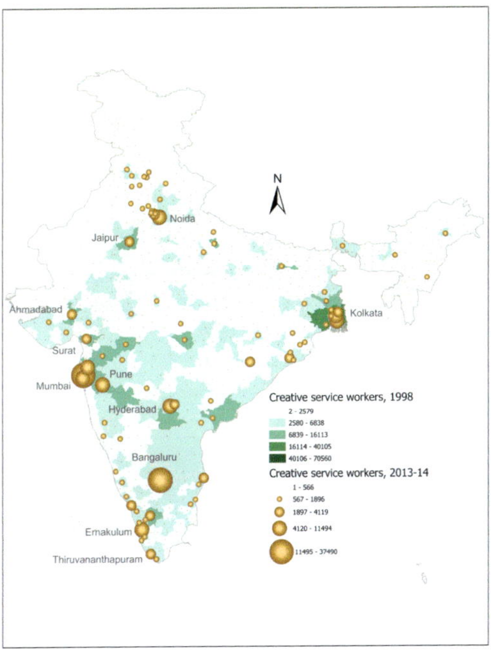

Figure 4.11 Location of workers of creative service sector by district, 1998 and 2013–14

Source: Computed using data from MoSPI (1998, 2016).

Table 4.12 Growth of creative service enterprises, worker, and location quotient by states, 1998 and 2013–14

States	*Enterprises (000)*		*Workers (000)*		*CAGR (%)*		*LQ for workers*	
	1998	*2013–14*	*1998*	*2013–14*	*Enterprises*	*Workers*	*1998*	*2013–14*
Andaman and Nicobar Islands	0.2	0.1	0.6	0.4	−8.1	−2.9	1.1	5.9
Andhra Pradesh	43.4	1.7	76.3	5.3	−19.5	−16.2	1.2	0.4
Arunachal Pradesh	0.4	0.1	0.8	0.3	−7.0	−5.9	0.9	3.5
Assam	9.8	0.6	27.7	3.4	−16.9	−13.0	1.2	0.4
Bihar	27.2	0.9	47.1	2.1	−20.6	−18.6	1.5	0.5
Chandigarh	0.9	0.2	3.5	1.2	−8.8	−6.8	0.9	1.3
Chhattisgarh	14.0	0.4	22.1	1.2	−21.3	−17.5	1.5	0.5
Dadra and Nagar Haveli	0.1	0.1	0.1	0.2	1.3	4.1	0.6	6.8
Daman and Diu	0.1	0.0	0.2	0.1	−15.6	−6.3	1.1	3.3
Delhi	21.3	1.5	70.6	13.0	−16.1	−10.7	0.8	3.0
Goa	1.3	0.4	3.4	1.7	−8.3	−4.4	0.9	5.8
Gujarat	38.2	4.5	73.5	13.0	−13.3	−10.9	0.5	0.9
Haryana	15.8	1.5	27.5	5.0	−14.5	−10.7	1.2	1.4
Himachal Pradesh	3.8	0.4	6.7	1.5	−13.7	−9.4	0.8	1.3
Jammu and Kashmir	3.5	0.3	5.5	0.9	−15.4	−11.1	0.4	0.2
Jharkhand	9.4	0.8	17.7	2.1	−15.5	−13.4	1.9	0.8
Karnataka	34.2	4.1	74.5	43.6	−13.2	−3.5	1.2	3.4
Kerala	33.1	6.4	63.9	20.4	−10.4	−7.3	1.0	2.0
Lakshadweep	0.0	0.0	0.1	0.0	−100.0	−100.0	0.8	0.0
Madhya Pradesh	46.3	1.4	81.8	5.0	−21.0	−17.0	1.4	0.8
Maharashtra	82.7	9.6	181.3	60.2	−13.4	−7.1	1.2	2.1
Manipur	0.9	0.5	1.8	1.1	−4.7	−3.2	0.5	0.3
Meghalaya	0.5	0.3	1.4	0.6	−3.7	−5.1	1.0	1.5
Mizoram	0.2	0.0	0.5	0.1	−13.6	−10.8	0.7	0.3
Nagaland	0.4	0.0	1.1	0.1	−20.5	−16.7	1.4	0.1
Odisha	33.5	6.1	60.3	16.0	−10.8	−8.5	1.7	1.0
Puducherry	0.8	0.1	5.6	0.9	−11.2	−11.5	1.5	1.7
Punjab	13.9	4.1	24.1	7.8	−7.9	−7.2	0.9	2.0
Rajasthan	32.4	2.9	63.4	7.8	−14.8	−13.0	1.1	0.5
Sikkim	0.2	0.1	0.5	0.2	−8.6	−7.5	1.3	1.6
Tamil Nadu	47.3	3.5	94.3	12.7	−15.9	−12.5	0.8	0.5
Telangana	23.1	1.6	52.1	11.6	−16.3	−9.5	0.7	0.6
Tripura	2.6	0.2	3.7	0.5	−16.3	−13.2	1.2	0.5
Uttar Pradesh	68.6	3.3	134.1	17.6	−18.4	−12.6	1.0	0.4
Uttarakhand	4.3	0.4	8.1	1.6	−15.3	−10.1	1.2	1.2
West Bengal	65.7	8.2	174.3	26.0	−13.0	−11.9	1.0	0.7
Total	679.8	66.0	1410.3	285.5	−14.4	−10.1	1.0	1.0

Note: CAGR = Compound annual growth rate; LQ = Location quotient.

Source: Computed using data from MoSPI (1998, 2016).

distribution of creative service workers is very marked. The western flank of the country from southern states, Maharashtra, Gujarat, Rajasthan, Delhi, and Punjab has a higher number of workers in this sector. Only southern West Bengal (Kolkata region) has a sizeable presence of workers in the eastern region. Third, the district level data shows that there are marked clusters/centres of the location of such workers (Figure 4.11). Mumbai and Bengaluru are the two primary centres of such industries. The secondary centres are Ernakulum, Hyderabad, Noida and Kolkata. There are a few tertiary centres but mainly located in Haryana and Punjab, Orissa, and coastal Kerala. Figure 4.11 also shows that many districts of south India which had relatively higher number of workers in creative services in 1998 have lost them by 2013–14 (see the shades in the map for 1998). In terms of the number of creative service workers among districts of India in 1998, Mumbai ranked first (with 40,105 creative service workers), and was followed by Kolkata (32,398), North 24 Parganas (25,213), Bengaluru (22,740), Medinipur (19,422), Hugli (19,397, and Pune (12,113). However, in 2013–14, Bengaluru ranked first (37,490 creative workers), and was followed by Mumbai Suburban (20,487), Mumbai district (11,494), Thane (8,483), Noida (8,007), and Pune (7,683).

4.5 Determinants of creative sector workers

What are the determinants of the concentration of CI workers? The most likely factors which can impact the development of creative industries are per capita income, higher education (Di Giacinto and Ferrante 2007), and urbanization rate (Lazzeretti et al. 2008). The per capita income leads to an increase in purchasing power which enables individuals to consume more creative goods and services. Higher education can be another determinant of creative goods and services, while urbanization is more associated with conspicuous consumption and display of creative goods and services, as CIs are usually associated with the status of families and individuals in the society. Given that we do not have data available for gross or net value addition by CI sectors by state or districts, the other indicators of the development of creative industries can be the number of creative enterprises or number of workers normalized with some appropriate denominators. We consider that number of workers in the creative sector per million of the population can be an appropriate indicator in this regard. The number of enterprises may not be a meaningful indicator of creative sector development as they can be large or small and even a few enterprises in a region can produce more goods and services than a large number of small enterprises in another region.

Once we identified the dependent and the interdependent variables, the problem becomes how to estimate the parameters using the data of the two reference years, 1998 and 2013–14, for 28 different states, including Union Territories. As the data belong only for two reference years for the same group of states, one could use the usual panel data model by taking difference of the variables. However, for simplicity, we have avoided the panel regression and instead have computed separate equations for each of the years, 1998 and 2013–14. The additional problem which could arise out of this cross-sectional data is spatial autocorrelation. As the data are for the state (located in spatial contiguity) of the same country, the spatial autocorrelation is strongly expected in the data (see Chapter 6 for a detailed discussion on spatial regression models). To overcome the spatial autocorrelation, we employed spatial econometric methods wherever we encountered spatial autocorrelation. We used the queen contiguity matrix in the estimation of our spatial regression equations. To save space, we have directly produced the best results yielded by ordinary least square (OLS), spatial lag model (SLM), or spatial error model (SEM).

The basic regression model used is as follows:

$$Y = \alpha + \beta_1 I + \beta_2 E + \beta_3 U + \xi \;...\; (1)$$

where Y is CI workers per million population in different sectors at the state level; I is the natural log of per capita net state domestic product; E is the percentage of population in 14–59 years age group with undergraduate and above level of education; U is the urbanization rate of the states; and ξ is the error term. We have estimated the equation separately for both the reference years, 1998 and 2013–14. We found that some of the estimations are affected by spatial lag or errors. To overcome the problems, we have augmented the equation using appropriately spatial lag or spatial errors.

We can make the following major observation based on the estimates of the regression equations of total and sectoral CI workers per million population presented in Table 4.13.

First, the higher educated class has been an important determinant of creative workers in the states in both the reference years. Urbanization was a significant determinant in 1998, while per capita income in 2013–14. In 1998, with an increase of 1% of undergraduate and above level of population (higher education), the increase in state CI workers per million of population was about 481, which increased to about 1,260 in 2013–14. In 2013–14, with an increase of 1% in per capita income of the state, the number of creative sector workers increased by about 6,134. This shows that as the economies shift upward (per capita income increases) creative sector becomes more dominant. This is expected as the demand for cultural and creative goods and services increases with the increase of income.

Second, with regard to the determinant of the art craft workers (*HHW*) of states, in 1998 none of the factors show any impact on the workers, but in 2013–14, per capita income and percentage of population with undergraduate and above levels of education were found to be having significant impact on the workers per million of population. It is interesting to note that the impact of per capita income is negative on *HHW*, indicating that as income rises the workers

Table 4.13 Determinants of the CI workers by sector, 1998 and 2013–14

Variables	*CIW*		*HHW*		*CSTW*		*PAW*		*VAW*	
	1998	*2013–14*	*1998*	*2013–14*	*1998*	*2013–14*	*1998*	*2013–14*	*1998*	*2013–14*
α	−5503.53	64630.20***	−7349.45	63090.50***	−910.20	−189.06	−131.37	−928.752	214.67	−403.69
	(0.541)	(0.007)	(0.121)	(0.006)	(0.226)	(0.774)	(0.352)	(0.404)	(0.785)	(0.596)
NSDP/ capita	419.26	−6134.36***	750.35	−5984.49***	84.78	20.52	−19.66	91.80	−41.55	43.18
	(0.648)	(0.007)	(0.113)	(0.006)	(0.648)	(0.747)	(0.168)	(0.395)	(0.598)	(0.558)
Higher education	481.49**	1260.27***	159.86	1135.50***	38.34**	−9.78	19.84***	−5.92	52.31***	5.55
	(0.020)	(0.002)	(0.144)	(0.004)	(0.017)	(0.329)	(0.000)	(0.725)	(0.007)	(0.631)
Urbanization rate	158.47***	−50.80	− 8.03	−69.47	0.274	4.10*	0.498	5.98	6.17	1.84
	(0.000)	(0.530)	(0.714)	(0.373)	(0.932)	(0.066)	(0.455)	(0.120)	(0.107)	(0.47)
Ω (spatial lag)	− 0.213	–	–	–	–	–	–	–	–	0.24
	(0.197)									(0.226)
Λ (spatial error)	–	0.62 λ***	–	0.60***	− 0.44	0.35*	–	–	–	–
		(0.000)		(0.000)	(0.197)	(0.060)				
R-squared	0.856	0.351	0.375	0.359	0.557	0.298	0.794	0.335	0.747	0.319
Variables	*AUW*		*PPMW*		*NMW*		*DSW*		*CSW*	
	1998	*2013–14*	*1998*	*2013–14*	*1998*	*2013–14*	*1998*	*2013–14*	*1998*	*2013–14*
α	−511.78	−564.10	1904.31	−316.68	−426.39	1955.27	2451.56	130.25	−51.27	−1411.25
	(0.201)	(0.271)	(0.644)	(0.337)	(0.444)	(0.630)	(0.715)	0.777)	(0.986)	(0.116)
NSDP/ capita	61.93	58.43	−418.86	36.33	10.16	−228.06	−195.15	−7.101	−11.49	126.20
	(0.123)	(0.239)	(0.313)	(0.255)	(0.854)	(0.561)	(0.771)	(0.873)	(0.986)	(0.146)
Higher education	−3.07	−2.75	344.01***	2.12	32.56**	62.42	−205.51	−12.55*	114.97	−6.50
	(0.740)	(0.720)	(0.001)	(0.669)	(0.017)	(0.313)	(0.194)	(0.082)	(0.099)	(0.628)
Urbanization	1.12	0.92	47.69**	−0.06	9.84***	10.11	53.00	3.76**	42.31***	6.96**
	(0.553)	(0.590)	0.021)	(0.955)	(0.000)	(0.461)	(0.105)	(0.022)	(0.005)	(0.020)

(*Continued*)

Table 4.13 (Continued)

Variables	*AUW*		*PPMW*		*NMW*		*DSW*		*CSW*	
	1998	*2013–14*	*1998*	*2013–14*	*1998*	*2013–14*	*1998*	*2013–14*	*1998*	*2013–14*
Ω (spatial lag)	−0.49** (0.029)	–	–	–	–	0.449** (0.011)	–	–	–	−0.29 (0.098)
Λ (spatial error)	–	–	–	–	–	–	–	–	–	–
R-squared	0.289	0.167	0.836	0.187	0.873	0.360	0.121	0.214	0.794	0.585

Note:

1 CIW = total number of creative sector workers per million population; HHW = number of workers in handloom and handicraft sector per million population; CSTW= number of workers engaged at cultural sites per million of population; PAW = number of workers in performing arts per million of population; VAW = number of workers in visual art sector per million of population; AUW = number of workers in audio-visual sector per million of population; PPMW = number of workers in publishing and print media sector per million of population; NMW = number of workers in new media sector per million of population; DSW = number of workers in design sector per million of population; CSW = number of workers in creative services per million of population.

2 Probability values are in parentheses; and

* = significance at 10% level,

** = significance at 5% level, and

*** = significance at 5% level of significance.

Source: computed by authors.

move out from this traditional industry, as often it is the industry with low remuneration and some of the enterprises being run even at subsistence level.

Third, in terms of determinants of cultural site workers (*CSTW*), the share of population with higher education had significant impact in 1998 but its impact has declined in 2013–14. Fourth, regarding determinants of performing arts workers in states of India (*PAW*), higher education was a major determinant in 1998, but in 2013–14 none of the independent variables are found to be having any significant impact on the workers of the *PAW*. Fifth, with regard to determinants of visual arts workers (*VAW*), only higher education exercised a significant impact in 1998. In 2013–14, none of the independent variables had statistically significant impact on the concentration of visual art workers.
Sixth, in case of audio-visual workers (AVW), we do not find any of the independent variable having any significant impacts. Seventh, publishing and print media workers' share was impacted by higher education in 1998, but in 2013–14 we do not find any of the factors having significant impact on the workers share.

Eighth, none of the factors, income, higher education, or urbanization rate has any significant impact on the concentration of workers of new media (*NMW*) in 2013–14, but in 1998 higher education and urbanization rate had significant impacts on the concentration of the workers. The reason for the no relationship with the independent variable of *NMW* in 2013–14 may be because higher education, income, and urban population characterize many cities and districts, but not all of them have developed new media industries. There may be some other historical or idiosyncratic factors behind the location patterns, not accounted for in the regression equations.

Ninth, urbanization is the only factor that has had a statistically significant impact on the location of design workers in 2013–14. Finally, urbanization is again the only factor that has had a significant impact on the share of creative service workers (CSW) in both the years at the state level. The reasons for this may be that demand for these services is higher in urban centres, and second the internet penetration in urban areas is much higher than that in rural areas. As per Census of India (2011), only 3% of the total households in India had access to the internet in 2011, while the figure for rural and urban areas was 8% and 1%, respectively, showing a very wide gap.

4.6 Conclusions

This chapter presents the first known attempt in India to examine the number of CIs, workers engaged in them at the national, state, and district levels in 1998 and 2013. It was challenging to present the major aspects of growth and spatial distributions of CIs in the country in the limited space of this chapter. Some of the important findings emerging from this chapter are as follows. First, at the aggregate level, CIs have grown significantly between 1998 and 2013–14. However, some of the sectors like design, creative services, and publishing and print media have contracted. They may have been affected by digitalization and globalization.

The southern and western states of the country have significant concentrations of CIs. However, we also find cities like Kolkata and Delhi, and states like Haryana and Punjab performing better in some specific sectors, specifically in art crafts. Second, today, art crafts constitute the major share of workers in CIs in the country. Relatively underdeveloped states have more workers engaged in art crafts. In fact, in this phase of globalization, these states can benefit much from this sector by promoting their crafts products and integrating the same with local, national, and international markets. To have more complete insight into the creative industries in India, it is recommended that creative industries be marked and presented as separate categories in economic census data, as has been attempted for handloom and handicraft industries in EC 2013–14. Further, the EC can collect data on some more variables like net and gross value added by economic establishments, which will help in understanding the economic value or size of CIs.

References

Archaeological Survey of India (2011a). Monuments. Ministry of Culture, New Delhi. Available at: https://asi.nic.in/monuments/ (last accessed on 25 March 2022).

Archaeological Survey of India (2011b). World heritage sites. Ministry of Culture, New Delhi. Available at: https://asi.nic.in/world-heritage-sites/ (last accessed on 25 March 2022).

Bandoypadhyaya, S. (1970). *The Music of India: A Popular Handbook of Hindustani Music.* Mumbai: D.B. Taraporevala Sons & Co. Pvt. Ltd.

Biswas, R. R. (2004). Making a technopolis in Hyderabad, India: The role of government IT policy. *Technological Forecasting and Social Change*, 71(8), 823–835.

Britannica (2021, 14 January). Taj Mahal. *Encyclopaedia Britannica.* Available at: www.britannica.com/topic/Taj-Mahal (last accessed on 25 March 2022).

Census of India (2011). Press note on release of data on houses, household amenities and assets, census 2011. Available at: www.censusindia.gov.in/2011census/hlo/Data_sheet/India/HLO_Press_Release.pdf (last accessed on 25 March 2022).

Choudhary, C., and Julka, T. (2018). SEZ in India: A study of gems and jewellery industry with special reference to Rajasthan. *Quarterly Journal of Management Development*, 49(1), 72–77.

D'Costa, A. P. (2009). Economic nationalism in motion: Steel, auto, and software industries in India. *Review of International Political Economy*, 16(4), 620–648.

Di Giacinto, M., and Ferrante, F. (2007). Idiosyncratic learning, creative consumption and well-being. In Bianchi, M. (ed.), *The Evolution of Consumption: Theories and Practices (Advances in Austrian Economics)*, Vol. 10, pp. 41–73. Bingley: Emerald Group Publishing Limited.

Government of India (2013). Brief industrial profile of Kancheepuram district, 2012–13. MSME-Development Institute, Ministry of MSME, Government of India, Chennai.

Hung, S.-W. (2009). Development and innovation in the IT industries of India and China. *Technology in Society*, 31(1), 29–41.

Jenks, G. F. (1977). *Optimal Data Classification for Choropleth Maps*. Lawrence, KS: University of Kansas, Department of Geography (Occasional Paper No. 2).

Khilnani, S. (1997). *The Idea of India*. New Delhi: Penguin India.

KPMG (2013a). Human resources and skill requirements in the media and entertainment sector (2013–17, 2017–22). Available at: https://skillsip.nsdcindia.org/knowledge-products/human-resource-and-skill-requirements-media-and-entertainment-sector (last accessed on 25 March 2022).

KPMG (2013b). Human resources and skill requirements in the gems and jewellery sector (2013–17, 2017–22). Available at: https://skillsip.nsdcindia.org/knowledge-products/human-resource-and-skill-requirements-gems-and-jewelry-sector (last accessed on 25 March 2022).

KPMG (2020). KPMG in India's Media and Entertainment Report 2020. KPMG, Mumbai.

KPMG-FICCI (2018). Visual Industry in India: Painting the Future. FICCI, New Delhi.

Kulkarni, P. (2012, 30 March). Rajiv Gandhi Infotech Park in Hinjewadi facing infrastructural problems. *The Economic Times*. Available at: https://economictimes.indiatimes.com/west/rajiv-gandhi-infotech-park-in-hinjewadi-facing-infrastructural-problems/articleshow/12467920.cms?from=mdr (last accessed on 25 March 2022).

Lazzeretti, L., Boix, R., and Capone, F. (2008). Do creative industries cluster? Mapping creative local production systems in Italy and Spain. *Industry and Innovation*, 15(5), 549–567.

Massey, R., and Massey, J. (1996). *The Music of India*. New Delhi: Abhinav Publications.

Matthew, J. (n.d.). Creative economy. The British Council. https://creativeeconomy.britishcouncil.org/guide/creative-manufacturing-india/ (last accessed on 25 March 2022).

Mohan, S. (2005). *Urban Development and New Localism: Urban Politics in Mumbai*. Jaipur: Rawat Publication.

MoSPI (1998). All India Report of Fourth Economic Census. Government of India, New Delhi.

MoSPI (2016). All India Report of Sixth Economic Census. Government of India, New Delhi.

Murthy, S. V. R. (2019). Measuring informal economy in India: Indian experience. Paper presented at 7th IMF Statistical Forum: Measuring the Informal Economy, November 14–15. Available at: file:///C:/Users/shaba/Downloads/seventh-imf-statistical-forum-ramana-murthy-presentation.pdf (last accessed on 25 March 2022).

Naidu, B. V. (2003). Tracing the history of IT in India. In Jussawalla, M. and Taylor, R. D. (eds.), *Information Technology Parks of the Asia Pacific: Lessons for the Regional Digital Divide*, pp. 119–150. Armonk, NY: M.E. Sharpe, Inc.

Patnaik, M. (2020a, 29 January). Just how big in India's creative economy. *Mint*. Available at: www.livemint.com/opinion/online-views/just-how-big-is-india-s-creative-economy-11593446149540.html (last accessed on 25 March 2022).

Patnaik, M. (2020b). *Measuring India's Creative Economy*. New Delhi: Esya Centre.

Rey, S. J., Stephens, P., Laura, J. (2016). An evaluation of sampling and full enumeration strategies for Fisher Jenks classification in big data settings. *Transactions in GIS*, 21(4), 796–810.

Sanga, P., and Shaban, A. (2017). Regional divergence and inequalities in India. *Economic and Political Weekly*, 52(1), 102–110.

Shaban, A. (2021). Growth and determinants of the middle class in rural and urban India in the post-liberalisation period. In Batabyal, A. A., Higano, Y. and Nijkamp, P. (eds.), *Rural-Urban Dichotomies and Spatial Development in Asia*. Singapore: Springer.

Shaban, A., and Vermeylen, F. (2015). Trade in the creative sector: Comparing India with China, Brazil and UK. *Economic and Political Weekly*, 50(20), 68–75.

UNCTAD (2010). *Creative Economy Report 2010*. Geneva: UNCTAD.

Verma, P.K. (2021, 16 July). How we fail our culture: India is a great civilisation. But no government makes institutional investment protecting its heritage. *The Times of India*. Available at: https://timesofindia.indiatimes.com/blogs/toi-edit-page/how-we-fail-our-culture-india-is-a-great-civilisation-but-no-government-makes-institutional-investment-protecting-its-heritage/ (last accessed on 25 March 2022).

Wade, B. C. (Ed.). (1983). *Performing Arts in India: Essays on Music, Dance and Drama*. Berkeley, CA: University Press of America.

APPENDIX

Table 4A.1 Percentage distribution of creative enterprises and workers by nature of operation, 1998 and 2013–14

Sectors	*Perennial*		*Non-perennial*		*Perennial*		*Non-perennial*	
	1998				*2013–14*			
	Enterprises	*Workers*	*Enterprises*	*Workers*	*Enterprises*	*Workers*	*Enterprises*	*Workers*
1. Total art crafts	82.6	88.0	17.4	12.0	88.7	89.9	11.3	10.1
1.a Food related	71.2	79.8	28.8	20.2	90.0	90.9	10.0	9.1
1.b Non-food related	92.8	94.2	7.2	5.8	88.7	89.9	11.3	10.1
2. Cultural sites	97.6	97.3	2.4	2.7	94.2	93.6	5.8	6.4
3. Performing arts	92.1	93.5	7.9	6.5	83.3	82.3	16.7	17.7
4. Visual arts	98.0	97.3	2.0	2.7	97.1	97.5	2.9	2.5
5. Audio-visuals	95.5	97.0	4.5	3.0	96.7	98.0	3.3	2.0
6. Publishing and print media	97.7	98.4	2.3	1.6	94.3	95.5	5.7	4.5
7. New media	96.9	97.3	3.1	2.7	97.6	98.0	2.4	2.0
8. Design	97.7	98.0	2.3	2.0	93.1	94.7	6.9	5.3
9. Creative services	96.7	95.8	3.3	4.2	90.7	94.0	9.3	6.0
Total	93.8	94.7	6.2	5.3	90.0	91.9	10.0	8.1

Source: Computed using data from MoSPI (1998, 2016).

Table 4A.2 Share of different types of creative enterprises and workers, 1998 and 2013–14

Sectors	*OAEs (%)*		*NDEs (%)*		*DEs (%)*		*Not registered enterprises (%)*	
	1998							
	Enterprises	*Workers*	*Enterprises*	*Workers*	*Enterprises*	*Workers*	*Enterprises*	*Workers*
1. Total art crafts	78.2	47.4	15.4	15.5	6.3	37.0	97.1	88.8
1.a Food related	85.8	56.8	11.0	11.0	3.2	32.2	97.5	90.4
1.b Non-food related	71.4	40.3	19.4	19.0	9.1	40.7	96.8	87.6
2. Cultural sites	57.7	38.5	38.5	34.1	3.8	27.4	96.0	93.6
3. Performing arts	49.1	19.0	41.1	34.1	9.7	46.9	96.2	93.9
4. Visual arts	68.4	50.3	30.1	39.9	1.5	9.9	97.3	94.3
5. Audio-visuals	49.0	21.3	39.5	25.1	11.5	53.5	93.2	89.3
6. Publishing and print media	33.4	12.1	50.1	31.6	16.5	56.3	90.3	74.5
7. New media	34.6	9.6	45.6	23.9	19.8	66.4	90.0	85.0
8. Design	63.5	30.4	27.6	23.3	8.9	46.3	96.0	93.0
9. Creative services	75.6	50.5	20.6	25.3	3.7	24.2	97.6	95.2
Total	69.9	39.9	24.1	24.1	6.0	36.0	96.6	90.4
2013–14								
1. Total art crafts	78.9	58.1	17.8	22.4	3.4	19.5	–	–
1.a Food related	74.4	48.4	21.6	23.5	4.0	28.1	–	–
1.b Non-food related	79.0	58.4	17.7	22.4	3.4	19.2	–	–
2. Cultural sites	34.1	24.8	61.5	52.6	4.4	22.6	–	–
3. Performing arts	61.8	33.9	30.2	31.8	8.0	34.3	–	–
4. Visual arts	66.4	46.1	32.2	45.2	1.4	8.8	–	–
5. Audio-visuals	47.4	15.9	40.6	30.1	12.0	53.9	–	–
6. Publishing and print media	48.6	17.7	41.4	32.1	10.0	50.2	–	–
7. New media	46.8	6.0	40.8	11.3	12.4	82.7	–	–
8. Design	52.2	23.9	39.4	39.0	8.4	37.1	–	–
9. Creative services	52.0	20.1	36.0	23.2	12.0	56.7	–	–
Total	72.4	43.3	23.2	23.4	4.4	33.3	–	–

Note: Own Account Establishments or Enterprises (OAEs) are those which do not employ any hired workers on fairly regular basis, that means they are largely run by households; Non-Directory Establishments (NDEs) employ on fairly regular basis 1–5 hired workers; Directory Establishments (DEs) employ 6 or more hired workers on regular basis (MoSPI 1998).

Source: Computed using data from MoSPI (1998, 2016).

Table 4A.3 Percentage distribution of creative enterprises by sources of finance and workers, 1998 and 2013–14

Sector of Cis	*Self-finance (%)*		*Financial assistance from government sources*		*Borrowing from financial institutions*		*Borrowing from non-institutions/ moneylenders*		*Others (including, loan from SHGs)*		*Donations/transfer from other agencies*	
	Enterprises	*Workers*	*Enterprises*	*Workers*	*Enterprises*	*Workers*	*Enterprises*	*Workers*	*Enterprises*	*Workers*	*Enterprises*	*Workers*
	1998											
1. Total art crafts	86.1	77.6	3.0	2.7	2.1	5.2	2.0	6.4	6.7	8.2	–	–
1.a Food related	87.9	73.2	3.3	3.1	1.6	5.1	1.7	11.0	5.6	7.6	–	–
1.b Non-food related	84.6	80.9	2.8	2.3	2.5	5.3	2.2	2.9	7.8	8.6	–	–
2. Cultural sites	68.3	61.2	1.0	0.9	3.1	4.1	1.6	1.6	26.1	32.1	–	–
3. Performing arts	81.1	67.9	1.3	0.7	2.7	16.6	1.4	1.2	13.5	13.7	–	–
4. Visual arts	90.4	88.3	1.1	1.1	2.9	3.5	1.2	1.4	4.4	5.7	–	–
5. Audio-visuals	72.5	64.6	1.8	1.3	3.3	5.0	1.6	1.6	20.8	27.5	–	–
6. Publishing and print media	85.5	78.1	1.2	1.2	5.7	7.8	1.9	1.7	5.7	11.3	–	–
7. New media	81.7	64.9	1.0	0.9	6.1	8.4	2.3	3.4	8.9	22.4	–	–
8. Design	90.5	89.9	0.9	0.8	1.8	1.7	1.2	1.0	5.7	6.5	–	–
9. Creative services	88.3	81.8	1.3	1.4	1.5	2.4	1.0	1.4	7.9	13.0	–	–
Total	87.0	80.5	1.6	1.5	2.2	3.9	1.3	2.7	7.9	11.3	–	–
	2013–14											
1. Total art crafts	85.9	83.0	1.8	3.3	1.2	2.5	3.8	3.5	0.5	0.6	6.8	7.1
1.a Food related	79.1	74.1	3.8	6.5	1.5	3.4	2.5	3.0	0.5	0.6	12.5	12.3
1.b Non-food related	86.1	83.2	1.8	3.2	1.2	2.4	3.8	3.5	0.5	0.6	6.6	7.0

(*Continued*)

Table 4A.3 (Continued)

Sector of Cis	*Self-finance (%)*		*Financial assistance from government sources*		*Borrowing from financial institutions*		*Borrowing from non-institutions/ moneylenders*		*Others (including, loan from SHGs)*		*Donations/transfer from other agencies*	
	Enterprises	*Workers*	*Enterprises*	*Workers*	*Enterprises*	*Workers*	*Enterprises*	*Workers*	*Enterprises*	*Workers*	*Enterprises*	*Workers*
	2013–14											
2. Cultural sites	29.2	33.7	32.5	30.8	0.7	1.3	0.4	0.6	0.4	0.4	36.9	33.4
3. Performing arts	78.3	75.8	4.6	6.4	1.3	2.6	0.6	0.8	0.3	0.4	14.9	13.9
4. Visual arts	88.0	87.1	2.8	2.7	2.2	2.8	0.6	0.8	0.2	0.2	6.2	6.4
5. Audio-visuals	80.0	72.6	6.6	11.0	2.7	5.4	0.8	0.8	0.2	0.2	9.6	10.0
6. Publishing and print media	80.8	72.6	7.2	9.7	2.6	8.1	0.7	0.6	0.2	0.4	8.5	8.5
7. New media	82.3	78.2	5.5	5.6	3.5	8.1	0.8	0.7	0.3	0.2	7.7	7.1
8. Design	85.5	81.8	3.0	5.2	2.2	3.9	0.7	0.8	0.7	1.0	7.9	7.1
9. Creative services	71.0	64.6	5.8	11.9	2.5	7.6	0.6	0.7	0.2	0.3	19.9	14.9
Total	83.2	79.6	3.4	5.2	1.4	3.8	3.0	2.4	0.4	0.5	8.5	8.5

Source: Computed using data from MoSPI (1998, 2016).

Table 4A.4 Percentage distribution of creative enterprises by ownership category, 1998 and 2013–14

Sectors	*SC*		*ST*		*OBC*		*Others*		*Non-proprietary (% of the total)*	
	Enterprises	*Workers*	*Enterprises*	*Workers*	*Enterprises*	*Workers*	*Enterprises*	*Workers*	*Enterprises*	*Workers*
	1998									
1. Total art crafts	21.0	15.3	4.4	3.7	37.4	35.6	37.2	45.3	1.4	3.2
1.a Food related	11.0	8.9	3.8	3.8	51.2	47.2	34.0	40.0	1.9	4.9
1.b Non-food related	29.8	20.0	5.0	3.7	25.1	27.1	40.0	49.3	1.0	2.0
2. Cultural sites	5.5	5.4	2.6	3.0	29.4	25.9	62.5	65.7	25.4	31.9
3. Performing arts	8.8	6.5	2.5	2.3	23.1	15.8	65.6	75.4	9.4	12.1
4. Visual arts	5.6	5.1	2.0	2.7	27.5	27.3	64.9	64.9	0.7	2.4
5. Audio-visuals	5.8	4.3	2.7	2.4	37.2	32.1	54.4	61.2	17.0	24.8
6. Publishing and print media	3.7	2.7	2.0	1.6	23.7	18.4	70.6	77.3	1.1	7.0
7. New media	2.6	2.0	1.4	1.2	19.1	13.8	77.0	83.0	2.5	14.0
8. Design	3.1	2.4	1.4	2.1	42.3	27.9	53.2	67.6	0.7	0.9
9. Creative services	7.7	8.4	2.4	2.6	54.5	44.4	35.5	44.6	3.0	8.8
Total	9.6	8.0	2.7	2.7	43.8	34.1	44.0	55.3	3.2	6.8
2013–14										
1. Total art crafts	13.9	12.4	6.5	6.0	47.6	45.3	32.0	36.3	8.0	15.4
1.a Food related	15.3	13.1	8.5	7.0	43.6	43.2	32.5	36.6	3.3	7.4
1.b Non-food related	13.8	12.4	6.5	6.0	47.7	45.4	32.0	36.3	3.4	7.6
2. Cultural sites	7.1	6.7	2.6	2.5	29.8	31.4	60.5	59.4	57.6	53.3
3. Performing arts	19.3	18.1	3.8	3.5	34.9	33.5	42.0	45.0	14.4	21.2
4. Visual arts	10.6	9.6	2.8	2.9	39.6	39.5	47.0	48.0	7.6	8.5
5. Audio-visuals	9.0	7.9	3.3	2.8	33.8	29.9	53.9	59.4	15.4	32.4
6. Publishing and print media	9.6	9.5	2.9	2.5	37.8	31.4	49.7	56.6	14.4	31.1
7. New media	7.6	6.0	3.0	1.9	32.6	21.2	56.9	70.8	15.5	63.4
8. Design	12.5	11.4	4.1	5.4	33.9	32.7	49.5	50.5	9.0	16.6
9. Creative services	13.1	9.4	3.4	2.4	31.5	32.2	52.0	56.0	24.9	40.4
Total	13.3	11.7	5.7	5.1	44.8	41.3	36.1	41.9	7.4	21.2

Source: Computed using data from MoSPI (1998, 2016).

Table 4A.5 Percentage of creative enterprises (and workers employed in them) owned by female, 1998 and 2013–14

Sectors	*1998*		*2013–14*	
	Enterprises	*Workers*	*Enterprises*	*Workers*
1. Total art crafts	7.2	5.9	21.9	16.5
1.a Food related	6.3	5.4	31.5	24.4
1.b Non-food related	8.1	6.3	21.7	16.3
2. Cultural sites	2.1	2.4	20.6	19.5
3. Performing arts	2.9	1.8	8.9	8.1
4. Visual arts	1.6	2.2	3.6	3.8
5. Audio-visuals	2.7	2.6	6.2	5.8
6. Publishing and print media	2.8	2.3	5.4	5.7
7. New media	2.7	2.1	8.0	6.8
8. Design	2.1	1.9	12.6	10.1
9. Creative services	4.0	4.1	7.7	7.7
Total	4.1	3.8	18.5	14.0

Source: Computed using data from MoSPI (1998, 2016).

5

INDIA'S EXPORTS AND IMPORTS OF CREATIVE GOODS AND SERVICES

Comparison with China, Brazil, and the UK

Abdul Shaban and Filip Vermeylen

5.1 Introduction

The global economic growth, and international trade as a consequence, was hit by the financial crisis in 2008 (The World Bank 2021). In 2020 and 2021, it suffered another blow due to COVID-19. However, the growth of creative economy has been robust before and post 2008 (UNCTAD 2019). We do not have data yet available for the COVID-19 period to precisely examine the impact. The available data prior to the COVID-19 show the creative industries' (CIs) potential to stimulate economic growth (UNCTAD 2019). Interestingly, in creative economy trade, only developed countries do not exclusively benefit, but many developing countries like China and India have emerged as major leaders in the sector. In many developed countries, the production of cultural goods and services have now become more substantial (at least in employment terms) than a number of traditional industries like mining and car manufacturing (Barrowclough and Kozul-Wright 2008). CIs also helped in the revitalization of many deindustrialized cities, such as London, Baltimore, and Newark, since the 1970s and 1980s (Strom 1999; Rich and Tsitsos 2016). Evans (2005) shows that CIs generate more income and employ more people in London than financial services sector. It is not surprising then that, today, creative goods and services constitute a significant share of the global trade. The UNCTAD found that exports of creative goods and services were worth US$562 billion in 2008, showing 14% annual growth since 2000 (UNCTAD 2010: xxiii; Flew 2013). Of the total exports of creative industries in 2008, creative goods constituted 69% and creative services accounted for 31% (UNCTAD 2010). As mentioned earlier, the industry has shown robust growth, and during 2008–09 slow down, when the global exports contracted by 12%, the trade in creative goods and services continued to grow (Flew 2013).

DOI: 10.4324/9781003129370-7

Overall, the share of household expenditures on recreation and culture[1] has been rising for decades in Western countries. It was 4.5% in the US, 4.9% in Canada, 5.1% in the UK, and 4.3% in France in 1970, but in 2005 they rose to 6.4% in US, 5.5% in Canada, 7.7% in UK, and 5.2% in France (OECD 2007; Disdier et al. 2010). Available data show that between 1980 and 1998, the world imports of cultural goods[2] increased by 347%, from US$47.8 billion to US$213.7 billion (UNESCO 2000). The important factors fuelling this growth have been rising income, easing global transportation, emerging information technologies (ITs), and the development of leisure and cultural tourism. The cultural goods have been found to be mainly traded at a shorter distance (that is, within the cultural realms), and within countries having similar colonial experiences (Disdier et al. 2010). However, the rise of diasporic societies in the western developed countries has also created significant demand for cultural goods from many developing countries. These goods are also referred to as 'nostalgic goods' (Newland and Taylor 2010).

Notwithstanding the lack of effective policy measures to promote creative industries in India, international trade in the sector has been on the rise. The rise in disposable income within the country has also created a significant demand for creative goods produced elsewhere in the world. Further, emerging social changes in India have valorized the possession and consumption of creative goods produced in Western countries, and they have become a marker of the social and economic status of individuals and families. In this chapter, we attempt to assess the growth of international trade of creative goods and services from India in comparison to similar economies like Brazil and China and also the UK, a matured economy with respect to CIs. The data relating to exports and imports of creative goods and services have been taken from UNCTADstat and this chapter has followed the UNCTAD (2010) classification of creative industries. The rest of this chapter is organized as follows: Section 5.2 discusses the growth of trade in creative goods from India in a comparative framework with China, Brazil, the UK, and the world, while Section 5.3 examines the value of imports and trade surplus. Section 5.4 analyses the imports and exports of creative services. Section 5.5 concludes the chapter.

5.2 Growth of exports and imports

Trade in the creative economy worldwide has significantly expanded in recent years. At current prices, it doubled in 14 years from US$208 billion in 2002 to US$509 billion in 2015. The growth rate in trade in creative goods has been consistent with an average annual growth rate of more than 7% during the period (UNCTAD 2019). We have presented the value, share, ranks in terms of exports, and annual average growth rate of imports and exports of creative goods for India, China, Brazil, and the UK[3] in Table 5.1 through Table 5.6. The following salient observations can be made from the tables.

First, India and China have significant earnings from the exports of creative goods. For India, the total value of exports of CI goods was about US$3.32

Table 5.1 Value of exports in US$ million (current prices) from India, China, Brazil, the UK, and at the world level

Products	*India*		*China*		*Brazil*		*UK*		*World*	
	2002	*2015*	*2002*	*2015*	*2002*	*2015*	*2002*	*2015*	*2002*	*2015*
All creative goods	3319	16937	32000	168507	628	883	13592	25926	208493	509753
1. Art crafts	**581**	**1592**	**3569**	**17383**	**58**	**67**	**432**	**407**	**19918**	**35720**
1.1 Carpets	428	988	369	1578	9	3	163	124	4420	7954
1.2 Celebration	5	48	1125	4482	0	1	51	110	3325	6145
1.3 Paperware	8	9	12	17	0	0	5	3	68	60
1.4 Wickerware	4	6	716	1393	0	0	4	6	1255	1722
1.5 Yarn	103	419	803	7545	46	59	189	140	8438	15679
1.6 Other	35	122	544	2367	3	4	19	26	2413	4159
2. Audio-visuals	**25**	**110**	**168**	**1092**	**11**	**8**	**1186**	**978**	**10268**	**21875**
2.1 Film	17	5	0	0	0	0	60	1	472	17
2.2 CD, DVD, Tapes	8	105	168	1092	11	8	1126	978	9796	21859
3. Design	**2478**	**14664**	**22775**	**122357**	**522**	**560**	**4078**	**10266**	**118210**	**318216**
3.1 Architecture	1	3	42	9	0	0	7	52	229	134
3.2 Fashion	826	3117	9282	41734	10	34	929	1662	31693	87737
3.3 Glassware	1	0	84	299	15	1	33	27	1545	1096
3.4 Interior	235	1322	5801	41624	433	453	1187	1369	38347	88179
3.5 Jewellery	1406	10154	1568	21482	46	60	1512	6419	23995	102109
3.6 Toys	9	68	5998	17208	17	13	410	738	22402	38960
4. New media	**162**	**122**	**2354**	**14097**	**2**	**97**	**617**	**1194**	**10974**	**42194**
4.1 Recorded media	159	122	62	5094	1	92	195	742	2608	24476
4.2 Video games	2	0	2291	9003	0	5	422	452	8366	17717
5. Performing arts	**2**	**16**	**431**	**1499**	**3**	**1**	**83**	**111**	**2817**	**4387**
5.1 Musical instruments	2	16	431	1498	3	1	62	82	2729	4288
5.2 Printed music	0	0	0	0	0	0	21	29	88	98
6. Publishing	**59**	**252**	**535**	**3186**	**28**	**24**	**3010**	**3536**	**30326**	**33661**
6.1 Books	42	214	409	1798	12	13	1818	2645	11595	16475
6.2 Newspaper	17	6	7	41	12	2	835	542	12586	8731
6.3 Other printed matter	. .	32	118	1347	3	9	357	348	6145	8455
7. Visual arts	**12**	**181**	**2169**	**8894**	**5**	**125**	**4185**	**9433**	**15979**	**53700**
7.1 Antiques	1	0	5	68	1	1	1357	1757	2540	7416
7.2 Paintings	3	105	17	464	1	70	2394	6466	6329	28264
7.3 Photography	0	1	14	195	1	10	129	98	1616	2337
7.4 Sculpture	7	75	2133	8167	2	45	306	1112	5495	15682

Source: Based on data from UNCTAD (n.d.).

billion in 2002 and US$16.9 billion in 2015, while the same from China was US$32.0 billion in 2002 and US$168.5 billion in 2015 (Table 5.1). Whereas China had a much higher value of exports in the absolute term in this sector in comparison to a mature creative sector economy like the UK, the total value of exports from India is still significantly lower than that of the UK in 2015. The share of exports of creative goods from India constituted only 1.9% of the global exports from this sector in 2003, but rose to 3.3% in 2015, while the same from

China rose from 17.1% in 2003 to 33.0% in 2015 (Table 5.2). Whereas China has ranked first in terms of the value of exports of creative goods both in 2003 and 2015, India rose in the ranking from 12th in 2003 to 8th place in 2015. In 2015, besides China, the USA, France, Hong Kong (China), Italy, and the UK were other countries with higher shares in global exports of creative goods than India.

Second, during 2003–2015, India and China had a higher growth rate of exports of creative goods, almost twice the rate at the global level. In general, growth rates from the Asian countries have been significantly higher than that for the UK and also Brazil. This confirms that India and China are fast-growing countries in terms of exports of creative goods. This said, the value of exports of creative goods from India in comparison to China is considerably lower. The actual value of exports from India was only 10.4% in 2002 of the total Chinese export in the same year, which marginally declined to 10.1% in 2015 to that of the total exports of creative goods from China in the same year. In 2015, China's creative goods export was four times higher than that of the USA (UNCTAD 2019: 9). In fact, "China's performance has buoyed the global creative economy" (UNCTAD 2019: 9) during the period 2002–2015. Post-2015, China may have further expanded its presence in the global creative economy through film, television, and artificial intelligence.

Specifically, the two leading sectors in exports in terms of annual average growth rates during 2002–2015 have been performing arts (annual average growth rate 17.5%) and design (15.2%) in India, while the two fast growing sectors in China during the same period have been design (14.9%) and visual arts (14.8%). Brazil, on the other hand, has experienced a significant decline in growth rate during this period in all the major sectors of creative goods except for the visual arts (24.8%).

Table 5.2 Top ranked creative goods exporting countries and their global shares, 2003 and 2015 (exports in US$ million at current prices)

2003				*2015*			
Rank	*Country*	*Exports*	*Share (%)*	*Rank*	*Country*	*Exports*	*Share (%)*
1	China	38	17.1	1	China	168	33.0
2	United States	18	8.0	2	United States	39	7.7
3	Italy	18	7.8	3	France	34	6.7
4	Germany	17	7.4	4	Hong Kong (China)	27	5.3
5	UK	15	6.5	5	Italy	27	5.3
6	France	10	4.5	6	UK	25	4.9
7	Canada	10	4.3	7	Germany	23	4.5
8	Belgium	6	2.9	8	India	17	3.3
9	Switzerland	5	2.3	9	Switzerland	15	2.9
10	The Netherlands	5	2.1	10	Singapore	10	2.0
12	India	4	1.9		–	–	–

Source: Based on data from UNCTAD (n.d.).

Third, post-2012, India's creative goods export has experienced a significant decline. The growth rate during 2012–2015 has been negative in all the sectors (Table 5.3). India's rank which was 4th in the export of creative goods, therefore, has declined to 8th in 2015. This suggests that India is not able to effectively use the potential of this sector for its economic growth and development. There has been significant instability in the share of India in total creative

Table 5.3 Annual average growth rate (%) of Indian total exports and imports of creative goods during 2003–2015 and the sub-periods

Products	*2003–2015*		*2007–2011*		*2012–2015*	
	Exports	*Imports*	*Exports*	*Imports*	*Exports*	*Imports*
All creative goods	**13.2**	**18.9**	**23.3**	**33.9**	**−10.9**	**−15.3**
1. Art crafts	6.3	12.5	1.4	10.3	10.0	11.8
1.1 Carpets	4.2	10.0	0.2	2.8	8.4	7.1
1.2 Celebration	20.9	30.3	18.9	44.1	23.1	−2.1
1.3 Paperware	12.7	15.4	8.8	19.6	12.4	0.3
1.4 Wickerware	−4.6	16.5	−19.6	22.2	−9.1	−20.4
1.5 Yarn	1.6	25.6	−30.0	51.9	47.0	−8.5
1.6 Other	11.5	10.9	5.7	5.7	12.4	21.7
2. Audio-visuals	..	..	..	..	..	..
2.1 Film	−4.7	−17.7	8.7	−3.1	−29.7	−35.5
2.2 CD, DVD, Tapes	..	..	..	..	..	..
3. Design	**15.2**	**24.0**	**27.0**	**19.7**	**-11.7**	**-28.4**
3.1 Architecture	16.9	−0.9	66.7	−24.1	−24.0	−36.7
3.2 Fashion	10.3	29.3	10.8	29.4	4.8	9.9
3.3 Glassware	−19.1	11.3	−22.8	26.1	−32.8	1.8
3.4 Interior	12.0	21.7	5.3	16.4	6.8	7.9
3.5 Jewellery	17.0	24.2	34.2	18.3	−16.2	−44.3
3.6 Toys	16.0	26.6	17.9	45.8	28.0	8.2
4. New media	..	..	..	..	..	..
4.1 Recorded media	..	..	..	..	..	..
4.2 Video games	−8.8	21.4	36.9	40.1	−68.8	13.5
5. Performing arts	**17.5**	**19.9**	**38.2**	**24.8**	**−7.7**	**−1.5**
5.1 Musical instruments	17.7	19.9	38.3	24.9	−7.8	−1.5
5.2 Printed music	−13.6	17.5	18.3	−41.8	41.2	−18.3
6. Publishing	**9.9**	**8.2**	**4.2**	**10.7**	**−7.8**	**0.2**
6.1 Books	12.0	5.9	11.6	0.2	−7.5	8.2
6.2 Newspaper	−7.2	8.6	−27.3	13.2	−16.4	−2.0
6.3 Other printed matter	8.8	13.4	−2.3	9.3	−7.7	13.2
7. Visual arts	**−6.2**	**27.2**	**−14.5**	**7.2**	**−11.7**	**28.7**
7.1 Antiques	9.4	36.6	−82.0	78.5	45.2	4.6
7.2 Paintings	−11.4	29.7	−13.2	−11.6	−16.7	31.9
7.3 Photography	0.9	10.4	13.6	20.7	56.2	34.2
7.4 Sculpture	9.9	31.4	2.3	32.0	1.1	26.9

Note: Average annual growth rates are defined as the coefficient *b* in the exponential trend function $y = ae^{bt}$, where *t* stands for time.

Source: Based on date from UNCTAD (n.d.).

Table 5.4 Annual average growth rate of total exports and imports of creative goods from China, Brazil, the UK, and at the world level

Products	*China*		*Brazil*		*UK*		*World*	
	2003–2015		*2003–2015*		*2003–2015*		*2003–2015*	
	Exports	*Imports*	*Exports*	*Imports*	*Exports*	*Imports*	*Exports*	*Imports*
All creative goods	**14.3**	**16.1**	**−0.4**	**19.2**	**3.4**	**2.1**	**7.3**	**5.1**
1. Art crafts	12.1	5.0	−1.2	22.1	−2.5	0.5	4.4	2.1
1.1 Carpets	11.8	8.7	−11.8	27.8	−4.7	−0.3	4.1	2.8
1.2 Celebration	12.2	5.2	−8.9	24.0	4.8	2.0	5.7	1.2
1.3 Paperware	12.1	5.9	5.1	13.2	−1.9	0.6	4.3	−0.2
1.4 Wickerware	14.6	−19.3	9.9	−6.0	6.3	−1.8	−0.4	−2.4
1.5 Yarn	3.4	6.3	−2.0	14.1	−1.7	−1.7	1.5	−1.4
1.6 Other	15.6	4.8	0.1	25.2	−4.5	1.0	4.6	3.5
2. Audio-visuals	..	..	..	..	..	..	..	..
2.1 Film	9.5	0.6	9.5	1.3	−22.7	−31.7	−23.9	−24.0
2.2 CD, DVD, tapes	..	..	..	..	..	..	..	..
3. Design	**14.9**	**17.3**	**−3.0**	**24.8**	**5.8**	**2.3**	**8.6**	**5.5**
3.1 Architecture	−3.3	−18.8	−3.7	10.5	2.6	2.0	−5.8	−1.8
3.2 Fashion	12.5	21.6	3.7	24.6	4.4	5.7	8.4	6.2
3.3 Glassware	18.3	25.4	−20.2	19.3	−5.8	−3.3	1.1	−2.0
3.4 Interior	14.6	12.0	−3.1	30.4	−0.6	0.7	5.8	3.6
3.5 Jewellery	33.0	29.1	−2.1	26.9	9.7	2.4	14.7	10.5
3.6 Toys	7.0	6.1	−3.9	24.0	2.3	0.8	3.5	2.5
4. New media	..	..	..	..	..	..	..	..
4.1 Recorded media	..	..	..	..	..	..	..	..
4.2 Video games	8.3	18.6	4.6	46.0	3.3	3.2	6.5	6.1
5. Performing arts	**8.3**	**19.3**	**−10.8**	**17.8**	**−0.1**	**−0.8**	**3.3**	**2.5**
5.1 Musical instruments	8.3	19.3	−10.9	17.8	−0.3	−0.8	3.4	2.6
5.2 Printed music	19.3	13.1	12.7	32.6	0.7	−1.3	−0.6	−1.3
6. Publishing	**13.5**	**10.6**	**−5.2**	**4.7**	**−0.3**	**−3.1**	**−0.1**	**−0.6**
6.1 Books	12.0	10.4	−1.9	10.5	1.2	1.0	1.9	1.3
6.2 Newspaper	5.9	6.6	−17.7	0.1	−4.3	−10.2	−3.0	−3.5
6.3 Other printed matter	17.9	14.8	−0.6	12.4	−1.3	−3.0	0.8	0.7
7. Visual arts	**14.8**	**31.0**	**24.8**	**24.1**	**4.4**	**5.2**	**8.0**	**6.4**
7.1 Antiques	17.7	40.5	4.4	−3.1	−1.2	4.1	4.4	5.4
7.2 Paintings	32.5	60.2	29.0	55.0	6.3	5.8	8.5	8.9
7.3 Photography	27.2	16.0	9.8	5.1	−3.5	3.4	1.8	2.1
7.4 Sculpture	14.2	25.5	28.3	29.4	9.9	5.0	9.9	3.9

Note: Average annual growth rates are defined as the coefficient b in the exponential trend function $y = ae^{bt}$, where t stands for time.

Source: Based on date from UNCTAD (n.d.).

goods exports at the global level (Figure 5.1), in comparison to China, the UK, and Brazil.

Fourth, the design sector constitutes a significant share of the total value of the exports from India, China, Brazil, and also from the UK. The design includes

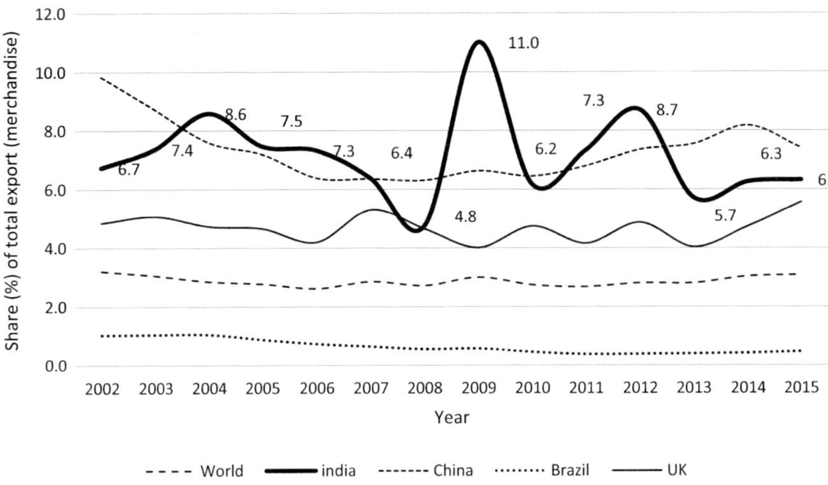

Figure 5.1 Share (%) of all creative goods to the total export (merchandise)

Source: Computed using data from UNCTAD (n.d.).

architectural (architectural design of buildings, etc., and interior objects), fashion design goods, glassware, interior design goods, jewellery, and toys. This sector constitutes more than two-thirds of exports of creative goods from India, China, and Brazil. The share of this sector in India's total exports of creative goods was 74.7% in 2003 which rose to 86.6% in 2015 (Table 5.5). In China, the share has shown a marginal increase from 71.2% in 2002 to 72.6% in 2015, while in Brazil the share of design relative to the total creative goods exports shrank significantly from 83.1% in 2002 to 63.4% in 2015. What is important to note here is that in the UK this sector constituted only 30.0% in 2002 and 39.6% in 2015 of the total exports of the creative goods. In the case of the UK, though the design sector remains the largest sector, the visual arts and publishing sectors also constitute significant shares of the total UK's creative goods export.

Fifth, India's exports are driven by the jewellery sector, which is part of design. The share of jewellery in India's total export has significantly increased over the years, from 42.4% in 2002 to 75.5% in 2012. However, its share later declined to 60.0% in 2015. Especially, the western regions of India (Mumbai, Ahmedabad, and Jaipur) have been important producers of gems and jewellery. Recognizing the importance of this sector in international trade, the Government of India has already created 10 Special Economic Zones (SEZs), in Mumbai, Surat, Gandhigram, Indore, Jaipur, Noida, Kolkata, Visakhapatnam, Chennai, and Cochin, to further promote exports of gems and jewellery (Gem & Jewellery Export Promotion Council, n.d.).

Sixth, the composition of goods exported from India reveals that the share of art crafts has significantly declined over the years 2002 to 2015 (Table 5.5). It can be noted that the sector employed 62.2% of the total creative workers in

Table 5.5 Share (%) of different sectors in the total value of creative goods exported from India

Year	*Share (%) in total export*							*Jewellery (as % of the total export of creative goods)**
	Art crafts	*Audio-visuals*	*Design*	*New media*	*Performing arts*	*Publishing*	*Visual arts*	
2002	17.5	0.8	74.7	4.9	0.1	1.8	0.3	42.4
2003	15.0	2.5	70.3	1.5	0.1	1.9	8.7	40.4
2004	11.8	1.9	77.5	0.9	0.1	1.6	6.3	52.2
2005	12.8	2.5	76.1	0.8	0.0	1.7	6.1	49.9
2006	11.9	2.1	78.8	0.3	0.0	1.8	5.1	54.9
2007	10.9	2.0	78.9	0.3	0.0	2.4	5.5	53.9
2008	11.0	1.0	82.1	0.1	0.1	2.1	3.7	50.7
2009	4.7	3.5	89.2	0.3	0.1	1.1	1.2	74.4
2010	7.8	2.9	85.7	0.5	0.1	1.4	1.6	64.8
2011	4.9	2.1	89.6	0.9	0.1	1.2	1.3	72.9
2012	4.5	2.4	90.1	0.7	0.1	1.2	1.0	75.5
2013	8.6	1.0	86.0	0.9	0.1	1.7	1.7	60.3
2014	7.6	0.6	88.6	0.6	0.1	1.2	1.2	65.5
2015	9.4	0.6	86.6	0.7	0.1	1.5	1.1	60.0

Note: Jewellery is part of design but has been presented separately as it forms the major share (%) of creative goods exported from India.

Source: Computed using data from UNCTAD (n.d.).

India, while the share of design sector workers was only 1.0% (see Chapter 4) in 2015. Art crafts mostly produce low-value goods, but the size of employment indicates that India is not using this sector effectively for its development while other countries such as China are much more successful in this regard. For instance, China's exports of art crafts increased about 5 times between 2002 and 2015, and the value of exports rose from US$3.5 billion to US$17.4 billion between the same years. India's export rose only about 2.7 times between the years and the value of exports was paltry (that is, US$0.58 billion in 2002 and US$1.59 in 2015) in comparison to China. In India, as most of the artisan class are engaged in this sector and they constitute a large share of the total poor in the country (Shaban and Vermeylen 2015), the modest growth in this sector is keeping the workers trapped in the poverty and with low economic returns.

Seventh, the share of creative goods exports in total exports at the global level from India has been very inconsistent. It has fluctuated much more than any of the other three countries covered in this chapter or regarding aggregate global figures (Figure 5.1). The spike in Indian exports has been because of the fluctuation of exports value in jewellery. The exports of jewellery from India rose to US$13.5 billion in 2009 from only US$4.7 billion in 2008, and then declined to US$9.1 in 2010 (see Table 5.5). The exports of jewellery again spiked from US$16.2 billion in 2011 to US$19.5 in 2012 and thereafter declined to US$10.8 billion in 2013. This has created a very wavy curve (showing instability) of India's share in the total global exports of creative goods (merchandise). This also shows that India has much potential to raise its creative goods exports by taking care of the factors causing these fluctuations.

Eighth, in comparison to China, India's share (%) in almost all the sectors of creative goods exports are far lower, about only one-tenth of China's exports in terms of all creative goods exports (Table 5.6). This shows that India has to cover a long journey to reach the level of China. Learning from China in terms of technology development for cost-cutting of the product and creating an effective creative economy policy are required to guide the development of this sector in the country.

Ninth, notwithstanding the rising exports, the growth rates of imports in India, China, and Brazil on average have remained far higher than the growth rate of exports from these countries during 2003–2015. This shows that despite emerging as significant players in the international market in creative goods, with rising income, they are also becoming important consumers of creative goods produced abroad. In India, only for architectural goods and books, the growth rates of exports have exceeded those of imports. The highest growth rate in imports during this period in India consisted of celebrations, which includes items associated with Diwali, Christmas, Carnival, and the like, (30.3%), fashion (29.3%), and toys (26.6%).

5.3 Imports and balance of trade

The imports of creative goods in India, China, and Brazil, as has been mentioned earlier, rose at higher rates than the growth rates of exports in the respective countries during 2002–2015. This implies that the trade balance is declining over the years. This also indicates that a developmental transition is taking place in these countries, where the creative and cultural contents in goods are appreciated over mass produced goods. The middle and higher classes in these countries are their main consumers who have over the years seen significant improvement in their incomes (Shaban 2021).

Table 5.6 Share of India, China, Brazil, and the UK in the world exports of major creative products

Products	*India (%)*		*China (%)*		*Brazil (%)*		*UK (%)*	
	2002	*2015*	*2002*	*2015*	*2002*	*2015*	*2002*	*2015*
All creative goods	1.59	3.32	15.35	33.06	0.30	0.17	6.52	5.09
1. Art crafts	2.92	4.46	17.92	48.67	0.29	0.19	2.17	1.14
2. Audio-visuals	0.24	0.50	1.64	4.99	0.10	0.04	11.55	4.47
3. Design	2.10	4.61	19.27	38.45	0.44	0.18	3.45	3.23
4. New media	1.47	0.29	21.45	33.41	0.01	0.23	5.62	2.83
5. Performing arts	0.08	0.37	15.31	34.16	0.10	0.03	2.95	2.52
6. Publishing	0.19	0.75	1.76	9.46	0.09	0.07	9.93	10.50
7. Visual arts	0.07	0.34	13.57	16.56	0.03	0.23	26.19	17.57

Source: Computed using data from UNCTAD (n.d.).

Whereas the total value of export of the creative goods from India was only about 11.4% and 10.1% of the total exports of China in 2002 and 2015, respectively, the share of India's total import to the Chinese total imports have been 43.7% and 34.2%, respectively, for the same reference years (Table 5.7). This shows that India, in relation to its exports, imports more than what China does. The total imports of creative goods by India were of US$1.1 billion in 2002, which increased to US$5.5 billion in 2015, while China's import was of US$2.5 billion in 2002, and increased to $14.8 billion in 2015. What is important to note here is the fact that the import of goods in design sector (which includes architectural goods, fashion design, glassware, interior design, jewellery, and toys) has shown significant increase. The share of the sector in total creative goods imports in the country was only 12.7% in 2002 but rose to 40.9% in 2015. This indicates that India's strategy in this sector is that of importing, adding value, and then exporting the finished goods. This is particularly true for the jewellery sector, which has both the higher imports and exports in relation to other sectors. India needs to strategize for import substitution in this sector to enhance the net surplus. After design, the audio-visual goods are another major imports in India in value term. India also has a higher growth rate of imports in art crafts than China. The value of China's imports of art crafts was 13.2 times that of India in 2002 but has declined to only 3.5 times in 2015. This shows that there is rising demand for foreign products in this traditional sector in India, and that the Indian arts and crafts sector needs to be suitably promoted and modernized to meet the demand of the domestic market. This, among others, will also help enhance the living conditions of the artisans involved in this sector.

Both India and China have relatively much smaller shares in the total world imports than their respective shares in the total world exports of creative goods (Table 5.8, compare with figures presented in Table 5.6). The share in imports have been almost three times lower for India in both the reference years 2002 and 2015 to that of its share in exports, but it has been almost 14 times and 10 times lower in case of China in the respective years. The UK and Brazil do not have much difference in their shares in world imports and exports of creative goods. Overall, these figures show that China has a huge advantage in the world trade in creative goods.

Concerning the overall trade in creative goods, India and China have trade surplus, while Brazil in 2015 and the UK in both the reference years 2002 and 2015 show trade deficits (Table 5.9). However, with respect to China, India's surplus is negligible. In comparison to India's trade surplus of US$2.2 billion in 2002 and US$11.9 billion in 2015, China's trade surplus in this sector was to the tune of US$29.5 billion and US$153.7 billion in the respective years. That shows that India's trade surplus to that of China was only 18.6% in 2002 and 7.7% in 2015. What is important to note here is that except in the audio-visual sector, China has surplus in all other sub-sectors, while India suffers from deficits (exports are lower than imports) in trade of goods related to audio-visuals, new media, and publishing. However, India is more internationally competitive than Brazil and the UK, where the aggregate levels have negative trade balance.

Table 5.7 Value of imports in US$ million (current prices) of India, China, Brazil, the UK, and at the world level

Products	*India*		*China*		*Brazil*		*UK*		*World*	
	2002	*2015*	*2002*	*2015*	*2002*	*2015*	*2002*	*2015*	*2002*	*2015*
All creative goods	1107	5053	2534	14777	515	2371	20573	31646	227469	454395
1. Art crafts	39	257	514	896	38	359	1398	1914	21139	28453
1.1 Carpets	6	32	21	66	6	46	593	815	4521	7113
1.2 Celebration	2	18	3	10	4	53	276	462	4820	6364
1.3 Paperware	1	3	5	0	0	0	2	2	125	97
1.4 Wickerware	0	2	8	11	2	8	69	79	1397	1350
1.5 Yarn	20	161	472	795	16	203	359	399	7246	10260
1.6 Other	11	41	5	15	10	50	99	158	3029	3269
2. Audio-visuals	367	1040	467	2984	93	26	1392	1274	12099	21483
2.1 Film	2	0	1	2	0	..	11	0	427	14
2.2 CD, DVD, tapes	365	1040	465	2982	93	26	1381	1274	11671	21468
3. Design	141	2067	1005	5778	133	1351	9296	16657	128857	267692
3.1 Architecture	33	11	69	2	0	0	3	7	220	113
3.2 Fashion	9	337	403	2559	68	599	1853	4335	35607	75255
3.3 Glassware	2	10	5	79	3	13	104	84	1258	986
3.4 Interior	31	627	296	1190	21	328	2827	4688	40663	76292
3.5 Jewellery	49	757	66	1422	5	75	2401	4391	20156	65974
3.6 Toys	18	325	166	527	35	336	2107	3153	30954	49071
4. New media	239	483	188	3468	10	187	1160	2416	12809	47145
4.1 Recorded media	236	459	133	3107	2	127	252	1160	2430	28537
4.2 Video games	3	24	55	360	8	60	908	1256	10379	18608
5. Performing arts	2	31	30	236	20	75	261	284	3264	4728
5.1 Musical instruments	2	31	30	236	19	75	252	270	3170	4644
5.2 Printed music	0	0	0	0	0	0	10	15	94	84
6. Publishing	314	1042	301	904	206	294	3168	2482	31617	32317
6.1 Books	78	213	97	287	85	147	1288	1589	12095	15745
6.2 Newspaper	236	797	147	283	106	112	1328	476	13916	9432
6.3 Other printed matter	..	32	57	334	15	35	552	416	5606	7141
7. Visual arts	5	134	29	511	16	79	3899	6618	17683	52577
7.1 Antiques	0	1	3	220	3	1	844	1439	3075	8234
7.2 Paintings	1	51	1	133	5	24	2539	4187	7569	31836
7.3 Photography	1	3	13	39	4	4	41	79	1526	2454
7.4 Sculpture	4	79	12	119	4	50	475	913	5514	10053

Source: Computed using data from UNCTAD (n.d.).

Table 5.8 Share (%) of India, China, Brazil, and the UK in the world imports of major creative products

Products	*India (%)*		*China (%)*		*Brazil (%)*		*UK (%)*	
	2002	*2015*	*2002*	*2015*	*2002*	*2015*	*2002*	*2015*
All creative goods	0.49	1.11	1.11	3.25	0.23	0.52	9.04	6.96
Art crafts	0.19	0.90	2.43	3.15	0.18	1.26	6.62	6.73
Audio-visuals	3.03	4.84	3.86	13.89	0.77	0.12	11.50	5.93
Design	0.11	0.77	0.78	2.16	0.10	0.50	7.21	6.22
New media	1.86	1.02	1.47	7.36	0.08	0.40	9.05	5.12
Performing arts	0.05	0.65	0.93	4.99	0.60	1.59	8.00	6.02
Publishing	0.99	3.22	0.95	2.80	0.65	0.91	10.02	7.68
Visual arts	0.03	0.25	0.16	0.97	0.09	0.15	22.05	12.59

Source: Computed using data from UNCTAD (n.d.).

Table 5.9 Balance of trade (exports–imports) in creative goods by India, China, Brazil, and the UK (in US$ million at current prices)

Products	*India*		*China*		*Brazil*		*UK*	
	2002	*2015*	*2002*	*2015*	*2002*	*2015*	*2002*	*2015*
All creative goods	2212	11884	29466	153730	114	−1488	−6982	−5720
1. Art crafts	542	1335	3055	16487	21	−292	−966	−1507
1.1 Carpets	421	956	348	1513	3	−43	−430	−691
1.2 Celebration	3	30	1122	4472	−4	−52	−225	−352
1.3 Paperware	7	6	7	17	0	0	3	1
1.4 Wickerware	3	4	708	1382	−1	−8	−65	−73
1.5 Yarn	83	258	331	6750	30	−144	−170	−259
1.6 Other	25	82	539	2353	−7	−46	−79	−132
2. Audio-visuals	−342	−930	−298	−1892	−83	−18	−205	−296
2.1 Film	15	5	−1	−2	0	–	49	0
2.2 CD, DVD, tapes	−357	−935	−297	−1890	−83	−18	−255	−296
3. Design	2337	12597	21770	116578	390	−791	−5218	−6391
3.1 Architecture	−32	−8	−27	7	0	0	4	45
3.2 Fashion	818	2780	8879	39175	−58	−564	−924	−2673
3.3 Glassware	−1	−9	78	220	12	−12	−71	−57
3.4 Interior	203	695	5505	40435	412	125	−1641	−3318
3.5 Jewellery	1358	9397	1503	20060	41	−16	−889	2028
3.6 Toys	−9	−257	5832	16682	−18	−323	−1697	−2415
4. New media	−77	−360	2166	10629	−9	−90	−543	−1221
4.1 Recorded media	−76	−337	−70	1987	−1	−35	−56	−418
4.2 Video games	−1	−24	2236	8642	−8	−55	−486	−803
5. Performing arts	1	−14	401	1263	−17	−74	−178	−174
5.1 Musical Instruments	1	−14	401	1263	−17	−74	−189	−188
5.2 Printed music	0	0	0	0	0	0	11	14
6. Publishing	−255	−790	233	2282	−178	−269	−158	1054
6.1 Books	−36	1	312	1511	−72	−134	531	1056
6.2 Newspaper	−218	−791	−140	−242	−94	−110	−493	66

6.3 Other Printed matter	0	0	61	1013	−12	−26	−195	−68
7. Visual arts	6	47	2139	8383	−11	46	287	2815
7.1 Antiques	1	0	2	−152	−2	0	513	318
7.2 Paintings	3	54	16	332	−3	46	−145	2279
7.3 Photography	0	−1	1	155	−3	6	88	20
7.4 Sculpture	3	−5	2121	8049	−2	−5	−169	198

Note: 0 shows very small values.

Source: Computed using data from UNCTAD (n.d.).

5.4 Trade in creative services

As the prosperity at the world level grows, the demand for creative services is likely to rise significantly. Recognizing the complex nature of creative services and their enmeshing in different emerging technologies, UNCTAD argues, "firstly, creative services are expanding alongside the digital and sharing economies. Secondly, creative services can be more resilient to economic pressures. Lastly, creative services are heavily enmeshed with emerging e-commerce activity" (2019: 10). As many countries are not reporting the data on trade in creative services, the UNCTAD has discontinued its compilation and, therefore, we use the available consistent data for 2004 to 2008 in this section. The data presented in Table 5.10 show that although India is considered as major pool of creative people, the country is not performing well in this sector in terms of the balance of trade. The value of imports of creative services by India has been higher than exports. The trade deficit was of US$ −86 million in 2004 which increased to US$ −316 million in 2008. This shows that where the country's exports of creative services have grown almost 4.6 times during 2004–2008 (from US$1.11 billion to 5.1 billion), the imports have also kept pace with exports and have risen 3.7 times. Although value of the exports of creative services from China is significantly lower than India, China has registered impressive improvement in the surplus from only US$15 million in 2004 to US$425 million in 2008. Brazil has registered massive improvement in trade surplus as well as value of exports of creative services during the period. The data for the UK shows that developed countries are often characterized with higher number of creative persons and technologies and as such they dominate in exports of creative skills.

The major source of deficit in trade in creative services in India in 2004 has been advertising, market research, and public opinion polling sector. A growing domestic consumption market and its intensive promotion through advertisement may be contributing to this rise in imports. In 2008, the major sectors which show deficits in trade is architectural, engineering, and other technical services. This sector registered a deficit of US$1.27 billion in 2008. While in comparison to India, Brazil performed much better in trade of creative services and had registered a trade surplus of US$2.24 billion in 2008. Among others, the rising aspiration of Western-style/modelled cities and houses may be immensely contributing to these higher imports of creative services.

Table 5.10 Exports, imports, and net exports of creative services by country (US$ at current prices in millions)

Economy	*Services*	*Exports*		*Imports*		*Net-export*	
		2004	*2008*	*2004*	*2008*	*2004*	*2008*
India	**All creative services**	**1,108**	**5,096**	**1,194**	**5,412**	**−86**	**−316**
	1. Advertising, market research, and public opinion polling	103	573	334	1,178	−231	−605
	2. Architectural, engineering, and other technical services	841	2,131	761	3,397	80	−1,266
	3. Research and development	118	1,684	38	512	80	1,172
	4. Personal, cultural, and recreational services	46	707	61	325	−15	382
	4.1 Audio-visual and related services	..	..	..	..	..	..
	4.2 Other personal, cultural, and recreational services	46	707	61	325	−15	382
China	**All creative services**	**890**	**2,620**	**874**	**2,195**	**15**	**425**
	1. Advertising, market research, and public opinion polling	849	2,202	698	1,941	150	262
	2. Architectural, engineering, and other technical services	..	..	..	..	..	..
	3. Research and development	..	..	..	..	..	..
	4. Personal, cultural, and recreational services	41	418	176	255	−135	163
	4.1 Audio-visual and related services	41	418	176	255	−135	163
	4.2 Other personal, cultural, and recreational services	..	..	..	..	..	..
Brazil	**All creative services**	**2,171**	**6,331**	**1,678**	**4,089**	**493**	**2,242**
	1. Advertising, market research, and public opinion polling	111	334	87	291	24	43
	2. Architectural, engineering, and other technical services	2,014	5,595	1,182	2,918	831	2,678
	3. Research and development	..	315	..	11	..	304
	4. Personal, cultural, and recreational services	47	86	409	869	−362	−783
	4.1 Audio-visual and related services	15	26	300	589	−285	−563
	4.2 Other personal, cultural and recreational services	32	60	109	281	−77	−220
UK	**All creative services**	**25,675**	**30,851**	**9,704**	**16,052**	**15,971**	**14,799**
	1. Advertising, market research, and public opinion polling	3,598	4,839	1,542	3,622	2,056	1,217
	2. Architectural, engineering, and other technical services	9,971	11,378	3,237	3,570	6,734	7,807
	3. Research and development	8,179	10,446	3,307	6,850	4,872	3,596
	4. Personal, cultural, and recreational services	3,927	4,190	1,619	2,011	2,309	2,178
	4.1 Audio-visual and related services	2,856	2,502	1,238	1,719	1,619	783
	4.2 Other personal, cultural, and recreational services	1,071	1,688	381	292	690	1,395

Source: Based on data from UNCTAD (n.d.).

5.5 Conclusions

During 2002–2015, the share of creative goods has grown consistently in the total exports at the global level. Among the developing countries, China and India have emerged as major players. However, due to the lack of any comprehensive policy framework for CIs in India (see Chapter 1), the sector remains under-developed. Both the growth rate of exports of creative goods and value of exports from India have been far lower than that in the case for China. Only in exports of services, India has an advantage over China, but overall, India suffers from a negative trade balance for creative services between 2008 and 2015.

Drawing from the discussions presented in Chapter 1, we can argue that the 'create in China' policy of the Chinese government has succeeded, and traditional sectors of the country have seen their modernizations, including improvement in skills of workers engaged in the sector. While the 'make in India' policy of India still has to show any of its impact (Babu 2020). In India, the traditional sector of art crafts, on which a significant share of Indian population depends for its livelihood, remains the most impoverished, under-marketed, and little penetrated with modern skills and technologies. In fact, due to these reasons, the art crafts are losing their hold even in the domestic market. This shows that, among others, the rising middle and upper classes of India prefer the art crafts from other countries over the domestically produced ones. This must be a wake-up call for the government of India. Further, Bollywood cinema holds huge potential not only for the earning revenues from other countries but also creating a sense of cultural and social belonging and harmony among people of other countries of South Asian, Western Asian, and Southeast Asian countries, which have large markets for Bollywood movies and also cultural affinities to India. A special emphasis needs to be placed on easing finance and marketing of the movies and promoting consolidation and modernization of the industry. India's exports of creative goods remain dominated by jewellery sector. Our analysis of the quantitative data suggests that there is an urgent need to adopt effective and coherent policy measures for the CIs in India to unleash its potential for the development of the country.

Acknowledgements

An earlier version of this chapter appeared in Economic & Political Weekly in 2015, in issue 50, number 20, Page 68–75. The authors are grateful to Economic & Political Weekly for providing the needed permission to republish the paper in this volume with updated data and other additions.

Notes

1 This includes audio-visual photographic and computer equipment; music instruments; CDs and DVDs; caravans; camper vans; sport equipment; domestic pets and related products; toys; gardening tools and plants; newspapers; tickets to sporting matches, cinema and theatres; and spending on gambling (including lottery tickets) less any winnings (OECD 2007) and tourism in general.

2 Includes printed matter, literature, music, visual arts, cinema, photography, radio, television, games, and sporting goods (UNESCO 2000).
3 These four countries were selected for the case studies as three of them (including India) are major economies of the Global South and the UK is one of the matured and developed economies with regard to this sector. These comparisons help us to better situate India's position in creative economy trade.

References

Babu, M. S. (2020, 20 January). Why 'Make in India' has failed. *The Hindu*. Available at: www.thehindu.com/opinion/op-ed/why-make-in-india-has-failed/article30601269.ece

Barrowclough, D., and Kozul-Wright, Z. (2008). Voice, choice and diversity through creative industries: Towards a new development agenda. In Barrowclough, D. and Kozul-Wright, Z. (eds.), *Creative Industries and Developing Countries: Voice, Choice and Economic Growth*, pp. 3–36. London: Routledge.

Disdier, A.C., Tai, H. T., Fontagne, L., and Mayer, V. (2010): Bilateral trade of cultural goods. *Review of World Economics*, 145(4), 575–595.

Evans, S. (2005). Creative clusters, creative industries, symposium on culture based development strategies. *Seminar*, 553(September). Available at: www.india-seminar.com/2005/553/553%20simon%20evans.htm

Flew, T (2013). *Global Creative Industries*. Cambridge, UK: Polity Press.

Gem & Jewellery Export Promotion Council (n.d.). SEZ: The pulse of India's gems & jewellery export. Available at: https://gjepc.org/assets/images/statistics/sez/SEZ-Pulse-of-India-Gem-and-Jewellery-Exports.pdf (last accessed on 25 March 2022).

Newland, K., and Taylor, C. (2010). *Heritage Tourism and Nostalgia Trade: A Diaspora Niche in the Development Landscape*. Washington, DC: Migration Policy Institute.

OECD (2007). *Factbook 2007: Economic, Environmental and Social Statistics*. Paris: OECD.

Rich, M., and Tsitsos, W. (2016). Avoiding the 'SoHo effect' in Baltimore: Neighborhood revitalization and arts and entertainment districts. *International Journal of Urban and Regional Research*, 40(4), 736–756.

Shaban, A. (2021). Growth and determinants of the middle class in rural and urban India in the post-liberalisation period. In Batabyal, A. A., Higano, Y. and Nijkamp, P. (eds.), *Rural-Urban Dichotomies and Spatial Development in Asia*, pp. 249–274. Singapore: Springer.

Shaban, A., and Vermeylen, F. (2015). Trade in the creative sector: Comparing India with China, Brazil and UK. *Economic and Political Weekly*, 50(20), 68–75.

Strom, E. (1999). Let's put on a show! Performing arts and urban revitalization in Newark, New Jersey. *Journal of Urban Affairs*, 21(4), 423–435.

UNCTAD (2010): Creative economy report 2010. Available at: http://unctad.org/en/Docs/ditctab20103_en.pdf (last accessed on 25 March 2022).

UNCTAD (2019). *Creative Economy Outlook: Trends in International Trade in Creative Industries, 2002–2015*. Geneva: UNCTAD.

UNCTAD (n.d.). UNCTADstat. Available at: http://unctadstat.unctad.org/wds/ReportFolders/reportFolders.aspx (last accessed on 25 March 2022).

UNESCO (2000). *International Flows of Selected Cultural Goods 1980–98*. Paris: UNESCO Institute for Statistics.

The World Bank (2021). GDP growth (annual %). World Bank national accounts data, and OECD National Accounts data files. Available at: https://data.worldbank.org/indicator/NY.GDP.MKTP.KD.ZG (last accessed on 25 March 2022).

6

IMPACT OF DIGITAL TECHNOLOGIES AND INDUSTRIES ON CREATIVE INDUSTRIES AND ITS GEOGRAPHIES IN INDIA

Abdul Shaban, Filip Vermeylen and Zinat Aboli

6.1 Introduction

Digital technologies have revolutionized the creative industries (CIs). The growth and development of digital industries (DIs) have impacted the CIs in all the three important spheres – production, consumption, and exchange. The easy and inexpensive availability of digital technologies have not only added to content creation but has also opened possibilities for amateurs to experiment, produce, and grow. The development of and accessibility to Information and Communication Technologies (ICT) have further strengthened the exchange of ideas and opened possibilities for multi-geographic and multicultural cooperation and knowledge creation leading to further enhancement of creative contents. This in turn has galvanized the consumption market of CI goods and services – be it arts, photography, films, music, books, heritage, or craft.

Although, it was expected that geographies of CIs (production, consumption, labour, and exchange) would get significantly altered with the development of ICT. Many argued that spaces would be annihilated by digital technologies. However, we still find that not only creative class exists in certain geographies but also at large, there are marked geographical concentrations or clustering of both the digital industries and CIs (see also Chapter 4). As both the DIs and CIs for their localization require skilled labour, capital, and developed means of transportations, they are significantly concentrated in major urban centres like Hyderabad, Bengaluru, Delhi, Mumbai, Pune, and Kolkata. Thus, there are clusters and agglomerations of these industries in India. These urban centres offer economies of scale to CIs enabling them to remain competitive. The clustering patterns and agglomerations of CIs and digital industries can partially be explained by new economic geography (Marshall 1890; Krugman

DOI: 10.4324/9781003129370-8

1991; Venables 2005) literature which focusses on increasing economies of scale (Krugman 1980; Gardiner et al. 2011), free trade, and factors (land, labour) immobility, thick (labour) market effect (Helsley and Strange 1990), and knowledge spill-over (Henderson 1988), and productivity increase (Rosenthal and Strange 2004). In addition, Storper and Venables (2004) have emphasized the importance of face-to-face contact, and the resulting 'buzz' which can fuel innovation in urban economies. However, in literature, there has been too much emphasis on urbanization economies and externalities, which have often masked the impact of other factors leading to the localization of creative industries, for instance, inter-firm inter-linkages or availability of digital technologies by spatial proximity of DIs.

In this context, the present chapter attempts (a) to understand how the digital technologies are helping in the production of creative content, marketing, and consumption, (b) spatial concentration and clustering of DIs and CIs in India, and (c) the impact of DIs on localization of CIs in India. The rest of this chapter is divided into seven sections. After this introductory section, Section 6.2 deals with a brief review of the literature concerning the impact of digital technologies (industries) on production, consumption, and exchange of CI goods and services and localization of CIs. Identification of DIs and CIs, which are then separated from Indian Economic Census data of 2013–14 (MOSPI 2017), is presented in Section 6.3. Section 6.4 deals with the methodology adopted for analysis of the data, Section 6.5 discusses the spatial clustering of DIs and CIs, while the impacts of digital industries and workers in the sector on localization of CIs and workers in that sector are presented in Section 6.6. The last section concludes the chapter.

6.2 Impact of digitalization and locational questions of CIs in India

Digitalization is the mass adoption of internet-connected digital technologies and applications by consumers, producers, and government (PricewaterhouseCoopers 2015). Penetration of digital technologies has fundamentally altered production, consumption, and trade in all the creative sectors, especially in book publishing, periodicals publishing, film and television, music, and gaming, etc. In Europe, "The vast majority of all growth generated in today's creative industries is digital. Depending on the sector, the non-digital part of the business is generally stagnating or even shrinking" (PricewaterhouseCoopers 2015: 6). In Europe, Oliver & Ohlbaum Associates (O&O) and Analysys Mason (2017) found a significant impact of digitalization on core copyrighted industries: television/film/video, music, books, and video games and on cultural and heritage institutions. It found that it has increased the quality of content and choices of consumers, without paying more, and thus creating consumer surplus. Oliver & Ohlbaum Associates (O&O) and Analysys Mason argue, which is true elsewhere as well:

> In most creative industries, content creators have benefited from reduced production and distribution costs, which have reduced barriers of entry and, in turn, allowed them to offer consumers increased choice, while delivering content on a wider range of devices. This direct link to consumers has spurred a competitive dynamic that has led to new business models and new types of content, often with a greater proportion of revenue flowing back to the content creators.
> (2017: 8)

In the cinema industry, as Brand (1988: 19) puts it, "With digitization, the content becomes totally plastic – any message, sound, or image may be edited from anything into anything else". With digitization, a movie is reproduced with 'total fidelity' during every screening and the associated costs for an exhibitor are four to five times less than for a traditional film print (Swartz 2004; Culkin and Randle 2006).

> Though Indian cinema is still largely celluloid-based, it is moving fast ahead on the tracks of digitization. Movies are increasingly being digitally recorded, encrypted, distributed to theatres via satellite, optical disks or fibre optic networks and the digitized movies are served to the digital projector for every screening. Digitized movies are not just restricted to cinemas but have also opened doors for exciting new business opportunities like animation, games, mobile serials, etc.
> (Stephanie et al. 2012: 8)

Digital technologies have made it easier to create and distribute content. Shooting and editing videos have become less tedious. The availability of apps also has made editing easier. Furthermore, digitalization has also enabled amateurs to engage in the creative sector (Arora and Vermeylen 2012).

Smart mobile phones have massified the digitalization of many sub-sectors of creative industries. In India, by mid-2017, there were about 650 million mobile phone users and over 300 million of them had a smartphone (Iyengar 2017). In fact, "the surge in mobile phone sales has helped India emerge as one of the world's largest markets for mobile music which is predominantly fuelled by film music" (Stephanie et al. 2012: 10). Mobile videos have grown significantly and the use of mobile cinema and mobile TV are on the rise. Roamware and Hungama Mobile have joined the GSM Association to launch the 'Mobile Bollywood Initiative' (Cybermedia News 2007). The opening of the 4G network, with a significant price cut, has further accelerated the demand for internet videos, games, and cinema. In India, not only in urban centres where the mobile networks work better, but even in rural areas with penetration of the 4G network the demand for music, games, and unprecedented viewing of videos has increased. About 90% of the smartphones shipped in 2017 were 4G enabled. In India, the LTE-capable device base grew to 218 million in 2017, with 74%

being Voice over LTE (VoLTE) capable as well (Khan 2018). By 2022, India is likely to have 520 million 4G subscribers while 3G subscribers will be 740 million (Rathee 2017).

In 2017, more than 90% of popular videos seen online comprised of Hindi and regional language movies (Khan 2018). In the same year, "On average, an Indian subscriber consumed 7.4 GB of data per user per month on their mobile devices over mobile networks alone, placing India ahead of developed markets like the UK, South Korea and France" (Khan 2018). The data consumption is expected to grow by annual compound growth rate of 40% during 2017–22, and the average monthly data consumption in 2022 is expected to be 11 GB per month (Rathee 2017).

The previous discussion reveals that the firm and technology relations between creative and digital industries have become quite strong. It, therefore, is expected that these firms will be clustered in space, as digital industries have strong impact on CIs. Marshall (1890), Weber (Fearon 2002) Hoover (1937), and Glaeser et al. (1992) have already argued about the externalities, raw material, labour, transport, and market determining the location and agglomeration of industries. Scott (2005), Cooke et al. (2007), Florida (2008), Florida et al. (2008), Cooke and Lazzeretti (2008), Lazzeretti et al. (2008), and Boix et al. (2012) characterize creative industries with tendency to concentrate in space, giving rise to creative clusters or creative regions. The creative clusters or regions are the result of the concentration by 'creative people' (Florida 2002) who come together in space where their diverse or similar talents can find meaningful expression in consonance of each other. The traditional approaches using external economies (localization and urbanization economies) have partially been able to explain why creative industries geographically concentrate (Tschang and Vang 2008; Cooke et al. 2007; Wenting et al. 2011; Hanson 2000; Vang 2005, 2007; Lazzeretti et al. 2008; Lazzeretti et al. 2012; Serra 2016). However, there has been little efforts to understand inter-industry (like digital to creative industries) causality, dependence, and localization, which this chapter attempts to find out.

6.3 Identification of DIs and CIs

The Sixth Economic Census (EC)[1] of India, 2013–14 (Government of India 2016), provides data up to 3-digit levels of National Industrial Classification (NIC) for districts. This 3-digit level data of DIs and CIs are used in this chapter (see also Chapter 3). The Greater Manchester Combined Authority (GMCA) in its report on Digital and Creative Industries (2016) identifies digital industries as:

> Made up of various subsectors such as communication equipment, communication services, computing and peripherals, film and TV broadcasting, ICT equipment, information processing, multimedia

communications, multimedia publishing, multimedia services, software, systems integration, vision and sound equipment.

(GMCA 2016: 3)

Taking cue from this definition, the digital industries from the Sixth Economic Census data have been identified (see Table 6.1).

Defining CIs has been trickier and there are many models for the same. Some of the models for identification of CIs are UK DCMS model, Symbolic text model, Concentric circle model, WIPO copyright model, and UNCTAD Model (UNCTAD 2010). Academics and practitioners equally accept these models. To define a handicraft industry, the Sixth EC has used two criteria: (a) predominant role of human skills, and (b) performed by hands using traditional knowledge and simple tools. For the EC, the term handicraft includes handlooms. Based on the UNCTAD Model and 3-digit level NIC, we have already identified CIs in Chapter 3.

6.4 Methodology of data analysis

We have used the CIs and its classification as mentioned in Chapter 3. However, this chapter presents the CI data in a slightly different form to that presented in Chapter 4. This chapter uses *clipping method* of ArcGIS 10.3 to aggregate the data on industry and workers in the clusters/regions marked on maps. It uses spatial econometric methods to understand the degree of clustering, and impact of DIs and workers on localization of CIs and workers. To understand whether the regional distribution of DIs and CIs are clustered or not, besides mapping spatial distribution, we have also computed Moran's I to find out degree of spatial clustering. The Moran's I measures value similarity with locational similarity (Anselin and Bera 1998). It ranges between +1 and −1. When values of an industry or worker are clustered in locations, it has positive value; when there are checkboards of high and low values (dissimilar values) in location, it has negative values. A value of 0 for Moran's I typically indicates no spatial association or autocorrelation. Moran's I in this chapter is computed as follows:

$$I = \left(\frac{n}{s_0}\right)\frac{\sum_{i=1}^{n}\sum_{j=1}^{n} w_{ij}x_i x_j}{\sum_{i=1}^{n} x_i^2} \quad (1)$$

where n is the number of observations, w_{ij} is the element in spatial weight matrix w corresponding to the district (i,j), the observations x_i and x_j are in deviation from their mean values for the district i and j, respectively, and s_0 is the normalizing factor equal to the sum of the elements of the weight matrix, i.e. $s_0 = \sum_i \sum_j w_{ij}$ (Anselin 1992).

Different types of weight matrix can be constructed for a given spatial distribution. This chapter adopts the simplest and the most powerful binary contiguity matrix, called queen's contiguity matrix, where the element *(i,j)* of the spatial weight matrix w_{ij} =1 if district *i* and *j* share a border and zero otherwise (Anselin 1992; Hanning 1990; Upton and Fingleton 1985). We have used row-standardized spatial weight matrix in which each row is equal to 1, and the expression of Moran's I given earlier then simplifies to (Lim 2003):

$$I = \frac{\sum_{i=1}^{n}\sum_{j=1}^{n} w_{ij} x_i x_j}{\sum_{i=1}^{n} x_i^2} \tag{2}$$

Or, in matrix notation:

$$I = \frac{X'wX}{X'X} \tag{3}$$

where *W* is spatial weight matrix and *X* is vector of observed values in deviation from mean.

Given that DIs are playing important role in development of the CIs, we expect significant causality from DIs to CIs. We also expect that neighbouring location of DIs and its workers exercise their influence on localization of CIs and its workers, respectively. Further, as we are dealing with spatial data, we also suspect that there will be spatial autocorrelation and therefore after testing the spatial autocorrelation, we use spatial lag and spatial error regression methods to overcome the possibility of model misspecification (Shaban 2006).

The conventional ordinary least squares regression model depicting the relationship between the CIs and DIs, spatial lag of DIs is as follows:

$$y_1 = \alpha + \beta_1 X_1 + \beta_2 X_2 + \varepsilon \tag{4}$$

where y_1 is number of CIs by district, α is the intercept, β_1 and β_2 are the regression coefficient for number of DIs by districts (X_1) and spatial lag of number of DIs by districts (X_2), respectively. The previous equation assumes that the random error term, ε, is normally distributed with zero mean and homoscedastic variance σ^2.

However, the equation does not take into account the spatial effect or spatial autocorrelation and treats districts as isolated islands (Quah 1996). It does not consider that concentration of enterprises in one district is also dependent on its neighbouring districts. In fact, the new economic geography (Marshall 1890; Krugman 1991; Venables 2005) tells us that economic evolution of a region is often dependent on the fate of its neighbouring regions. That means regional distribution of industries is unlikely to be spatially independent and random. As such, ignoring the spatial dependence in the model can cause serious problem of model misspecification (Anselin 1988; Lim 2003). In this chapter, we have adopted two methods to deal with the spatial dependence in the data, that is, through introduction of spatial lag of dependent variable and spatial error.

With spatial lag of dependent variable incorporated, the previous model (equation 4) can be expressed as follows:

$$y_1 = \alpha + \beta_1 X_1 + \beta_2 X_2 + \rho w y_1 + \varepsilon \tag{5}$$

where ρ is spatial autoregressive coefficient and wy is spatial lagged dependent variable for a spatial weight matrix w. The OLS model of the previous equation will yield biased and inconsistent estimates for the coefficients due to the simultaneity between the error term and the spatially lagged variable. Therefore, maximum likelihood (ML) method has been used for estimation of this model (Anselin 1988; Anselin and Bera 1998).

The spatial error model is considered when spatial dependence is expected to be working through the error process, which can result from a measurement problem (Rey and Montouri 1999). The spatial error dependence is often considered as a 'nuisance' as it reflects spatial autocorrelation in measurement errors in variables that are not important for the model (Shaban 2006). The spatial process relating to the error term can be expressed as (Lim 2003; Rey and Montouri 1999):

$$\varepsilon = \lambda w \varepsilon + \xi$$

$$\varepsilon = (1 - \lambda w)^{-1} \xi$$

where ε is a vector of error term, λ is a spatial error coefficient, and ξ is a vector of error term, which is normally distributed with zero means and homoscedastic variance σ_ξ^2. With inclusion of spatial autocorrelation of the error terms, the equation is expressed as follows:

$$y_1 = \alpha + \beta_1 X_1 + \beta_2 X_2 + (1 - \lambda w)^{-1} \xi \tag{6}$$

The OLS estimator will again provide inconsistent and biased estimates of the parameter's' variance, and therefore, it is again estimated with ML method (Anselin 1988; Anselin and Bera 1998).

Similar to the models for number of CIs, y_1, the locational determinants of the number of CI workers, y_2, can be modelled as follows:

For the OLS estimator, without consideration of spatial dependence in lag and error terms:

$$y_2 = \varsigma + \tau_1\phi_1 + \tau_2\phi_2 + \nu \quad (7)$$

where ς is the intercept; τ_1 and τ_2 are regression coefficients for ϕ_1 and ϕ_2 digital industry workers and spatial lag of digital industry workers, respectively. ν is the error term.

The spatial lag of the y_2 is estimated as follows:

$$y_2 = \varsigma + \tau_1\phi_1 + \tau_2\phi_2 + \vartheta w y_2 + \nu \quad (8)$$

where ϑ is the coefficient of spatial lag of the dependent variable y_2. The spatial error model of the y_2 is specified as follows:

$$y_2 = \varsigma + \tau_1\phi_1 + \tau_2\phi_2 + (1 - \lambda w)^{-1}\xi \quad (9)$$

6.5 Spatial clustering of digital and creative industries

As a continuity to the analysis presented in Chapter 4, we have attempted to map the spatial (using district level data) distribution of number of industries and workers of DIs and CIs, though identifying the patterns only at the aggregate level but using a different method that is ArcGIS clipping method to capture the data in a shape/area to find out the total number of workers and industries within that shape/area. We have purposefully used absolute data as we wanted to understand the absolute concentration of the industries and workers.

Out of the total 58.5 million firms in India in 2013–14, the share of digital industry was 0.95% (that is 554,294 establishments), while the sector constituted 0.72% of the total 131.3 million workers in all the industries (for CIs, see Chapter 4). The largest share in digital industries was of repair of computers and communication equipment (43.9% of the total digital industries) in which about 18.2% of the total workers of digital industries were employed (Table 6.1). It is also interesting to note that with about 8.6% share in total digital industries, the computer programming, consultancy, and related activities constituted 37.5% of the workers of the sector.

We find a significant spatial association/co-location between DIs and CIs, and DI workers and CI workers. In fact, from the bivariate mapping (Figures 6.1 and 6.2), one can identify 10 significant clusters of the digital and creative industries (this does not include handloom and handicraft industries, which are presented separately; see Figure 6.3) in India. These, from north to south, are:

Table 6.1 Number of digital industries and workers in India, 2013–14

NIC 3-digit code	*Name of industries*	*No. of Industries*	*% of the total digital industries*	*No. of workers*	*% of the total digital industry workers*
261	Manufacture of electronic components	25,362	4.6	167,390	7.4
262	Manufacture of computers and peripheral equipment	3,962	0.7	64,159	2.8
263	Manufacture of communication equipment	4,338	0.8	17,121	0.8
264	Manufacture of consumer electronics	7,113	1.3	59,905	2.7
267	Manufacture of optical instruments and equipment	4,743	0.9	13,403	0.6
268	Manufacture of magnetic and optical media	235	0.0	1,225	0.1
611	Wired telecommunications activities	102,734	18.5	301,777	13.4
612	Wireless telecommunications activities	33,164	6.0	87,564	3.9
613	Satellite telecommunications activities	12,245	2.2	40,886	1.8
619	Other telecommunications activities	16,532	3.0	52,921	2.3
620	Computer programming, consultancy, and related activities	47,467	8.6	846,249	37.5
631	Data processing, hosting, and related activities; web portals	18,467	3.3	63,143	2.8
639	Other information service activities	34,539	6.2	130,302	5.8
951	Repair of computers and communication equipment	243,394	43.9	410,414	18.2
Total		554,295	100.0	2,256,459	100.0

Source: Based on data from Sixth Economic Census of India, 2013–14.

i ***Bareilly-Amritsar region***: This includes a large number of districts with relatively sizeable number of DIs and CIs. Some of the districts in this region are – Bulandshahar, Bareilly, Moradabad, Bijnor, Muzaffarnagar, Meerut, districts of Delhi state, Ludhiana, and Jalandhar. This region has a

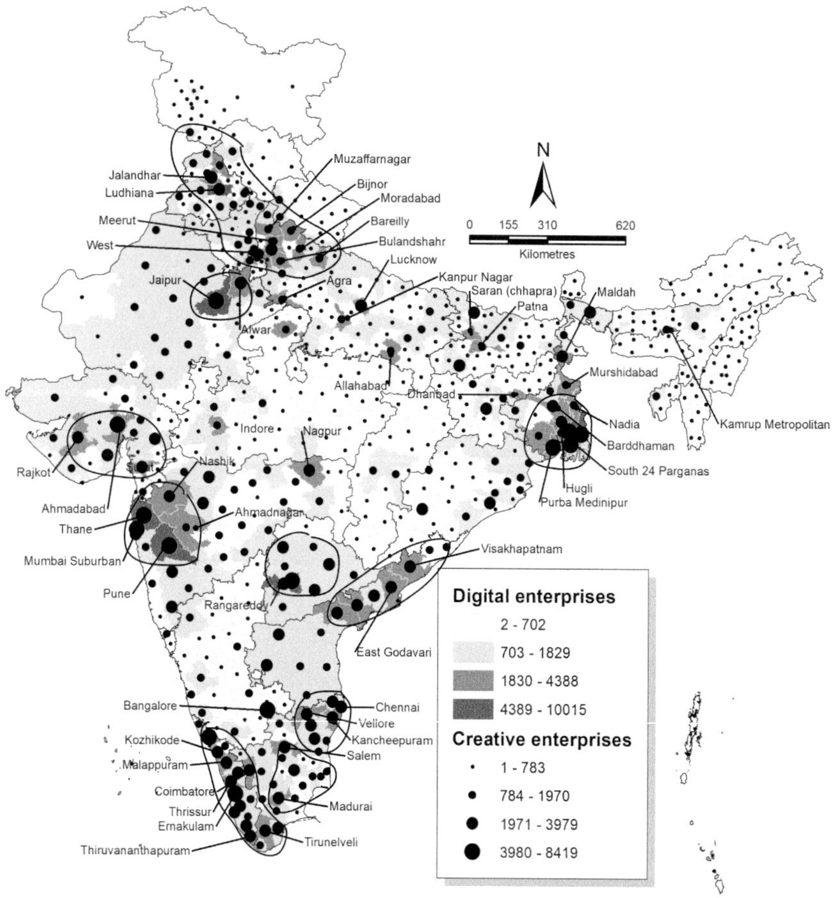

Figure 6.1 Distribution and clustering of digital and creative industries by districts in India, 2013–14

Source: Based on data from Sixth Economic Census of India, 2013–14.

quite diffused distribution of industries. This region constitutes 30.6% of the DIs and 25.1% of the workers engaged in DIs in India (Table 6.2). The share of this belt in the total CIs in India is 22.7% and the total 19.7% of the workers in CIs in India are concentrated in this region. A large number of DIs are located in this region, but the belt specializes in manufacturing of consumer electronic (with 47.3% of total industries and 72.3% of total workers at all-India level) and manufacturing of optical instruments and equipment (Figure 6.2). This region also has high concentration of workers (50.6%) in manufacturing of electronic components. In comparison to DIs and workers in the sector (Tables 6.2 and 6.3), the shares of CIs and workers in the sector in this region are relatively lower (Tables 6.4). However,

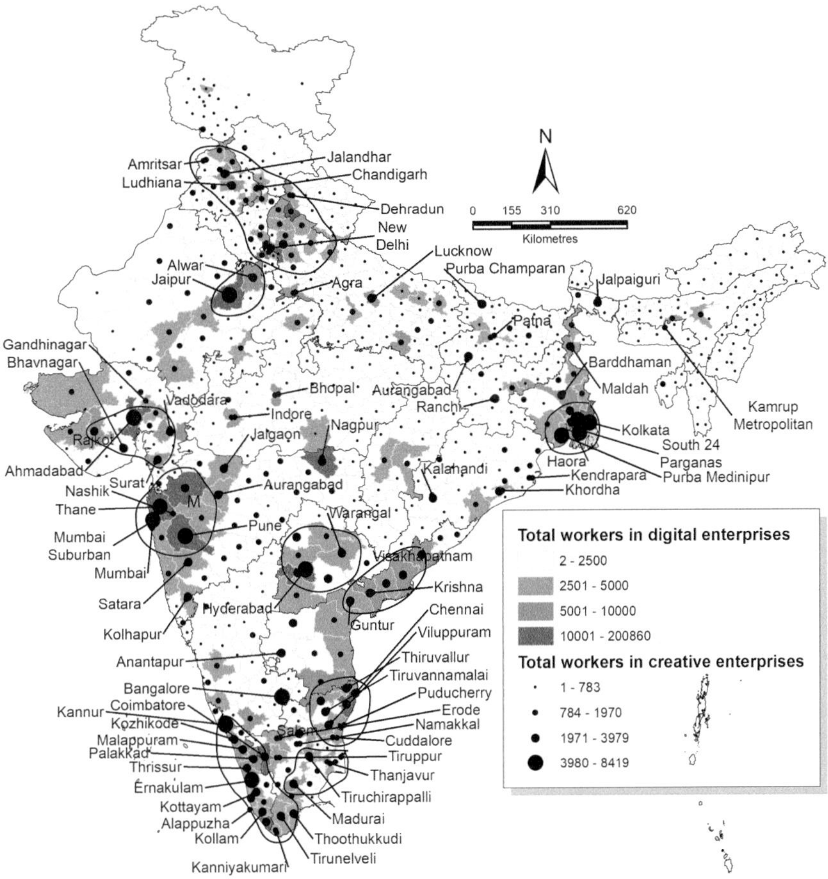

Figure 6.2 Distribution and clustering of workers in digital and creative industries by districts in India, 2013–14

Source: Based on data from Sixth Economic Census of India, 2013–14.

CIs with significant all-India share of the industries and workers in this region are sound recording and music publishing, photography, and other amusement and recreation activities (Figures 6.4 and 6.5).

ii ***Alwar-Jaipur region***: These two districts show significant concentration of DIs and CIs, and the node is Jaipur. This region is prominent in manufacturing of electronic components and general telecommunications, satellite communication, and manufacturing of magnetic and optical media. Moreover, this region has significant presence of industries of sound recording and music publishing, and publishing of books, periodicals, and other publishing. This small region accounts for 12% of the total workers of the country engaged in sound recording and music publishing and 5.7% of the

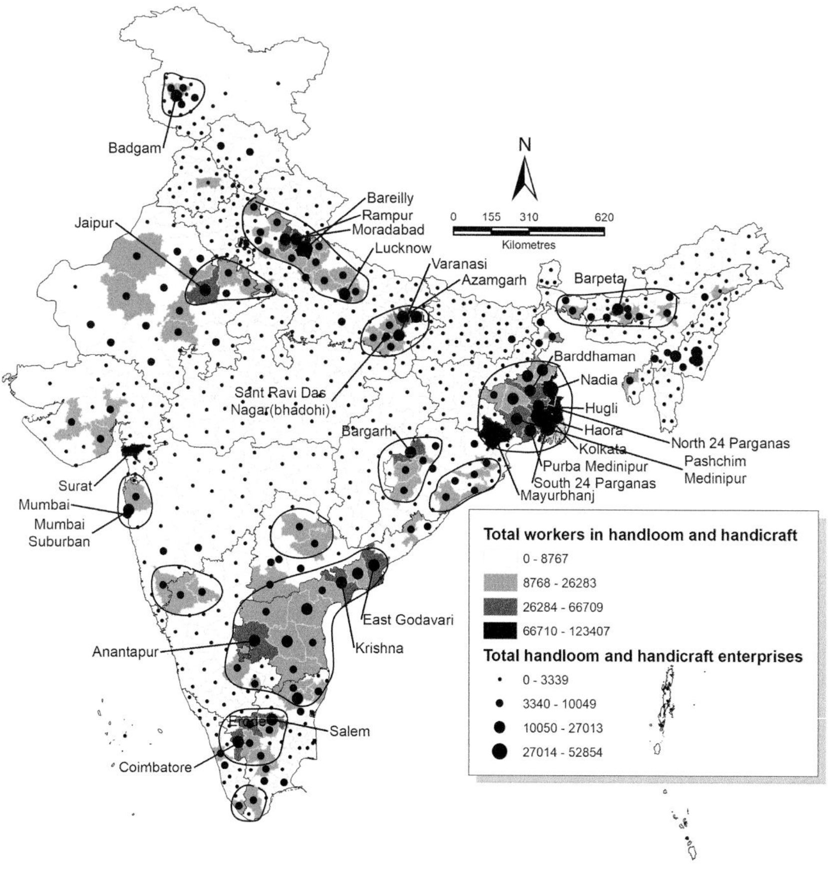

Figure 6.3 Distribution and clustering of industries and workers of handloom and handicraft by districts in India, 2013–14

Source: Based on data from Sixth Economic Census of India, 2013–14.

workers engaged in publications of books, periodicals, and other publishing activities.

iii ***Ahmedabad-Vadodara-Surat region***: This region has significant share of all-India number of CIs but low share of digital industries. We have also included Rajkot and Bhavnagar in this region, both of which have higher DI and CI concentration. This region has significant concentration of industries related to manufacturing computer and peripheral equipment (11.4% of all-India total), and manufacturing of optical instrument and equipment (11.4%) (Table 6.2). The region also has significant concentration of workers (10%) engaged in manufacturing of electronic components. With regard to creative industries, the corridor specializes in organization of convention and tradeshows. It has 65.3% of the industries and 54.9%

Table 6.2 Share (%) of the regions in digital industries to the respective national totals, 2013–14

Industry (NIC 2008)	*Bareilly-Amritsar region*	*Alwar-Jaipur region*	*Ahmedabad-Surat-Vadodara region*	*Kolkata and adjoining districts*	*Mumbai-Pune-Nashik region*	*Hyderabad and adjoining districts*	*Coastal Andhra Pradesh*	*Northern Tamil Nadu*	*South and central Tamil Nadu*	*Coastal belt of Kerala*	*Total*
All	30.6	3.8	7.0	12.9	13.4	6.0	3.8	6.8	4.0	11.7	100.0
261	37.6	6.4	8.0	7.7	27.1	4.7	1.1	4.1	1.0	2.4	100.0
262	30.0	3.8	11.4	7.8	22.4	6.0	5.4	6.2	1.7	5.4	100.0
263	15.5	0.7	10.8	7.5	14.0	5.9	2.3	6.2	9.3	27.9	100.0
264	47.3	2.7	4.0	2.3	25.9	10.1	2.1	1.5	0.3	3.7	100.0
267	40.6	5.9	11.4	27.0	4.8	0.9	0.3	4.5	1.5	2.9	100.0
268	30.7	6.3	1.6	34.6	12.6	4.7	1.6	3.9	0.0	3.9	100.0
611	30.2	1.7	6.1	13.2	10.8	5.3	6.9	6.2	5.1	14.6	100.0
612	29.3	2.8	3.8	15.2	5.4	14.4	4.9	13.5	1.5	9.0	100.0
613	17.3	3.4	1.1	12.0	3.8	3.3	11.7	11.5	14.1	21.8	100.0
619	31.3	5.1	0.1	31.8	10.4	3.5	0.7	8.1	3.7	5.2	100.0
620	15.2	4.6	6.1	10.6	19.2	9.2	3.1	7.1	4.7	20.2	100.0
631	8.2	3.1	5.3	17.2	15.8	5.4	4.4	9.2	7.2	24.2	100.0
639	30.3	2.6	7.1	12.2	22.2	8.8	2.7	1.8	0.6	11.8	100.0
951	36.2	4.7	8.8	12.2	11.8	4.5	2.6	6.8	3.8	8.6	100.0

Note: Please see Table 6.1 for the name of the industry (NIC 2008).

Source: Based on data from Sixth Economic Census of India, 2013–14.

of all-India workers of the sector (Tables 6.4 and 6.5). The region also has significant concentration of industries and workers engaged in software publishing, specialized design activities, and handloom and handicraft. In fact, this corridor is known for diamond-cutting and polishing, gems and jewellery manufacturing, and design activities.

iv ***Kolkata and adjoining districts***: Kolkata as a node of DI and CI concentration is well-evident from Figures 6.1 and 6.2. Around Kolkata, the districts with significant concentrations of DIs and CIs are South 24 Praganas, Bardhaman, Hugli, Howrah, Purba Medinipur, and Nadia. As shown in Tables 6.2 and 6.3, this region has significantly higher concentration of a digital industries and workers engaged in them. Prominent among them are manufacturing of magnetic and optical media (34.6% of the all-India total), manufacturing of optical instrument and equipment (27.0%), and industries engaged in other telecommunication activities (31.8%). This region has more than 30% of the industries and workers engaged in handloom and handicraft at all-India level, while having significant concentration of television programming and broadcasting activities, amusement and recreation activities, creative arts and entertainment activities, and libraries, archives, museums, and other cultural activities. It will not be an exaggeration to claim that Kolkata is a cultural city of India where traditional, ethnic, and modern arts and crafts are thriving with rising digital industry.

v ***Mumbai-Pune-Nashik region***: This is India's most industrialized and urbanized region and now includes Aurangabad within its fold. Thane, the neighbouring district of Mumbai, is a major district of concentration of DIs and CIs. This is one of the major and historically most important industrial regions of India. It has large concentration of industries and workers engaged in many digital industries and significant among them are manufacturing of consumer electronics, computer programming, consultancy, and related activities; manufacturing of electronic component; and manufacturing of computers and peripheral equipment. Significantly higher share of workers (to the all-India respective totals) are found to be engaged in manufacturing of magnetic and optical media (37.8%), other information activities (32.8%), data processing, hosting and related activities (28.5%), computer programming, consultancy and related activities (24.1%), and other telecommunication activities (24.6%). In fact, this region has predominantly modern industries and has significantly lower share of handloom and handicraft industries. It specializes in market research and public opinion polling (41.2% of all-India total industry in this sector and 60.7% of the workers), advertising (26.0% of industries and 39.4% of workers), creative arts and entertainment activities (15.3% of industries and 18.9% of workers), specialized design activities (20.8% of industries and 22.7% of workers), and motion picture, video, and television programme activities (13.2% of industries and 26.4% of workers). In fact, Bollywood, the Indian Hindi-language film industry (motion picture

Table 6.3 Share (%) of the regions in the digital industry workers to the respective national totals, 2013–14

(Industry) NIC 2008	*Bareilly-Amritsar region*	*Alwar-Jaipur region*	*Ahmedabad-Surat-Vadodara region*	*Kolkata and adjoining districts*	*Mumbai-Pune-Nashik region*	*Hyderabad and adjoining districts*	*Coastal Andhra Pradesh*	*Northern Tamil Nadu*	*South and central Tamil Nadu*	*Coastal belt of Kerala*	*Total*
All	25.1	1.8	3.7	6.3	21.2	19.2	1.6	10.1	1.6	9.3	100.0
261	50.6	2.0	10.0	2.0	21.1	4.6	0.3	5.3	0.3	3.8	100.0
262	46.5	0.7	3.9	0.9	25.7	14.2	0.4	6.2	0.2	1.3	100.0
263	41.7	0.6	4.3	5.0	15.9	7.3	0.8	3.2	2.9	18.2	100.0
264	72.3	0.4	1.1	0.6	15.9	4.0	0.4	1.3	0.0	4.1	100.0
267	36.5	3.8	10.9	22.7	9.2	1.0	0.3	8.6	1.1	5.9	100.0
268	39.8	4.0	0.2	11.0	37.8	1.8	0.4	2.0	0.0	2.9	100.0
611	31.1	1.3	5.3	9.9	15.9	8.0	5.3	6.1	3.7	13.3	100.0
612	21.2	2.0	4.7	11.7	9.8	20.1	4.4	12.9	1.4	11.8	100.0
613	40.0	5.7	0.8	7.2	8.8	2.3	5.3	7.6	8.6	13.8	100.0
619	29.3	2.0	0.1	16.9	24.6	13.0	0.4	5.9	2.5	5.4	100.0
620	11.5	1.1	0.9	3.9	24.1	33.2	0.5	14.8	0.5	9.5	100.0
631	9.0	3.6	6.0	11.5	28.5	6.1	2.0	11.6	4.7	16.9	100.0
639	31.4	2.9	3.9	6.3	32.8	13.0	1.2	1.6	0.3	6.7	100.0
951	31.7	4.0	8.6	11.6	14.5	4.9	2.8	7.6	3.9	10.3	100.0

Note and Source: as for Table 6.4.

Table 6.4 Share (%) of regions in the creative industries to the respective national totals, 2013–14

(Industry) NIC 2008	*Bareilly-Amritsar region*	*Alwar-Jaipur region*	*Ahmedabad-Surat-Vadodara region*	*Kolkata and adjoining districts*	*Mumbai-Pune-Nashik region*	*Hyderabad and adjoining districts*	*Coastal Andhra Pradesh*	*Northern Tamil Nadu*	*South and central Tamil Nadu*	*Coastal belt of Kerala*	*Total*
All	22.7	3.5	8.7	10.6	12.7	7.3	5.6	7.5	5.5	16.0	100.0
581	27.3	6.7	9.1	10.1	9.9	12.4	5.8	4.5	2.5	11.8	100.0
582	27.4	1.5	27.3	2.3	5.6	10.2	1.9	9.6	4.3	10.0	100.0
591	21.4	3.0	9.0	11.1	13.2	3.8	18.1	6.4	1.7	12.3	100.0
592	29.8	10.8	4.3	6.8	5.7	4.1	4.2	10.2	12.8	11.3	100.0
601	18.3	3.3	7.0	10.5	10.2	9.6	5.4	12.8	9.8	13.0	100.0
602	24.0	1.4	0.8	22.8	5.4	16.7	7.7	7.3	1.7	12.2	100.0
711	15.8	7.0	6.2	3.1	22.9	1.8	3.1	3.1	2.9	34.1	100.0
731	20.0	2.2	6.8	9.0	26.0	4.2	2.8	3.9	3.6	21.5	100.0
732	10.9	1.3	3.6	7.2	41.2	16.3	5.3	3.5	0.2	10.5	100.0
741	9.9	1.3	15.1	8.5	20.8	18.0	4.6	5.8	2.7	13.4	100.0
742	29.3	3.6	8.2	8.3	11.3	8.6	5.8	7.1	4.0	13.7	100.0
823	2.3	0.6	65.3	2.8	13.1	6.0	0.9	1.1	0.6	7.3	100.0
900	25.7	3.6	9.6	10.4	15.3	6.7	7.2	5.6	4.0	11.8	100.0
910	3.4	1.5	2.9	11.8	9.9	2.1	2.9	15.7	17.6	32.2	100.0
932	28.6	1.9	14.9	35.0	4.6	3.0	2.1	5.7	0.3	3.9	100.0
H&H	20.3	4.8	6.8	33.4	5.1	4.7	8.4	5.7	4.2	6.6	100.0

Note: Please see Table 6.2 for name of the industry (NIC 2008); H&H = handloom and handicraft industries.

Source: Based on data from Sixth Economic Census of India, 2013–14.

Table 6.5 Share (%) of regions in the creative industry workers to the respective national totals, 2013–14

NIC 2008	*Bareilly-Amritsar region*	*Alwar-Jaipur region*	*Ahmedabad-Surat-Vadodara region*	*Kolkata and adjoining districts*	*Mumbai-Pune-Nashik region*	*Hyderabad and adjoining districts*	*Coastal Andhra Pradesh*	*Northern Tamil Nadu*	*South and central Tamil Nadu*	*Coastal belt of Kerala*	*Total*
All	19.7	2.8	8.4	9.2	16.3	8.9	4.8	11.4	4.3	14.1	100.0
581	24.8	5.7	6.2	5.8	12.7	15.3	4.8	8.6	2.2	14.0	100.0
582	11.2	0.3	11.7	0.3	1.6	3.8	0.3	65.6	1.2	4.1	100.0
591	15.2	2.4	6.4	8.1	26.4	10.0	12.7	6.8	1.0	11.0	100.0
592	27.7	12.0	5.1	5.5	9.1	4.5	3.7	9.9	10.4	12.0	100.0
601	23.8	2.1	5.3	10.1	14.3	8.1	3.4	9.2	6.1	17.5	100.0
602	13.2	0.8	1.2	21.2	11.4	21.3	4.3	6.9	1.3	18.5	100.0
711	19.8	3.6	6.7	2.2	36.2	2.3	2.0	3.2	2.1	21.9	100.0
731	23.0	1.3	6.2	6.8	39.4	3.8	1.3	2.4	2.0	13.6	100.0
732	7.0	0.6	1.8	5.0	60.7	8.5	3.1	3.7	0.1	9.5	100.0
741	11.2	1.0	17.3	6.7	22.7	17.2	3.2	5.9	2.3	12.5	100.0
742	25.5	3.1	7.8	8.5	10.8	11.7	5.9	7.6	4.4	14.7	100.0
823	5.3	0.9	54.9	5.3	17.5	9.0	0.6	0.7	1.0	4.8	100.0
900	23.2	3.4	9.8	9.5	18.9	8.3	7.6	5.0	3.6	10.6	100.0
910	4.9	1.6	3.4	11.0	9.5	2.9	2.8	17.8	17.5	28.7	100.0
932	30.7	2.3	9.0	34.0	4.8	3.1	3.5	6.5	0.2	5.8	100.0
H&H	20.9	4.8	10.6	31.7	6.7	3.6	5.7	5.1	3.8	7.1	100.0

Note and source: As for Table 6.6.

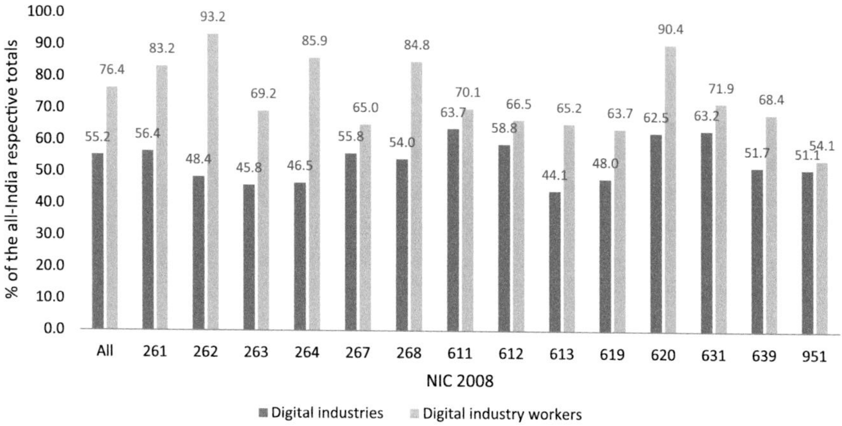

Figure 6.4 Percentage distribution of total DIs and workers in regions to the respective all-India totals, 2013–14

Source: Based on data from Sixth Economic Census of India, 2013–14.

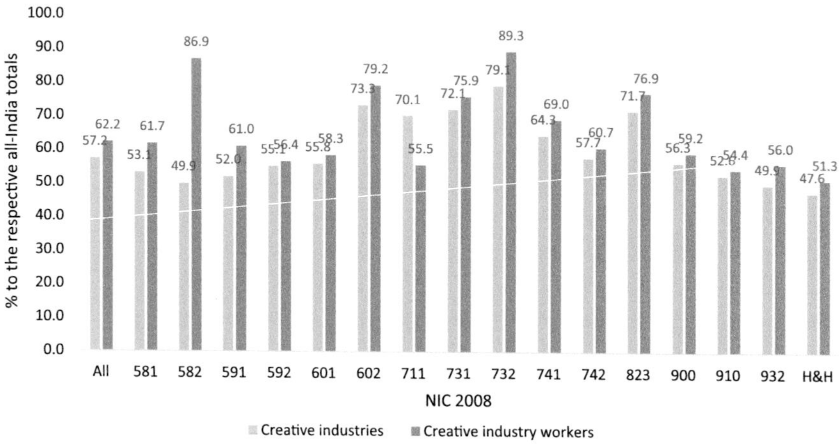

Figure 6.5 Percentage distribution of CIs and workers in region to the respective all-India totals, 2013–14

Source: Based on data from Sixth Economic Census of India, 2013–14.

production), is based in the city of Mumbai. In the city, there is also thriving design industry (gems and jewellery, and architecture).

vi ***Hyderabad and its neighbouring districts:*** Hyderabad has a significant concentration of both digital and creative industries in India. Its neighbouring and nearby districts due to its influence have also grown in significance in this regard and some of such districts are Rangareddy, Warrengal, Nizamabad, Karim Nagar, and Nalgonda. Hyderabad for the last two decades has emerged as centre for new media and software production, besides cultural industries. The region has 33.2% of the total workers engaged at all-India level in computer programming, consultancy, and related activities, 20.1% of the workers in wireless communication activities, and 14.2% of the workers in manufacturing of computer and peripheral equipment. In fact, major Information Technology (IT) industries like Google, Microsoft, etc. have their offices located in Hyderabad. Given the specialization of Hyderabad in IT sector, the motion picture editing and publishing have also emerged as major activities in this region. In fact, Hyderabad has its own Tollywood (Telugu Film Industry) known for action movies with content edited through digital technologies. Among the creative industries, it has a significant share of workers engaged in television programming and broadcasting activities, specialized design activities, photographic activities, and motion picture, video, and television programme activities.

vii ***Coastal Andhra Pradesh***: This includes districts of Vishakhapatnam, East Godavari, West Godavari, Krishna, and Guntur. In this belt, significant digital industry is satellite telecommunication, and among creative industries, motion picture, video, and television programme activities dominate.

viii ***Northern Tamil Nadu***: This includes Chennai, Vellore, Kanchipuram, Thiruvallur, and also Puducherry (which is a Union Territory of India). The major digital industries in this region are computer programming, consultancy, related activities, data processing, hosting and related activities, and wireless telecommunication activities. Among the creative industries, significant presence is seen of software publishing (65.6% of all-India total workers), and libraries, archives, museums, and other cultural activities.

ix ***South and Central Tamil Nadu***: Significant districts in this region are Tiruchirappalli, Madurai, and Tiruppur. This region has significant share of workers and industries engaged in satellite telecommunication activities, and among creative industries significant presence is seen of sound recording and music publishing activities, and libraries, archives, museums, and other cultural activities.

x ***Coastal belt of Kerala:*** A significant concentration of both DIs and CIs are seen in Coastal districts of Kerala. In fact, Kerala is one of the most literate and highly developed states of India, in terms of human development. The rise of tourism and relatively better income has created a significant concentration of both the DIs and CIs in the coastal districts of the state. Some of the significant districts in this regard are Ernakulam, Kannur, Malapuram, and Thiruvananthapuram. Among the digital industries, this belt has a significant presence of manufacturing of communication equipment, data processing, hosting and related activities, satellite telecommunication activities, and wired telecommunication activities. The belt has more than 10% share of many creative industries and workers engaged in them. The significant among them are libraries, archives, museums, and other cultural activities (28.7% of all-India workers in the sector), and architectural and engineering activities and related technical consultancy (21.9% of the workers).

Handloom and handicraft industries and workers: The handloom and handicraft sector shows its own spatial concentration and clustering. Although 10 digital and creative industry regions mentioned earlier account for 47.6% of the total industry and 51.3% of the total workers engaged in this sector at all-India level, there is significant spatial separation in concentration of handloom and handicraft activities to the digital and non-handloom and handicraft CIs. Only Kolkata, Alwar-Jaipur, and Coastal Andhra Pradesh regions seem to be neatly fitting with the earlier mentioned concentrations of digital and non-handloom and handicraft creative industries. Some other significant clusters of handloom and handicraft are Srinagar and adjoining districts, Lucknow-Chandigarh belt, Varanasi-Azamgarh-Mirzapur region, Mumbai-Thane region, Kolhapur-Belgaum-Bagalkot region, Karimnagar-Warangal region, Andhra Pradesh and Northern Tamil Nadu, Coimbatore-Salem region, Thiruvananthapuram and Tirunelveli region, coastal Odisha, and Assam Valley. These regions have significant concentrations of workers engaged in handloom and handicraft industries. As the data for all the handicraft and handicraft industries are clubbed together in the Sixth Economic Survey 2013–14, we are unable to make any distinction as in which industry a particular region specializes in. However, Kolkata is the largest and densest concentration of workers engaged in handloom and handicraft industries while Andhra Pradesh is spatially more expansive region in this context.

6.6 Spatial clustering and impact of digital industries on CIs' localization

The analysis in the previous section of DIs and CIs shows significant spatial concentration and co-locations. This spatial clustering of workers and industries is well-reflected from the significant Moran's I values (Table 6.6). Moran's I values for all the digital industries and workers, except for the workers engaged in manufacturing of computer and peripheral equipment, are statistically significant as 5% level of significance. The Moran's I values for creative industries and workers are also found to be statistically significant at 5% level (Table 6.7). This shows that there are significant spatial clustering of these industries in India.

The data also shows significant co-location of DIs and CIs. That means that they share the same geographies. This co-geography is possible when the industry also shares strong interdependence. Figures 6.6 and 6.7 further prove the strong spatial colocation of digital and creative industries and workers of both industries. Figure 6.6 shows that with the rise of 1 digital industry in a district, the creative industry in that district increases by 0.8, that is almost one-to-one relationship, while Figure 6.7 shows that with an increase of 1 worker in the digital industry in a district the number of workers in creative industries in that district rises by 0.71, again showing a very strong causality.

Table 6.6 Clustering of DIs and workers

Digital industries NIC 3-digit code	*Industries*		*Workers*	
	Moran's I value	*p-values*	*Moran's I value*	*p-values*
261	0.186	0.002	0.134	0.003
262	0.046	0.016	0.003	0.080
263	0.115	0.006	0.064	0.025
264	0.103	0.006	0.065	0.020
267	0.124	0.004	0.087	0.006
268	0.118	0.004	0.001	0.001
611	0.390	0.001	0.238	0.001
612	0.237	0.001	0.023	0.002
613	0.175	0.001	0.034	0.032
619	0.219	0.001	0.238	0.001
620	0.213	0.001	0.269	0.001
631	0.257	0.001	0.280	0.001
639	0.243	0.001	0.127	0.005
951	0.307	0.001	0.288	0.001
Total	0.368	0.001	0.296	0.001

Note and source: As for Table 6.4.

Table 6.7 Clustering of CIs and workers

NIC 3-digit code	*Industries*		*Workers*	
	Moran's I value	*p-values*	*Moran's I value*	*p-values*
581	0.235	0.001	0.206	0.001
582	0.087	0.008	0.019	0.013
591	0.204	0.001	0.251	0.001
592	0.232	0.001	0.179	0.001
601	0.100	0.005	0.073	0.012
602	0.237	0.001	0.171	0.001
711	0.217	0.001	0.034	0.016
731	0.286	0.001	0.349	0.001
732	0.449	0.001	0.443	0.001
741	0.147	0.001	0.118	0.004
742	0.442	0.001	0.387	0.001
823	0.285	0.001	0.266	0.002
900	0.287	0.001	0.329	0.001
910	0.289	0.001	0.329	0.001
932	0.143	0.004	0.218	0.001
H&H	0.402	0.002	0.392	0.001
Total	0.387	0.001	0.276	0.001

Note and source: As for Table 6.4.

From simple causality test as presented in Figures 6.6 and 6.7, we now move to a more rigorous and robust analysis of spatial causality of location from digital industries and workers to creative industries and workers. Table 6.8 shows that

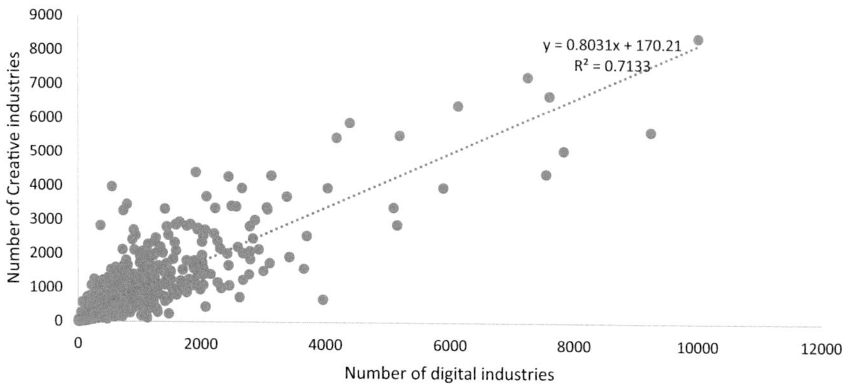

Figure 6.6 Relationship between the number of DIs and CIs in districts of India, 2013–14

Note: Excludes handloom and handicraft industries.

Source: Based on data from Sixth Economic Census of India, 2013–14.

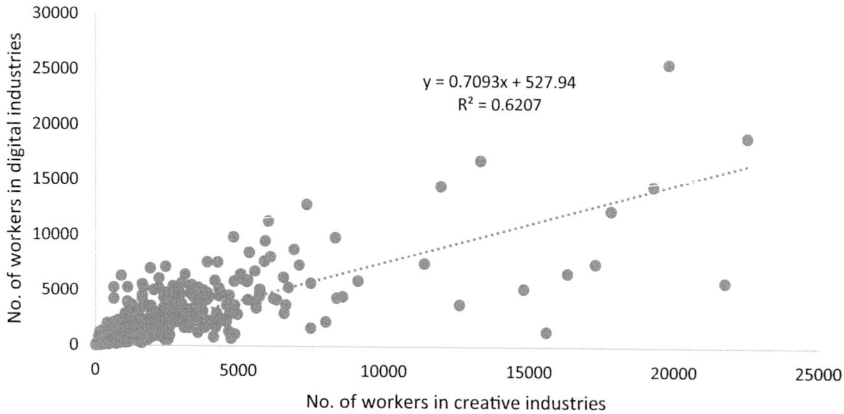

Figure 6.7 Relationship between the number of workers in DIs and CIs in districts of India, 2013–14

Note: 13 districts with very large size of workers in DIs and CIs have been excluded from scatter plot in order to show better distribution of dots in the chart. This excludes handloom and handicraft workers.

Source: Based on data from Sixth Economic Census of India, 2013–14.

the OLS model is not fit due to the spatial autocorrelation, as Moran's I is statistically significant. Among the spatial lag and spatial error models, the spatial error is the robust one as it has the lower Akaike-Information Criterion (AIC). We use AIC for the selection of the best model as lag and error tests have similar values. The result shows that on average with an increase of 1 digital industry in a district, the number of creative industries rises by 0.771 (β_1) in that district. However, it is found that spatial lag values of the digital industry also play a

Table 6.8 Impact of digital industries on creative industries

Parameters	*OLS model*	*Spatial lag model*	*Spatial error model*
α	204.925	−158.185	**188.119**
	(0.000)	(0.001)	**(0.000)**
β1	0.758	0.757	**0.771**
	(0.000)	(0.000)	**(0.000)**
β2	136.379	−266.386	**109.969**
	(0.000)	(0.000)	**(0.0144)**
$\lambda 1$			**0.429**
			(0.000)
$\rho 1$		0.423	
		(0.000)	
R2	0.718	0.762	**0.762**
AIC	9969.070	9888.630	**9887.380**
Moran's I	0.272	–	–
	(0.000)		
LM lag test	116.105	–	–
	(0.000)		
Robust LM-lag test	1.441	–	–
	(0.230)		
LM-error test	115.942	–	–
	(0.000)		
Robust LM-error test	1.278	–	–
	(0.258)		

Source: Computed using data from Sixth Economic Census of India, 2013–14.

significant role in the location of the creative industry in India. This means that the fate of a district's neighbouring district with regard to the location of the digital industry also shapes the fate of that district.

Table 6.9 shows the impact of DI workers on the localization of CI workers. Given that robust LM-lag test is significant, we chose the spatial-lag dependence model. The result shows significant causality from DI workers and lag of digital industry workers to CI workers. Further, the result also shows that the spatial lag of CI workers in a district also shapes the fate of that district with regard to the concentration of CI workers in those districts. Thus, the result points out a spatial process at work with regard to the geographic distribution and localization of CIs and CI workers in India.

The impact of DI is also quite significant on the handloom and handicraft industry (Table 6.10). The spatial error model shows that on average with an increase of 1 digital industry in a district, the handloom and craft industry increased by 1.051, more than 1 in the district, while the impact of spatial lag of digital industry is also quite significant on the location of handloom and handicraft industry. However, the impact of DI workers though statistically significant is not very high on the handloom and handicraft industry workers (Table 6.11). Computation shows that on average with an increase of 1 worker in digital DI, the workers in the district on an average rises by 0.089, a small increase indeed.

Table 6.9 Impact of DI workers on CI workers

Parameters	*OLS model*	*Spatial lag model*	*Spatial error model*
α	1499.050	**897.391**	1483.180
	(0.000)	**(0.000)**	(0.000)
β1	0.214	**0.209**	0.216
	(0.000)	**(0.000)**	(0.000)
β2	1146.270	**533.087**	1456.530
	(0.000)	**(0.030)**	(0.000)
λ	–	**–**	0.295
			(0.000)
ρ	–	**0.279**	–
		(0.000)	
R2	0.555	**0.583**	0.584
AIC	12153	**12123.000**	12121.000
Moran's I (error)	0.156	–	–
	(0.000)		
LM lag test	45.696	–	–
	(0.000)		
Robust LM-lag test	5.967	–	–
	(0.0145)		
LM-error test	41.475	–	–
	(0.000)		
Robust LM-error test	1.746	–	–
	(0.186)		

Source: Computed using data from Sixth Economic Census of India, 2013–14.

Table 6.10 Impact of DIs on handloom and handicraft industries

Parameters	*OLS model*	*Spatial lag model*	*Spatial error model*
α	1788.07	**550.631**	1715.130
	(0.000)	**(0.037)**	(0.000)
β1	1.247	**1.051**	1.222
	(0.000)	**(0.000)**	(0.000)
β2	1966.8	**674.615**	1693.490
	(0.000)	**(0.053)**	(0.000)
λ	**–**	**–**	0.481
			(0.000)
ρ	**–**	**0.480**	–
		(0.000)	
R2	0.183	**0.343**	0.341
AIC	12776.8	**12671.800**	12671.500
Moran's I	0.306	–	–
	(0.000)		
LM lag test	148.629	–	–
	(0.000)		
Robust LM-lag test	1.701	–	–
	(0.000)		

LM-error test	147.183 (0.000)	–	–
Robust LM-error test	0.192 (0.661)	–	–

Source: Computed using data from Sixth Economic Census of India, 2013–14.

Table 6.11 Impact of DI workers on handloom and handicraft workers

Parameters	*OLS model*	*Spatial lag model*	*Spatial error model*
α	6127.120 (0.000)	**2453.520** **(0.000)**	5742.11 (0.000)
β1	0.114 (0.000)	**0.089** **(0.010)**	0.103 (0.003)
β2	1498.480 (0.000)	**636.874** **(0.337)**	1405.940 (0.048)
λ			0.561 (0.000)
ρ		**0.560** **(0.000)**	
R2	0.028	**0.299**	0.297
AIC	14039.7	**13879.100**	13879.000
Moran's I	0.382 (0.000)	–	–
LM Lag test	233.325 (0.000)	–	–
Robust LM-lag test	5.248 (0.022)	–	–
LM-error test	229.275 (0.000)	–	–
Robust LM-error test	1.198 (0.273)	–	–

Source: Computed using data from Sixth Economic Census of India, 2013–14.

6.7 Conclusions

Digital technologies have reshaped the geographies of production, consumption, and distribution of goods and services. Creative industries have also been significantly impacted by it, and, in fact, new production and trade in the sector are largely driven by digital technologies. Not only the content, process, and real-time of production have changed with the penetration of digital technologies, but it has also created new consumers, producers, and tradesmen, and impacted the prices. The geographical concentration of digital technologies and industries has in many ways maintained the production, consumption, and trade of CIs spatially fixed, even as they offer opportunities for content augmentation and the destruction of time and space of consumption, commerce, and prices. The present chapter shows that, in India, there is a strong spatial dependence of creative and digital industries.

The DIs and CIs and workers in the sectors are largely concentrated in clusters. This chapter shows that there are 10 major spatial concentrations of digital and creative industries and workers in India. The handloom and handicraft industry is also largely spatially concentrated, but its clustering does not much coincide with the other creative and digital industries. This case study also shows a strong spatial process at work that co-localizes the digital and creative industries. Spatial econometric models show a strong impact of the digital industry and spatial lag of this on the location of creative industry; and of digital industry workers, spatial lag of digital industry workers, and a spatial lag of creative industry workers itself on the localization of creative industry workers. The similar process and impact of the digital industry and spatial lag of it are seen on the localization of handloom and handicraft industry, but the impact of workers in the digital industry and its lag is not very high on the localization of handloom and handicraft workers. The results indicate that distribution of digital and creative industries in India is spatially very lumpy and digital industry plays a significant role in shaping this spatial lumpiness.

Note

1 The EC captures all the economic establishments in the country "except those involved in crop production and plantation, public administration, defence and compulsory social security, related to production and/or distribution of goods and/or services other than for the sole purpose of own consumption" (Government of India 2016: 5). The EC also excluded illegal activities (like smuggling, gambling, etc.), drivers and domestic servants, and households depending on remittance, rent, interest, pension, etc.

References

Anselin, L. (1988). *Spatial Econometrics: Methods and Models*. Dordrecht, The Netherlands: Kluwer Academic Publishers.

Anselin, L. (1992). *SpaceStat Tutorial: A Workbook for Using SpaceStat in the Analysis of Spatial Data, National Centre for Geographical Information and Analysis*. Santa Barbara, CA: University of California.

Anselin, L., and Bera, A. K. (1998). Spatial dependence in spatial regression model with an introduction to spatial econometrics. In Ullah, A. and Giles, D. E. (eds.), *Handbook of Applied Economic Statistics*. New York: Marcel Dekker.

Arora, P., and Vermeylen, F. (2012). The end of the connoisseur? Experts and knowledge production in the visual arts in the digital age. *Information, Communication and Society*, 16(2), 194–216.

Boix, R., Lazzeretti, L., Cappone, F., and Sánchez-Serra, D. (2012). The geography of creative industries in Europe: Comparing France, Great Britain, Italy and Spain. In Lazzeretti, L. (ed.), *Creative Industries and Innovation in Europe. Concepts, Measures and Comparative Case Studies*. London: Routledge.

Brand, S. (1988). *The Media Lab: Inventing the Future at MIT*. New York: Penguin Books.

Cooke, P., De Laurentis, C., Tödtling, F., and Trippl, M. (2007). *Regional Knowledge Economies*. Cheltenham: Edward Elgar.

Cooke, P., and Lazzeretti, L. (Eds.) (2008). *Creative Cities, Cultural Clusters and Local Economic Development*. Cheltenham, London: Edward Elgar.

Culkin, N., and Randle, K. (2006). Digital cinema: Opportunities and challenges. *Convergence: The International Journal of Research into New Media Technology*, 9(4), 79–98.

Cybermedia News (2007, 16 January). Bollywood movies go mobile. *Cybermedia India Online Limited*. Available at: www.ciol.com/ciol-techportal/Content/Mobility/News/2007/20701161144.asp (last accessed on 25 March 2022).

Fearon, D. (2002). Alfred Weber, theory of the location of industries, 1909. *CSISS Classics*. UC Santa Barbara, Center for Spatially Integrated Social Science. Available at: https://escholarship.org/uc/item/1k3927t6 (last accessed on 25 March 2022).

Florida, R. (2002). *The Rise of the Creative Class*. New York: Basic Books.

Florida, R. (2008). *Who's Your City?: How the Creative Economy Is Making Where You Live the Most Important Decision of Your Life*. New York: Basic Books.

Florida, R., Mellander, C., and Qian, H. (2008). *Creative China? The University, Human Capital and the Creative Class in Chinese Regional Development*. CESIS Electronic Working Paper Series.

Gardiner, B., Martin, R., and Tyler, P. (2011). Does spatial agglomeration increases national growth? Some evidence from Europe. *Journal of Economic Geography*, 11, 979–1006.

Glaeser, E., Kallal, H., Scheikman, J., and Shleifer, A. (1992). Growth in cities. *Journal of Political Economy*, 100, 1126–1152.

GMCA (2016). *Deep Dive: 04 – Digital and Creative Industries*. Manchester, UK: Government of the UK.

Government of India (2016). All India Report of Sixth Economic Census. Ministry of Statistics and Programme Implementation, Central Statistical Office, New Delhi.

Hanning, R. (1990). *Spatial Data Analysis in the Social and Environmental Sciences*. Cambridge: Cambridge University Press.

Hanson, G. H. (2000). Firms, workers, and the geographic concentration of economic activity. In Clark, G., Gertler, M. and Feldman, M. (eds.), *Handbook of Economic Geography*, pp. 477–496. New York: Oxford University Press.

Helsley, R. W., and Strange, W. C. (1990). Matching and agglomeration economies in a system of cities. *Regional Science and Urban Economics*, 20(2), 189–212.

Henderson, J. V. (1988). *Urban Development: Theory, Fact and Illusion*. London: Oxford University Press.

Hoover, E. M. (1937/1971). *Location Theory and the Shoe and Leather Industries*. Cambridge, MA: Harvard University Press.

Iyengar, R. (2017, 28 September). India poised for smartphone revolution. Available at: http://money.cnn.com/2017/09/26/technology/india-mobile-congress-market-numbers/index.html (last accessed on 25 March 2022).

Khan, D. (2018, 22 February). 4G LTE captures 82% of India's overall mobile data traffic in 2017: Nokia. Available at: https://telecom.economictimes.indiatimes.com/news/4g-lte-captures-82-of-indias-overall-mobile-data-traffic-in-2017-nokia/63029086 (last accessed on 25 March 2022).

Krugman, P. R. (1980). Scale economies, product differentiation and the pattern of trade. *American Economic Review*, 70, 950–959.

Krugman, P. R. (1991). Increasing returns and economic geography. *Journal of Political Economy*, 49, 137–150.

Lazzeretti, L., Boix, R., and Capone, F. (2008). Do creative industries cluster? Mapping creative local production systems in Italy and Spain. *Industry and Innovation*, 15(5), 549–567.

Lazzeretti, L., Boix, R., and Capone, F. (2012). Why do creative industries cluster? In Lazzeretti L. (ed.), *Creative Industries and Innovation in Europe: Concepts, Measures and Comparative Case Studies*, pp. 45–64. London: Routledge.

Lim, U. (2003). A spatial analysis of regional income convergence. *Planning Forum*, 9, 66–80.

Marshall, A. (1890/2009). *Principles of Economics*, Unabridged 8th edition. New York: Cosimo Publications.

MOSPI [Ministry of Statistics and Programme Implementation] (2017). Sixth Economic Census Data, 2013–14. Data on CD. Government of India, New Delhi.

Oliver & Ohlbaum Associates and Analysys Mason (2017). *The Impact of the Internet and Digitalization on the European Creative Sector*. North West Wing, Aldwych, London: Bush House.

PricewaterhouseCoopers (2015). The digital future of creative Europe: The impact of digitization and the Internet on the creative industries in Europe. Available at: www.strategyand.pwc.com/media/file/The-digital-future-of-creative-Europe-2015.pdf (last accessed on 25 March 2022).

Quah, D. (1996). Regional convergence clusters across Europe. *European Economic Review*, 40, 951–958.

Rathee, K. (2017, 15 June). India likely to have 520 million 4G subscribers by 2022: Ericsson. *Business Standard*. Available at: www.business-standard.com/article/companies/india-likely-to-have-520-million-4g-subscribers-by-2022-ericsson-117061401010_1.html (last accessed on 25 March 2022).

Rey, S. J., and Montouri, B. D. (1999). US regional convergence: A spatial econometric perspective. *Regional Studies*, 33, 143–156.

Rosenthal, S. S., and Strange, W. C. (2004). Evidence on the nature and sources of agglomeration economies. In Henderson, V. and Thisse, J. (eds.), *Handbook of Urban and Regional Economics*, Vol. 4, pp. 2119–2172. Amsterdam: North-Holland.

Scott, A. J. (2005). *On Hollywood: The Place, the Industry*. Princeton: Princeton University Press.

Serra, D. S. (2016). Location determinants of creative industries' firms in Spain. *Investigaciones Regionales–Journal of Regional Research*, 34, 23–48.

Shaban, A. (2006). Regional structure, growth and convergence of income in India. *Economic and Political Weekly*, 41(18), 1803–1815.

Stephanie, L., Sharma, R. S., and Ramasubbu, N. (2012). The digitisation of Bollywood: Adapting to disruptive innovation. *Media Asia*, 39(1), 3–16.

Storper, M., and Venables, A. (2004). BUZZ: Face-to-face contact and the urban economy. *Journal of Economic Geography*, 4, 351–370.

Swartz, C. S. (2004). *Understanding Digital Cinema: A professional handbook*. Burlington, MA: Focal Press.

Tschang, T. F., and Vang, J. (2008). Explaining the spatial organization of creative industries: The case of the U.S. Videogames industry. Paper presented at the 25th Celebration Conference 2008 on Entrepreneurship and innovation–organizations, institutions, systems and regions, Copenhagen, CBS, Denmark, June 17–20.

UNCTAD (2010). *Creative Economy Report 2010*. Geneva, Switzerland: UNCTAD.

Upton, G. J., and Fingleton, B. (1985). *Spatial Data Analysis by Example, Vol I: Point Pattern and Quantitative Data*. New York: Wiley.

Vang, J. (2005). *Rethinking the Spatial Organization of Creative Industries*. CIRCLE Electronic Working Paper Series, Paper no. 2005/10.

Vang, J. (2007). The spatial organization of the news industry: Questioning assumptions about knowledge externalities for clustering of creative industries. *Innovation: Management, Policy and Practice*, 9(1), 14–27.

Venables, A. J. (2005). New economic geography. Available at: www.rrojasdatabank.info/newecongeogven05.pdf (last accessed on 25 March 2022).

Wenting, R., Atzema, O., and Frenken, K. (2011). Urban amenities and agglomeration economies?: The locational behaviour and economic success of Dutch fashion design entrepreneurs. *Urban Studies*, 48(7), 1333–1352.

Section III

COMMUNITIES AND CREATIVITY

India is characterized by vast cultural diversity across communities and regions. The chapters in Section III zoom in on particular creative products and related local practices. All contributions provide inspirational insights into the sources of cultural creativity in India. They document the communities that generate, sustain, and cherish various specific creative products. They illustrate the intricate relationship between CCI and religious traditions, social stratification, and remnants of the caste system, as well as generational change. They also discuss the association between specific cultural and creative practices and market institutions. Chapter 7 addresses the snake charming community of Kalbeliya in Rajasthan. Chapter 8 contains a sophisticated study of Mahbubani painting in its wider social context. Chapter 9 focuses on the elderly, who are increasingly engaged in cultural life from dance to music and painting. It discusses how this helps in generating income, support dignified aging, and social participation of older Indians. We hope these case studies provide inspiration and templates for further case studies on the rich and diverse cultural and creative practices in India.

DOI: 10.4324/9781003129370-9

7

THE TRADITIONAL CREATIVE COMMUNITIES OF RAJASTHAN

A case study of Kalbeliyas, the snake charmers and the gypsies of Rajasthan

Ujjwal Dadhich

7.1 Introduction

रे काळ्यो कूद पड्यो मेले में, साईकल पंक्चर कर ल्यायो
हो दो दनि ढब जा रे डोकरयिा, छोरी म्हारी बाजारयिों काढ़
रे बाजा बाज रया डूंगर में, छोरी तने लेबालो आयो.

– Local version of a Kalbeliya song

Kalyo has fallen in carnival, punctured his cycle
Two days be patient old lady, my girl has gone to market
Music band is played in hills; girl will be taken to her in-laws.

– Translated version of Kalbeliya song

Visit to the State of Rajasthan is incomplete if one has not heard the *Kalyo Kood Padyo* song. The famous song is frequently played in taxis, public places, radio, and fairs. The song lyrics are humorous where a mother talks about her son-in-law who is coming to receive her daughter after marriage. Many such songs centred around marriage, relationships, seasons, and materialistic desires are quite common in Rajasthani local dialects. What enriches these songs are the amusing lyrics and the dance moves which are performed on them. The community which is mainly known for such song composition and acrobatic dance are the Kalbeliyas which is the focus of the present chapter.

Kalbeliyas are an indigenous tribe of the Rajasthan. They are considered as socially outcastes. Kalbeliyas along with Bopas are the only two surviving gypsy tribes in the country. Kalbeliyas follow Hinduism and are descendants of the Romani artisans who emerged in Rajasthan during 3000 BCE (Snodgrass 2016). They are native to the regions of Jaisalmer, Barmer, Jodhpur,

DOI: 10.4324/9781003129370-10

Ajmer, and Jaipur. Traditionally, Kalbeliyas are non-pastoral nomadic tribes and are identified by the unique profession of their men, who hypnotize cobra with their *pungi or been* (wind instrument). Based on their snake charming act, Kalbeliya men are popularly known as *saperas* (snake charmers) or *Jogi Naths* (Jogi = yogi, Naths = sorcerer) or cobra gypsies in modern India (Robertson 1998).

While men perform snake charming tricks, Kalbeliya women, also known as *Jogins (yoginis)*, go on *pheri*, i.e. door-to-door roaming to beg for food, clothes, and money while singing self-composed songs. These self-composed songs have a rich oral history as they are passed from one generation to another. Alongside singing, women also perform dance manoeuvres which typically resemble snake movements and involve acrobatics.

Changing social-economic conditions, the Wildlife Protection Act, 1972, and the development of other means of entertainment have negatively affected this community's traditional profession. Snake charming is neither legally permissible anymore nor a sustainable economic activity for livelihood. Also, door-to-door singing and begging are viewed as a downgraded social activity by younger generations. The younger ones in the community have therefore taken up mainstream economic activities while many still play musical instruments in social gatherings.

The shift in livelihoods and cultural activities has created a knowledge gap between younger and older generations. Middle and older people, both men and women, are relatively well-versed with the details and nuances of performing acts. It is their knowledge and sustained efforts that have preserved the community's ethnic heritage over time.

Recognizing the creative efforts of the community to preserve and evolve its culture, UNESCO in 2010 included Kalbeliya folk songs and dances in its Representative List of the Intangible Cultural Heritage of Humanity. The present chapter discusses these traditional art forms of the community, its various elements, and evolution which has shaped Kalbeliyas' unconventional and rich cultural life.

7.2 Data and methodology

This chapter has two broad objectives. The first is to examine the community background and its cultural beliefs, and the second is to discuss the details of their performing arts – snake-charming, self-composed songs, musical instruments, and dance moves.

The discussion present in the chapter is an outcome of detailed qualitative fieldwork with eight Kalbeliyas and their families intermittently from March to October 2018 in Bhilwara (Rajasthan) and Gurgaon (Haryana). The discussions helped to gain in-depth ideas of the everyday life of community members, their beliefs, the importance they place to the art, and details of their artistic acts. Additionally, informal interactions were also done with a few non-community members and tourists who have interacted with Kalbeliyas in the past or/and have witnessed their performance.

7.3 Snake charming – the identifying act of Kalbeliyas

> Ramath Sa ka naam 100 gaavo mein chalta tha . . . mere pardada the aur unke jaisa sapera aaj tak nahi ssuna . . . . darbaar mein raja maharaja bhi unke kartab dekhke ke stabdh ho jaate . . . 20 ft ke naago ko kaabu karte the . . . unke jaisi dhun aur kartab koi na dikha paaya.
>
> – Mahendra (72 years)

> Ramnath's name was famous across 100 villages . . . he was my great grandfather and there has not been a snake charmer like him . . . even kings and royal members of the court were amazed with him . . . he used to tackle 20 ft long cobra snakes . . . nobody has been able to play tone like him or show such skills.
>
> – Translated version

Remembering his great grandfather, Mahendra exaggerates the galore of snake charming in old days. His eyes glitter when he remembers age-old tales, talks about his great grandfather, and recalls the pride of his family in performing at royal courts. As per Mahendra, "those were the old times when saperas used to tackle even 20 ft cobras but now there are neither such long snakes nor masters like my grandfather . . .".

To acquire mastery over snake charming, one must learn the art and science of *been* making, playing it, and reacting spontaneously to snake's movements. All three activities require years of practice and patience to master. Among the three, the steppingstone is *been* making. *Been* also known *pungi* is a creative innovation comprising a hollow bulged surface at the middle and a long opening at one end. The bulged surface and opening are made from dried bottle gourd. A single or two reed or bamboo pipes are then inserted from another end. One of these pipes has holes that helps to modulate air movement with fingers just as in the case of a flute. The honey wax paste is spread at the joint of the bulged surface and rods to avoid any air leakage.

As the Kalbeliya regulate air movement with *been*, a distinctive sound is produced, probably due to the large, bulged surface and material used. The *been* sound needs no introduction and soon gathers an inquisitive crowd. To an outsider watching the snake charming act, *been* seems to be a magic wand that helps in enchanting snakes. Contrary to the deception, snake movement is regulated not by *been* but by hand and body movement of Kalbeliyas. As snakes do not have ears, they move in response to the vibrations around them. Therefore, when a Kalveliya plays been (pungi) and moves both of his hands in a whirling circle and up-side-down, it is these movements that cause a snake to react and move.

The degree to which a snake moves and reacts also depends on their behavioural attributes. Kalbeliyas classify snakes as *nugra* and *sughria* (Robertson 1998). The former is of fierce nature, repeatedly makes *hiss* sound in retaliation, and does not submit easily. The latter is calm and generally bows down easily to training. Kalbeliyas generally perform with nugra snakes in festivals as the encounter is thrilling for the crowd and makes more money. To have better money prospects, many Kalbeliyas have also moved to tourist cities over time. Foreigners enjoy this bizarre entertaining act and give a good amount as a token of respect and enjoyment. For Kalbeliyas anything from a foreigner is a memory to recapitulate and showcase to others. They, therefore, decorate their *beens* with coins and trinkets given by foreigners

Before performing the snake charming act, Kalbeliyas must first make the snake docile. For this purpose, the wild snake after being caught is kept in a cane or bamboo basket for a period of 5 to 15 days. The captive period in a small space does not allow the snake to move, reduces its agility, and makes it lethargic. The venom fangs of the snake are also removed before keeping it in captivity. Whether this removal is temporary or permanent is debatable (Angelillo 2013). The snake is fed milk, water, egg, etc. through hollow bones or/and pipes being inserted through its mouth. Many snakes are not able to cope with changing environments and die within 5–10 days. Those which survive then became passive and familiar with regular Kalbeliya activities. Nirmala (60 years), a resident in Rajasthan, recalls her childhood Kalbeliya experience:

> *I still remember I was 20 years old and was spending the summer holidays at my maternal grandmother's house. A 8–10 ft cobra entered our house and a sapera was called to catch it . . . . The sapera played his pungi for around 20–30 min but could not find the snake. He then tied ghungroo i.e. anklet bells on the pungi and started playing pungi while anklet bells ring continuously. The snake came in another 15 minutes . . . The Kalbeliya then told that he put ghungroo because the vibrations make the snake feel that the female snake is nearby which excites it. The sapera then made the snake dance for about an hour and being completely exhausted, the snake was then guided easily to a cane basket.*

The Kalbeliyas do recognize the damage they cause to snakes while subjecting them to hardships, particularly in the capitivity period. To repent, Kalbeliyas then give love and affection to snakes like their other family members and believe that such behaviour will surpass their wrongdoings. In fact, when a snake is caught and brought to the home for the first time, *pooja*, a religious ritual, is performed as snakes are the source of income for the family. Kalbeliyas also vow to release the snake in about two and a half months from the time of capture. The festival of Nagpanchami is of special significance for this community, during which they worship snakes and also release them. Special care of snakes is also taken with seasonal variations. In summer, water is sprinkled on cane baskets and care is taken not to overexpose snakes to scorching heat. In the winter season, during which snakes hibernate, care is taken to ensure their safety and comfort (DownToEarth 2015).

As snakes become familiar with the surrounding environment over time, they then roam around freely in the Kalbeliya premises. Snakes come and go to the cane basket at their will or upon command by the family members which they give by gently striking on the basket. The same touch and soft strike vibration on the basket guides the snake movement during the snake charming act.

Roaming to perform from one place to another, Kalbeliyas generally use a large cloth bag to put cane basket, pungi, and other instruments called *dhapli* and *khanjari*. Both dhapli and khanjari are made of wood from the jackfruit tree and one side of it is covered by the skin of monitor lizard (Khati 1998). While *dhapli* is a small hand drum, *khanjari* is larger in size and both are used alongside singing and dance performances.

7.4 About Kalbeliyas – etymology and religious affiliation

It is uncertain how the word Kalbeliya originated or what it means. Some believe that Kal means death and beliya means who control, i.e. one who controls death by commanding snakes. Some others believe that kal means black and beliya refers to catchers, i.e. one who catches snakes. Additionally, Kalbeliyas are also referred to as black sorcerers (kal = black + beliya = sorcerer) who with their meditation and hymes '*mantras*' drive away evil spirits and cure diseases. Bhagchand (54 years) recalls his medical experience with one Kalbeliya:

> *I recall, it was a Kalbeliya man . . . around 25 years ago, one of my son who was 4 years old suffered from high pneumonia fever. The medicine that we gave was not having much effect and the city hospital was around 2–3 hours away with bad roads. On a suggestion from known persons, we called a Kalbeliya man for treatment. He brought some needles of a porcupine, dried faeces of elephant and some other things. He then lit the mixture and my son was exposed to the smoke of the mixture . . . my son's high fever became less and eventually after two-three such exposures in a week, it was gone . . . I think finding such Kalbeliyas would be difficult now and also people will not be willing to undergo such treatment citing it non-scientific . . . but I have witnessed it and believe that they help people with their hymes and traditional knowledge.*

Kalbeliyas belong to Nath Sampradaya (Mallinson 2011) who are worshippers and followers of Lord Shiva. Lord Shiva referred to as *maha yogi* (greatest saint) is the creator and destroyer of the world and is the supreme God. The ideas of Nath Sampradaya are based on the teachings of influential guru Goraksanatha, who is considered to be the incarnation of Lord Shiva during the 12th century.

The Nath sect combines ideologies of Shaivanism, Buddhism, and Yoga, particularly hath yoga, where the body is transformed to higher spiritual levels by practicing hardships over a longer duration.

The Nath sect is further subdivided into *panths* (paths or ways), each of which is led by different idols, *gurus*. Kalbeliyas belong to *pa panth* led by great *siddha yogi*[1] Kanipa. Kanipa is the son of Shiva and is mythologically believed to be born from his ear (Robertson 1998). Kanipa is believed to sit on Mount Kailash along with Lord Shiva. He is also cited to be the initial disciple of Goraksanatha according to Goraksavijaya. However, as legends go, Kanipa once disobeyed Goraksanatha. In return, the guru cursed him to carry poisonous snakes and beg for money (Angelillo 2013). Another story states that Lord Shiva once tested all his disciples and offered Kanipa a bowl of poison. Kanipa exhibiting faith in Shiva drank the entire bowl. Impressed by his faith and dedication, Lord Shiva blessed him and his descendants with a unique occupation where they would have control over poison and poisonous creatures and could also beg without shame. Since then, Kalbeliyas are believed to be abiding instructions of Lord Shiva to protect people and have dominion over poisonous creatures.

Furthermore, paying reverence to Lord Shiva, Kalbeliyas imitate some of his physical features. This includes having large split ears, *kanphata*, decorated by earrings and wearing a garland of *vauki naga*, deadly cobra. Kalbeliyas also wear a necklace of rudraksha seeds to please Lord Shiva. Rudraksha, etymologically signifying tears or eyes of Lord Shiva, are worn to attain concentration, courage, and calmness which are fundamental for any ascetic. Bheru Nath (56 years) expresses his devotion for Lord Shiva:

> *hum sab uske ansh hai . . . uska na koi ant hai . . . woh tto anant hai.*
>
> – Original version

> *We are all his parts . . . he has no end . . . he is infinity in himself.*
>
> – Translated version

Alongside these sacred ornaments, Kalbeliyas wear an ochre or orange turban, a robe, and carry a stick on their shoulder. One end of the stick, snake basket is tied and the other end carries clothes and alms they have gathered. Kalbeliyas agree that a traditional appearance attracts more crowds and thereby more money.

Although widely known for snake charming, Kalbeliyas have sought other livelihood activities that include basket making, stone grinding, catching snakes from homes, selling traditional herbal medicines, sand trade, surma or kajal stone, etc. The younger generations consider snake charming to be thrilling but refuse to practice it as a livelihood activity as it involves begging. They are more interested in other activities which can be respectful and monetarily rewarding.

7.5 Folk songs

बाटड़ल्यां थांरी जोवती, म्हारी आंखड़ल्यां दनि रात
आवो म्हारा साएबा, तो कोई करल्यां मनड़े री बात.

– Local version of a Kalbeliya song

Waiting for you, my eyes are opened day and night
Come, my dear, then we can talk through our heart.

– Translated version of Kalbeliya song

Kalbeliyas compose songs while observing environment, society, and relationships, and changing social dynamics over time. As Kalbeliyas are mainly confined to western Rajasthan, most of these songs enumerate regional geography, physical features, culture, and everyday life and are dedicated to local gods. What makes these songs special are the rhyming words and usually the high pitch tome in which these are sung. Few of the famous Kalbeliya songs are around *rohiro* which is the local tree, *amal* which is illegal opium grown in the region, *kangasiyya* which is a decorative wooden comb and is given during farewell ode to bride, local sweet dishes of *labsi and halwa made* of wheat, ghee and moong dal, *odhni* which is a medium size cloth used to cover head and face, and *ghagra* which is a traditional Rajasthani women attire similar to flaked skirt and a top etc. One can therefore find Kalbeliya songs around almost every aspect of life, emotions, and day-to-day objects. All these together reflect the observational and articulation skills of the community.

Most of the Kalbeliya songs are composed and sung by women. As such, they involve a central woman character who is narrating a story or/and expressing her feelings in a particular situation. Robertson (1998: 260) well captures these elements of women's songs as follows:

> Women relatives sing songs in admiration of the groom, extolling his virtues, his good looks, and the prestige the bride will gain by marrying their boy. They also sing admiringly about the boy's relatives. Folk and film music is played and sung.

Both Kalbeliya men and women generally have low literacy levels and therefore all the composed songs are orally transmitted from one person to another and through generations. Such an effective oral transmission is not because that community members sit and learn with each other but mainly because songs are a part of daily lives for women. They whisper lines during their everyday chores and regular conversations. Some of these become songs when lines become paragraphs by either an individual or collective contributions. Also, songs are an expression of both happiness and sadness, and means of leisure for them. With these activities and embedded culture, Kalbeliya women seem to be both natural lyricists and perfect singers.

Like men, Kalbeliya women also roam around from door to door, asking for alms while singing. Usually, these women are in groups of 2–3 and may even be accompanied by male children for their security. While begging, women groups may also split in the neighbourhood and ask alms individually. Standing on the main gate of houses, they then call the residents while singing songs, giving good wishes, and predicting fortunes. Calling residents from outside of the house makes women speak and sing at high pitches. As such, high pitch singing became a natural behaviour among the community members. Also, as women usually sing in groups, they demonstrate a perfect chorus together. While one could recognize different voices, one can also recognize the symmetry and timing that they together have. Claps and hand pinches are also used to create distinctive sounds in between. But unlike men who also perform at public places, women don't sing and beg at public places on ordinary days. Gita (32 years) recalls her childhood memories concerning Kalbeliya women:

> *Around 12–15 years back, Kalbeliya women used to come almost once in 12–15 days They used to sing for around 5 minutes and people used to give them food, flour and clothes. Now I rarely see them, may be twice in a year at Nagpanchami and Holi, don't know why, maybe younger generation does not beg and do some other work or maybe I wish their financial condition has improved over time or maybe they have gone somewhere else. Lots of possibilities.*

Women as narrated by Gita usually come to beg on festivals of *Nagpanchami, Holi, and Mahashivratri.* On other days, they can be seen begging outside goddess temples on a regular basis. They generally put a stone idol (Higgins 2010: 91–129) or decorate a small picture in a cane basket or steel bowl to beg. As pilgrimage sites have a huge influx of tourists on an everyday basis, begging at these places assures a greater income. Household begging on the other hand offers limited income and is equally physically tiring. But on occasions of Nagpanchami and Holi, people are usually at home spending family time. Also, these festivals have cultural significance, and giving alms is considered to be a holy deed. As such, begging at the house doorstep is economically beneficial during these festivals.

Begging in the name of God made women compose many devotional songs. Like women, men have also been involved in composing and singing devotional songs. They usually participate and even perform during *Jagran* which are devotional nights to deities. This according to community members is not an exceptional quality as everyone expresses their feelings and prays to gods and goddesses. Singing songs, men also play pungi, khanjari, dhapli, manjira, and khartal (the latter two are percussion instruments) which add music to the words and voice modulations. Community members, particularly men, also acknowledge that their engagement in songs and music became more prominent as the Wildlife Protection Act, of 1972 prohibited snake catching. Community members then practiced music and dance in all solemnity and made those their supreme means of survival.

Kalbeliya songs represent a community culture that kept on improving as per changing social-economic conditions. However, despite the originality and creativity, Kalbeliya songs were not recognized legitimately as an important cultural capital for long. Residents of the regions viewed Kalbeliya activities including songs, music, and snake charming to be mere means to beg. And begging was seen in relation to the community's low position in the social hierarchy. As such, the entire community and their activities were seen in stereotypical ways. The recognition of the community's songs and music first came with appreciation from foreigners who came as tourists. As more and more global visitors witnessed the community's lifestyle and culture, wrote about it, the community songs and music were then legitimately included under the folk category.

7.6 Dance, acrobatic moves, and attire

This is my third trip to Rajasthan and this is the second time I will be visiting to see Kalbeliya dance. The dance is a treat to watch.

– Views of a foreign tourist

One of the most important cultural heritage of Kalbeliyas for which they are now renowned globally is their dance. The dance is performed by women who demonstrate flexibility, vigour, and charisma through their acrobatic moves. The dance manoeuvres are inspired by snake movements, thereby leveraging community's traditional knowledge of snakes. Bherunath (54 years) explains:

We know only about snakes, so our dance also uses this knowledge. How a snake rises, sits, how a snake moves forward, backward, sideways . . . these are the fundamental steps in our dance.

Imitating snakes, women perform torso, hand, and body movements barefoot. These movements start at a slow tempo and the pace increases as one proceeds into the performance. An alluring aspect of this dance is the bending and circular movement of the dancer at an unbelievable speed which is complemented by the dress and make-up of the performer. A foreign tourist recalls his experience of Kalbeliya dance as here:

The dance is a treat to watch . . . it is full of energy, speedy wrist, hand, hip and body movements which are combined with fast footwork as per the music . . . I think those women are made of extraordinary flexible bones.

– Views of a foreign tourist

As acrobatic moves consume energy and are tiring, usually two or more dancers perform together. This allows women to swap positions during the performance and alternatively execute the tiring steps. Sometimes a male dancer, called *faqir*, also performs with a woman (Joncheere 2017). The duo performs romantic and comedy songs that sound humorous to audiences. Unlike women, *faqir* does not perform acrobatic moves but rather complements the performance through expressions, body language, and basic hand and footsteps.

A notable aspect of Kalbeliya dance is that it is not rehearsed. Dancers perform it spontaneously on the music being played by men. This demonstrates the familiarity and perfectionism that women have in responding to the music with their steps. However, public performances, particularly dance, were not appreciated locally and also within the local community. In fact, women dancers who used to perform in public for money were equated with prostitutes (Joncheere 2017, 2015). Such a mindset changed once the dance was recognized globally and together with it also brought economic benefits.

In addition to dance moves, women's attire, jewellery, and make-up are also an ecstasy for the viewers. Their dress consists of an *angrakhi* (blouse or top), *ghahgra* (a skirt like lower wear), and *odhani* (stoll used to cover head with pins and goes up till lower torso). All these are made of black cotton which women generally stitch and sew by themselves. The use of black colour is to reproduce the image of cobras. It is not clear whether black was the original colour that women used to dress during performances. An important difference here to be noted is that men wear a saffron colour dress as they do snake charming but women do not while dancing. Bherunath (56 years) explains the difference as follows:

> *Saffron is the colour of jogi, it is a scared colour that signifies ascetism . . . men wear it during snake charming as they beg for alms . . . even women can wear it asking for alms . . . but during dance women don't wear it as they are not begging . . . they are doing it for money.*

Making the plain black dress attractive, women do patch, tassel, and lacework on their dress and embellish it with small mirrors, silver lattice, and embroidery. Largely the decorative work is done on angrakhi and ghagra. Odhanis with the smaller surface area have wide decorated borders with no or relatively less patchwork in the middle. Angrakhi can be short or long sleeve. Depending on the sleeve length, women wear armlets and bangles, the latter stretch up to the lining of their sleeves. One can therefore see 10–12 bangles worn by women in the case of short sleeve angarakhis. The circumference of these bangles increases from wrist to shoulder area.

Apart from bangles, women also join colourful hanging thick threads with a *buta* (braided lump of cloth) around their elbow at angarakhi's sleeve. Such hanging threads are also joined at the waist and back. When women dance, these threads create a vibrancy of colourful display as dancers swirls and turn around at a dynamic speed. Mary (36 years), an attendant of Kalbeliya dance, narrates her observation:

> *The dress, the moves, make-up, everything is so detailed . . . everything has a significance to create a positive atmosphere. From top to bottom you will see vivid colours on black base and artefacts all shining to catch the viewer's eye.*

With decorated dress, Kalbeliya women usually wear silver, pearl, and bead work jewellery. Their ornaments are in line with regional Rajasthani culture. It consists of *maang-tika*, a head ornament worn in the upper part of forehead; a silver ring type and matted bead necklace; *kamar bandh*, waist chain which shines and dazzles during dance; nose ring, anklets, and dangling earrings. Citing ornaments an important desire, Kalbeliya women have composed a number of songs urging their fiancé or husbands to bring jewellery for them. Additionally, women put *kajal or surma* in eyes, bright coloured lipstick, a prominent *bindi* on forehead, and make-up on face to enhance their features.

> Jab mein jau bazaar mein, chahu chudi or kamarbandh
> Thhe motorcycle pe aajo aur diaaljo mane cheez manapasand.
> – excerpts from Meera (20 years)

> When I go to market, I want bangles and waist chain
> You should come on motorcycle, buy things which I want.
> – translated version

Women are the main actors in Kalbeliya dance. But equally important are men who play musical instruments during the performance. Male musicians usually sit in a horizontal line or semi-circle and play an array of musical instruments that provide tempo to women to which she frisks her movements. The music is predominantly provided by playing *been* and the act personifies the snake charming. Other instruments like dholak (another percussion instrument), harmonium, khanjari, morchang, dafli, and khuralio are also played and they together create a wistful, playful, and a seductive atmosphere. Alongside musicians, sometimes women folk singers also accompany the group. Their high-pitch singing further entwines vocal and instrumental music with live performance.

To maintain audience attention and thrill, a lot of modifications and improvisations have been made in dance. This includes women balancing pots on their heads while dancing, picking up money from the floor with the mouth, picking rings with eyelids, dancing on broken glasses, dancing with swords and blades, etc. On the one hand, these additions exhibit the creative aspects of the community; on the other hand, it presents the necessity on part of the community to innovate for livelihoods. With these innovations, Kalbeliya women have earned global recognition with their dance and music.

7.7 Conclusion

Kalbeliyas are the creative community that has conserved its cultural heritage over time. The cultural capital of the community includes snake hypnosis, rich oral traditions, and dance which has gained global recognition. Each of these activities involves age-old traditions in practicing and doing innovations to improve it further. While snake charming is now practiced on a small scale, songs and dances are being performed mainly in tourist areas. However, the youth does not practice these activities as the main source of livelihood anymore. Being seen as socially derogatory, men have now taken up informal jobs which ensure regular and higher income. Women, on the other hand, do continue these legacies at the household levels in their daily lives and only a few get a chance to perform at the national and international stage. Through these activities, women in the community play the leading role in conserving and continuing the community's customs. Practicing beliefs and customs, Kalbeliyas exhibit a distinctive cultural adherence which has been widely acknowledged in recent times and has been able to improve the economic well-being of the community as well.

Note

1 Siddha yogis are the ones who have given up worldly desires, knows to channelize their energy by having command over the seven chakras and five elements that make all of us.

References

Angelillo, M. (2013). Rethinking resources: Service Nomadism adjusted. *Communication and Culture Online*, Special Issue 1, 79–95.

DownToEarth (2015, 7 June). Charming no more. Available at: www.downtoearth.org.in/coverage/charming-no-more-12843

Higgins, C. (2010). *Charming Images of History: Kalbeliya Memories of Itinerancy, Begging, and Snake Services*. Master's Thesis, Masters of Arts, Arts Department, Cornell University, Ithaca.

Joncheere, A. (2015). Intangible inventions: The kalbeliya gypsy dance form, from Its creation to UNESCO recognition. *Archiv Orientální*, 83(1), 71–93.

Joncheere, A. (2017). Kalbeliya dance from Rajasthan: Invented gypsy form or traditional snake charmers' folk dance? *Dance Research Journal*, 49(1), 37–54.

Khati, A. S. (1998). *National Parks Of India*. Noida: Pelican Creations International.

Mallinson, J. (2011). *Nāth Sampradāya*. Leiden: Koninklijke Brill NV.

Robertson, M. (1998). *The Kalbelias Of Rajasthan: Jogi Nath Snake Charmers*. Michigan: Illustrated Book Publishers.

Snodgrass, M. E. (2016). *The Encyclopedia of World Folk Dance*. Maryland: Rowman & Littlefield Publishers.

8

CAUGHT IN THE WHEELS OF COMMERCE? THE COMMERCIALIZATION OF MADHUBANI PAINTING IN INDIA

Filip Vermeylen and Bhagyalakshmi Daga

8.1 Introduction

The contemporary Indian art market has been growing over the past couple of decades. This is said to be fuelled by both a robust economy and the exponential growth of a new demographic of art buyers – the expanding middle class. Stakeholders in the art market now cater to these new affluent buyers with carefully developed artistic interests. These collectors, along with the private and non-profit sector investing in market infrastructure, have altogether contributed to the emergence of an ecosystem that is gaining widespread attention. Indian art is increasingly sought after by collectors both in India and abroad, and more and more contemporary Indian artists are now appearing in international biennials, exhibitions, and fairs (Vermeylen 2015; Komarova 2018; KPMG 2018). India's art market infrastructure is also expanding with the India Art Fair established in capital New Delhi since 2008 and the Kochi-Muziris Biennale in the Southern Indian town of Kochi since 2012. At the same time, India's inclusion in the global art market is also having a visible impact on traditional and folk-art practices.

The arts and crafts sector is said to be particularly sophisticated in India, forming the second-largest source of employment in the country after agriculture (Mohi-ud-din et al. 2014). The case of Madhubani painting gives us an understanding of the impact of globalization and commercialization on a traditional folk art. For years, the women of Madhubani have participated in wall and floor paintings depicting not just spiritual images but also certain rites of passage in Hindu culture, such as marriages, births, etc. It was only in the late 1960s that these wall paintings were transferred to paper and sold nationwide. Today, Madhubani art is witnessing a surge in national and international popularity with a growing demand for diversified products, such as sarees, tiles,

DOI: 10.4324/9781003129370-11

notebooks, etc., all of which can easily be purchased both offline and online. The commercialization of this art form brings a combination of various opportunities and challenges for the different artist clusters in the region. There is little doubt that many families in the Madhubani region depend on their art for their livelihoods. At the same time, one could argue that while globalization and the establishment of a modern style market for the visual arts in India have transformed it into a marketable fine art, the engulfing process of commercialization may be eroding the traditional meanings of this unique expression of Indian folk art and culture.

Fieldwork undertaken by the authors in November 2016 in the two artist villages Ranti and Jitwarpur in Madhubani, in the Northern State of Bihar in India, reveals not just the process and impact of the transformation of this art form and the market on the artists but also the strategies they employ to deal with the increased demand for their work. The authors have visited the homes of 16 artists in both the villages, most of whom either speak the local language Maithili or Hindi to communicate. In addition to in-depth semi-structured interviews and collective discussions that were recorded, direct observations and field notes also aid in this analysis of the Madhubani art market.

The rest of this chapter is organized as follows. Section 8.2 presents an introduction to Madhubani art comprising of a brief history as well as unique characteristics of the traditional art. Section 8.3 explores the discovery and the subsequent transformation of the art form. The process of commercialization of Madhubani art and its implication for the artists as well as the market forms are the focus of Section 8.4. Section 8.5 investigates the role of middlemen who have made themselves all but indispensable in the market, while Section 8.6 evaluates the impact of the digital revolution on the market, and its gradual inclusion in the global art market. Section 8.7 presents a discussion on the role of institutions such as art schools and cooperative societies in protecting artists from exploitation. The final section discusses the transformation of Madhubani art into a near fine arts practice and concludes by posing questions on the possible erosion of traditional meanings attached to this unique expression of Indian art.

8.2 Madhubani art – historical context

Madhubani, a small town and district in the Indian state of Bihar, boasts a rich cultural heritage that goes back over 2,500 years (Kaushik 2019). It is also the home of the traditional art style called Madhubani or Mithila art. In its earliest form, this art served a distinct purpose in the lives of Madhubani dwellers. Essentially, a day-to-day domestic ritual activity, for centuries it was practiced by rural women living in closed societies in the Madhubani region. It is believed that "the original inspiration for Madhubani art emerged out of women's craving for religiousness and intense desire to be one with God" (Madhubani Art Centre 2015: para 13). Based on the earliest references to these artworks dating back to 14th century texts (Mishra 1979), they were originally painted by the women of *Brahmin and Kayasth* (upper) castes on the walls (*kohbar*) and floors (*arpana*) of their houses during auspicious events such as wedding and births.

Vermeylen and Sarkar (2019) describe how the participation in the art practice relates to various rites of passage from birth to death:

> Sathhudi, a ritual observed during the seventh and ninth months of pregnancy; Chatiyar puja, done on the sixth day after the birth of a child; Annaprashan, the child's rice-eating ceremony; Akshararambh, to mark a child's entry into the world of learning; Janaur, to mark the symbolic rebirth of young Brahmin boys and also marriages and deaths. Festivals like Chhath and Chauth Chand are also occasions for practicing this ritual art.
>
> (Vermeylen and Sarkar 2019: 166)

The *arpana* or floor decorations, painted using *arva chawal* (rice) and *sindoor* (vermillion), usually depicted spiritual figures as well as motifs and images from life and nature.

The *kohbar* (Figure 8.1), painted on the walls of the *kohbar ghar* or the nuptial chamber, incorporated symbolic images of the lotus, fishes, birds, turtles, and snakes, to represent union and fertility. According to artist Godavari Dutta, the occasion of Ram and Sita's wedding from the Hindu epic *Ramayan* led to the creation of the *kohbar*, ultimately becoming the symbol of Madhubani art.[1] Initially, the paintings were limited to the walls and floors of mud houses. The process first included a coating of cow dung on walls to ensure absorption of colours, followed by another layer of smoothened mud to flatten out the walls. The colours were naturally prepared, using extractions from different leaves and flowers.

Studies suggest that this folk-art first came to be known to the outside world in the early 1930s following a massive earthquake in Bihar (Rekha 2010; Heinz 2006). The damaged painted walls were discovered by British officer William G. Archer during his inspection of the region. Intrigued by its similarities to the works of Miro and Picasso, he took back several black and white photographs to London which became the first known documentation of this art (Ghosh 2013).

However, it wasn't until the critical drought and consequent famine that struck Bihar in the late 1960s that the exploration and research of Madhubani art officially began, under the orders of then Prime Minister Indira Gandhi. As Ghosh (2013) describes, the agricultural economy of Madhubani was severely crippled and consequently, representatives of the All India Handicrafts Board were sent to the villages as part of a larger initiative to alleviate the acute poverty in the area. For several years, aid worker and artist Bhaskar Kulkarni and his team researched not just the marketability of the art and its potential as a source of income but also strategies that might help bring attention to the artists that needed support and nurturing.

National Awardee Bibha Das recalls her late mother-in-law and master artist Mahasundari Devi as one of the first women to lead the transformation of Madhubani art.[2] In spite of the stringent *purdah* (veil) customs – a form of female segregation that prevented women from communicating with outsiders or possessing an occupation outside of the domicile – she was encouraged by Kulkarni to replicate her wall compositions on the handmade papers and colours he provided. Ultimately Kulkarni went on to inspire scores of women in the villages to do the same, periodically selling their paintings all over the country and providing the women with a steady source of income. As Gita and Arun Wolf (2015: 65) highlight, state interventions such as these "turned a household practice into a vivid art form that was commercially viable".

8.3 Madhubani art – a transformation

As illustrated earlier, the very first steps towards the commercialization of this art form were taken in the 1960s. The transfer of wall paintings to paper had vast consequences for Madhubani and its inhabitants. Heinz (2006: 18) explains this slow detachment and transformation of the art by from its traditional meanings to an artistic product as Kulkarni "created a class of artists, consciously attempted to professionalize them and successfully turned some into international celebrities". Heinz further states that not only had this attempt to bring economic relief to the poverty-stricken region of Bihar been successful in providing formerly segregated women in a patriarchal society with a steady source of income, it was also empowering them to be more independent, take ownership of their art, and live with dignity. At the same time, the growing prestige of Madhubani art started to draw the interests of both national and international buyers, filmmakers, and scholars to a previously overlooked part of Bihar.

Commissioned works for hotels, fairs, as well as in private domains steadily brought attention to these artists (Rekha 2010). Encouragement of artists from all backgrounds through state and national level awards also saw a surge in interest for the art form, especially among international collectors. The foreign currency being increasingly spent in the area did not go unnoticed by the government and private funders, as various schemes, NGOs, and societies such as Gowri Misra's SEWA Mithila and Parampara Project,[3] as well as The Ethnic Arts Foundation by Raymond Owens[4] were set up in collaboration with the artists to develop the art form and set up an outlet for sales.

Madhubani painting has no discernible association to any conventional school of art, and therefore stood out for its raw originality. "Mithila art has its own style, its own identity, its own model . . . it represents something for us" notes Godavari Dutta.[5] Women of Madhubani were not educated, nor possessed any formal art training. The artistic practice, therefore, has been confined to the geographical range of Madhubani and has simply been handed down from mother to daughter, one generation to the next. Wolf and Wolf (2015) illustrate how even when exploring different themes in their works, artists continue to frame their works with traditional borders and patterns in order to keep "a common visual vocabulary alive" (66). Thus, any personal artistry aside, the overall formal art style of Madhubani has remained more or less unchanged.

However, the differences between works become more apparent when the caste system – a social order system in India based on traditional occupations – comes into play. In Madhubani, too, caste-based art styles began to slowly emerge in the 1970s, each caste employing certain unique characteristics, images, and styles in their works (Donier 2009). The paintings from the lower castes (*Dalits*) were considered simpler and less ornate in comparison to the ones from the upper castes (*Brahmins, Kayasthas*). As Berger and Heidemann (2013) describe, most discourses on the art had been limited to the works of upper castes for decades until the visit of anthropologists Erika Moser and Ray Owens to the Dalit village Jitwarpur in the 1970s. Moser encouraged the Dalit women to provide for themselves by creating artworks like the Brahmin and Kayastha women. Unfamiliar with the elaborate styles and images of the upper caste artists, the Dalit women began creating their own style of works inspired by their traditions and lives. Thus, while the Brahmins and Kayasthas focused primarily on religious themes in their paintings, the Dalits allowed themselves a greater freedom of expression by capturing their oral history in their works and illustrating the lives and struggles of their community. Dalit women were persuaded to work on handmade papers and use colours employed exclusively by the upper castes. At the same time, inspired by the growing prestige of the Madhubani art community, a marked gender shift was witnessed with several men also participating in the practice of the art form. As evidenced by field observations and the interviews conducted, this shift has become even more pronounced over time, with an increasing amount of men practicing this art.[6]

Thus, a fascinating development in this earlier process of commercialization has been the organic emergence of the different styles of Madhubani painting such as *Bharni* (color), *Kachni* (line), and *Godna* (tattoo), all of which originated from different castes. While *Bharni* or colour paintings use solid and vibrant colours to fill in enclosed areas, the Kachni or line paintings (Figure 8.2) make use of thin, delicate lines to create patterns (Vermeylen and Sarkar 2019). Godna or tattoo style painting initiated by artist Chano Devi[7] was derived from the simple tattoos that Dalit women had on their arms and legs.

While at first the *Kachni* and *Bharni* style were limited to the upper castes and the *Godna* style to the lower ones, these established demarcations are slowly starting to blur with time, at least for several young Dalit artists who are actively employing the different art styles and merging them with their own (Figure 8.3). These distinctions still seem to exist for the upper caste artists, however. When asked about the merging art styles today in the interviews conducted, some upper caste artists appeared rather affronted, quickly rushing to deny their participation in them,[8] indicating some ongoing tensions within the art community, at least as far as the caste-based art styles are concerned.

8.4 Process of commercialization

Older generation artists could not fully comprehend the economic dimension of their craft, as they lacked entrepreneurial skills. Most artists, even today, take more of a 'wage worker' approach to their activities rather than an entrepreneurial one, whereby they would take the initiative.[9] However, the establishment of various cottage industries and handicrafts organizations in the state was instrumental in selling the artworks through their outlets, popularizing them both nationally and internationally. Several NGOs and organizations such as the *Mithila Art Institute, Mithilasmita, Ethnic Arts Foundation*, and *Jeevika* have contributed towards empowering thousands of artists, by providing them with support, training, and exposure, as well as facilitating nationwide exhibitions and direct sales with buyers.

An area of discourse is the disassociation with the status of 'art' which influences the treatment of the artists' works. The creators often refer to themselves as artisans and not artists, suggesting a divide in how their work is perceived, not just by them but also by the market. Kaushik Jha of Mithila Art Institute finds that the treatment of Madhubani art as a handicraft reduces it to a tradeable decorative commodity, devoid of the unique characteristics usually associated with art.[10] The commercialization of this art form has led to its display and expression on various diversified products, and derivatives of the original Madhubani imagery and prototypes (Figure 8.4). Beginning with the transfer of the wall paintings to handmade papers in the 1960s, the traditional art can now be found on a broad range of products and materials such as sarees, cushion covers, drapes, t-shirts, tiles, jewellery boxes, cups, glasses, notebooks, toys, etc. Such objects make for a more widespread commodity than a painting and increase the range of its uses (Sarkar 2016).

Artists in the village of Ranti assert that the demand for diversified products is substantially more than paper paintings, usually bringing them twice the earnings. Artist Abha Das sells around 12 sarees with Madhubani imagery a year, each fetching her nearly €130, compared to 3–4 large paintings per year for roughly €60.[11] Artists are also hired on commission by the private sector to display visual commentaries and interpretations of themes for events and festivals (for example, Indian spices brand *MDH Masala* commissioning a Rajasthani Holi scene in Madhubani style of painting[12]). Although overall, paper paintings continue to be the largest sellers, the market for diversified products is, without a doubt, developing. Local co-operatives like Shilp Sangh are increasingly involved in this commodification process, encouraging their artists to create new products that possess a distinct market advantage (see later).

8.5 The role of intermediaries

In markets where intermediaries exist due to any sort of market imperfections, situations concerning power imbalances can transpire. Intermediaries like art dealers have been very perceptive in assessing the commercial potential of

Madhubani art, making them all but indispensable in the market. Dealers control the information concerning demand for these goods in distant markets, and are uniquely positioned to organize transport and sales.

Artist village Jitwarpur, which houses most of the artists belonging to lower castes, consists of scores of unregistered artists working from their homes. While official statistics are unavailable on the total number of artists employed in the Madhubani art market, multiple studies have attempted to evaluate the size of the clusters in Madhubani. It is estimated that of the 400 houses in Jitwarpur, approximately 250 houses in Jitwarpur have multiple household members partaking in Madhubani paintings (Ghosh 2013). It is also estimated that in 2015, more than 26,000 workers engaged in the process of production, sales, and promotion of Madhubani art were registered at the Office of the Development Commissioner (Handicrafts) in Madhubani (Jha et al. 2017).

In most households in Jitwarpur village, every family member, from young children to seniors, is involved at some level in producing artworks. A single-family member is often responsible for the entire production process, with other members assisting them at different stages, such as mothers doing the illustrations and outlines while the children colour in. Artists of Jitwarpur primarily work with *Bharni* or colour paintings, which can be produced at a fast rate, especially when the division of labour is applied. There is also hugely demanded in the market because of the rich colours used.

However, based on Godavari Dutta's narrative,[13] as well as the accounts of families interviewed, major obstacles for the artists happens to be uncertainty and information asymmetry. Most artists have little to no connections outside the village to take their paintings around.[14] For example, participation in exhibitions requires access to either national or state government agencies, or financial resources to purchase a spot in them, both of which are severely lacking for the villagers. Furthermore, while several artists had information concerning prices at which the dealers were selling their works, they also reported having no contacts in the larger market, who could be willing to aid in direct sales. Additionally, most of the artists can only properly converse in the local language *Maithili*, not to mention that a majority of artists are women who cannot move out of the village to sell their works, which further limit the sales opportunities for Madhubani artists.

As a result, these artists face many entry barriers which impede access to the market (Figure 8.5). It is therefore no surprise that a large section of the market for *Bharni* paintings from this village is now occupied by a growing horde of middlemen or dealers with a well-connected network of buyers, both within the country and globally. At the same time, the dealers are aware of the different artist families in the villages. "They know us and our work because our mothers and grandmothers . . . are famous. So, they know the houses, the districts, and where we live. That's why they keep coming here to take our works to the cities", comments artist Sheela Devi of Jitwarpur.[15] And while we lack solid evidence to support this claim, it appears that dealers collude rather than compete, in that they tacitly agree which artists will supply a particular dealer, thereby maintaining a stronghold on the market as well as limiting entry of new dealers into the market. These dealers, then, facilitate exchange by buying or commissioning hundreds of paintings every month in bulk, generally for a negligible fixed price for a batch of paintings featuring popular motifs such as the tree of life, and ultimately selling them to bigger buyers in the major cities.[16]

Dealers employ various techniques to ensure and safeguard their position in the market. Primarily, artists are discouraged from signing their works, so as to avoid any future direct contact with the buyers.[17] This further increases the artists' dependence on a steady monthly income from the middlemen. According to artist Runa Das:

> Earlier foreigners would come to the artist's house to buy paintings. Now the hotels they stay in tell them where to buy the paintings from because they have deals with dealers. . . . And other times these dealers even show up at the hotels to make sales.[18]

This observation was echoed by several other artists interviewed as well, which suggests that this may be a common occurrence. Dealers purchasing in bulk also particularly consider works that incorporate repetitive styles, designs, and themes befitting the demands of the urban market. Artist Ranjan Paswan laments that heavy exploitation, often by uncertified middlemen, is rampant, rendering the artists helpless as they settle for poor compensations for their hard work, especially in lean periods.[19] Thus, due to fewer opportunities for direct sales, the market appears to be almost entirely intermediary-driven, instead of customer-driven. In this business model, it is clearly in the best interest of the dealers to separate the end-buyers from the creators, making them all but indispensable.

8.6 The promise of digital revolution and inclusion in the global art market

Some alternatives do exist, however. Media and telecommunication access are less of a challenge for the artists today. While a minority of older established artists rely chiefly on fairs and direct contact with patrons for business, some younger artists make use of social media platforms such as Facebook pages and groups, Amazon, and smaller web portals, such as *eMithilaHaat, mithilapaintings.com, worldofmadhubani.com, madhubaniart.co.in, localqueen.com*, etc., to promote and sell their products. These websites list not just paintings, but a variety of different Madhubani products created by artisans. However, based on anecdotal evidence as well as an analysis of the websites, we ascertain that nearly all platforms tend to solely promote works of established artists. Especially sales on popular Indian e-commerce websites, such as *snapdeal.com, engrave.in, and chumbak.com*, tend to be larger for derivative works and crafts than paintings. Some artists informed us that often works are bought by middlemen or businesses and put up for sale on e-portals, but the artists themselves have no means of addressing these issues.

Some business is also conducted through WhatsApp, where artists communicate with existing buyers and share images of their current works.[20] But it presents little scope in connecting with potential buyers and the practice is not too common. Artist Ranjan Paswan acknowledges that younger artists are more active on social media and "are much further in the race because they can reach their customers directly".[21] In general, artists are not tech-savvy and have not been able to fully take advantage of digital marketing due to a lack of knowledge and training in the matter, ultimately finding themselves disadvantaged due to a lack of direct interface to communicate with their customers. This further illustrates the scope and need for policy intervention.

At the same time, the global interest in the art form has contributed to the growth and recognition of some artists. Vermeylen and Sarkar (2019) elaborate on the apparent increase in the visibility of contemporary Madhubani artists in the art market over the years. Renowned artists such as Dulari Devi, Amrita Jha, and Bharti Dayal participate in yearly exhibitions and fairs across the country. Paintings of the more popular artists have also made it to various museums and exhibitions in France, Germany, and the United States, significantly helping to familiarize the Western audience with this kind of folk art. Godavari Dutta has been instrumental in setting up the Mithila Museum in Niigata, Japan, considered a treasure house with over 15000 paintings.[22] International interest has gradually piqued with not just returning foreign buyers and collectors but also academics and filmmakers such as Ray Owens and Joe Elder, curious about the dynamics of this art form. Despite the surge in popularity, however, the market is restricted to selective fairs and exhibitions in the country for most artists. While the state and national level awardees are invited to special events and exhibitions organized by the government, most artists depend on their own network of intermediaries and returning buyers to sell their works.[23]

8.7 The role of institutions and co-operatives

Some creator-driven initiatives in Madhubani despite, or perhaps due to, the intermediary-driven market situation appear to yield fascinating outcomes. Finding themselves disadvantaged as a result of limited access to their buyers, the people of Madhubani have been resourceful in joining forces in distinct ways to overcome their adversities. In this section, we explore two different models for the provision of skills and resources as well as protection of artists' interests identified in our fieldwork in Madhubani.

8.7.1 The academic approach: Mithila Art Institute

Troubled by the pronounced exploitation of artists, the Ethnic Arts Foundation (EAF) was set up by anthropologist Raymond Owens in 1980 to contribute to the continual development of Madhubani Art, and to ensure these artistic skills are passed on to new generations of artists. Since then, EAF has focused on making the production of original and aesthetic Madhubani artworks an economically viable activity. The Mithila Art Institute (MAI) (Figure 8.6) was consequently set up in the heart of the town of Madhubani, offering free one-year training programmes to support, encourage, and develop new generations of Madhubani artists, irrespective of their castes.[24] The MAI trained over 400 young artists since the founding of the institute in 2003, until it closed its doors in 2019.[25]

Out of hundreds of applicants, 25 students were competitively selected every year. During the first year, training took place for 4 hours every day, and while students did not receive any stipends, they also do not pay any tuition or material fees. Operational costs were covered by the foundation and donors. In essence, MAI aspired to get students motivated to learn to paint out of love and respect for their cultural heritage and not for immediate monetary gains. At the end of each year, a select number of exceptional students were encouraged with scholarships to continue for the second year of advanced training and special projects.[26]

Various master artists were involved in designing the curriculum and teaching at the institute. While the first six months were dedicated towards "the culture and command of traditional Mithila iconography", the last six months allowed students to work on any range of subjects. Kaushik Jha, the Chief Administrator of MAI, asserts that the institute aimed to develop the artistic skills of students, encouraging them to create works that are rooted in tradition while at the same time allowing them to express their original interests and ideas. Ranjit Paswan, a graduate of the programme told us he finds it important to have a unique style and message so his work "stands out in the crowd and interests the public . . . especially when everybody is making the exactly same thing several times".[27]

Students were also taught interpersonal and presentation skills, and networking to establish contact with buyers and ultimately build their brand. Furthermore, the institute also acted as a gallery and an agent for the graduates, with 70% of the revenues from sales going to the students. Thus, the students have a strong incentive to continue producing their best work. In contrast to the works produced in the villages, the paintings were all signed, with small descriptions of the work written by the artists on the back of each painting.[28] As a result, prices for paintings offered for sale through the MAI website were substantially more expensive than the ones which can be purchased in the villages.

Thus, the MAI has been instrumental in the recognition of this art form almost as a fine arts practice. It is important to note, however, that the certificate provided by the institution has not been recognized by any formal educational organization or board. Considering the general preference towards formal education, an uncertified diploma may not have seemed encouraging to students, especially since it is a rigorous programme that runs at the same hours as formal courses in colleges and art academies.

Right until they closed their doors, MAI maintained a strong digital presence; the institute website was frequently updated with hundreds of paintings on display by graduates that could be purchased through any one of the sophisticated digital payment methods.[29] Additionally, MAI promoted engaging content such as exhibitions, artworks, and market and artist news on their Facebook page, enabling a global reach and interaction. Then manager Kaushik Jha stressed the value of hand-made works, but recognized a possible market for digital paintings, believing this could create unique opportunities for the artists. However, the focal point of the institution remained paintings, and deviation from the norm was highly discouraged. Overall, MAI trained artists work primarily in the traditional sense, on paper paintings, wall paintings, or murals. Cloth and other products are just pure business and have nothing to do with art, Kaushik Jha stated.[30] Thus, the focus of MIA was not to operate as a business enterprise but to create value for original Madhubani paintings.

As traditional as the teachings at MIA may seem, it did not stop the artists to experiment with new and contemporary subject matter: graduates presented powerful critiques of contemporary issues in their paintings, ranging from global issues of terrorism to ones more intimately tied to their biographies such as sexism, violence, and poverty. Some even create their own painting styles, while others combine existing ones such as line and colour painting. Consequently, there is a discernable difference in the quality and style of works from graduates compared to the artists of Ranti and Jitwarpur. The works by the MIA artists also tend to be in much better condition due to adequate storage facilities, which are lacking in the villages. Furthermore, the association with MAI and its network provides most graduates with a greater chance to expand their reach and establish themselves as professional artists, as evidenced by their roster of alumni achievements.

The main reason given for the closure of MAI in the Summer of 2019 is the foundation of a Mithila art academy by the state of Bihar: the Mithila Chitrakala Sansthan. This new government-funded institution employs salaried instructors and promises to provide a range of facilities for students and the opening of a museum dedicated to Madhubani art. These are amenities that MAI could not provide as it operated on donations, volunteers, and to some degree on the revenues from the sales of artworks.[31] Bittersweet as it may have been for the staff and students of MAI, the launch of a proper state-run and certified academy also signifies the ultimate recognition of Madhubani art as a part of Indian heritage – something MAI always sought to accomplish.

8.7.2 The commercial approach: Shilp Sangh

Far removed from the academic environment is Shilp Sangh. A co-operative society in the village of Ranti, it comprises 52 women skilled in Madhubani art.[32] Set up with the support of multiple foundations and organizations (such as The Asian Heritage Foundation, Japan Social Development Fund, Jiyo!, and the Bihar Rural Livelihoods Project-Jeevika), Shilp Sangh was established in 2008. The initial investment was provided by Jiyo! and Jeevika. Shilp Sangh has since worked towards providing sustainable livelihoods and ownership to the women of Ranti through their own skills while at the same time promoting the art form. Women are routinely provided with skill development training and mentoring during training sessions held every 3 months. This is done to ensure support for budding artists as well as a constant flow of artisans being brought into the co-operative.

Unlike the individual entrepreneurs in the villages or a training ground like MAI, Shilp Sangh is essentially structured as a democratically operated producer collective (Figure 8.7). There is a centralized core of decision-makers in place (such as an appointed president, secretary, and treasurer), who handle day-to-day management. The women gather to work every day in their outdoor open studio, and hold regular meetings to discuss their orders, payments, and expenses, as well as potential products and markets to explore.

Co-operatives like Shilp Sangh also protect these artists from exploitation from middlemen, helping them by negotiating fair trade prices. Artists have lamented that they were forced to accept the lower prices set by the middlemen who purchased from them until they joined Shilp Sangh. Furthermore, for hundreds of women who aren't allowed to work outside of their home, the economic contribution made by Shilp Sangh helped legitimize the activity of making and selling Madhubani artworks. This has added value to their lives and given them dignified means of providing for themselves.

Shilp Sangh focuses on design-led development, encouraging artists to be creative about producing new works under the traditional art domain that may have a distinct market advantage. They target a lot of their products towards the ever-increasing young/urban markets. This presents the most interesting case of the effects of commercialization. The organization boasts of a wide variety of commodities being produced by the collective. From home furnishings such as cushion covers, curtains, bedspreads, and napkins; to apparel such as dupattas, scarves, and sarees; to even toys for children. In addition to these, small trinkets and boxes, wedding cards, bookmarks, diaries, and calendars, kitchen, as well as garden accessories are also produced. The women maintain that these diverse products tend to be bigger sellers compared to paper paintings. The works are generally affordable, and while heavily ornate, carry qualities of being mass-produced; it is difficult to tell one piece apart from the other.

On average, Shilp Sangh makes Rs. 5–6 lakhs (6000–7000 euros) in sales per year (BRLP 2016). While the bulk of the works is sold to local wholesalers and retailers who further supply their goods to the major cities (e.g. Delhi Haat), Shilp Sangh also facilitates some trade by participating in fairs and exhibitions (BRLP 2016). Commissioned works are also undertaken, such as the Lotus Pond installation at the Mumbai International Airport. Some business is conducted directly with regularly visiting customers, but there is no direct export system in place (BRLP 2016).

Shilp Sangh has some digital presence with an appointed representative to handle their Facebook page, although it shows irregular activities and updates. There is no direct way to make online purchases nor are products for sale displayed on their page. However, dozens of artworks are available for sale on amazon.in, usually with the title 'Shilp Sangh Jeevika (material) (subject/theme) (size)'. Thus, the works are sold as products of a faceless collective, with no means of reaching the creative person behind it. In the end, in light of the intended audience which is not prepared to pay a premium for unique works by a branded artist, this model has proven to be viable for all parties concerned.

8.8 Conclusions

The hidden traditional folk art of Madhubani paintings is now recognized as not just fine art but also an important expression of Indian heritage. In addition to the more customary paintings, the age-old tradition got commodified through the application of the Mithila iconography onto a wide variety of objects. With the dissemination of this colourful imagery both within India and abroad, Madhubani art has become an export commodity and has entered the international art scene and market. This is evidenced by several featured exhibitions in Europe, Japan, and the United States and their visibility on offline and online trading platforms. The growing popularity of Madhubani imagery and increasing trade has also led to a more segmented market, whereby the high-end artists supply (signed) unique paintings to veritable art collectors, while a wide variety of mass-produced derivatives finds its way to buyers less concerned with quality and originality.

Furthermore, our evidence shows that this is a market very much dominated by the dealers. Middlemen have been instrumental in connecting the production centres in remote Bihar with the market outlets in the major cities, and beyond. As a result, they are in a position to control and steer the production, rendering most artists in Bihar dependent on the demands of the dealers and which allows dealers to charge high commissions. During our fieldwork, artists complained of this lack of independence, which also explains the emergence of local artists' cooperatives such as Shilp Sangh to gain some negotiating power and claim a larger share of the profits. At the same time, while the digital revolution does open some avenues for trade and independence for the creators, the overall potential seems untapped and unexplored.

It should be recognized that the trade in Madhubani paintings and all its derivatives has lifted many families in the district out of poverty. Hundreds of family production units in the villages of Ranti and Jitwatpur alone now earn their livelihood practicing Madhubani art. Furthermore, we observed that the growth of this creative industry holds the promise of paving the way for upward social mobility by attempting to break deeply rooted caste barriers, although this will be a slow process. Finally, when asked whether they lamented the loss of spiritual meaning resulting from the commercialization of their beloved art form, the artists pointed to the roof over their heads, suggesting that it was a small price to pay.

Figure 8.1 *Kohbar* painting by Godavari Dutta, 2016

Source: Photograph by authors.

Figure 8.2 Line painting by unknown artist, 2016

Source: Photograph by authors.

Figure 8.3 A *Bharni-* and *Godna-*style painting by artist Ranjan Paswan, 2016

Source: Photography by authors.

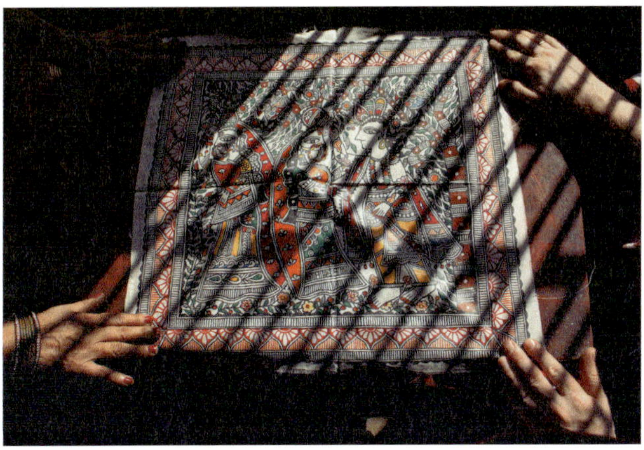

Figure 8.4 Cushion cover with Madhubani art, 2016

Source: Photograph by authors.

Figure 8.5 Art dealer selling Madhubani paintings at Dilli Haat, 2020
Source: Photography by authors.

Figure 8.6 Student at Mithila Art Institute, 2016
Source: Photography by authors

Figure 8.7 Outdoor open studio of Shilp Sangh, 2016

Source: Photograph by authors.

Notes

1 Dutta, Godavari. (Artist), in discussion with the authors. Madhubani, November 2016.
2 Das, Bibha. (Artist), in discussion with the authors. Madhubani, November 2016.
3 "Gauri Mishra – The folk paintings of Mithila (Madhubani)", Parampara Project, accessed January 22, 2020, www.paramparaproject.org/individuals_gauri-mishra.html
4 "About" Ethnic Arts Foundation, accessed January 22, 2020, https://ethnicartsfoundation.com/about/
5 Dutta, Godavari. (Artist), in discussion with the authors. Madhubani, November 2016.
6 Multiple artists in discussion with the authors. Madhubani, November 2016.
7 Paswan, Vinod (Son of Chano Devi), in discussion with the authors. Madhubani, November 2016.
8 Identities hidden (Artists) in discussion with the authors. Madhubani, November 2016.
9 Multiple artists in discussion with the authors. Madhubani, November 2016.
10 Jha, Kaushik. (Administrator, MAI), in discussion with the authors. Madhubani, November 2016.
11 Das, Abha. (Artist), in discussion with the authors. Madhubani, November 2016.
12 Das, Bibha. (Artist), in discussion with the authors. Madhubani, November 2016.
13 Dutta, Godavari. (Artist), in discussion with the authors. Madhubani, November 2016
14 Multiple artists in discussion with the authors. Madhubani, November 2016.
15 Devi, Sheela. (Artist), in discussion with the authors. Madhubani, November 2016.
16 Multiple artists in discussion with the authors. Madhubani, November 2016.

17 Multiple artists in discussion with the authors. Madhubani, November 2016.
18 Das, Runa. (Artist), in discussion with the authors. Madhubani, November 2016.
19 Paswan, Ranjan. (Artist), in discussion with the authors. Madhubani, November 2016
20 Jha, Sudhir. (Artist), in discussion with the authors. Madhubani, November 2016.
21 Paswan, Ranjan. (Artist), in discussion with the authors. Madhubani, November 2016.
22 Dutta, Godavari. (Artist), in discussion with the authors. Madhubani, November 2016.
23 Paswan, Vinod (Artist), in discussion with the authors. Madhubani, November 2016.
24 "Home", Mithila Art Institute, accessed January 22, 2020, http://mithilaartinstitute.org/Home/Index
25 "A Message from Prof. Parmeshwar Jha. President", Mithila Art Institute, accessed January 22, 2020, www.facebook.com/MithilaArtInstitute/
26 Interview with Kaushik Jha; http://mithilaartinstitute.org/Home/Index
27 Paswan, Ranjit. (Artist), in discussion with the authors. Madhubani, November 2016.
28 "History", Mithila Art Institute, accessed January 22, 2020, http://mithilaartinstitute.org/Home/History
29 At the time of writing, the website was still active and paintings from the extant stock could be purchased online: http://mithilaartinstitute.org/Home/Paintings
30 Interview with Kaushik Jha
31 "A Message from Prof. Parmeshwar Jha. President", Mithila Art Institute, accessed January 22, 2020, www.facebook.com/MithilaArtInstitute/
32 Situation at the time of fieldwork, in 2016.

References

Berger, P., and Heidemann, F. (2013). *The Modern Anthropology of India: Ethnography, Themes and Theory*. London: Routledge.

BRLP. (2016). *Study on the Back End Value Chain Analysis of Cluster*. Bihar: BRLP.

Centre, M. A. (2015). About Madhubani art. Available at: www.madhubani.com/about-madhubani-art.aspx

Donier, W. (2009). *The Hindus: An Alternative History*. New York City: Viking Press.

Ghosh, S. (2013). *An Interactive Need Assessment Survey and Design Study of Madhubani Painting of Jitbarpur, Madhubani district, Bihar*. Patna: Design Clinic Scheme.

Heinz, C. B. (2006). Documenting the image in Mithila art. *Visual Anthropology Review*, 22(2), 5–33.

Jha, A. K., Mishra, J. M., and Chandran, A. (2017). Indigenous tourism in India: Evaluating the strengths of Mithila painting art and heritage and suggesting integrated marketing development approach for sustainable promotion. *Atna-Journal of Tourism Studies*, 1–34.

Kaushik, S. (2019). Madhubani–the exotic art of Mithila. *Researchers' Guild*, 1(3), 1–6.

Komarova, N. (2018). Between the market and noncommercial art institutions: Early career strategies of contemporary artists in emerging art scenes. *Poetics*, 71, 33–42. doi:https://doi.org/10.1016/j.poetic.2018.11.004

KPMG. (2018). *Visual Arts Industry in India: Painting the Future*. KPMG – FICCI. Delhi, India.

Mishra, V. (1979). *Cultural Heritage of Mithila*. Allahabad: Mithila Prakasana.

Mohi-ud-din, T., Ahmad Mir, L., and Bhushan, S. (2014). An analysis of current scenario and contribution of handicrafts in Indian economy. *Journal of Economics and Sustainable Development*, 5(9), 75–78.

Rekha, N. (2010). From folk art to fine art: Changing paradigms in the historiography of Maithil painting. *Journal of Art Historiography*, 2, 1–20.

Sarkar, A. (2016). *'In Stock' on Amazon: The Cultural Globalisation and Deterritorialisation of Madhubani*. Rotterdam: Erasmus University Rotterdam.
Vermeylen, F. (2015). The India art fair and the market for visual arts in the global South. In Velthuis, O. and Curioni, S. B. (eds.), *The Globalization of Markets for Contemporary Art*, pp. 31–54. Oxford: Oxford University Press.
Vermeylen, F., and Sarkar, A. (2019). The commodification of art: Moving Indian painting in the global market. *Proceedings of the 34th World Congress of Art History*, 16, 166–169.
Wolf, G., and Wolf, A. (2015). *Between Memory and Museum: A Dialogue with Folk and Tribal Artists*. Chennai: Tara Books.

9

CREATIVITY AMONG INDIA'S ELDERLY

Few case studies

S.S. Sripriya

9.1 Introduction

Population ageing – the process by which older individuals come to form a proportionately larger share of the total population – is one of the most distinctive demographic events in the world today. Initially experienced in the more developed countries, the process is now rapidly approaching the developing world. In 1950, the number of persons elderly (60 years or older) was 205 million. Their numbers surged to 606 million in 2000. By 2050, the number is projected to rise to two billion. In terms of percentage, the elderly constituted 8.2% of the world's population in 1950; this percentage rose to 10% of the total population in 2000 and is projected to rise to 21.1% by 2050, by that time the world population of the elderly will be larger than the population of children between the ages 0 and 14 years. The oldest age segment (80 years and above) will be the fastest-growing segment, and by 2050, about 20% of older persons will be 80 years and above (UNFPA 1999). This will have significant implications for the older persons themselves, as well as the families and societies they live in.

As per the Census of India (2011), India's elderly constitute over 100 million. The female elderly constitute a little more than half of the population. Over three-fourths of the elderly are living in rural areas. About poverty among them, one-third of the elderly are living below the poverty line, and another one-third of them are just above the poverty level. Yet their contribution to society is significant and must be noted. For example, it can be said that the elderly population contributes to the livelihoods of households approximately in the same proportion as their share in the population. Further, elderly from poor households contribute to household income largely from self-employed activities, while elderly from higher-income households have better access to wage labour markets and contribute significantly to total wage earnings of households.

DOI: 10.4324/9781003129370-12

The elderly are the storehouse of the culture accumulated with their experience and innovations and also those received from previous generations. Further, as they retire from active 'work', they devote more time to the creation and cultural expressions. They become active in creating abstract designs, crochet craft, weaving, knitting, braiding, storytelling, singing, dancing, etc. These activities may be for economically supporting themselves, quasi-economic, or only for entertainment without any economic gains. However, these activities have consequences for positive ageing.

Historically it is recorded that creative ageing programmes started in the United States of America in the 1970s with combining art and activities for older adults (Klimczuk 2017). The creative ageing movement in Europe also emerged in the 1970s (Cutler 2009). In Europe, various initiatives were (and still are) established through universities of the Third Age movement, such as courses, workshops, and debates focused on the arts and humanities. The creative ageing movement has become widespread around the world in recent years (United Nations 2002).

Ageing has a positive influence on creativity which may be due to the accumulation of knowledge and experience. The research study undertaken by Cohen et al. (2007) have demonstrated that the cultural program participants reported a better overall degree of physical health, fewer doctor visits, less medication usage, fewer falls, and fewer other health problems than the comparison group. Castora-Binkley et al. (2010) observed that the engagement of older adults in creative activities in care settings may lead to increased quality of life for staff, improved retention of personnel, facilitation of points of communication for visitors, increased social cohesion, the development of volunteering, and the establishment of new programs or activities. Creative activities have been shown to have a positive effect on both physical and mental health. Even though art therapy has made inroads into health care, the effects of creativity on elderly health is less examined.

The creative activity contributes to successful ageing by giving the elderly a sense of purpose, personal growth, and interaction with others. Engaging in a creative pursuit like painting and knitting can motivate seniors to manage their lives and boosts self-esteem. Art crafts can also slow the deterioration of cognitive function in elders. It can also alleviate symptoms of anxiety and depression. Elderly people who engaged in art activities report benefits like a higher rate of physical health and a decrease in the number and type of medications they need. However, according to Klimczuk (2017), the relationship between the creative industries and old age is ambiguous. On the one hand, there are plenty of examples of 'worst practices' in the fields of advertising and mass media that repeat negative stereotypes of older people as slower, weaker, outdated, lonely, or poor. On the other hand, there are also 'best practices' of products and services in fields such as architecture, consumer electronics, and fashion, often based on the ideas of the 'user-centred design' or 'universal design'. Such projects tend to involve older adults at all stages of research and development, highlighting positive features of old age such as experience, knowledge, free time, and freedom from work-related duties.

In this context, the present chapter attempts to (a) examine the creative activities undertaken by the elderly for economic and non-economic purposes, and (b) know how do these activities impact positive ageing. The research in this area is limited and we do not have many documented and organized forms of data available on the same. Therefore, we have based this paper on case studies. The rest of this chapter is organized as follows. Section 9.2 through case studies attempts to understand the creative activities being undertaken by the elderly in Mumbai. Section 9.3 studies the impact of creativity on positive ageing and the last section concluded the chapter.

9.2 Elderly and creative activities: case studies

Ageing and creativity are generally viewed in contrast with each other. There is a general stereotype that creativity decreases after the age of 60 years. Case studies and laboratory research, however, do not support this notion. These studies suggest that ageing does lead to physical deterioration, but creativity is seen in individuals across all age groups. What affects creativity is not age but a combination of cognitive factors, social environment, and inner motivation. However, society tends to have a negative view of ageing and elderly people are viewed as devoid of skills to tackle any problem innovatively. With such misconception, public opinion on creativity is usually associated with relatively younger cohorts rather than with adults and the elderly. To create interventions for the promotion of active ageing, an attempt is made here to highlight the participation of the elderly in the field of yoga, dance, creative writing, and organizer of recreational centres, by a few case studies.

Case study 1: creativity through dance

Mrs Navanita, 72 years old, resides in Goregaon, Mumbai. She is married and currently living with her husband and her daughter. Her son is living abroad with his family. She has done a Master's programme in statistics and a course on banking. Till her formal retirement, she was working in a bank. Her focus on classical dance – Bharatanatyam (Indian classical dance form originated from Tamil Nadu, a state in India), developed while she started learning it along with her daughter at the age of 44 years. After she completed the course at the age of 54 years, she started her dance academy through which she started training people of different age groups. She was interested in dance from the early stages of her life. However, in those days girls in the community were generally not permitted to learn dance and because of it, she could not pursue her dream. Her parents and other elders in the family felt that by learning dance she won't gain anything and also perceived that it will not fetch any financial support to her. They felt that Navanita should complete her studies, get married, and form a family of her own. Accordingly, she fulfilled her parents' wish though she was always keen on learning Bharatanatyam which was a very famous classical dance in those days. But she used to do the Garba (one form of dance during Navratri festival), for which her parents used to allow her when she was young and unmarried. After marriage, though she got busy with her family responsibilities, her interest in dance was still lingering in her mind. Her interest in Bharatanatyam crept in her mind after she started taking her daughter to Bharatanatyam classes. This led to her joining the dance classes along with her daughter. Though initially, she felt awkward to go to classes at that age and with her daughter, she was determined to fulfil her dream of learning Bharatanatyam. Over a period she became a professional in this art and she started participating in various dance competitions. After she retired from a job she started to train specially abled children in dance and recently she started teaching senior citizens as well, whom she met in a social work course at Nirmala Niketan, a college of social work in Mumbai. Given her financial independence, she is not depending on the earnings from this activity. However, to add financial value to this activity that she is doing and also to continue this activity more sustainably, she started charging each student per month. Though the amount is not specified by her, she receives the payment based on their affordability and willingness to contribute. Usually, the amount that she gets from the students ranges from Rs 100–500 per student per month. No employees are working in her centre on a payment basis. She has been assisted by her friend who was trained in this profession and they are working as partners. According to her, the senior citizens are very enthusiastic and are very much interested to learn. She faced new challenges during Covid-19, as she could not continue to teach off-line.

Given this situation, she opted to learn digital technology with the help of her daughter. She started teaching her students online and other social media platforms. She even uploads videos on YouTube and other social media sources to reach out to wider groups. She is thankful to her family members for their constant support which enabled her to fulfil her dream. She fondly remembers how her mother-in-law who initially expressed her reservation, after seeing her on the stage performing Bharatanatyam for the first time, started encouraging her till her last breath.

Though Navanita had not received any awards or recognitions in her academic career, through dance she started receiving recognition and other forms of appreciation. Recently, she has received a gold medal for her participation in a dance competition by the name 'Sitare – The Rising Stars'. Her interest in other forms of dances continues, as she started learning Kathak (an Indian classical dance form that originated from Uttar Pradesh). According to her, everybody should take out time for themselves and learn something they like. In her own words, "follow *your heart, follow your dreams and try to fulfil it because age is just a number*". She feels that every elderly should try to take care of themselves without depending on others. She narrated her own experience recently as she had a fall in the bathroom which led to a fractured hand. Despite this limitation, she continued to teach her students.

This case reflects how a woman determined to pursue her passion for dance, despite experiencing several hurdles in the form of conventional ideas and involvement in familial roles and responsibilities. As soon as she was free from these hurdles, she not only fulfilled her dreams but also started teaching other senior citizens and specially abled persons residing in the locality.

Case study 2: creative production through creative writing

Mrs Hira Mehta, 65 years old, resides in Andheri, Mumbai. She is living with her husband and daughter. Her son is living abroad with his family. She is a Graduate and has a Diploma in Event Management and Voice. She worked as a Manager in internal communications in a bank. She had a passion for writing short stories even before her retirement. Her first book which is a compilation of short stories won an award. Her second book is a non-fictional one and more like a self-help book titled 'Young and Sixty' which depicts the life of a senior citizen. After retirement, Mrs Mehta wanted to be involved in social work activities and that is when she came across the Silver Innings Foundation that works on dementia. During a contest announced by Yes Bank called, "Yes I am the change", she came up with a film called 'A selfless soldier' by depicting the activities of Silver Innings Foundation led by Mr Sailesh Mishra. She made another film on a lady named Ms Sona Kumar, who runs a Trust for the education of street children. Besides making short films, she also acted in them. One such film called 'Blue Helmet' where she played the protagonist had won a critics award. She also does many web series. Currently, she is working on her third book. Due to Covid-19 she started doing a Podcast called 'GupShup' (indiscreet discussions) diaries on Instagram where she talks on different subjects and shares her thoughts, provides facts, and motivates the viewers on those subjects besides inviting those who have similar interest to contribute. Mrs Mehta carries out all the activities voluntarily without any financial support from the foundation. Her financial sources mainly include payment from acting, dubbing, film direction, royalty from publishing books, and regular pension being a retired bank employee. She is financially independent which has helped her to carry out other activities voluntarily. This way she continues her social participation and keeps herself occupied. She has always been proactive for change. She learnt to be like this from her mother, whom she lost in an accident. She says that since then she started living the life that her mother wished and also living the life that she wants. Among her achievements, she listed that she won a REX Karmaveer Global Fellowship award, 1st prize for a poetry reading contest, and twice her podcasts were played on international homegrown radios. Her proudest moment she recalls was when as a retiree of the bank she was assigned the work of archiving the history of the bank. She recollects how she was also invited when they launched it. Even though she was a banker, she used to be scared of doing online transactions. However, with the help of her daughter, she overcame this fear and now she is at ease at doing online transactions. She feels that as seniors who are used to following certain routines find it difficult to deviate and to accept any change. When the pandemic situation arose, she felt like a double retiree, one which was a formal one from her job and the other being not able to meet people physically. For a person like her who was always in the midst of people, not being able to interact with them now due to the lockdown is very stressful. To come out of this adverse situation, she started learning digital technology with the help of her daughter and started using social media and doing live streams and interacting with people. According to her, your life is not meant to be lived for others, it is meant to be lived for yourself. She quotes by saying, "Love *the face in the mirror first, because if you don't love the face in the mirror you won't be able to make anybody happy*".

Mrs Mehta's case depicts how a working woman pursued her interest in writing short stories and after retirement continued her passion not only in writing but also in other activities like doing podcasts, acting, and dubbing and for which she utilized various social media platforms like Facebook, Instagram to reach out to larger groups. With her determination, she has changed the perception of the elderly that they are passive receivers of care in society. Her success is an indication that we can create the "society for all ages", as quoted by the United Nations (United Nations 1999).

Case study 3: creative production through Yoga

Mr Ramagopal, 71 years old, resides in Andheri, Mumbai. He is living with his wife and their two children who have settled abroad. He is a science graduate from Madras University and holds a certificate in Enterprise Resource Planning (EPR) from the Indian Institute of Technology, Mumbai; an MBA with specialization in Retail Management from Madhurai Kamaraj University; and a postgraduate diploma in spirituality and health care from Annamalai University, Tamil Nadu. After he retired from a private company in 2009, he took up a visiting faculty position in management colleges. He also became a volunteer (Business Wing) for the Brahma Kumaris programme on Raja Yoga Meditation. During the last 13 years, he has been a certified laughter yoga teacher. He has been recognized by The Laughter Yoga International University, and he has been nominated as a Laughter Ambassador. His other activities also include several social work programmes. In the current pandemic situation, people are facing psychological distress like depression, isolation, and other mental health issues, for which laughter is the best medicine. He is of the view that these psychological problems, which are widely prevalent among the residents of the old age homes or shelter homes, have started penetrating into the society, especially among the elderly, due to Covid-19. When asked about his initiation in the laughter programmes, he recollects that when he was young he used to accompany his aunts, uncles, and father to various shelter homes and old age homes or in any social work-related activities carried out during events such as birthdays, anniversaries, or any special occasions. The elders in the family taught him that if he earns 16 Annas (1 Rupee = 16 Annas, as per currency equivalent in 1957 in India), 15 Annas is yours and the rest 1 Anna you should spend on others as a charity. His company which has a pan India presence has helped him to visit various places in India and in each of these places he used to visit various shelter homes and old age homes. When he started to settle in Mumbai, he came across the activities of Dignity Foundation for the well-being of senior citizens in the city. He remembers the quote of Ms Sheilu Sreenivasan the founder of the Foundation where she quoted in one of the articles that "Do not plan your retirement after retirement but plan it when you are 55years". Also, his interest in social work started developing whenever he was accompanying his wife for Brahma Kumaris Raja Yoga Meditation programmes. Besides his regular work in groups, he particularly mentions his leadership on International Yoga days where he gathers all the senior citizens in his locality and started teaching various programmes like Laughter Yoga and Raja Yoga Meditation. To propagate the importance of laughter yoga among the young generation, he started organizing various programmes in different educational institutions and clubs. He feels that people have forgotten to laugh, since their mind is conditioned that way, and thereby the necessity of promoting laughter yoga among them. During this pandemic everyday, he claps around 5 pm for 5 minutes as he feels that the vibrations will reach the pandemic warriors. Since most of the senior citizens do not know how to use smartphones, he has also started teaching them various applications like Hangout, Zoom, and Skype systematically. He recollects his experiences 13 years back when he started with laughter yoga in public parks, people who used to come there for walks or to jog and also those who reside in the nearby buildings found it as a nuisance. Also at the same time, a few of them used to be very happy as no alarm was required for them to wake up. Initially, youngsters used to perceive that laughter yoga is not for them but older people. As part of mobilizing elderly for the programme, he started an initiative like 'each one brings one' through which more number of people started joining the programme. Given the high mortality among elderly and migration, the membership for the programme started dwindling and currently, they have 35 members only. In addition to that during the pandemic, the challenge of being not able to meet physically has come up. In this situation, they have moved to virtual meetings by using online platforms like Zoom and Skype. Recently, online they celebrated Rakshabandhan (Indian festival), among their members. He found that ladies used to feel shy in laughter yoga especially when conducted in public parks. But due to their virtual meetings from their homes, they are at ease and even dress up, sing, and dance for the occasions. He feels that more youngsters should join laughter yoga programmes as they are knowledgeable and aware of the benefits of the programme. Thanks to virtual meetings the laughter yoga ambassadors interact and exchange frequently. In his own words, Mr Ramagopal says about the programme, *Everything needs practice, nothing happens overnight, don't expect benefits immediately.*

From the case study of Mr Ramagopal, it is clear how the value of philanthropy, when inculcated to a child by the elders of the family, can continue to progress at later stages of life. Also, his efforts have yielded in changing the mindset of the young generation and others towards the benefits of laughter yoga programmes. Further, his knowledge of digital technology enabled him to reach out to wider audiences across the globe for propagating laughter programmes. All these activities he is carrying out without any fee from the participants.

9.3 Impact of the creativity on positive ageing

Given the economic, physical, and social dependence that the elderly require, it is important to focus on aspects of positive ageing and support for maintaining a decent quality of life. Several different terms are used when referring to positive ageing, e.g. healthy ageing, active ageing, productive ageing, and successful ageing. However, the concept is consistent and refers to enhancing the quality of life by providing opportunities for improving and maintaining physical and mental health, independence, participation, and security. As positive ageing leads to a better quality of sustenance through physical and mental health, their longer participation would ensure more inclusive societies.

Becoming aware of the importance of ageing and the need to formulate policies upon it, various governments across the world particularly in the developed countries have devised certain strategies to deal with ageing. The regional development authority of Alpine Shire, Australia (Asquith 2009) has devised similar strategies, which are also important to replicate in developing countries like India. Among the five strategies, two of them viz promote social and civic engagement and build a supportive culture for positive ageing are highly relevant for promoting positive ageing.

According to Klimczuk (2017), the ageing population and the development of creative industries are often perceived as an issue that affects only the Global North. Yet, the rapid ageing is also a major challenge for countries of the Global South where creative industries play a crucial factor for the fast growth of local economies. Older adults cannot only be treated as passive consumers by creative industries. Older workers and volunteers are a valuable resource of tacit knowledge and skills for sectors such as the crafts, music, and heritage protection. He also emphasized that many older people are already active policy actors who through cultural and creative activities are being empowered. A number of 'new' ageing interest groups include the creative ageing movement, the Men's Sheds movement, the University of the Third Age movement, the elder co-housing movement, the Elder-hostel movement, the senior rights movement, the encore career movement, and the age-friendly movement. Further, he opines that selected creative industries such as architecture, fashion, software, design, and household goods are very close to the fields described through the concept of the silver economy. Having said that, Klimczuk (2017) opines that cautious research in creative sectors could improve our understanding of creative processes related to the ongoing development of the silver markets, the silver brands, the silver industries, the silver cities, and the silver regions.

Dance has recently been recommended as a physical activity to improve motor ability, fitness, and balance, as well as to facilitate successful aging (Olsson 2012). Studies have shown that older social dancers have better balance, posture, and gait than do non-dancers (Zhang et al. 2008)

The concept of positive ageing which has been debated widely in developed countries has started to gain its importance in developing countries like India, as these countries started becoming developed ones. However, as the majority of elderly reside in developing countries, there is a strong need to conceptualize a policy on ageing, which is largely holistic in its approach and specific in its application by identifying and addressing various physical, psychological, and mental issues related to older persons, and also encourage them to have a positive outlook by enhancing their creativity.

Positive ageing looks to change societal perceptions about ageing so that it is viewed with acceptance and with positivity or a new phase of life. This is particularly important given that research on ageing tends to come with a problem-oriented approach that tends to explore the negative aspects of ageing, which in turn affects interventions. However, taking on a different approach to positive ageing will impact how interventions and solutions are sought.

Given positive ageing, tips are offered on how to keep active in old age ranging from keeping fit, meditating, and engaging in cultural activities, as well as healthy eating, focusing on good conduct, good thoughts and good behaviour with others, and recreation, which are all part of ancient practices in India to keep healthy even in old age. The importance of knowing about ageing, understanding it as a stage of life much like youth or infancy, and plans need to be made ahead of time in to prepare for it. Understanding ageing is important so as not to dismiss problems as being part of old age, and also to have a fuller sense of life in the later years, and also for policymakers and planners to accordingly be sensitized and prioritize work accordingly. Promoting skill-based training programmes for elderly for developing countries like India is thus important not only for the elderly population to benefit them personally but also for the country as a whole as it brings out the quality human resource and adds to the productivity of ageing.

The digital inclusion, which can significantly help in the facilitating access to and participation in creative programmes, of the elderly is only in India are in the initial stage. The digital literacy inclusion programmes are conducted in different geographical regions of India by organizations like HelpAge India and other community-based organizations in India. These programmes mainly cover the day-to-day aspects of computers and the internet. But effective enrolment and indulgence are yet to take place. The illiteracy among the members, the absence of immediate need and the lack of full-fledged infrastructure and financial support are the bottlenecks for the expansion of digital inclusion programmes for the elderly in India. The coverage of the digital programme will take more time for the elderly to get accustomed to the technology and it also requires an inter-generational approach. However, efforts should be made to provide the necessary digital literacy like usage of the internet for communication with employers, family members, customers, peer group members, cultural groups, and other stakeholders. These measures will not only address their social participation but also connect them to the local cultural economy which will enable them to participate in the production and consumption of various cultural products. While accepting their limitations of illiteracy and lack of immediate necessity, the elderly in a recent survey (Siva Raju 2019) observed that they are in favour of digital training on the day-to-day aspects.

9.4 Conclusions

Creativity is not only about the pursuit to be a renowned person or for economic gains but it's about individual happiness and contentment that a person gets even for an hour on an everyday basis. If older adults show an inclination towards a particular activity or hobby like photography or dancing, then they should be given a boost and motivation to nurture their talent. There has been significant lack of literature on participation of creative industries of elderly, but these are cultural industries which can play very significant role in positive ease by making the living joyful with economic gains. Though many centres offer various classes and courses in cultural activities including, exercise programs, crafts and arts, paintings, etc., yet they are limited in number.

The crucial issues faced by older people that have been identified till now are inadequately addressed by existing elderly services and intervention approaches due to various factors such as lack of awareness, poor implementation, mismatch with their needs, and lack of political will. Efforts should be made to identify suitable and effective programmes and schemes which will help in enhancing the creativity among the elderly and thus to address their well-being in family and society. The following are the specific measures that require the attention of the policymakers and program managers who are associated with the promotion of creativity among the elderly population in a country like India:

1. There is a need to re-look into the National Policy of Older Persons (Government of India 1999) and emphasize positive ageing with a special focus on creativity among the elderly and its associated factors.
2. A national-level survey may be undertaken among the elderly to identify the existing industries on creativity which are elder-friendly. Such a survey

is expected to help us in understanding the elderly's potentials for further contribution to these industries and to identify the required skills to further enhance their involvement in such industries.

3. A stakeholder analysis is required to understand all the relevant actors associated with creative industries with a special focus on the role of senior citizens associations and organizations.
4. Efforts are needed to identify suitable mechanisms through which the products that the elderly create need to be marketed in the local economy. Such an effort is necessary to enhance the productivity of ageing.
5. Efforts should be made to evolve a grassroots model of advocacy that would involve the emergence of local leadership and typical motivational, needs defining, goal-setting, and organizational processes – instead of services being initiated by the official planning processes of the ageing network. Such an effort will bring the elderly in the communities to the mainstream of development.
6. As part of advocacy, efforts should be made to change older people from passive clients into active and empowered individuals with a positive self-image. Such an effort will help us in strengthening elderly people's contact with the community, eliminating elderly people's negative self-image, protecting elderly rights, and increasing their capacity to influence policy-making.
7. The success of the Digital Inclusion Programme of Elderly though at this stage is at a low level, adequate emphasis should be made for its continuation, given the future implication of digitization in developing countries like India. Such an effort will in turn help in promoting creativity among the older population of India.

References

Asquith, N. (2009). Positive ageing, neoliberalism and Australian sociology. *Journal of Sociology*, 45(3), 255–269. https://doi.org/10.1177/1440783309335650

Castora-Binkley, M., Noelker, L., Prohaska, T., and Satariano, W. (2010). Impact of arts participation on health outcomes for older adults. *Journal of Aging, Humanities, and the Arts*, 4(4), 352–367.

Census of India (2011). Population enumeration data (final population): Age data. Available at: https://censusindia.gov.in/2011census/population_enumeration.html

Cohen, G. D., Perlstein, S., Chapline, J., Kelly, J., Firth, K.M., and Simmens, S. (2007). The impact of professionally conducted cultural programs on the physical health, mental health, and social functioning of older adults – 2-year results. *Journal of Aging, Humanities, and the Arts*, 1(1–2), 5–22.

Cutler, D. (2009). *Ageing Artfully: Older People and Professional Participatory Arts in the UK*, London: Baring Foundation.

Government of India (1999). *National Policy on Older Persons*. New Delhi: Ministry of Social Justice and Empowerment.

Klimczuk, A. (2017). How the creative industries can positively impact ageing and old age. International Network for Critical Gerontology. Available at: https://criticalgerontology.com/creative-impact-ageing/ (last accessed on 25 March 2022).

Olsson, C. J. (2012). Dancing combines the essence for successful aging. *Frontiers in Neuroscience*, 2(31). https://doi.org/10.3389/fnins.2012.00155

Siva Raju, S. (2019). End-term Evaluation of Project ASTITVA-II of HelpAge India on Livelihood and Empowerment of Elderly. Report Submitted by Tata Institute of Social Sciences, Mumbai.

UNFPA (1999). Population and Family Study Centre, Population Ageing: Challenges for Policies and Programmes in Developed and Developing Countries, UNFPA and Population and Family Study Centre, New York and Brussels.

United Nations (1999). Towards a society for all ages. Available at: www.unmultimedia.org/avlibrary/asset/1996/1996564/ (last accessed on 25 March 2022).

United Nations (2002). Madrid plan of action and its implementation. Available at: www.un.org/development/desa/ageing/madrid-plan-of-action-and-its-implementation.html (last accessed on 25 March 2022).

Zhang, J. G., Ishikawa-Takata, K., Yamazaki, H., Morita, T., and Ohta, T. (2008). Postural stability and physical performance in social dancers. *Gait Posture*, 27(4), 697–701.

Section IV

CINEMA AND MUSIC INDUSTRIES

India is known for its cinema and music, and these industries exhibit swift and broad changes with digitalization. Bollywood is one of the largest film production clusters in the world, reaching billions of consumers. Yet, India also hosts regional varieties of film production. Regional production of works with wide appeal and high production values is found, for instance, in Telugu, Tamil, Bhojpuri, Bengali, and Assamese. There are also many alternatives, more rough-and-ready productions, so-called spoof cinema, also referred to as Mollywood. Chapter 10 analyses data on production and commercial success factors in contemporary mainstream, Bollywood cinema. Quite uniquely, Bollywood has played a particularly major role also in the formation of the Indian recorded music industry, especially Hindi music with all its regional and community nuances. Chapter 11 documents how the Indian recorded music industry is gradually claiming its own territory, over and beyond the traditional ties with cinema. Audio-visual entertainment in India has long been shaped by limited access to permanent cinema venues or to media hardware in many private households, especially in rural communities. Chapter 12 documents the fascinating case of how travelling cinemas in Maharashtra evolved in this context, experienced decline, and started to explore new niches for their services with the diffusion of new media technology. Chapter 13 focuses on low-budget Mollywood film production in Malegaon, which integrates contributions from amateurs with working-class backgrounds. While this seems to reflect blurring boundaries between professional and amateur production in contemporary CCI, this chapter also documents the transformation and decline of this specific Mollywood tradition since the 2010s.

DOI: 10.4324/9781003129370-13

10

BOX OFFICE SUCCESS OF BOLLYWOOD FILMS

An analysis of influencing factors

Zinat Aboli

10.1 Introduction

The Indian Hindi film industry, located in Mumbai, is one of the largest film industries in the world in terms of the number of feature films produced and audience base. The industry emerged in the early nineteenth century through an idiosyncratic mix of factors in Mumbai – the legacy of Parsi theatre, the availability of capital in the city, and its multicultural ethos, among other things (Johnston 2012). *Alam Ara* was the first sound film made in India in 1931 and since then the industry surged ahead adopting new technologies.

Bollywood films have a wide audience and demand from countries in the global south like Morocco in the west to the Philippines in the east. The demand for Bollywood films had significantly grown in Russia during the Nehruvian time in the 1950s and 1960s (Swaminathan 2017). In recent years, the industry has become truly global with vast demand and audience in Europe and North America. The rise of the Indian diaspora (overseas market) and the emergence of India as an economic power (domestic market) have further helped in generating these demands. Bollywood also has significant economic importance for India and specifically for Mumbai. It is considered as one of the largest film-making industries globally, having a 27% share of revenue in the overall Indian entertainment sector (Jones 2010).

However, Bollywood as a production industry is not very organized; instead, it has enormously scattered small and medium units. Over the years, Mumbai city has gathered a critical mass of creative people who at the individual, group, and organizational levels have been engaged in the production of the films. The creative class is largely concentrated in the western suburb of the city, and one can commonly find poets, scriptwriters, directors, and actors occupying cafés and restaurants discussing their projects. They more often are joined by financiers who are ready to make good money in the short run through investments in Bollywood films.

DOI: 10.4324/9781003129370-14

For a long time, the Government of India did not recognize Bollywood as an industry and therefore the finance from organized sectors at concessional rates to the industry was limited and also expensive. The Indian film industry was given "industry" status by the Indian government in 2001. Institutional finance, which became available thereafter at comparatively modest credit rates, made it easy for aspiring and talented filmmakers to make their films.

According to the FICCI-EY Media and Entertainment report 2019 (FICCI-EY 2019), the Indian film segment grew 10% in 2019 to reach INR 191 billion (about US$2.71 billion) driven by the growth in domestic theatrical revenues and both rates and volume of digital/Over the Top (OTT) rights sold. Moreover, domestic film revenues crossed INR 115 billion (about US$1.63 billion) with Gross Box Office collections for Hindi films at INR 49.5 billion (about US$0.71 billion) – the highest ever for Hindi theatricals. Totally 17 Hindi films entered the desired INR one billion club of earnings in 2019. Interestingly, six films made it to the INR 2 billion clubs in 2019, as compared to three in 2018.

The films produced vary according to their budget and genre. A large number of the industry's total films are low-budget films that offer investors significant returns but are often high-risk investments. In this context, the present chapter attempts to examine the number of Bollywood films of various genres produced, the budget range, the impact of star actors and different production and distribution houses, season of release, and their box office success in terms of gross earnings and profits. The rest of the chapter is divided as follows. Section 10.2 situates Bollywood in the global film production arena and reviews the relevant literature, while Section 10.3 discusses the data and method of analysis adopted in this chapter. Next, Section 10.4 deals with the production and release of the number of films by star actors, budget category, genre, production and distribution houses, season/month of release. Section 10.5 examines the impact of various factors on profits and gross box office earnings of these films using a multivariate regression approach. The last section concludes the chapter.

10.2 Situating Bollywood in the global film industry

With revenues second only to those of the US film business, the Indian film industry produces more films and sells more tickets internationally than any other film industry. The Indian film industry churned out an impressive 1,255 feature films in 2011 and 1,986 in 2016, higher than any other countries in the world (Table **10.1**). The USA, the second-largest producer of feature films, produced less than one-third to that of India in 2016 (González et al. 2013, also see Scott 2005). The number of screens in India were almost one-fourth to that in the USA, which were 10,020 in India as compared to 39,641 in the USA in 2011, and 11209 in India as compared 40,393 in the USA in 2017 (UNESCO Institute for Statistics 2021).

The film industries of other leading countries like Japan, South Korea, France, and Germany have been much smaller than that of India in terms of number of films produced. However, this ranking does not assure Bollywood as the number

Table 10.1 Number of films produced by country, 2011–17

Country	*2011*	*2012*	*2013*	*2014*	*2015*	*2016*	*2017*
Brazil	99	83	129	114	129	142	160
China	584	745	638	618	686	853	874
France	272	279	270	258	300	283	300
Germany	212	220	223	229	226	244	233
India	1255	1602	1724	1868	1907	1986	–
Japan	441	554	591	615	581	610	594
Republic of Korea	216	204	207	248	269	339	494
United States of America	819	738	738	649	663	656	660

Source: UNESCO Institute for Statistics (2021).

one earner of profits from the same. As we will demonstrate later in this chapter, most of the films made in Bollywood are of low budget and earn relatively lower profits than those from Hollywood or other European film industries.

The decision to finance a film is quite perilous and is based on both artistic and commercial aspects (Eliashberg et al. 2006). Every new film is like a roll of the dice or a spin of a slot machine with every player trying to calculate odds that might well be incalculable (Paul 1994). In recent years, Over the Top (OTT) platforms have become very crucial for determining success of films. Nevertheless, theatrical channels remain crucial for the film success (Litman and Ahn 1998).

It is not, therefore, unexpected that there is a sizable and expanding body of research on the economics of the cinema industry, much of it focusing on empirical examination of the characteristics and distribution of commercially successful films (Albert 1998; Litman 1983; Litman and Kohl 1989; Smith and Smith 1986; Hennig-Thurau et al. 2006).

Some other such studies specifically related to Hollywood films have been those by Basuroy, Chatterjee and Ravid (2003), Chang and Ki (2005), Hennig-Thurau et al. (2001, 2007), King (2007), Neil et al. (2005), and Walls (2005). However, as mentioned earlier, few studies look at the variables that make non-US films successful, like Italian films (Bagella and Becchetti 1999), German films (Jansen 2005), and Dutch films (Gemser et al. 2007). Moreover, there have been a very few studies that have examined the factors determining the success of Bollywood films. Fetscherin (2010) examined determinants of domestic and total foreign earnings of a sample of 330 Bollywood films produced during 1997–2007. He examined determinants like genre, rating, star power, director power, season, distribution power, screens, ratings, and reviews. Among others, Fetscherin (2010) found that genre (drama) was an important factor for box office success, while other influencing factors were ratings, star power, and director power. Reviews were not found affecting the success of films. Masih and Ihsan (2019) using data from various sources for the year 2013 to 2017 found that reputation of actor, director, budget, genre, and awards play important role in the success of Bollywood films.

The contribution of this chapter is twofold. First, it analyses a relatively large sample of films of 1,148 films in comparison to other studies (Fetscherin 2010; Lehmann and Weinberg 2010), using both the combined foreign and domestic earnings. As such the data becomes a good representative to study Bollywood. Second, it uses the multivariate regression approach to further decompose the data, for instance actor influence into male and female actor influence, seasons into months, but due to lack of consistent data does not include factors like reviews, number of screens, and first week collection in the equation to examine the box office success of the films. As Fetscherin (2010) chose only 330 Bollywood films released in the UK or the USA to examine the contribution of various factors in their success, it can be said that the study suffered from sample bias as only certain groups of distributors and producers have access to releasing their films in the overseas market.

10.3 Data and methods

Obtaining micro data on Bollywood films is rather difficult. Whereas the Central Board of Film Certification(CBFC), Government of India, Mumbai, provides data on number of films in different languages and genre produced in the country and by major regional centres in India, it does not provide details of actors, distribution and production houses, and also month of release. As such the data remains diffused and located with individual units rather than available in an organized form. Some websites have attempted to organize these data, prominent among them being IMDB and boxofficeindia.com. These websites provide details related to films, their budgets, actors, director, release months and box office earnings, etc. Data from 2009 to 2018, that is for 10 years for 1,148 films, have been gathered from the above source for the present paper. Moreover, to ensure reliability, data from books, websites, newspapers, and magazines have also been referred and compared. These data are better representative of Bollywood reality as they include the movies released in India rather than only the overseas market and also are listed in two websites: IMDB and boxofficeindia.com. Although many lesser films may not have made to the list and the list itself may still be biased, it is the only organised source of information that is publicly accessible.

Various ratios and percentages based on these data have been computed for analysis and comparison. Bivariate tables have also been generated to understand the relations between different factors and various aspects of the films. Also, multivariate pooled regression analysis has been used to further examine impacts of various factors on the success of films in a more precise and statistically reliable way. Though there are many potential elements that may have an impact on the revenue and profit of the movies, this study focussed on the effects of star power, budget, genre, production company, distribution company, and time of release on the profitability of films. The lack of data prevented the use of other determinants or factors. The descriptions of the independent variables used in the regression model are produced in Table 10.2.

Table 10.2 Description of variables used for the pooled regressions

Variables	*Condition*	*Descriptions*
Dummy value of Months =1	*if*	June, July, Oct, Nov, Dec =1
Dummy value of Male superstars =1	*if*	Shahrukh Khan, Salman Khan, Aamir Khan, Saif Ali Khan, Sanjay Dutt, Anil Kapoor, Akshay Kumar, Hrithik Roshan, Ajay Devgan, Ranbir Kapoor, Ranveer Singh, and Amitabh Bachchan
Dummy value of Female superstars =1	*if*	Deepika Padukone, Priyanka Chopra, Alia Bhatt, Kareena Kapoor, Aishwariya Rai, Kangna Ranawat, Anushka Sharma, Katrina Kaif, Kajol, and Rani Mukherjee
Dummy value of Star directors=1	*If*	Anand Rai, Anubhav Sinha, Anurag Basu, Anurag Kashyap, Ashutosh Gowarikar, Dibakar Banerjee, Farhan Akhtar, Hansal Mehta, Imtiaz Ali, Kabir Khan, Karan Johar, Madhur Bhandarkar, Neeraj Pandey, Prabhu Deva, Pradeep Sarkar, Rajkumar Hirani, Rakesh Roshan, Rakeysh Omprakash Mehra, Rohit Shetty, Sajid Nadiadwala, Sajid-Farhad, Sanjay Gupta, Sanjay Leela Bhansali, Shoojit Sircar, Sooraj Barjatya, Sriram Raghavan, Vikas Bahl, Vikram Bhatt, Vishal Bhardwaj, and Zoya Akhtar
Dummy value of Star production houses=1	*if*	Aamir Khan Film Productions, Ajay Devgn Films, Anurag Kashyap Films, Balaji Motion Pictures Mumbai, Bhansali Productions, Dharma Productions, Excel Entertainment, Fox Star Studios, Jar Pictures, Phantom Films, Rajshri Productions, Red Chillies Entertainment, Reliance Entertainment, T-Series Films, Tips Industries, UTV Motion Pictures, Viacom 18, Motion Pictures, Vinod Chopra Films, Walt Disney Pictures India, Yash Raj Films, and Warner Bros.
Dummy value of Star distribution houses=1	*if*	Dharma Production, Eros International, Fox Star Studios, Nadiadwala Grandson Entertainment, Pen India Limited, Percept Picture Company, PVR Cinemas, Rajshri Productions, Red Chillies Entertainment, Reliance Entertainment, Shree Ashtavinayak CineVisions Ltd, Sony Pictures, T-Series, Tips Films, UTV Motion Pictures, Viacom 18, Motion Pictures, Walt Disney Studios, Warner Bros, Yash Raj films, and Zee Studios
Action films =0 (reference category)	*if*	Drama, Comedy, Thriller, Horror, Romance, Biopic, Children films, Avant Garde, Period drama =1
Budget	=	Total expenses in production of the films
Box office earning	=	Total national and international earning of the films
Ln	=	Natural logarithm

Note: In the absence of any other criteria available, star actors, star production, and distribution houses were identified subjectively based on their popularity in producing successful films.

10.4 The influencing factors for box office success

There are many empirical studies which have attempted to study one or more determining factors of success of films at box office. However, these studies have largely been based on non-Bollywood films. The positive role of star power and directors in the box office success as such has been highlighted by Basuroy et al. (2003), Chang and Ki (2005), Elberse (2007), Elberse and Eliashberg (2003), Hennig-Thurau et al. (2007), Litman and Kohl (1989), Ravid (1999), Walls (2005), and Zuckerman and Kim (2003); while relationship of genre on the success has been studied by Chang and Ki (2005), De Vany and Walls (2003), Litman and Kohl (1989), Simonoff and Sparrow (2000), Wallace et al. (1993), Walls (2005), and Zuckerman and Kim (2003). Season of release as component of success has been investigated by Basuroy et al. (2003), Chang and Ki (2005), Elberse and Eliashberg (2003), Litman and Kohl (1989), Simonoff and Sparrow (2000), Walls (2005), Zuckerman and Kim (2003). The role and importance of distribution houses on success of films have been highlighted by Chang and Ki (2005).

Across the spectrum, whether in Hollywood or closer home in Bollywood, the films with star actors (superstar actors) have more likelihood to achieve box office success (Fetscherin 2010). Usually, the audience is driven by the fan factor to these stars rather than the other aspects of films itself (Basuroy et al. 2003; Chang and Ki 2005; Elberse 2007). However, it is also true that in recent years the hold of the established star actors has been weakening in India. A quick scan of many publications revealed that, specifically, post-2008 the success of not so well-known actors in low-budget films was based on other factors like storyline, the quality of screen presentation, genre, marketing, etc. In India, the role of film critics and reviewers has not been so effective in determining the success of the films as the audience do not generally attention to them. This section attempts to understand the success of films based on star power, budget, genre, production house, distribution house, and time of release of films.

10.4.1 Star actors and film earnings

As has been mentioned earlier, among others, the success of films depends on largely the star power. However, in literature, the impact of stars on film's success remains a contested issue as other researchers question this relationship (De Vany and Walls 1999; Elberse 2007).

Bollywood since its inception has been driven by star power. For instance, during 1950–70s, these were Dilip Kumar, Raj Kapoor, Dev Anand from male actors whose films were big hits. During 1970–90s, Amitabh Bachchan, Rajesh Khanna, Dharmendra ruled Bollywood as male super stars and the period also saw the emergence of female superstars like Sridevi and Rekha. From 1990 onwards the male star actors have been Shahrukh Khan, Aamir Khan, Salman Khan, Ajay Devgan, and Akshay Kumar along with female super stars like

Madhuri Dixit, Kajol, Rani Mukherjee, etc. Although they typically only appear in two films a year (with the exception of Akshay Kumar), they generate significant box office revenue (Table 10.3).

In recent years, the films of Aamir Khan, Salman Khan, Alia Bhatt, Rani Mukherjee, and Hrithik Roshan have performed relatively better than those of other stars or not-well established/known actors. Films starring Aamir Khan have on an average shown spectacular box office success. On an average, his films have an earning-budget ratio of 9.4. That is one rupee spent on his films brings an earning on an average of 9.4 rupee. Although, Bollywood is known for its male superstars. However, the films of two female actors Rani Mukherjee and Alia Bhatt have shown spectacular success in terms of box office earning (Table 10.3).

Table 10.3 Star actors and number of films with earnings, 2009–18

Actors	*No. of films*	*% of total films*	*Average budget (INR in million)*	*Average box office earning (INR in million)*	*Box office earning – budget ratio*
Rani Mukherjee	3	0.3	92.0	1151.0	12.5
Aamir Khan	6	0.5	741.7	6970.2	9.4
Alia Bhatt	3	0.3	320.0	1730.7	5.4
Salman Khan	17	1.5	698.0	2812.0	4.0
Hrithik Roshan	8	0.7	612.5	1750.5	2.9
Akshay Kumar	32	2.8	475.0	1217.2	2.6
Ajay Devgan	19	1.7	441.8	1165.1	2.6
Ranveer Singh	11	1.0	766.0	1967.8	2.6
Kareena Kapoor	4	0.3	272.5	714.0	2.6
Ranbir Kapoor	13	1.1	604.2	1484.2	2.5
Priyanka Chopra	3	0.3	213.3	528.3	2.5
Shahrukh Khan	10	0.9	1188.0	2559.4	2.2
Anushka Sharma	3	0.3	193.3	395.3	2.0
Others	943	82.1	153.3	291.5	1.9
Saif Ali Khan	14	1.2	426.2	640.0	1.5
Anil Kapoor	4	0.3	720.0	1104.8	1.5
Amitabh Bachchan	17	1.5	497.6	686.9	1.4
Shahid Kapoor	11	1.0	355.5	501.2	1.4
Kangana Ranawat	7	0.6	243.6	349.1	1.4
Deepika Padukone	2	0.2	670.0	793.5	1.2
Katrina Kaif	1	0.1	530.0	626.0	1.2
Aishwariya Rai	2	0.2	310.0	335.0	1.1
Sanjay Dutt	9	0.8	263.8	217.3	0.8
Kajol	1	0.1	200.0	65.0	0.3
Total for all films	1143	99.6	241.2	558.3	2.3
SD	190.9	16.6	257.6	1420.2	2.8

Note: data for 5 films were not available.

Source: Computed using data mentioned in Section 10.3.

10.4.2 Films by budget categories

Film production budgets have garnered attention of studies by Litman (1983), Litman and Ahn (1998), Litman and Kohl (1989), Prag and Casavant (1994), Ravid (1999), Basuroy et al. (2003), and John et al. (2002). These studies show a positive correlation between budget and returns. For instance, Ravid (1999) and John et al. (2002) show that big budgets films are correlated with higher revenues.

Out of 1,148 films in our sample, budget and box office earning data for 821 films are available. The minimum and maximum budget films during the period have been of INR 0.6 million and INR 3000 million, respectively, while the mean and median of the budget over the period are INR 241.2 million and INR 150 million, respectively (Table 10.4). A wide gap between mean and median of the budget shows that higher share of the films is made with lower budgets. About 41% of these films were of very low budget films, that is less than INR 100 million (Table 10.5). Only about 10% of the films had a budget of more than INR 500 million. This also shows that cost of production of films in India is relatively low – mainly due to lower factor costs and use of relatively lower grade technologies. The trained workforce is easily available at cheaper rates and the cost of actors is lower, except in the case of a few high-ranking superstar actors.

The films have been categorized into seven groups as presented in Tables 10.4 and 10.5. An analysis of success of very low budget films (below INR 50 million) shows that on an average these films are made with an expenditure of INR 28.11 million (minimum INR 0.26 and maximum INR 50 million). The average earning of these films is 22.8 million (minimum 0.1 and maximum INR 700). Overall, very low budget films on an average are losing business ventures as total spending in 188 very low budget films during 2008–18 was INR 5,286 million, but the total earning was only INR 4,292 million. Only about 12% of these films had earning above INR 50 million, and two films had

Table 10.4 Descriptive statistics related to budget of the films, 2009–18

Budget type	*Minimum (INR in million)*	*Maximum (INR in million)*	*Mean (INR in million)*	*Median (INR in million)*	*Std. Deviation*
1. Very low	0.6	50	28.1	30	13.9
2. Low	54	100	81.1	80	15.9
3. Low medium	110	250	175.1	180	43.0
4. Medium high	260	500	366.6	350	72.0
5. High	510	750	628.7	630	67.2
6. High-high	760	1000	882.9	865	78.3
7. Very high	1040	3000	1513.2	1380	499.6
Total	0.6	3000	241.2	150	305.8

Source: As for Table 10.3.

Table 10.5 Budget of Bollywood films, 2009–18

Budget type	*Budget (INR million)*	*Number of films*	*% of films*
1. Very low	Below INR 50	188	22.9
2. Low	50–100	148	18.0
3. Low medium	100–250	235	28.6
4. Medium high	250–500	165	20.1
5. High	500–750	46	5.6
6. High-high	750–1000	14	1.7
7. Very high	Above INR 1000	25	3.0
Total		821	100.0

Source: As for Table 10.3.

extraordinary success by earning more than INR 500 million. The earning-expenditure ratio of this category films was 0.81, which means on an average these films made 19% of losses (earned below the expenditures).

The box office earning of *low*-budget films (INR 50–100 million) has been spectacular. The average cost of production of such 148 films during 2008–2018 was INR 81.1 million (minimum 54 and maximum 100 million), but the average earning was 207.6 million (minimum 0.2 million and maximum INR 9700 million). About 15% of such films had earning above INR 250 million while six such films registered box office earnings more than INR 1000 million. As such the earning expenditure ratio of these films was 2.56, that is on an average, film under this budget category had likelihoods of earning of more than 2.5 times of the expenses on them.

Low *medium* budget films (INR 100–250 million) on an average have also registered spectacular earning performance. However, about three-fifths of this category films (total 235 films) had earnings less than INR 250 million, and about 42% earned below INR 100 million. This shows that only about 40% of such films succeeded to earn more than INR 250 million, but about 25% of them earned more than INR 500 million. Among such films, 10.6% made earnings of more than INR 1000 million. Overall, the average spending on make of these films was INR 175 million (minimum 110 and maximum 250 million) while the average earning was INR 452.4 million (minimum 0.5 million and maximum 9770 million). The earning-expenditure ratio of such 235 films was 2.58, and as such on an average they have been huge profit makers.

The *high medium* budget films (INR 250–500 million) also had on average good earning performance. The average spending on make of these total 165 films was INR 366.59 million (minimum 260 and maximum 500 million) while the average earning was INR 824.16 million (minimum 25 and maximum INR 7916). The earning-expenditure ratio of such films was 2.25. However, a quarter share of such films had earnings lower than INR 100 million, surely the loss makers, while about 48.5% had earning above INR 500 million, the profit makers.

The films produced under *low high* budget (INR 500–750 million), on an average, also registered spectacular performance in terms of box office earning. The average spending on make of these films was INR 628.67 million (minimum 510 and maximum 750 million), while the average earning is INR 1,620.1 million (minimum 3.20 and maximum INR 21,000). The total spending on such 46 films for their production was INR 28,919 million, but total earning by these 46 films was INR 74,524 million. As such, the earning-expenditure ratio of these films was 2.58. In other words, these were, on an average, huge profit-making films. The failure ratio of this budget category films was significantly low as more than 63% of these films registered earnings above INR 750 million.

The performance of *high*-budget films (INR 750–1000 million) had also been good. Totally 14 films during 2008–2018 were produced under this budget category. The average spending on make of these films was INR 882.85 million (minimum 760 and maximum 1000 million), while the average earning was million INR 2214.9 (minimum 410 and maximum INR 8540). On these films, total spending was INR 12,360 million while total box office earning on these 46 films was INR 31,009 million. As such, the earning-expenditure ratio was 2.51. Only about 14% of such films had earnings less than INR 750 million, but 10 of them had above INR 1000 million. As such, these films also have been on an average huge profit-making films.

On an average, the number of films decline as we move up in the budget category. Only 25 films were produced under *very high* budget (Above INR 1000 million) category. Average spending on make of these films was INR 1513.20 million (minimum INR 1040 and maximum INR 3,000 million), while the average earning is million INR 3,018.96 (minimum 430 and maximum INR 5,892). The total spending on 25 such films was INR 37,830 million, while total earning by them was INR 75,474 million. Out of 25 such films, only three films earned below INR 1,000. The earning-expenditure ratio of this category films was 2.00, and as such, very high budget films are also big money makers.

10.4.3 Genre of films made and earnings

Film audiences consider films genre important before making up their minds to watch a specific film (Austin and Gordon 1987; De Silva 1998). Hence there are many studies that focus on relevance of genre for success of the film as suggested in the review of literature. Furthermore, some studies like that of Elliot and Simmons (2008) suggest that in the UK films targeting children are usually successful. On the other hand, Zuckerman and Kim (2003) identify crime theme as significant for the success of Hollywood films. Many studies suggest that comedy as a genre is significant (Litman and Kohl 1989; Sochay 1994). Also, the popularity of the sci-fi/fantasy and horror genres for box office success is empirically supported in other literature (Litman 1983; Litman and Kohl 1989; Wyatt 1991). However, Litman and Kohl's (1989) study suggests success at the box office was negatively correlated with drama, but Chang and Ki (2005) find that drama genre is related with success of films. However, Walls (2005) finds no individual genre classification significant for box office success.

In terms of genre, out of 1,140 films for which data are available for the period 2009–2018, drama (27.9% of the total 1140 Hindi films), comedy (22.6%), action (12.5%), and romance (12.5%) constituted more than 75% of the total Hindi films made in India during 2009–18, while thrillers constituted about 16% of the total films produced during the same period. Indian masses have specific orientation towards drama, comedy, and romance (Table 10.6). In fact, historically many epics like Mahabharata, Ramayana, etc. are the portrayal of these genre. The demand for thrillers and sci-fi films remains low.

In Bollywood, all the genres of films, on average, had good earnings (Table 10.7). However, the earning was relatively higher by drama films (earning-expenditure ration 3.1), biopics (3.0), romance (2.4), comedy (2.2), and action (2.1). Avant garde and children related films registered relatively low success on box office and had earning-budget ratio of 1.1 each. Thriller and horror category films had medium-level performance in terms of earning. Overall, the Bollywood films generate good profit, as the average earning-budget ratio of the films is 2.3. This shows that on an average, the films generate income of 2.3 times to the expenditure.

10.4.4 Production houses and film earnings

Although a large share of Bollywood films does not get finance from the organized sector for the production, a few important production houses have emerged. Among the well-known national production houses are Yash Raj Films, Red Chillies Entertainment, Rajshri Productions, T-Series, Reliance Entertainments, Nadiadwala Grandson Entertainment, Zee Studios, Balaji

Table 10.6 Number of films produced by genre in Bollywood

Genre	*No. of films*	*% of total films*
Action	142	12.5
Drama	318	27.9
Comedy	258	22.6
Thriller	180	15.8
Horror	45	3.9
Romance	142	12.5
Biopic	20	1.8
Children	23	2.0
Avant Garde	3	0.3
Period drama	9	0.8
Total	1140	100.0

Source: As for Table 10.3.

Table 10.7 Bollywood films by genre, budget, and earning-budget ratio, 2009–18

Genre	*Number of films*	*Minimum (in INR million)*	*Maximum (in INR million)*	*Mean (in INR million)*	*Median (in INR million)*	*Std. deviation*	*% of total films*	*Earning-budget ratio*
Action	112	4.2	2100.0	398.9	290.0	394.8	13.6	2.1
Drama	195	2.0	2700.0	204.5	120.0	285.8	23.8	3.1
Comedy	199	0.6	1310.0	203.1	150.0	206.8	24.2	2.2
Thriller	135	5.0	1500.0	218.3	150.0	225.4	16.4	1.9
Horror	30	5.0	310.0	114.9	90.0	84.1	3.7	1.7
Romance	109	2.0	1800.0	225.1	140.0	265.6	13.3	2.4
Biopic	15	10.0	1450.0	417.7	290.0	437.1	1.8	3.0
Children	17	15.0	340.0	83.5	50.0	87.0	2.1	1.1
Avant garde	2	30.0	80.0	55.0	55.0	35.4	0.2	1.1
Period drama	7	30.0	3000.0	1118.6	630.0	1110.9	0.9	1.4
Total	821	0.6	3000.0	241.2	150.0	305.8	100.0	2.3

Note: the statistics is based on 821 films on the number of films for which budgets and earning are available.

Source: As for Table 10.3.

Motion Pictures, Aamir Khan Productions, Ajay Devgan Films, etc. Some of the international production houses have also, of late, joined Bollywood in film production, and these are Warner Bros, Walt Disney studios and its subsidiaries. It is interesting to note that some of the aforementioned Indian production houses have been established by the major male superstars like Shahrukh Khan (Red Chillies Entertainments), Aamir Khan (Aamir Khan Productions), Ajay Devgan (Ajay Devgn FFilms), etc. Though these production houses have been financing major films, more than 60% of Bollywood's films are financed by less known production houses and/or by the informal sector (Table 10.8). Although, the data available from 2009 to 2018 from different sources provides significant insights at the aggregate level, it also suffers from some limitations. For instance, out of total 1148 films for which data were gathered, by production houses data are available for 911 films (Table 10.8), but the data are available for only 699 films by budget and earnings (Table 10.9). Still with these limitations, the overall sample is large to provide us meaningful insights of various aspects of the Bollywood films.

Some of the production houses are known for creating films which can bring good earnings. As can be seen from Table 10.9, the major money-maker production houses through the films have been Aamir Khan Productions (earning-budget ratio 24.4), Viacom 18 (5.5), Maddock (5.2), Ajay Devgn Films (3.2), and A.A. Films (3.0). Some of the failures have been Reliance Entertainment and Rajshri Productions with the earning-budget ratio of 0.1 each. Well-known production houses like Yash Raj Films, Red Chillies, Nadiadwala Grandson Entertainment, Fox Star Studios, T-Series, and Zee-Studios had on an average earning-budget/expenditure ratio of 2.

Table 10.8 Number of films produced by production houses, 2009–18

Production houses	*2009*	*2010*	*2011*	*2012*	*2013*	*2014*	*2015*	*2016*	*2017*	*2018*	*Total*
Yash Raj Films	1	4	2	3	3	5	3	3	3	3	30
T-Series	0	1	2	0	1	3	5	4	7	7	30
Balaji Motion Pictures	0	2	3	1	4	4	0	4	1	2	21
Viacom 18	0	0	1	2	3	3	4	2	2	1	18
Eros International	2	1	1	0	0	2	1	4	2	2	15
A A Films	3	0	1	2	1	1	3	2	1	1	15
Red Chillies Entertainment	1	1	2	0	1	1	1	3	2	2	14
Nadiadwala Grandson Entert.	1	2	0	1	0	2	2	3	2	1	14
UTV Motion Pictures	5	0	4	1	1	1	0	1	0	0	13
Fox Star Studios	0	1	0	1	1	1	2	2	3	0	11
Phantom Films	0	0	0	0	0	3	3	1	1	3	11
Zee Studios	1	0	0	0	0	0	1	1	1	3	7
Ajay Devgn FFilms	1	0	0	2	0	1	0	2	0	1	7
Maddock	0	0	0	0	0	1	1	0	2	1	5
Aamir Khan Prod.	0	1	2	0	0	0	0	1	1	0	5
Reliance Entertain.	0	0	0	1	1	0	0	0	0	0	2
PVR Pictures	0	1	0	0	0	0	0	0	1	0	2
Rajshri Productions	0	0	1	0	0	0	0	0	0	0	1
Others	30	97	76	36	59	94	68	79	83	68	690
Total	45	111	95	50	75	122	94	112	112	95	911

Note: Out of 1148 films, for 237 films the details of production houses are not available.

Source: As for Table 10.3.

10.4.5 Major distribution houses and films with earnings

In Bollywood, there is a large overlap between production and distribution houses. Many production houses also engage in the distribution of the films (Table 10.10). Almost 30% of the Bollywood films during 2008–18 were distributed by the companies which were also engaged in production of films. The year-wise number of films distributed for which data is available shows that Eros International, UTV Motion Pictures, and Fox Star Studios are three major distribution players in for Bollywood films.

In terms of earnings, most successful films have been from Zee Studios, UTV Motion Picture, Dharma Production, Viacom 18, while that of failures have been from Rajshri Productions (Table 10.11).

10.4.6 Time of release and earnings

There are studies that have shown correlation of the time of release of films with box office success. It has been observed that internationally films released

Table 10.9 Major production houses, budgets, and earning-budget ratio, 2009–18

Production houses	*N*	*Minimum (INR in million)*	*Maximum (INR in million)*	*Mean (INR in million)*	*Median (INR in million)*	*Std. Deviation*	*Earning-budget ratio*
Aamir Khan Product.	5	100	700	266.0	150.0	249.1	24.36
Viacom 18	11	30	320	142.7	100.0	92.6	5.83
Maddock	5	120	470	246.0	230.0	135.8	5.21
Ajay Devgn FFilms	7	200	730	352.9	300.0	186.7	3.20
A A Films	14	30	310	144.3	100.0	89.6	2.97
Zee Studios	5	200	500	330.0	300.0	123.7	2.82
Fox Star Studios	11	60	1400	443.6	200.0	435.5	2.69
Yash Raj Films	28	100	3000	547.7	225.0	705.6	2.64
Nadiadwala Grandson Entert.	14	100	1150	549.3	570.0	269.4	2.54
T-Series	27	35	589	246.5	200.0	142.4	2.05
Red Chillies Entertainment	13	30	2700	1004.6	1190.0	745.5	2.05
UTV Motion Pictures	12	17	580	227.5	156.5	182.0	1.98
Balaji Motion Pictures	21	13	950	353.0	390.0	240.0	1.81
Eros International	12	50	630	202.9	180.0	168.2	1.64
PVR Pictures	1	190	190	190.0	190.0	–	1.51
Phantom Films	10	35	1200	278.5	112.5	377.8	1.44
Rajshri Productions	1	120	120	120.0	120.0	–	0.08
Reliance Entertainment	2	20	120	70.0	70.0	70.7	0.08
Others	470	2	2150	213.5	130.0	249.9	2.12
Total	669	2	3000	260.1	160.0	322.6	2.41

Note: Out of 1148 films, data for budget and earnings are available for only 669 films as produced in this table.

Source: As for Table 10.3.

in summer and at Christmas give better yields (Krider and Weinberg 1998; Litman 1983). Detailed data for 1,148 films produced and released during 2009–2018 were collected. This 10-year period does not show any major difference of year-wise release of films, except that in recent years, there has been marginally more production of films (Table 10.12). Also, except that October gets marginally more releases, there is not much difference in month-wise variations in release of films in Bollywood.

Time of release as a factor plays a very important role in determining the box office earnings of films. The films released during holidays and festivals generally perform better over the films released during usual times. A pattern can be observed which distributors of films have followed in India. Firstly, all the distributors generally release the new films on Fridays so that the following

Table 10.10 Distribution of films by distribution houses and year, 2009–18

Distribution houses	*2009*	*2010*	*2011*	*2012*	*2013*	*2014*	*2015*	*2016*	*2017*	*2018*	*Total*
Eros International	5	8	5	12	11	6	11	9	5	4	76
UTV Motion Pictures	11	7	7	8	10	10	4	4	1	0	62
Fox Star Studios	1	2	3	4	4	5	7	6	6	3	41
Reliance Entertainment	3	4	8	3	2	6	1	3	4	5	39
Viacom 18	3	0	3	8	7	4	2	3	4	4	38
Yash Raj Films	3	4	2	2	4	5	3	3	4	3	33
A A Films	0	0	0	1	1	4	2	2	9	10	29
T-Series	2	1	1	0	3	1	3	8	4	4	27
PVR Pictures	1	5	1	1	0	2	0	3	4	5	22
Balaji Motion Pictures	0	1	3	0	3	3	0	3	3	0	16
Zee Studios	0	0	0	0	0	0	2	3	3	4	12
Warner Bros	0	5	1	0	0	0	0	0	0	0	6
Red Chillies Entertainment	1	0	2	0	0	0	1	0	1	0	5
Dharma Production	1	1	0	0	1	0	0	0	1	0	4
Rajshri Productions	0	1	1	1	0	1	0	0	0	0	4
Shree Ashtvinayak Prod.	2	2	0	0	0	0	0	0	0	0	4
Others	34	64	32	20	29	34	27	34	40	39	353
Total	67	105	69	60	75	81	63	81	89	81	771

Table 10.11 Major distribution houses, average budget, and earning, 2009–18

Distribution houses	*N*	*Minimum (INR in million)*	*Maximum (INR in million)*	*Mean (INR in million)*	*Median (INR in million)*	*Std. deviation*	*Earning-budget ratio*
Zee Studios	7	150.00	500	381	410	121	6.3
UTV Motion Pictures	61	2.00	1380	345	250	329	4.0
Dharma Production	4	15.00	300	181	205	125	3.5
Viacom 18	33	27.00	2150	313	190	390	3.3
Reliance Entertainment	37	30.00	1390	291	250	255	3.2
A A Films	25	70.00	590	272	280	129	3.0
Fox Star Studios	39	30.00	1800	434	280	412	2.6
Eros International	73	13.00	1450	337	250	264	2.5
Shree Ashtvinayak Prod.	4	300.00	1100	548	395	372	2.2
Yash Raj Films	31	50.00	3000	568	250	761	2.1
Red Chillies Entertain.	5	40.00	1600	872	1190	693	1.9
T-Series	25	22.00	589	208	170	139	1.8
Balaji Motion Pictures	15	13.00	950	310	260	291	1.6
PVR Pictures	13	3.50	600	170	110	181	1.3
Warner Bros	6	30.00	180	98	83	57	1.0
Rajshri Productions	4	20.00	150	93	100	56	0.1
Others	243	.60	1500	175	110	197	1.4
Total	625	.60	3000	277	190	326	2.4

Note: data by distribution houses, budget, and earnings are available for only 625 films.

Source: As for Table 10.3.

Table 10.12 Year- and month-wise releases of Bollywood films, 2009–18

Year	*Year-wise releases*		*Month of release*	
	Number	*% of total*	*Month*	*% of total*
2009	96	8.36	Jan	7.6
2010	125	10.89	Feb	8.6
2011	102	8.89	Mar	9.7
2012	103	8.97	Apr	8.8
2013	112	9.76	May	9.3
2014	136	11.85	Jun	6.4
2015	112	9.76	Jul	7.8
2016	122	10.63	Aug	8.4
2017	125	10.89	Sept	9.6
2018	115	10.02	Oct	10.5
–	–	–	Nov	7.9
–	–	–	Dec	5.5
Total	1,148	100		100.0

Source: As for Table 10.3.

Saturdays and Sundays viewers can watch it over the weekend. Secondly, some of the distributors have found some specific occasions associated with some festivals in a year to release their films. For instance, Dussehra-Diwali break (which coincides with the months of October and November every year) when educational institutions and government departments generally go on a week or two week-long holiday breaks. Some distributors also prefer to release their films during the new year break beginning from the last week of December, i.e. around Christmas (mid-December and December last week), while others prefer to release their films during Eid (a Muslim festival). In the international Gregorian calendar, the dates vary from year to year shifting 11 days earlier each year, as the Muslims follow Islamic Lunar calendar for Eid. Hence it is difficult to assign any specific month for Eid, but other festival times can be well recorded. It has also been observed that a few distributors release their films during the months of May-June, i.e. the holiday break for educational institutions.

Data presented in Table 10.13 shows that the films released in December, October, June, and July have shown better successes. As mentioned earlier, these months coincide with New Year, Dussehra-Diwali, and Eid (in recent years). The earning-budget ratio of the films released on these occasions has been better than those released in other months. Films released in December earn the highest (earning-budget ratio 3.5), followed by those released in October, June-July (has coincided with Eid for last few years).

10.5 Impact of individual factors on earning of films

Previously, we discussed the bivariate association of earning of films with budget of the films, star power, production houses, distribution houses, production

Table 10.13 Months of release, budget, box office earning of films, 2009–18

S. no.	*Month*	*Number*	*% of total*	*Average budget (INR in million)*	*Average box office earning (INR in million)*	*Box office earning-budget ratio*
1	Jan	87	7.6	256.0	486.6	1.9
2	Feb	99	8.6	210.0	412.4	2.0
3	Mar	111	9.7	134.1	256.9	1.9
4	Apr	101	8.8	163.3	312.0	1.9
5	May	107	9.3	185.1	381.4	2.1
6	Jun	73	6.4	254.5	625.1	2.5
7	Jul	89	7.8	252.7	710.9	2.8
8	Aug	96	8.4	248.3	513.5	2.1
9	Sept	110	9.6	218.8	486.8	2.2
10	Oct	121	10.5	268.9	688.8	2.6
11	Nov	91	7.9	358.4	633.9	1.8
12	Dec	63	5.5	470.8	1650.7	3.5
	Total	1148	100.0	241.2	558.3	2.3

Source: As for Table 10.3.

houses, genre, and time of release as factors. In this section, we use pooled Ordinary Least Square (OLS) regressions and many dummy variables to better illustrate the impact of specific factors on the profit and box office earnings of the films, controlling for other factors, on which we have data (see Tables 10.2 and 10.14). We find that the models with level of dependent variable *profits* (of which *Ln* cannot be taken as there are many films with negative values) do not have much explanatory powers as R-squared are around 0.15. However, when we use the *Ln* of box office earning and budget, the explanatory powers of the equations (see models 1 and 2 in Table 10.14) significantly improve.

Results with profits as dependent variable are of particular interest. Female superstars have no apparent impact on film profits, either. Male superstars, star directors, star producers, star production houses, and the budget of the films all positively impact the box office success of the films in our sample. Among all the aforementioned factors, the highest impact on profit is of male superstars. The model 4 shows that, *ceteris paribus*, on an average, films of male superstars earn INR 392 million more than films of male non-superstars. Similarly, films of star production houses, on an average, earn INR 306.1 million more than those from non-star production houses. This shows that for the box office success of the films, the start power and production houses play an important role.

Time factor has not been found significant in any of the equations in determining the profit or box office earnings of films. It seems that in Bollywood time factor often mentioned by distribution and production houses is a myth rather than any scientific reality in determining the success of films. What matters for success of Bollywood films is not the time of release but male superstars, star directors and production houses, and budgets of the films. Elberse (2007) study on the 'power of star' in Hollywood also shows that star actor does impact positively

Table 10.14 Regression results showing impacts of various factors on revenue and profit of Bollywood films

Variables	*(1)* *Ln of box office earning*	*(2)* *Ln of box office earning*	*(3)* *Profits (INR million)*	*(4)* *Profits (INR million)*
Month	−0.211	−0.194	145.4	150.3
	(0.134)	(0.134)	(92.08)	(92.52)
Male superstars	0.327**	0.359**	397.7***	392.0***
	(0.165)	(0.165)	(113.8)	(115.6)
Female superstars	0.712**	0.766**	−2.221	−33.57
	(0.305)	(0.306)	(206.8)	(208.8)
Star directors	0.476**	0.503***	320.0**	288.7**
	(0.188)	(0.189)	(128.5)	(130.0)
Star prod. houses	0.623***	0.610***	325.7***	306.1***
	(0.142)	(0.142)	(97.23)	(97.81)
Star distrib. houses	0.788***	0.819***	231.1***	243.1***
	(0.121)	(0.122)	(81.41)	(81.94)
Budget (INR million)			0.483***	0.542***
			(0.152)	(0.163)
Log Budget (INR)	1.540***	1.543***		
	(0.0557)	(0.0571)		
Drama		0.0172		205.3
		(0.190)		(130.0)
Comedy		0.0909		−2.419
		(0.188)		(129.6)
Thriller		0.111		−16.20
		(0.203)		(139.4)
Horror		0.949***		47.25
		(0.327)		(224.4)
Romance		−0.214		11.85
		(0.215)		(147.6)
Biopic		0.387		296.9
		(0.434)		(297.8)
Children films		−0.307		−110.1
		(0.414)		(283.0)
Avant Garde		1.282		33.73
		(1.119)		(767.0)
Period drama		−1.022*		−481.5
		(0.613)		(433.3)
Constant	−3.855***	−3.945***	−119.3**	−178.1
	(0.251)	(0.314)	(57.11)	(117.1)
R-squared	0.674	0.681	0.147	0.156

Note: Standard errors in parentheses;

* *p<0.1;*
** *p<0.05;*
*** *p<0.01, the reference category for the genre is 'action' not included in the equation to avoid dummy trap.*

Source: As for Table 10.3.

Table 10.15 Regression results showing impacts of various factors on revenue-budget ratio of Bollywood films

Variables	*(1)*	*(2)*	*(3)*	*(4)*
	Revenue-budget ratio	*Revenue-budget ratio*	*Revenue-budget ratio*	*Revenue-budget ratio*
Month	0.272	0.300	0.117	0.139
	(0.482)	(0.485)	(0.481)	(0.483)
Male superstar	1.827***	1.869***	1.377**	1.369**
	(0.595)	(0.606)	(0.590)	(0.597)
Female superstar	1.027	0.811	1.076	0.806
	(1.082)	(1.094)	(1.092)	(1.104)
Star director	1.708**	1.594**	1.529**	1.447**
	(0.672)	(0.681)	(0.673)	(0.683)
Star prod. houses	1.478***	1.441***	1.338***	1.274**
	(0.509)	(0.512)	(0.510)	(0.512)
Star distr. houses	1.697***	1.738***	1.672***	1.704***
	(0.426)	(0.429)	(0.435)	(0.438)
Budget (INR million)	−0.00260***	−0.00256***		
	(0.000795)	(0.000852)		
Drama		1.134*		1.299*
		(0.681)		(0.687)
Comedy		−0.0805		0.156
		(0.679)		(0.678)
Thriller		0.0275		0.200
		(0.730)		(0.732)
Horror		0.274		0.499
		(1.176)		(1.179)
Romance		0.286		0.470
		(0.773)		(0.776)
Biopic		0.402		0.319
		(1.560)		(1.567)
Children		−0.602		−0.297
		(1.482)		(1.493)
Avantgarde		−0.449		−0.265
		(4.018)		(4.039)
Period drama		0.343		−1.222
		(2.270)		(2.210)
Ln Budget (INR million)			−0.335*	−0.262
			(0.200)	(0.206)
Constant	0.989***	0.673	2.175**	1.385
	(0.299)	(0.614)	(0.898)	(1.133)
Observations	821	821	821	821
R-squared	0.070	0.077	0.061	0.069

Note: Standard errors in parentheses;

* *p<0.1;*

** *p<0.05;*

*** *p<0.01, the reference category for the genre is 'action' not included in the equation to avoid dummy trap.*

Source: As for Table 10.3.

the revenue of the films. We also estimated the models with revenue-budget ratio (which is non-negative, unlike profit) as dependent variable but found that explanatory powers of the equations were very low. The estimations we have produced in Table 10.15.

10.6 Conclusions

Bollywood is one of the largest film industries of the world in terms of its customer base. It produces more than 1000 films every year and entertains billions of people around the world and more specifically in Asia and Africa. The present study attempted to understand the box office success of Bollywood films during 2008–2018. The study finds that Bollywood films on an average provide good returns (global revenue) on the investments. Especially relatively big budget films generate higher revenues. The star power of lead male actors plays a very important role in the success of the films as they are often produced by large production houses. Some specific male actors like Aamir Khan have been very successful on the box office, as his films have made sizeable earnings both in India and abroad. Though, we have attempted to measure the success of Bollywood films through their box office success, but the film industry has huge cultural impact and followers across the world, often extending the soft power of India. The industry is currently in a transformative stage and is becoming more digital not only in the production process but also with the distribution. This transitions, as has been evident in COVID-19 period, has posed a challenge to the earnings by the films as most of the Indian and South Asian audiences still lack access to digital technologies and do not prefer to watch them on small screens like mobile phones and TV.

Unlike Hollywood films, Indian films are still largely based on the local themes rather global. This limits the scope for earning from foreign countries. The Indian diaspora are the main consumers of Indian films in the foreign countries. The producers of Bollywood films also face the dilemma about the making films on global context as large section of Indian audience are still not aware about the same, while the success in foreign market may not be guaranteed. As such, the domestic demands become the main drivers of Bollywood films. However, some of the Bollywood films like that of Dangal by Aamir Khan became a huge hit in China. In this context, it will interesting to further examine themes which can have global appeal/market for Bollywood films.

India is also undergoing significant change in the viewing platforms of films. The fast expanding cheaper broadband internet are leading to the rise of OTT and websites, viewing of films on TV, mobile phones, and computers rather than in theatre. The COVID-19 lockdown has further popularized the OTT and online viewing of the films. The Bollywood distributors therefore may need to fast change their strategies of the distribution of films from screen based to OTT- and online-based viewing. In this context, studies need to be taken to examine the factors that are accelerating the online- and OTT-based viewing of films and the strategies the producers and distributors can adopt to prevent the copyright violations to enhance their revenues.

References

Albert, S. (1998). Films stars and the distribution of financially successful films in the motion picture industry. *Journal of Cultural Economics*, 22(4), 249–270.

Austin, B. A., and Gordon, T. F. (1987). Films genres: Toward a conceptualized model and standardized definitions. *Current Research in Film: Audiences, Economics and the Law*, 4, 12–33.

Bagella, M., and Becchetti, L. (1999). The determinants of motion picture box office performance: Evidence from films produced in Italy. *Journal of Cultural Economics*, 23, 237–256.

Basuroy, S., Chatterjee, S., and Ravid, A. (2003). How critical are critical reviews? The box office effects of film critics, star power, and budget. *Journal of Marketing*, 67(4), 103–117.

Chang, B.-H., and Ki, E.-J. (2005). Devising a practical model for predicting theatrical films success: Focusing on the experience good property. *Journal of Media Economics*, 18, 247–269.

De Silva, I. (1998). Consumer selection of motion pictures. In Litman, B. R. (ed.), *The Motion Picture Mega-Industry* (pp. 144–171). Needham Heights, MA: Allyn and Bacon.

De Vany, A., and Walls, D. (1999). Uncertainty in the films industry: Does star power reduce the terror of the box office? *Journal of Cultural Economics*, 23(4), 285–318.

De Vany, A., and Walls, D. (2003). Films stars, big budgets, and wide release: Empirical analysis of the blockbuster strategy. Latin American Meeting of the Econometric Society, São Paulo, Brazil, 2002.

Elberse, A. (2007). The power of stars: Do star actors drive the success of films? *Journal of Marketing*, 71(4), 102–120.

Elberse, A., and Eliashberg, J. (2003). Demand and supply dynamics for sequentially released products in international markets: The case of motion pictures. *Marketing Science*, 22(3), 329–354.

Eliashberg, J., Elberse, A., and Leenders, M. (2006). The motion picture industry: Critical issues in practice, current research, and new research directions. *Marketing Science*, 25(6), 638–661.

Elliott, C., and Simmons, R. (2008). Determinants of UK box office success: The impact of quality signals. *Review of Industrial Organization*, 33(2), 93–111.

Fetscherin, M. (2010). The main determinants of bollywood films box office sales. *Journal of Global Marketing*, 23(5), 461–476.

FICCI-EY. (2019). *A Billion Screens of Opportunity: India's Media and Entertainment Sector*. Kolkata: Ernst and Young LLP.

Gemser, G., Van Oostrum, M., and Leenders, M. A. (2007). The impact of film reviews on the box office performance of art house versus mainstream motion pictures. *Journal of Cultural Economics*, 31(1), 43–63.

González, R., Deloumeaux, L., and Pessoa, J. (2013). Emerging markets and the digitalization of the film industry: An analysis of the 2012 UIS international survey of feature film statistics. Unesco.

Hennig-Thurau, T., Houston, M. B., and Walsh, G. (2006). The differing roles of success drivers across sequential channels: An application to the motion picture industry. *Journal of the Academy of Marketing Science*, 34(4), 559–575.

Hennig-Thurau, T., Houston, M. B., and Walsh, G. (2007). Determinants of motion picture box office and profitability: An interrelationship approach. *Review of Managerial Science*, 1(1), 65–92.

Hennig-Thurau, T., Walsh, G., and Wruck, O. (2001). An investigation into the factors determining the success of service innovations: Case of motion pictures. *Academy of Marketing Science Review*, 6, 1–29.

Jansen, C. (2005). The performance of German motion pictures, profits and subsidies: Some empirical evidence. *Journal of Cultural Economics*, 29(3), 191–212.

John, K., Ravid, S. A., and Sunder, J. (2002). *The role of termination in employment contracts: Theory and evidence from film directors' careers*. working paper, Stern School of Business, New York University.

Johnston, B. (2012). The 2012 World Cities Culture Report. London City Council.

Jones, M. (2010) Bollywood, Rasa and Indian cinema: Misconceptions, meanings and millionaire. *Visual Anthropology*, 23(1), 33–43.

King, T. (2007). Does film criticism affect box office earnings? Evidence from films released in the US in 2003. *Journal of Cultural Economics*, 31, 171–186.

Krider, R. E., and Weinberg, C. B. (1998). Competitive dynamics and the introduction of new products: The motion picture timing game. *Journal of Marketing Research*, 35(February), 1–15.

Lehmann, D., and Weinberg, C. (2000). Sales through sequential distribution channels: An application to films and videos. *Journal of Marketing*, 64(3), 18–33.

Litman, B. R. (1983). Predicting success of theatrical films: An empirical study. *Journal of Popular Culture*, 16(4), 159.

Litman, B. R., and Ahn, H. (1998). *Predicting Financial Success of Motion Pictures: The Motion Picture Mega-Industry*. B. R. Litman. Boston, MA: Allyn and Bacon Publishing, Inc.

Litman, B. R., and Kohl, L. S. (1989). Predicting financial success of motion pictures: The '80s experience. *Journal of Media Economics*, 2(2), 35–50.

Masih, S., and Ihsan, I. (2019). Using academy awards to predict success of bollywood films using machine learning algorithms. *International Journal of Advanced Computer Science and Applications*, 10(2), 438–446.

Neil, T., Butler, M., and De' Armond, D. A. (2005). The determinants of domestic box office performance in the motion picture industry. *Southwestern Economic Review*, 32(1), 137–148.

Paul, W. (1994). The K-Mart audience at the mall films. *Film History*, 6(4), 487–501.

Prag, J., and Casavant, J. (1994). An empirical study of determinants of revenues and marketing expenditures in the motion picture industry. *Journal of Cultural Economics*, 18(3), 217–235.

Ravid, S. A. (1999). Information, blockbusters and stars: A study of the film industry. *Journal of Business*, 72, 463–486.

Scott, A. J. (2005). *On Hollywood: The place, the industry*. Princeton, NJ: Princeton University Press.

Simonoff, J., and Sparrow, I. (2000). Predicting films grosses: Winners and losers, blockbusters and sleepers. *Chance*, 13(3), 15–24.

Smith, S. P., and Smith, V. K. (1986). Successful films: A preliminary empirical analysis. *Applied Economics*, 18(5), 501–507.

Sochay, S. (1994). Predicting performance of motion pictures. *Journal of Media Economics*, 7(4), 1–20.

Swaminathan, R. (2017). *Bollywood Boom: India's Rise as a Soft Power*. New Delhi: Penguin Random House.

Wallace, W. T., Seigerman, A., and Holbrook, M. B. (1993). The role of actors and actresses in the success of films: How much is a films star worth?" *Journal of Cultural Economics*, 17(1), 1–24.

Walls, D. (2005). Modeling films success when 'nobody knows anything': Conditional stable-distribution analysis of film returns. *Journal of Cultural Economics*, 29, 177–190.

Wyatt, J. (1991). High concept, product differentiation, and the contemporary US film industry. *Current Research in Film: Audiences, Economics and Law*, 5, 86–105.
UNESCO Institute for Statistics (2021, March). Feature film production. Available at: http://data.uis.unesco.org/ (last accessed on 31 March 2021).
Zuckerman, E., and Kim, T.-Y. (2003). The critical trade-off: Identity assignment and box-office success in the feature film industry. *Industrial and Corporate Change*, 12(1), 27–67.

11

INDIA BEYOND BOLLYWOOD? EXPLORING THE DIVERSE INDIAN INDEPENDENT MUSIC INDUSTRY IN THE DIGITAL AGE

Bhagyalakshmi Daga

11.1 Introduction

The music industry is not considered all that detached from the film industry in India. Film music in Bollywood and other regional cinemas is not simply relegated to the background but is considered an integral part of the story, and for decades, film music has been the most popular and dominant form of popular music in India. However, fuelled by initiatives such as 'Digital India' and the proliferation of smartphones and 3G services, a transformation is observable in the Indian popular music industry. A thriving digital ecosystem has not only given way to new forms of music consumption but also aided in the creation and promotion of an industry attempting to appear out of the shadows of Bollywood and the like. The country is now witnessing the development of a nascent independent music industry that is addressing the apparently unmet demands of a growing population of largely urban middle-class music creators and consumers. Equipped with digital tools of production and consumption, as well as knowledge of global trends, this demographic is championing DIY (Do it Yourself) culture, informal business practices, and entrepreneurial spirit to bring national attention to new alternatives to the mainstream music.

Rapidly advancing digital technologies in the past decade in India have both greatly driven and benefitted the creative economy. At the same time, a key question is whether for all its benefits, digital technologies truly empower the individual creator or is it the established superstars who continue to reap most of the benefits. The role and importance of digital technologies in the creative economy, therefore, have become a crucial part of the discourse.

To examine these questions, fieldwork was undertaken by the author in April 2018 in two Indian cities Bangalore and Mumbai with the most prominent developments in the independent music industry. In-depth semi-structured

 DOI: 10.4324/9781003129370-15

interviews with 12 creative workers – from independent artists, record label executives, and artist collectives, to music journalists, along with direct observations and field notes are utilized in the analysis of industry practices. Additionally, analysis of industry reports and raw data acquired by foundation Indian Music Industry (IMI) and International Federation of the Phonographic Industry (IFPI) on the Indian market (Digital Music Study, Global Music Study) aid in shedding light on the market shares and user-adaptability of the digital platforms. The findings reveal the transformations brought about in the popular music industry in India with a thriving digital ecosystem.

This chapter proceeds as follows. After this introductory section, Section 11.2 presents a brief history of the role and dominance of the popular music industry in India – the Bollywood. Section 11.3 investigates the digital revolution in India which brings about many transformations, particularly with music streaming and the development of non-film/indie music. Section 11.4 delves deeper into this growing demand for non-film music, whereas Section 11.5 investigates how the term 'indie' has evolved in the Indian context. Section 11.6 presents the persistence of informal practices in the industry. The commonplace culture of free consumption among Indian consumers becomes the focus of Section 11.7. Section 11.8 explores the growth of the live industry in relation to the independent industry. The chapter concludes with discussion over the transformation of the popular music industry in India with the emergence of the digital revolution and poses questions over the possible challenges, pitfalls, and opportunities for this uniquely emerging market.

11.2 Dominance of Bollywood in popular music

Film music is considered an essential component of popular culture in South Asia (Manuel 1988). Indeed, one of the distinct characteristics of the Indian popular music industry is its strong association with the film industry. In fact, popular music can be considered all but synonymous with film music in India (Booth 2015). According to Booth and Shope (2013), post-independence (1947) hardly any popular music was being recorded and commercially produced outside of film music. Even up until the 1980s, there was virtually no concept of commercial non-film music apart from traditional and folk music in India (Ganti 2013). Therefore, for a long period of time there existed a unique situation in India as nearly all music production was under the control of the film industry with no popular music industry outside of it. Thus, the close association between film and music led to film music dominating nearly all the popular music disseminated to and consumed by the masses for several decades. Hence, Bollywood along with the regional film music contributed to shaping India's popular music culture.

The inclusion of music in Indian films is a very persistent phenomenon, wherein the music acts not just as background music but is considered wholly integral to cinematic storytelling, and particularly essential to tap into the full potential of the market. The popularity and continued relevance of film songs in India go far beyond the three hours and four walls of cinema halls. Often the music acts as a primary reason for audience to watch a film multiple times in the cinema (Manuel 1988). Often the music of a film is released prior to the release of the film, and its popularity with filmgoers and consumers often provides first indications of the possible success of the film. Creekmur (2005) argues that if the music isn't a hit upon release, the film isn't likely to be either. As Rehman (2016: 326) states, "hit movies are remembered not only for their stars, but also for their songs". This illustrates the intriguing, yet vital role film music plays in the commercial success of films in India.

At the same time, though film songs appear to be a significant social and cultural phenomenon, they remain economically insignificant for the producers when compared to the film. Morcom (2008) in her interview with film producer Rajkumar Barjatya describes how producers would essentially make 'peanuts' of songs. Booth (2015) also argues that film producers were considered the persons also producing the music. The active producers and creators of the songs (composers, musicians, lyricists, singers) have historically operated on a work-for-hire basis with the film producers, making the employer (the film producers) the first owners of the songs. A kind of package deal has long existed in the film industry, wherein creators are offered up front payments to give up their rights to the music. Therefore, film producers become music producers and consequently right holders; essentially also acting as record labels and music publishers.

Up until recently music in India has served more of a playback role, highlighting how in the creative process, importance is primarily given to the persons on the screen – the actors – and the music and singers follow accordingly. This also alludes to how film culture has dominated popular music culture in India to the extent that unlike in the West, there is no visible culture of 'superstar musicians' outside of the film music industry in the country. Popular film music singers such as Kishore Kumar and Lata Mangeshkar in the past, and Sonu Nigam and Shreya Ghoshal in the present have managed to carve a space for themselves as musical superstars from India on the global platform. While contemporary film music superstars do manage to release music not featured in movies, they are primarily known for performing Bollywood music live, both domestically and worldwide.

Fascinatingly, also unlike in the West, the global major labels – Sony, Warner, and Universal, face quite some competition in the Indian market from what is often called "local majors" in the country – Zee Music and T-Series. These local music labels and publishers do not just produce the music but also the films these are featured in, "allowing labels to build their own monopoly" (Hu 2017). Bollywood music albums also account for nearly 80% of revenues for the music industry in India, with the local majors essentially capturing the largest share of the market (Gurbaxani 2019).

11.3 The burgeoning digital music ecosystem

In recent decades, the considerable economic and cultural impacts of technology, particularly digital technology, has led to remarkable transformations of both the global and Indian music industries. Post-economic liberalization of India in the 1990s, there has been rapid growth of the use of technology in everyday lives in India, and the music industry is no different. The country's rapid digitalization since 2015, with the 'Digital India' initiative, the provision of cheap 4G and broadband service 'to every Indian' by telecom company Reliance Jio, followed by other players like Airtel, Vodafone, etc., and the availability of cheap smartphones have been catalytic in transforming the Indian digital ecosystem, and ultimately disrupting traditional media content and consumption in India (Peto 2017). Today, India is now second only to China in the largest smartphone market in terms of users, roughly around 502 million (Newzoo 2020).

The growing audio and video streaming platforms (also referred to as 'over-the-top platforms') in the country have been significant in shaping both the creative content that is being produced, as well as the way it is being consumed. Unlike the Western markets, Indian consumption has essentially bypassed both CDs as well as digital downloads (Hu 2017). With both record sales and digital downloads being an unfeasible source of revenue for the Indian music industry, India's swift transition to online streaming is proving to be both remarkable and possibly lucrative. Audio streaming platforms are currently experiencing considerable growth in consumption with revenues only expected to rise over time. The Indian music industry accounted for a total of INR 10,680 million (roughly $156 million) in revenues in 2018 (about 0.006% of the country's GDP). Digital music revenues of the country accounted for about 78% of the recorded music revenues in the same year (Figure 11.1), as demonstrated by data acquired from the Indian music industry (IMI) and the International Federation

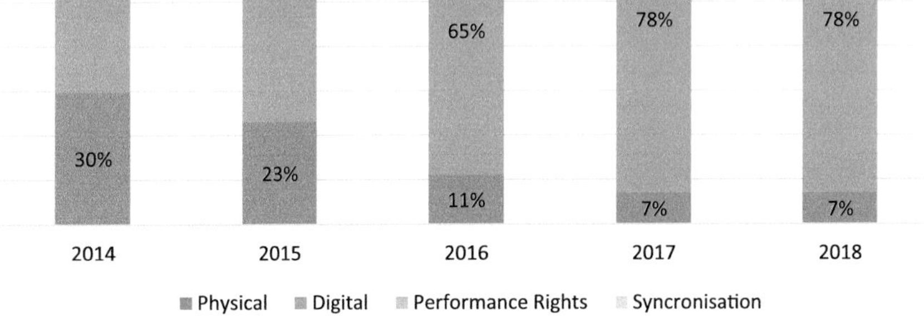

Figure 11.1 Indian music industry revenue share

Source: based on IMI-IFPI (2019).

of the Phonographic Industry (IFPI)'s digital study report (2019). In addition to these figures, the music streaming revenues from subscriptions also grew by 33.3% and the free/ad-supported streaming revenues grew by 43.6% in 2018 (IMI 2019). Multiple local streaming services exist on the market such as JioSaavn, Gaana, and Hungama, in addition to the global industry giants Spotify, Apple, and Amazon Music, all of which stream English language and international music in addition to Bollywood and regional language songs. According to IMI (2019), streaming services including JioSaavn, Gaana, Wynk Music, Apple Music, and Amazon music have collectively accounted for 150 million users in India in 2018.

However, despite the great number of users, the Indian music industry's revenues was merely 2% of the US music industry revenues in 2018 (around $7.65 billion) (IFPI 2019). Thus, while the digital infrastructure has facilitated music consumption in India, the Indian music industry still faces some critical issues that hinder its digital reach and revenue potential.

The concept of subscription-based streaming for content is still something of an uphill climb for India. Despite the country boasting of the lowest mobile data costs in the world and paid streaming services being provided for minimal prices (Table 11.1), both of which should ideally come in support of online music consumption, the actual consumer willingness to pay is extremely low. According to IMI (2019), the current conversion of free to subscription-based model on streaming platforms among the 150 million music listeners is roughly at about 1%. Therefore, while the consumption of free/ad-based streaming continues to grow, the development of subscription-based streaming in the country still has a long way to go.

Additionally, the innumerable homegrown music streaming platforms are competing with not just global leaders for the lion's share of the market, they also seek an edge over alternative forms of entertainment and media consumption. The most prominent form of music consumption in India continues to be YouTube, with an online reach of over 225 million monthly active users in India (IANS 2018). A possible explanation for the popularity of audio and video

Table 11.1 Monthly subscription prices for streaming platforms in India, 2019

Service	*Monthly subscription price*
Apple Music	Rs. 120 ($1.60)
Spotify	Rs. 119 ($1.67)
Google Play Music	Rs. 99 ($1.39)
Amazon Music	Rs. 129 ($1. 72)
YouTube Music	Rs. 125 ($1.76)
JioSaavn	Rs. 99 ($1.39)
Gaana	Rs. 99 ($1.39)
Hungama	Rs. 99 ($1.39)

Source: Compiled by the author.

synced content on YouTube over other services in India may be tied to the visual, cinematic tradition of film music. As mentioned earlier, Indian listeners are inclined to consume music for both the audio and visual element, that is not fulfilled by strictly audio streaming platforms.

Furthermore, the presence of media piracy with weak IP enforcement in place is still cited as a big barrier to growth in the Indian music industry. There is a massive shadow economy of pirated music in the country, estimated to be more than a $1 billion industry (UNESCO 2005). Shops in small towns and villages in India provide services such as sideloading MP3s on phones or selling SD cards full of MP3s for a nominal fee. Simultaneously, the digital space is ripe for piracy among young consumers, who generally prefer file-sharing and stream-ripping websites to premium/paid streaming services. Nearly 67% of listeners continue to pirate music, a number much higher than the global average of 27% (IMI 2019).

Ultimately, however, in spite of the possible pitfalls, strong digital infrastructure in the form of inexpensive electronic devices and cheap broadband and data and a plethora of digital services and platforms are creating a space for India's digital ecosystem to flourish. At the same time, these exceptional circumstances are also creating a fertile ground for a whole new music industry to emerge alongside Bollywood. As Booth (2015) states, for long the popularity and accessibility of film music in India have carved out very little economic or cultural scope for the development of distinct musical 'stars' to materialize out of the shadows of Bollywood. However, independent artists are now utilizing these new digital channels, increasingly creating content, and interacting with their audience directly, while symbiotically exploiting the offline space, as the live music sector experiences an accelerating boom in the country.

11.4 Growing demand for non-film and live music

Independent or Indie music (also referred to as non-film music) in India has come to comprise of any music, irrespective of genre, that does not fall under Bollywood, regional films, classical, devotional, and folk music. In the Indian context, it also includes artists producing and distributing independently. Indie music has truly come of age in less than a decade in India. Shashidhar (2013) argues that non-film music has historically never been lucrative enough to be the focus for record labels in India. While time and time again, creators of non-film music have tried to make a space for themselves in the industry – whether it was the "indi-pop" wave in the 1990s (Bora 1996), or the programming efforts of television shows such as Pepsi MTV Indies and Channel V Launchpad in early 2000s – most of these initiatives have been short-lived or overshadowed by Bollywood. The economic and cultural significance of Bollywood and other regional cinema is so widespread that creators and artists are often compelled to create content for the film industry if they wish to make a name for themselves.

As producer Karsh Kale succinctly puts it "Before this, there was Bollywood, and everything else was deep underground" (The Guardian 2018). Over the last decade, the Indian music landscape has seen a transformation with the rise of multiple independent music scenes, subcultures, and movements outside of Bollywood. One of the biggest contributing factors to this changing musical ecosystem has been the growth of domestic live music festivals such as the Sunburn Festival in Goa, Magnetic Fields in Rajasthan, and NH7 Weekender, a multi-city music festival. In addition to bringing down international artists, the music festival industry has also championed new and homegrown talents at various editions over the years.

Economic developments in India have also led to the growth of new creators and consumers in the music market – the rising young and urban middle class. Booth (2015) notes the transformation of the Indian music industry over the years, with steadily growing nightlife in elite hotel bars in urban centres providing the earliest performance spaces for independent artists. Specially-designed music venues for independent artists in urban centres, as well as growing informal and underground events such as small 'home' concerts and 'listening room' concerts, have continued to pop up in less than a decade despite unsuitable political climate is indicative of a growing demand for alternatives to mainstream Bollywood and regional film music.[1] It is also interesting to note that while the underground and informal music movements in Western Europe were largely led by underprivileged and disenfranchised youth, it is the urban and upper middle class that is primarily leading the movement in India. This same period has seen a multifold increase in the number of artists and music genres, ranging from folk, hip hop and rap, and indie rock to techno, trance, and drum and bass, all under the umbrella term of 'indie music', as well as a significant growth in the influence of these independent music scenes on not just the development of music cultures but also Bollywood.[2]

The growing digital presence in the country has also provided independent artists with a space to produce and simultaneously connect with their audience, allowing them to create new expressions and styles of music, and promote their works without going through channels (Nayan 2017). Social media platforms are also helping creators build global networks, making it easier for artists to find like-minded individuals and collaborate. With music labels and creators increasingly shifting towards digital business models, and a progressive young demographic exposed to global trends, demand for homegrown independent creators is steadily increasing, not just on streaming platforms but also for live performances in urban areas. At the same time, Indie acts are more dependent on social media than Bollywood artists, because social media likes and follows play a significant role in decisions regarding being signed for live acts.[3] The slowly emerging independent music industry is also seeing a rise in the number of indie record labels, artist management companies, and artist collectives in the major urban centres.[4] Indie artists such as Nucleya, The Local Train, Sandunes,

Ankur Tewari, and Prateek Kuhad, for instance, have successfully carved out a space for themselves in the music industry, not just nationally, but also on the global stage.

This evolving Indie music scene in India is not only enjoying increasing demand from listeners but also corporations and brands that are attempting to leverage new sounds to attract young consumers while supporting the indie music ecosystem. Large corporations ranging from beer and alcohol brands to clothing and sneaker companies have all jumped the bandwagon of utilizing the indie music space to create new advantageous marketing strategies. Indian beer brand Bira 91's collaboration named Freeflow with Indian and international hip hop artists is one of the more popular examples, with a series of concerts aimed at promoting Indian hip-hop acts (Wildcity, n.d.). At the same time, while experiential marketing projects like these certainly bring visibility and income to both the artists and the brands, in general artists within the indie industry seem to frown upon the associations, citing differences in visions and motives as an important factor.[5] Some artists also find that "shaping a cultural community that is built around and through the music is severely hindered when events are heavily corporatized".[6]

Additionally, despite digital platforms exacerbating the popularity of independent music, they haven't successfully unseated the powerful behemoth that is Bollywood music. Bollywood music continues to be the most consumed on all the streaming services, accounting for nearly 70% of streaming revenues, further indicating a clear dominance of major Indian labels in the digital market as well (Hu 2017). IFPI's survey of 3000 internet users in India revealed that over 60% of respondents named new and old/vintage Bollywood music as their top favourite, making those the most popular genres on streaming platforms (IFPI 2019). This also strongly ties to the culture of music consumption in India, where algorithmic recommendations do not necessarily work but music consumption rather depends on individual search and discovery of music. In the case of the average music consumer in India, these searches usually circle around known Bollywood actors, directors, and singers, making the discovery of non-film music more difficult. Furthermore, with Bollywood music being consumed the most on all streaming platforms and generating about 70% of the streaming revenues (IMI 2019), there appears to be a clear dominance of the major Indian labels in the digital space as well.

Regardless, as small concentrations and clusters of independent music scenes have started to emerge in different urban sectors in the country, with growing numbers of creators, agencies, collectives and labels, substantial corporate spending, and a thriving playground for live music and performance venues, there happen to be clear indications of increasing demand for alternatives to mainstream film music. At the same time, what also becomes clear is the visible growth of nascent progressive youth culture and entrepreneurial spirit that is rather steeped in informality, as far as the activities and processes of function are concerned.

11.5 The evolution of indie

It is interesting to note that the concept of underground and indie music, while often considered a Western import, does tend to go beyond the Westernized idea of mere creators producing independently or signed to independent labels within the Indian context. At first glance, the Western influence is certainly visible in the beginnings of the independent music movement in India in the 1990s–2010s, primarily in the music stylings. Earlier Indian bands were often inspired by popular Western bands such as Radiohead, Tame Impala, Arctic Monkeys, etc. and would employ subgenres such as Indie rock, Indie electro, etc. to label their works. Over time, however, genres and scenes that embrace the local culture, instruments, and traditional sounds have also been included in the understanding of Indian indie, including niche genres such as folk music and Dalit music, etc. This 'indie' recognition of these small concentrations of music scenes and subcultures in the different urban sectors is something of a recent phenomenon. Bangalore's nascent experimental and noise music, the lo-fi and folk music scene in Delhi, or the electronic music explosion through the country are just some of the examples.

The underground hip-hop subculture in the slums of Dharavi in Mumbai has also been fast-growing, increasingly catching the attention of the mainstream. While commercially driven hip-hop has been popular in India in film music, songs with more socially conscious and politically charged messages have been developing only in recent years. This growing subculture has also led to socially innovative projects, such as the creation of the After School of Hip-Hop in the heart of Dharavi – a rented public school space that transforms into a school of hip-hop learning for the children of Dharavi every evening. These small clusters of creators and artists in different spaces lead to lot of learning, collaboration, and competition, simultaneously helping create niche communities of creators and consumers in different urban areas.

The earlier Western influence was limited to not just musical stylings but also language. Earlier Indian bands in the indie circuit, Pentagram, Soulmate, Junkyard Groove, and Sky Rabbit to name a few, primarily recorded in English, perhaps as a way to set themselves apart from Bollywood. However, over the past decade, the number of artists performing and recording multilingually or bilingually has increased substantially, the language association to Bollywood no longer appearing to be a deterrent. Artists such as Prateek Kuhad, Taba Chake, and When Chai Met Toast increasingly release music in both Hindi and English. Many indie artists have started by releasing music only in English and shifting to bilingual releases over time. Interestingly, within the rap community, artists from Dharavi, Mumbai but also other parts of the country rap not just in English and Hindi but also in Marathi, Tamil, Punjabi, Marwari, and dozens of regional languages and dialects.

This evolution could be attributed to multiple reasons. One reason may be that indie artists find that singing in Hindi eliminates any possible linguistic barrier and allows them to reach and connect with a larger audience. Providing film-goers with alternatives to Bollywood music by singing in Hindi can also increase the chances of artists to secure stardom of some kind in the country, much like the Bollywood singing superstars. This becomes evident when looking at Hindi Rapper DIVINE, which has gained nearly 3 million monthly listeners on Spotify (as of Jan 2021) comparable to current top Bollywood singer Neha Kakkar's 6 million (as of Jan 2021). Furthermore, a reason often cited by several bilingual artists is that like most young urban Indians who transition easily between languages, a lot of artists find it natural and comfortable to express themselves in both Hindi and English. Therefore, it is often just a spontaneous choice, depending on the need for the music.

11.6 The informal networks and practices

Creative industries are often characterized by the existence of a substantial number of SMEs largely located in the informal economy, marked by a high degree of self-employment, independent, and project-based work (Barrowclough and Kozul-Wright 2008). The informal economy, as defined by International Labour Organization (ILO), comprises any form of employment in both formal or informal organizations that occurs without formal contracts, labour benefits, and any kind of social security (Alter Chen 2005). Informal actors tend to produce goods and services that address an important segment of otherwise unmet consumer demand. High regulatory costs in India have been considered vital in the creation of an informal economy that witnesses large volumes of unregulated economic activity. The informal cultural economy certainly is not a new phenomenon in India; informal activities have always existed in some form or another in many different industries, and the independent music industry in India is no different.

A large portion of the main stakeholders in this industry – the artists, the independent record labels, and the artist management agencies among others, seem to operate *off the books* and are generally beyond the reach of official regulation. Most of the businesses functioning in the independent music space are not registered entities.[7] Entrepreneurs often find that the cost of formalizing activities far outweighs the benefits, especially when not enough revenues are being generated. In this sense, a lot of the indie organizations work on volunteer effort, tend to operate on a small-scale, and are largely informal. DIY home studios and setups and equipment on loan are also commonplace, to avoid large expenses.

Independent artists are also all too familiar with 'napkin deals' organized around oral contracts, as they consciously steer away from written commitments and legal jargon. A large part of this is due to a very apparent lack of knowledge among creators on various matters of the process of production, from the nuances of intellectual property rights and ownership to contract negotiations and legalities.[8] Some of this also has to do with the fact that most of this industry is made up of familiar social circles and known communities, which allow for informal arrangements. Furthermore, as multiple interviewees noted, every year dozens of new indie record labels enter the market, but many of these initiatives end up being doomed ventures within years.[9] This may, of course, be due to disadvantages that specifically labels within the niche market tend to face. For instance, major labels benefit from economies of scope – the ability to invest in a diverse, large, and stable roster of artists and ultimately mitigate the inherent uncertainty of their artists' success and spread out their risk. Indies, however, do not have this advantage and often fail to manage their financial risks over time. For independent artists and labels, financing is primarily required at the production stage of the value chain.

In addition to low access due to informality, financing within the creative industries faces several barriers in the form of information asymmetry, weak institutional support, low levels of entrepreneurial capability, and piracy (Cunningham et al. 2008). In developing countries, informal networks of people become extremely important in order to leverage any form of financial support, with crowdfunding and pooling being the most common modes of finance. In general, however, stakeholders in the indie space tend to have limited access to finance, and any revenues made from one project by a creator or a label are simply reinvested to finance another project. Due to the nature of these informal career trajectories, creators and labels face high levels of personal risks in the form of financial losses. Simultaneously, it makes it difficult for creators, labels, and agencies to scale production and distribution activities. Attracting an international audience and any kind of foreign investment is also challenging when brand spending and promotion become expensive undertakings, although new technologies and social media platforms do provide avenues to create awareness and overcome distribution barriers.[10] Overall, however, the livelihood of most creators continues to be threatened as they struggle to find a sustainable niche for themselves.

11.7 The apparent culture of 'free'

What is considered, among different stakeholders, as something of an ingrained cultural obstacle in the success of this music industry is the average Indian consumer's low willingness to pay for music. According to the Nielsen Music Survey of 1570 online Indian consumers in the age range of 16–45, Indians spend over 20 hours a week listening to music compared to the global average of 17.8 hours, and that more than 70% of the participants consider music a very important part of their lives (Nielsen 2018). Despite that industry experts claim that more than half of those consumers are unwilling to pay for it.[11] As one music journalist argues "there has never been a strong culture of paying for music in India",[12] suggesting that for as long as music has existed, the *jugaadu* or the ever-improvising Indian consumer has found a way to dodge any kind of payments and maximize their benefit – be it the recording of radio music on cassettes or the use of P2P networks and torrents in the online space. This is also seen to some extent globally with the shutdown of Napster in 2001 leading to the proliferation of several decentralized competitor platforms. As Farchy (2011) argues, the perception of cultural goods formed over time leads to assuming differentiated costs for different goods, and the culture of 'free' is another byproduct of the direct and unlimited access of cultural goods over the internet. However, assessing the average Indian consumer's unwillingness to pay not only raises the question of how much of essential expenditure music may be for them but also indicates something larger about the value system that shapes consumption in India, i.e. how consumers value the necessity of cultural and creative goods in the country.

Different levels of music engagement translate to different kinds of consumer behaviour, with core fans more likely to have a higher willingness to pay for the music they consume. But free access to music is essentially assumed among most Indian consumers. This becomes evident by the two most common consumption practices in India highlighted earlier – pirated music and ad-supported streaming preference. According to IFPI's survey (2019), 58% of the 3000 respondents claimed the use of stream-ripping websites for music downloads. When asked about their unwillingness to pay for subscriptions, 51% responded that they preferred Youtube's virtually no-cost access to an abundant collection, whereas nearly half additionally considered paid audio streaming to be an expensive endeavour. Freely shared music and the particularly easy availability of music through piracy in the Indian market is considered rather commonplace, a fundamental trait of informal media economies. This has also seemingly established the expectation among consumers that digital music should be free or priced extremely low. This has an impact on the pricing decisions of the subscription services in India which are priced relatively low (Table 11.1) when compared to the global averages, undoubtedly taking into consideration both the low willingness to pay as well as lower disposable incomes. Naturally, slow progress is being made in converting users for whom a few ads are a small price to pay for the privilege of free music into paid subscribers, and an overall lack of willingness to pay for content is witnessed among Indian consumers.

Interestingly, this unwillingness to pay also extends towards the live industry, where venue and event organizers often have to provide a large number of free tickets and passes to various funding, authorizing, and licensing bodies that provide them with the resources to arrange concerts, and overtime struggle to make any sort of profits.[13] Thus, an intriguing sort of free culture exists not just in the physical and digital consumption of music but also within the live industry, which ultimately ties to the value system in India and possibly leads to devaluing both the music as well as the paying consumers.

11.8 The promises and challenges of the live industry

Considering Bollywood music's large market share in the country, breaking into the streaming market on its own appears to be quite a challenge for the non-film/independent artist. As indie artists tend to settle for negligible transactional per stream revenues (numbers revealed to be somewhere between Rs. 0.07 and 0.12 per stream[14]), it appears as no surprise that live performances and concerts become the main source of income for them, with festivals providing seasonal income, i.e., income earned during festival season in autumn-winter. By and large for all interviewed artists, digital platforms serve merely as a promotional tool, used primarily to gain access to performances at bars and venues.[15]

On average, upcoming, and new artists are paid anywhere between Rs. 10,000 and 30,000 ($130–400) by venues in the major cities like Delhi and Mumbai.[16] Furthermore, venues often operate at a loss when hiring independent artists to perform, further impacting the rewards received by the artists, as hiring a DJ and hosting regular Bollywood music nights would prove to be much more lucrative for them.[17] The pop-up, informal, and underground gigs that are put together by music-loving organizers with their own funds, often pay next to nothing or nothing at all in exchange for an opportunity to perform and promote. For some artists, being employed as session musicians for other acts allows them to pursue music full-time. But the overall picture suggests that employment in this industry is often part-time and supplemented by multiple job holdings in related (teaching music) and unrelated domains (IT/bank), to make ends meet.

Many artists also agree that the live industry is rather disorganized and disconnected, with little collaboration outside of the local networks in each major city.[18] Concert tours, a popular concept in the West, of artists touring in different cities every (other) day of the week is also rather unexplored in the country. A reason for this may be that tours become an expensive endeavour as live music attendance is largely reserved for the weekends and people are less likely to go to a concert on the weekday. Furthermore, the existence of a handful of booking agencies across the country such as Unmute, Krunk, and Gently Altered help arrange tours for some independent artists and mitigate some uncertainty in the live industry, but overall, artists find arranging tours when not connected to known agencies remains cumbersome due to a general lack of information about venues, regulations, or access.

Censorship and an unfavourable political climate are other concerns cited by various artists. As Times (2015) reports, freedom of expression for the creative and cultural industries is rather limited in many Asian economies like India. This is certainly echoed by multiple artists who reveal their inability to make music a lucrative career as being tied to a lack of institutional and political support for the arts in the country.[19] Several instances of artists critical of the government, political authorities, or religious icons in their performances being charged with sedition have provoked outrage among the artistic community in the country (Stalin 2018). An example also cited by some artists of regulatory obstruction is the police crackdown and consequent shutdown of dozens of live music venues in Bengaluru since 2018. These venues were required to procure special permits and licenses in order to continue live performances at their premises, which were considered difficult to acquire by the owners, ultimately putting the venues out of business (Swamy 2018).

At the same time, as Caves (2000) has noted, creative industries are marked by an excess supply of creators and content, which doesn't just weaken their bargaining power but also makes attracting and retaining potential consumers' attention that much more difficult. This excess supply of creators and content is also visible in India, as the use of digital technologies certainly allows independent creators to grow in numbers. At the same time, it can be observed that these artists are still struggling to capture the imagination of a large enough section of society to make their works commercially viable.

11.9 Conclusions

As observed so far, the music culture in India continues to be inseparable from film culture, a phenomenon that also differentiates the Indian music industry from the global one. Not only is Bollywood music experiencing a consumption growth, it also remains on top of the charts even in the streaming economy. The concept of global 'superstar' musicians is largely limited to popular artists within the Bollywood space.

Even so, growing economic developments and the widespread use of digital technology have opened up new avenues in support of alternative creative sectors that serve the young and urban in the country. While the emergence of digitization in the west had led to the disruption of the music industry globally, digitization along with socio-economic change in India has instead helped creators and entrepreneurs lay the foundation for an Indian music industry that has so far succeeded in operating without close ties to the domestic film industry.

This research shows the emergence of various informal networks and *off the books* enterprises and activities in urban sectors that are helping develop small communities of independent and niche music creators and consumers. The burgeoning digital ecosystem supported by a vibrant live industry is facilitating the growth of independent music and allowing for various underground and independent music cultures to thrive in many ways. Independent music, although considered a Western import in its earliest form, is now a genuinely homegrown form of cultural expression, comprising genres, languages, sounds, and instruments native to various parts of the country. Finally, the independent music industry is not just creating a space for innovation, collaboration, and artistic expression but also inviting mainstream recognition and an enormous amount of promotional spending from brands.

It should be noted that familiar problems in the music industry worldwide are also visible in India. First, low barriers to entry and an oversupply of creators can be observed. The Indian indie market is marked by large output, with revenues spread among a large number of creators and distributors. Furthermore, despite the demand for new forms of music, financial rewards for most creators, apart from the more well-known ones, remain unpredictable. Most artists receive poor revenues from streams as well as live performances, making multiple job holdings practically a prerequisite in the industry, at least for the first few years of a musician's career. This also raises questions about the apparent culture of 'free' in the consumption patterns of Indian consumers, and it is important to consider the social, cultural, and economic dimension of the value system that dominates the consumption behaviour of cultural goods in the country. Conversion of subscriptions on streaming platforms may help support the huge range of content being produced and demanded by the diverse Indian consumers. Ultimately, with film music so integral a part of the daily life in Indian society, and with major Indian music labels also consolidating market power in the digital and streaming platform, it will be fascinating to observe how the independent music industry carves out a larger space for itself moving forward, from under the shadows of Bollywood.

Notes

1 Multiple independent artists in discussion with the author. Bangalore and Mumbai, April 2018.
2 Multiple independent artists in discussion with the author. Bangalore and Mumbai, April 2018.
3 Independent artist A in discussion with the author. Bangalore, April 2018.
4 Multiple independent artists in discussion with the author. Bangalore and Mumbai, April 2018.
5 Multiple independent artists in discussion with the author. Bangalore and Mumbai, April 2018.
6 Independent artist A in discussion with the author. Bangalore, April 2018.
7 Record label executive S in discussion with the author. Mumbai, April 2018.
8 Music journalist B and Independent artist A, in discussion with the author. Bangalore and Mumbai, April 2018.
9 Multiple independent artists and record label executives in discussion with the author. Bangalore and Mumbai, April 2018.
10 Multiple independent artists in discussion with the author. Bangalore and Mumbai, April 2018.
11 Multiple record label executives in discussion with the author. Bangalore and Mumbai, April 2018.
12 Music journalist B, in discussion with the author. Mumbai, April 2018.
13 Multiple independent artists and record label executives in discussion with the author. Bangalore and Mumbai, April 2018.
14 Multiple independent artists in discussion with the author. Bangalore and Mumbai, April 2018.
15 Multiple independent artists in discussion with the author. Bangalore and Mumbai, April 2018.
16 Multiple independent artists in discussion with the author. Bangalore and Mumbai, April 2018.
17 Multiple independent artists in discussion with the author. Bangalore and Mumbai, April 2018.
18 Multiple independent artists in discussion with the author. Bangalore and Mumbai, April 2018.
19 Multiple independent artists in discussion with the author. Bangalore and Mumbai, April 2018.

References

Alter Chen, M. (2005). *Rethinking the informal economy: Linkages with the formal economy and the formal regulatory environment* (No. 2005/10). WIDER Research Paper.

Barrowclough, D., and Kozul-Wright, Z. (Eds.) (2008). *Creative Industries and Developing Countries: Voice, Choice and Economic Growth.* New York: Routledge.

Booth, G. D. (2015). Copyright law and the changing economic value of popular music in India. *Ethnomusicology*, 59(2), 262–287.

Booth, G. D., and Shope, B. (Eds.) (2013). *More Than Bollywood: Studies in Indian Popular Music.* Oxford: Oxford University Press.

Bora, P. (1996). Channel V and MTV create never-before market for global music. *India Today*. Available at: www.indiatoday.in/magazine/indiascope/story/19961115-channel-v-and-mtv-create-never-before-market-for-global-music-834080-1996-11-15 (last accessed on 25 March 2022).

Caves, R. E. (2000). *Creative Industries: Contracts between Art and Commerce* (No. 20). Cambridge, MA: Harvard University Press.

Creekmur, C. (2005). Popular Hindi cinema and the film song. In Linda Badley, R. Barton Palmer and Steven Jay Schneider (eds.), *Traditions in World Cinema*, pp. 193–202. Edinburgh: Edinburgh University Press.

Cunningham, S., Ryan, M., Keane, M., and Ordonez, D. (2008). Financing creative industries in developing country contexts. In Diana Barrowclough (ed.), *Creative Industries and Developing Countries: Voice, Choice and Economic Growth*, pp. 65–110. New York: Routledge.

Farchy, J. (2011). The internet: Culture for free. In *A Handbook of Cultural Economics, Second Edition.* Cheltenham: Edward Elgar Publishing.

Ganti, T. (2013). *Bollywood: A Guidebook to Popular Hindi Cinema.* Abingdon, UK: Routledge.

The Guardian (2018). India's clubbing scene rises up–but is it a rich man's game?

Gurbaxani, A. (2019). The best of Music Inc 2019: Discussions on the dominance of film music, streaming services in India. *First Post.* Available at: www.firstpost.com/entertainment/the-best-of-music-inc-2019-discussions-on-the-dominance-of-film-music-streaming-services-in-india-6902511.html (last accessed on 25 March 2022).

Hu, C. (2017). How India, the global music industry's sleeping giant, is finally waking up. *Forbes.Com.*

IANS (2018). Youtube watched by 80 percent internet users in India with 225 million active mobile users every month. Available at: www.firstpost.com/tech/news-analysis/youtube-watched-by-80-percent-internet-users-in-india-with-225-million-active-mobile-users-every-month-4403107.html (last accessed on 25 March 2022).

IFPI (2019). IFPI Global Music Report.

IMI (2019). *Audio OTT Economy in India – Inflection Point.* New Delhi: Deloitte.

IMI-IFPI. (2019). Digital music study. Mumbai: IMI-IFPI. Available at: http://indianmi.org/be/wp-content/uploads/2019/09/output.pdf (last accessed on 25 March 2022).

Manuel, P. (1988). Popular music in India: 1901–86. *Popular Music*, 7(2), 157–176.

Morcom, A. (2008). Tapping the mass market: The commercial life of Hindi film songs. *Global Bollywood: Travels of Hindi Song and Dance*, 63–84.

Nayan, R. (2017). *Indie 101: The Ultimate Guide to the Independent Music Industry in India.* New Delhi: Music Gets Me High.

Newzoo (2020). Newzoo global mobile market report 2019-light version. *Newzoo.* Available at: https://newzoo.com/insights/trend-reports/newzoo-global-mobile-market-report-2019-light-version/ (last accessed on 25 March 2022).

Nielsen. (2018). India Music 360. Industry Report, Nielsen.

Peto, E. (2017). Interim economy: An introduction to India's digital music industry. *MediaNama.* Available at: www. medianama.com/2017/07/223-india-digital-music-industry (last accessed on 25 March 2022).

Rehman, S. (2016). The role of music in Hindi cinema. *Synergy*, 12(2), 314–329.

Shashidhar, A. (2013). Freedom song. Available at: www.businesstoday.in/magazine/features/india-music-industry-non-bollywood/story/200971.html (last accessed on 25 March 2022).

Stalin, S. D. J. (2018). Tamil singer Kovan arrested for song criticising PM Modi, Rath Yatra. Available at: www.ndtv.com/tamil-nadu-news/for-song-criticising-pm-modi-trichy-police-arrest-tamil-singer-kovan-1837366 (last accessed on 25 March 2022).

Swamy, R. (2018). Bengaluru has shut down 27 joints that play live music. *The Print*. Available at: https://theprint.in/india/governance/bengaluru-has-shut-down-27-joints-that-play-live-music-heres-why/68783/ (last accessed on 25 March 2022).

Times, C. (2015). *The First Global Map of Cultural and Creative Industries*. London, UK: EY.

UNESCO (2005). The persistence of piracy: The consequences for creativity, for culture, and for sustainable development. UNESDOC, Paris, 1–20.

Wildcity (n.d.). FreeFlow. Available at: www.thewildcity.com/directory/5026-bira-91-freeflow.

12

THE CHANGING LANDSCAPE OF TRAVELLING CINEMA IN MAHARASHTRA, INDIA

Gandharva Pednekar and Purushottam Bhandare

12.1 Introduction

Travelling cinema is a mobile/touring cinema. It can visit and offer services to customers living far away from fixed-site theatres. Over the last century, travelling cinema has tried to bring the magic of moving pictures to audiences across Western countries like the United Kingdom, Germany, and France. In India, travelling cinema had a massive draw in the rural parts. It is an act of watching a movie that we do all the time, but a sense of escapism from reality was presented by travelling cinema was far more significant in the rural parts.

Ben-Ghiat (2003) discusses the growing scholarly work about colonial narratives and representations centred on the Italian colonial cinema. It focuses on the double-edged power of the visual in colonial films concerning both Italian and African audiences. The enthusiasm for visual tools such as cinema links colonial movies to different parts of a colonial culture established on an ethos of ownership and show. Ben-Ghiat (2003) also mentions that the outdoor film projection in Ethiopia has brought the experience of watching films to the colonial people. In the case of outdoor screenings of films, the setting up of projection equipment used to begin in light. This marks commencement of the event, sounds of the generator, screen size, and, after dusk, the truck's headlights; these all have played an integral part in the cinematic experience.

Also, in an African context, the Nigerian Film Industry (Nollywood) has a history of travelling cinema. In Nigeria, filmmaking is mainly divided along with regional and marginally ethnic and religious lines (Olayiwola 2011). Olayiwola (2011) finds that film exhibition in Nigeria took two forms: first, the government and the church operated through the mobile film units (a van), a 16mm projector, a reel of 16mm film, and a motion-picture screen; second, commercial distributors operated through showings in the big halls and film theatres with films brought in through the British Council in London and the Crown Film Unit. According to Adesanya (1998), The Yoruba travelling

DOI: 10.4324/9781003129370-16

theatre, i.e. travelling cinemas, was perhaps the most promising single factor in the evolution of an indigenous cinema in Nigeria. Hence, having established a rich tradition of touring plays, the travelling theatre introduced a regional dimension to the Nigerian film.

> *When the cinema came, the manager was often a blend of the fairground show-man, the travelling theatre proprietor, and the panorama lecturer.*
>
> John H. Bird (1949: 21–22)

Low and Manvell (1948), in their classic study of British film, mark 1906 as the year that witnessed the widespread realisation of permanent purpose-built palaces for the exclusive showing of living pictures. The entertainment environment in the United Kingdom in the 1890s was a dynamic and bewildering mixture of low-class unauthorised venues and practices alongside legitimate theatre, music halls, circuses, operas, lectures, and reading halls, and, of course, the burgeoning cinematograph industry (Toulmin 2010). British fairground is a large outside area used for public events. On these fairgrounds, travelling cinematograph shows are conducted. These shows catered to large urban populations and audiences in smaller market towns and villages, which still presented more traditional and less urbanised forms of leisure events such as the local feast or wake fair (Toulmin 2010). The fairground audience used to be the holiday crowd in Britain. The crowd comprises people who enjoy a break from the everyday work routine and were similar in composition to the seaside audience, who viewed the cinematograph show as part of their escape from monotonous work routines. According to Low and Manvell (1948), the travelling cinema audience is mainly working-class and is composed of entire communities holidaying together or enjoying the attractions of their local fair. Film viewing was not a habit but a one-off occurrence to be enjoyed as part of their trip to the fair or the seaside.

Toulmin (2001), in his article about travelling show-men in Britain in the early 1900s, assessed the feasibility of the travelling cinema (theatre/ exhibitions). He critically evaluated the contextualisation of the films and theatre in local areas. In Britain, the primary focus on films got transformed into the local context rather than fictional stories. This has attracted the local public towards the travelling cinema as they could relate the stories in cinema to the everyday happenings around them.

12.2 Travelling cinema in India and Maharashtra

Bhaumik (2001) has done a comprehensive study on the emergence of the Bombay film industry during the period 1913–1936. According to him, the period from 1900 to 1918 was the era of the cinematographic performance rather than the cinema. The term 'cinematograph exhibitions' therefore denoted the entire institution of film exhibition encompassing the machine, the films shown, the site of the exhibition, the commercial company owning the machine, as well as the audience. These semi-permanent tent-show companies transformed the context of film exhibition, from travelling shows to more permanent cinema halls by being transitory yet stable. Even when cinema halls replaced tent shows, the new halls continued to be called 'cinematographs' for several years. In the 1920s and 1930s, more cinema halls appeared in Bombay. Despite this, there was a rapid increase in the number of touring cinemas in Bombay in that period. Those days films were shown at the Mahim fair, an annual event drawing thousands of people on the occasion of *urs* the *pir* to whom the Mahim dargah was dedicated.

In 1927, Bengal had 36 travelling cinemas compared to only five in Bombay. At the same time, there were approximately 275 permanent cinemas (including seasonal cinemas) in India, while licensed travelling cinemas were 354 (Mahadevan 2010). Before independence, the colonial government provided subvention in loans to construct movie theatres conceiving cinema as a tool for public education. But post-independence, the Indian government followed developmental and 'nation-building' objectives, and a moratorium on 'non-essential building' in the 1950s restricted the construction of new movie theatres (Mahadevan 2010).

Indian cinema and the many domestically produced films they show have attracted vast viewership throughout the country. Apart from Hindi language cinema, which has more outreach due to Hindi speaking hinterland regions of India, the medium is very well developed as regional film industries in Marathi, Telugu, Tamil, Malayalam, Bengali, and Punjabi speaking states. An interesting case of the regional film industry is Maharashtra. Maharashtra's rural population grew from 16.1 million in 1901 to 22.8 million till 1950, while it grew exponentially to 61.5 million in 2011 (Census 2011). Due to infrastructural limitations, cinema in India was largely limited to the urban centres in its early days. As India moved to become a rural agriculture-based economy post-Independence, the entertainment needs of the rural populace brought the cinema to their doorsteps in the form of travelling cinema, also known as touring talkies. In the 1960s, touring companies started flourishing in rural areas in Maharashtra State, which had limited modes of entertainment. The business continued to grow in the coming decades until the period of economic liberalisation in the 1990s.

Travelling cinemas followed the religious calendar to decide exhibition venues where it was enjoyed by the large audience. Watching a movie in a tent pitched by the travelling cinema used to be a communal experience. Travelling cinema's total extravaganza was mainly part of a religious *mela* (fair). Pilgrims travelled from interior villages to offer their prayer at the temple and enjoy the movie shown by travelling cinema (Khan 2016).

Post-liberalisation, satellite television gave access to a world of entertainment within the confinements of households. In Maharashtra, ownership of television sets in households has increased from 67 per cent in 2012 to 90 per cent

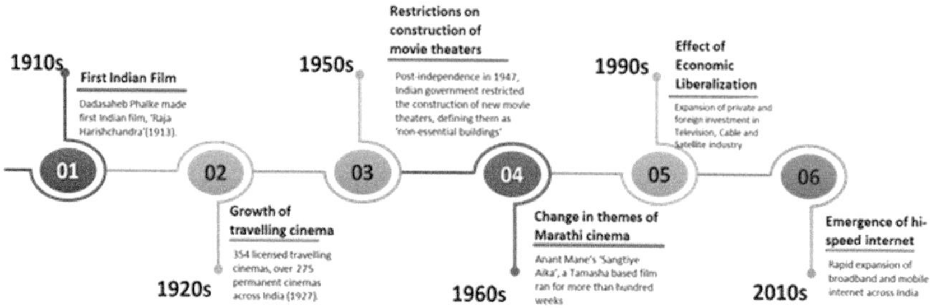

Figure 12.1 Major timelines of travelling cinema in India

Source: Based on Mahadevan (2010), Khan (2016), Hafeez and Ara (2016), KPMG (2019).

in 2019 (FICCI-EY 2019; FICCI-KPMG 2013). Easy access to video home system (VHS)/ video compact disk (VCD)/ digital versatile disc (DVD) players also resulted in declining demands for travelling cinema. With rural India's changing social and economic landscape, the touring talkies were disappearing gradually. Yet considering the rural market potential, several alternatives to touring talkies have emerged in the 2010s (Figure 12.1).

In this regard, the present chapter focuses on exploring the culture of travelling cinema in Maharashtra, its functioning, and perspectives. The chapter also decodes the socio-economic factors that affected the popularity of travelling cinema and how the same factors are building the alternatives for the future of travelling cinema in Maharashtra.

12.3 What are travelling cinemas?

Since its inception, the Indian film industry has witnessed massive growth and transformation in technology and filmmaking. Maharashtra was a case in point. Travelling cinema was the most popular form of film exhibition in the rural parts of Maharashtra. Travelling cinema constitutes many things at a place. This includes projection-related equipment and technicians, promotion activities, art, cultural exhibits, etc. Typically, travelling cinema is shown during the carnival/ pilgrimage known as '*Jatra*' in rural areas.

Jatras are popular cultural theatres/ festivals run by touring groups in rural areas and have been around for many years in India. They are the most popular form of entertainment and celebration for farmers and their families. Over time, live performances like circus acts, magic shows, and travelling cinemas replace plays and theatres. Every year, jatras are held across several villages in Maharashtra after harvesting season. These are held around religious places or district headquarters, having better transport linkages that allow thousands of families to visit and get entertained at the touring talkies. The seating arrangement often reflected on the social hierarchy at that time. Some sections of the community occupy the reverse side of the screen, while the other social groups occupy the front of the screen. The type of seating also differed as economically influential community members were provided chairs or sofas on the side of the front row.

In contrast, others used to sit on the ground. There was no electricity in the rural area and no TV at that time, and not everyone could afford to travel to the cities to watch movies. So, touring talkies were the only option for watching movies.

In primarily rural Maharashtra, travelling cinemas started operating in the 1960s. A travelling cinema company has a truck that carries projectors, film tents, and everything else they need to set up the cinema along with the crew. After setting up the tent, during the daytime, people carrying trumpets used to announce the arrival of travelling cinema in nearby villages. There was only one show from 9 pm to 12 pm the night. The film reels were brought from nearby big cities such as Kolhapur, Sangli, Pune, etc. Each film is recorded in about four to six reels, and there used to be an interval at the end of each reel. A movie used to last two to five days in one village. Most of the Marathi films have played for a long time, only from touring talkies.

Over the decades, the announcement mode changed to megaphones attached to auto-rickshaws, which used to ride all day long in the villages. With the use of tents, the number of shows grew from four to films continuously being played day and night. On the side of the tent, there used to be a ticket counter. The pricing used to be the same amount for everyone. As the business started declining, the travelling cinema owners adopted innovative ideas like getting the actor from the film to stand at the ticket counter to cheer the crowds and take out lucky draws from sold tickets. The winner of the draw received small household items gifts. The alternative sources of income, like advertising of local brands, promotion campaigns of local political leaders through sponsored shows, were also tried. Yet the operating costs of travelling cinema kept increasing while revenues did not improve as per the expectations of travelling cinema owners.

Eventually, the Marathi film industry has transformed with the changing themes. Table 12.1 depicts the transformation of the Marathi film industry. The films were based on Sanskrit epic and devotional folklore stories like 'Raja Harishchandra', the first Indian feature film made by Dadasaheb Phalake in Bombay 1913 (Hafeez and Ara 2016). The theme was transformed into the

Table 12.1 Changing film themes in Maharashtra over decades

Decade	*Social and family drama*	*Comedy*	*Tamasha*	*Other*
1967–70	38 (54%)	6 (8%)	12 (17%)	15 (21%)
1971–80	101 (59%)	24 (14%)	8 (5%)	37 (22%)
1981–90	142 (62%)	50 (22%)	5 (2%)	31 (14%)

Source: adapted from (Kamble 2013)

modern art of music and drama (known as Tamasha) in the 1960s. A Marathi film came in 1959, 'Sangtiye Aika' (Listen, I am speaking), directed by Anant Mane, was run for more than a hundred weeks to break all the records. Then the comedy films have picked up momentum along with the films on social and urban issues. In recent years, Marathi family drama and Hindi films are being shown in travelling cinemas in Maharashtra.

12.4 Studies on travelling cinema

British colonial establishment has a significant influence on Indian cinema (Hughes 1981). The author put factful insight into historical perspective about films, urban mobility, and the beginning of cinema in Chennai, India. He links access to the cinema with the improved transport facilities in urban space. Earlier cinema used to be a part of only urban space where people in and around the city would travel to the cinema tents. The theatre and drama companies started to travel to rural spaces to scale up the people's movements through the cinemas of different genres.

Nair (1999) commented on the beginning of cinema in India. He explored the historical events in the Indian Film Industry and elaborated the efforts and contexts that have changed the face of the Indian film industry. Earlier films were based on stories from mythology. Nair (1999) cites the reason for including mythological stories in the films. Dadasaheb Phalke, a pioneer of Indian cinema, came from an orthodox Hindu household – a family of Brahmin priests with strong religious roots. So, when technology made it possible to tell stories through moving images, it was but natural that the Indian film pioneer turned to his very own rich cultural heritage, the epics, and Puranas for source material. Moreover, the characters, incidents, and plot outlines were very much part of rich Indian traditions and, therefore, close to the heart of every Indian.

Maharashtra has been the birthplace of the Indian film industry (Mujawar 1969). The cultural heritage of India in all its diverse forms is not only the common property of the people of India but of the whole of humankind, and it involves an obligation on the part of all of the film industry to enrich it. Mujawar (1969) portrays the history and culture of the Indian film industry and the relentless efforts of early filmmakers and artists. From 1913 to 1963, the film industry has grown rapidly to be one of the major industries in the Indian economy in terms of revenue generation. Mujawar (1969) also argued that the institutional tradition of film making that studio-based movie productions had descended post-independence. Individual filmmakers started experiencing the success and failure of their films, which led to the growth of the Indian film Industry. Theatre and film companies started taking cinema to travel outdoors to increase the audience and market their films.

Marathi cinema has contributed immensely to the Indian film industry. Ingle (2017) has analysed two historical characteristics of Prabhat. Prabhat is a Marathi film studio and has produced many popular Marathi films. First, how the studio imagined a cinema through linguistically specific regional content and forms of performance. Secondly, how this filmmaking was institutionalised is an example of artistic excellence, therefore conforming to the notion of social respectability. This article accesses anecdotal biographies, archival materials, and existing Prabhat films to evaluate this tendency towards social respectability. He asserts that filmmaking in provincial spaces served to re-align traditional craft with the aid of an emergent form of entertainment. Marathi cinema has been instrumental information of a regional film industry in India as it provided a self-referential prism of cultural production.

This extensive literature review highlights the situation of travelling cinemas around the world. There are very few explorations on the travelling cinema in Maharashtra. The specific focus of this chapter is to establish whether there is still a niche for travelling cinemas in India/Maharashtra and what travelling cinema firms can do to provide valuable services (e.g. attracting paying audiences or public funding, promoting local culture and social cohesion) and operate sustainably.

12.5 Methodology

In this chapter, we employ qualitative empirical methods. Key informant interviews are conducted as a primary technique for the data collection. We selected four interviewees who have been part of the Marathi cinema industry for the last decades and have witnessed changes in the travelling cinema ecosystem. An interview guide was used for asking questions to these key informants. The interview guide listed the topics to be covered and focused on critical aspects of travelling cinema. In-person and telephonic interviews were conducted with these selected key informants. The in-depth interviews were conducted through multiple sessions depending upon the availability of key informants. Collected information has been transcribed, checked, and cleaned with qualitative data analysis tools such as Atlas.ti.

12.6 Insider perspectives on the Marathi film industry

12.6.1 Sameer Ramesh Surve

Sameer Ramesh Surve is one of the self-aware directors in the regional film industry. He has directed seven films since 2012, out of which four have been released until now, namely Shree Partner (2012), Nachaniya (Bhojpuri) (2017), Shubh Mangal (2018), and Judgement (2019). He likes to present societal issues through commercial cinema. His first film, Shree Partner, focused on the lack of communication among spouses, leading to a gradual breakdown of marriage as an institution. Nachaniya dealt with the discrimination faced by children of performing artists in the heartland areas of Bihar. Shubh Mangal underlined issues of live-in relationships in India, while Judgement dealt with topics like female feticide and mental health. Sameer has been associated with the Marathi film industry since 2001.

Sameer felt that the era of travelling cinema saw many transitions, from the time it ventured into the Jatras to the current time where the elite class is looked down upon. In the 1960s, when travelling cinema was entering the Jatras, the Marathi films largely showcased stories related to Gods, religious scriptures, and ardent devotees. This type of devotional story had a huge market in the untapped rural market as the urban areas now had several single-screen theatres and started watching stories related to vast genres. The reels of older films were available in abundance, and projectors were usually bought second-hand from urban theatres. As these were Japanese or American-made projectors, they had more extended durability and were low on maintenance. Tents were also rented in the initial years, but the owners procured their tents as the business increased. The stories moved from devotional to Tamasha, a local dance form in Maharashtra.

As a performing art, Tamasha already had a huge audience in the Jatras; the films having one or two dance acts of Tamasha started becoming audience favourites in Jatras in the 1960s and 1970s. During 1980–1990, the Marathi film industry had witnessed the great comedy phenomenon of Shri. Dada Kondke. His films primarily catered to a rural audience and usually had sexually suggestive dialogues in comic narration. Though these films earned money, they alienated the urban audience from Marathi films. This was the time when Marathi cinema survived by the profits it received from the travelling cinemas.

By the 2000s, Marathi cinema went through a transitional phase, exploring various new subjects, which had stories in rural regions but were made for an urban multiplex going audience. The travelling cinema owner started showing old Marathi or Hindi movies. This was the beginning of people losing interest in watching the cinema in a tent. By now, cable television also provided better access to Marathi content at the luxuries of one's own house. The rural economy also started to benefit from liberalisation. Many of the new investors were sugar cane farmers and mill owners, who enjoyed higher disposable incomes and could afford to invest in film production. The fascination of the cinema industry and the glamour associated with actors attracted these newly rich into film production. But with the limited amount they had to invest in films, the quality of films further deteriorated.

The A-listed actors from Marathi cinema did not want to associate them with Jatras anymore. This created the second rung of actors who started regularly acting in these films explicitly made for Jatras. Many producers started insisting that the actress sits at the counter while tickets were being sold as an added attraction. But by now, the spiral of loss had begun, with less income, the maintenance of projectors, tent, audio equipment all were affected. This had a direct negative impact on the experience of watching travelling cinema as a whole.

Sameer is also of the view that the one-time producers, who vanished after producing just one movie, did more harm than good to the Marathi film industry in general and travelling cinema in particular. The films were such formulaic clichés that they no more had an audience and sullied the reputation of travelling cinemas.

Overall, the interview highlights the changing genres of Marathi films over a period of time and how improvement in education and economy brought about a change in audience perceptions. It also highlights that post-liberalisation, the travelling cinemas could not match the rapid development in technology, which led to its closure.

12.6.2 Virendra Nevrekar

Virendra Nevrekar is the Director of Nevrekar Institute of Performing Arts and is also involved in filmmaking through his production house Veenveer vision. Being from the Art and Education field, Virendra had an overview of the emergence and decline of travelling cinemas, focusing on social and cultural values rather than financial aspects. He stated that, for the rural populace, travelling cinema acted as an avenue for entertainment and as a place for social and cultural cohesion where all the community members come together to experience the world of cinema. He elaborated that Laavani, Tarpa, Balya, and other such dance forms were largely cultural heritages of Maharashtra. The misconception of Laavani artists performing at Tamasha as courtesans developed a negative outlook towards Laavani as an art form. Laavani is a popular folk art in Maharashtra. It is a combination of traditional song and dance, which is particularly performed to the beats of Dholki, a percussion instrument. Laavani is noted for its powerful rhythm. It has contributed substantially to the development of Marathi folk theatre.

The female populace in rural areas was now averse to watching or participating in Laavani; the male members were also looked down upon if they visited Tamasha performances. At this point, the travelling cinema came, showing devotional films, the concept was new to the rural audience, and the films were family-friendly. Due to societal norms, the females never used to go alone to the Jatras. They used to take the entire family with them. The limited entertainment options in rural areas made watching films in travelling cinema an annual pilgrimage of sorts. Some Laavani artists joined the Marathi film industry themselves, but they were limited to dance numbers in the films.

Virendra felt that art constantly evolves and how we view it changes its popularity. The hunger for entertainment never dies; it only changes the medium. Tamashas' popularity declined and led to the blooming of travelling cinema to approximately 2000 such units across Maharashtra. The phase began its descent with the entry of satellite cable television in rural households. Television gave access to the entertainment needs of the rural population at a fraction of the costs of taking the entire family to a travelling cinema. The female audiences felt that they no longer had to venture into community spaces and sit with unknown men to fulfil their entertainment needs. The convenience of watching films or daily soaps at your own time was far greater than the willingness to watch a film on a big screen. The younger generation, who had limited say about the content they could watch on television, was distancing from it when the internet revolution took place. The consumption of art again changed formats, as entertainment became handheld with mobile devices. With the rise of YouTube channels based in rural areas, creating localised content was lapped up by the younger generation of audience. The utility of travelling cinema as a form of entertainment came to an end, and it became another relic of the past located in Maharashtra's famed Jatra's.

Overall, the interview underlines the decline of traditional folk arts and cultural aspects of the rural population in Maharashtra. It also highlights how technology changed movie viewing from a community-based experience to household experience to individual experience leading to a decline in travelling cinemas.

12.6.3 Sachin Zoting

The case of Sachin Zoting's Prakash Ganga production is very peculiar and illustrates how individual errors by travelling cinema owners lead to the decline of the industry. Sachin's father had a footwear shop in Dadar Market, one of the busiest commercial areas at the heart of Mumbai city. After graduation, Sachin also joined his father in the family business. Since college, he liked to act in one-act plays. A one-act play is a play that has only one act, as distinct from plays that occur over several acts. One-act plays may consist of one or more scenes. Through his interest in the performing arts, he became interested in producing films and established Prakash Ganga Productions for producing Marathi films in 2015. But as he explored the Marathi film industry, he became aware that the cost of promoting a film is almost equivalent to producing a film. As Sachin had limited resources, he tried to ascertain other ways of establishing himself as a producer. This was when he learned about the travelling cinema business in Jatras.

He heard stories of heydays of the travelling cinema and how so much money was pouring in that people used to stuff it in gunny bags and send it to city banks. As he got hooked on the idea, he believed that this was something that could target the limited funds he had and establish himself as a film producer. To lower the risks, he procured the rights of an already released Marathi film rather than making a fresh film. He procured the rights for the film "Sopanchi Aai Bahinabai" (Sopan's mother Bahinabai). The film showcased the life and times of poet Bahinabai Chaudhari, a famous poet in rural Maharashtra, through her Ovi's (short poems). Sachin made a verbal agreement with a travelling cinema owner and took the film to a local Jatra in Satara.

The travelling cinema owner painted a rosy picture of the business, making Sachin believe that he should witness the phenomenon himself. Sachin travelled to Satara along with the film. The film received a lukewarm response from the audience at the Jatra. After a week, the travelling cinema owner informed Sachin that the film failed to garner any audience and it won't be feasible to continue. Sitting at the ticket counter himself every day, Sachin could also see that he could not reach the expected number of footfalls to break even. Still, he continued to show the film until the end of the Jatra period.

As they moved to the next Jatra, Sachin was optimistic that they would earn profits and cover earlier losses, at least in this Jatra. But the same state of affairs followed in the second Jatra as well; with each passing day, Sachin was losing more and more of his investment. The travelling cinema owner suggested to Sachin to rent out another film. Through the contacts of the travelling cinema owner, Sachin rented a Hindi film released just one year ago. But it also followed the same fate, as most of the audience had already seen the movie on satellite television.

By the end of the second Jatra, Sachin felt it was better not to attend further Jatras as his financial situation deteriorated. The travelling cinema owner charged various taxes, electricity charges, Hindi movie rental charges, etc., so that he made a limited profit. Sachin was left with a considerable financial loss. Sachin chose to quit the industry and returned to managing his father's shop. His losses ran into millions, which he now had to pay through his father's business. Sachin feels that more transparency and proper advice from the travelling cinema owner would have helped him overcome the situation.

Overall, the interview provides an insider's perspective about the producers engaged in creating small-budget Marathi movies and their struggles to adapt to the rural entertainment industry's changing landscape. This also highlights the need for proper guidance to such entrepreneurs, who are willing to invest in travelling cinema but might be failing due to the limited know-how of the rural entertainment industry.

12.6.4 Vinay Nalawade

Cinebaazar is the brainchild of Vinay Nalawade, who had created the basic concept as a project during his MBA coursework. He then registered its intellectual property right and has started providing its services in six Indian states by 2012. He terms the experience as 'movie tourism', which integrates the rural audience's cultural, social, and economic spheres. Before the screening of the movie, Vinay organises various traditional games, folk dance competitions, in which members of a different classes, castes, and religions actively participate. Vinay explains that he pitched the idea of showing films for free as a marketing strategy to corporates and firms seeking to promote their brands. The brands decide on the villages and the number of shows. Vinay charges them a certain amount to take care of logistics to arrange the show.

Vinay has carried out more than 500 shows across villages in India since the model's inception and has partnered with brands like P&G, Lifebouy, Maruti Suzuki, Hyundai, Tata, Colours TV, and Videocon. Vinay chooses movies that have social relevance and family-friendly content. He carries out brand integration through car rallies, posters, pamphlets, and interactive games with villagers throughout the day and in the evening shows the movie at a public place for free. The brands often carry out customer satisfaction surveys in the chosen villages. Such surveys ascertain the output for brands, impact on sales, and recall of the product. He explained that for the venture to be financially viable to both partners in the activity, film shows need to be arranged in a large number of villages as it reduces the operational costs.

Overall, the interview provides a glimpse into the future of travelling cinema and the need to adapt to the technological changes in the entertainment industry. It shows that with the right amount of planning, networking, and financial support, it is possible to meet the entertainment needs of rural communities while running a successful business venture.

12.7 Issues faced by travelling cinema owners

The interviews brought out various issues faced by the owners of the travelling cinemas, like financial, regulatory, and cultural issues, which are believed to have led to the decline of travelling cinema in Maharashtra. The decline began post-liberalisation and continued for a long time until travelling cinemas in Maharashtra were almost extinct: in 2008, there were 10 touring talkies per village during the six-month season, and by 2009, there were only three (Sharma 2016).

Technology readiness – The travelling cinema owners could not foresee and adapt to the new and advanced projection techniques. The first generation of travelling cinema owners often learned about the use of analogue projectors on the job and did not have any formal training. The second or third generations of travelling cinema owners had moved on to more secure occupations. Hence adapting to new technologies proved difficult for the owners. Some owners tried to adapt digital projectors and improved sound systems, but their tents could not match the comforts of multiplexes. As the profit margins dwindled over the years, the capacity to invest in the upgradation of travelling cinema was reduced.

Access to television, internet, and multimedia mobile devices – In 2019, only 10 per cent of the households in Maharashtra did not have a television set. Cable and Satellite television provide access to different content for each family group, with 89 per cent of the households subscribed to these services (FICCI-KPMG 2013; FICCI-EY 2019). This has impacted the footfalls in the tents to a large extent. There is a need for further research in understanding the role of travelling cinemas for those households who do not have access to television and feel it is a luxury to spend on the fees for admissions and travelling costs to reach the central places where travelling cinemas pitch their tents.

The internet has reached most of the villages in India. The monthly cost of accessing the internet has also been reduced substantially in the recent past. This is accompanied by the constant reduction of prices of internet-ready devices. This made the entire gamut of the younger generation privy to entertainment on the go. The travelling cinema doesn't have the financial resources to catch up with the younger generation. The younger generation is fascinated by watching cinema in tents with poor audio and video quality. Travelling cinemas are yet to recognise the potential use of the internet as a promotion/marketing device or a means to do market research.

Non-exemption from entertainment tax – All Marathi movies running in theatres are exempted from payment of entertainment tax to the state. The State Government explicitly made this provision to enable exhibitors to provide tickets at a cheaper rate to Marathi film-going audiences. Eventually, to support the Marathi film producers against the onslaught of mega-budget Hindi films. But travelling cinema does not receive this exemption and has to pay local entertainment tax in each district, where they set up their operations at the Jatras. With the introduction of the Goods and Services Tax (GST) on 1 July 2017, the entertainment tax on movie tickets costing Rs 100 or less was revised to 18 per cent. Before GST, the price of a movie ticket was based on the entertainment tax levied by state governments. For Maharashtra, it was 45 per cent. The different tax rates for permanent cinema halls and travelling cinema in the state policy has impacted travelling cinema's revenue generation compared with single screens or multiplexes.

Movie Piracy – Easy availability of latest films, released through pirated DVDs/ VCDs/ torrents, has reduced the cost of watching a movie significantly, as pirated material prices are very low. Also, it provides an option to watch the movie from the convenience of one's own house. In rural Maharashtra, transportation is still a significant issue. Hence people have started preferring to watch movies at home. Limited action against those involved in piracy and the lack of stringent laws has made it difficult for the Marathi film industry to fight piracy.

Increasing operational costs – Electricity for running a film show is provided by using a diesel generator. The price of diesel keeps increasing year after year, thereby affecting the running budget of travelling cinema owners. The ticket prices are restricted in the bracket of Rs. 30–60, as the purchasing power of the rural populace is very low. This limits the profit while the operational costs keep on increasing, leading to the travelling cinema unit becoming financially unviable.

Natural and Man-made calamities – Rural households often have limited sources of income and focus more on subsistence rather than a luxury. Natural calamities like drought, floods, and sudden weather changes, or unnatural disasters like economic slowdown, policy changes, riots, and epidemics, directly affect the income levels of the rural audience. In such scenarios, the need is probably there, but the opportunity costs are too high when more basic needs are hard to satisfy for the rural populace. In 2020, the COVID-19 pandemic was one example that led to the entertainment industry's total closure due to lockdowns.

As the travelling cinema was already struggling with revenue generation, the pandemic has further deteriorated the financial health of its owners.

12.8 Impact of digital technologies

The digital divide between urban and rural India has been steadily narrowing in the last decade. The number of Indian internet users grew exponentially. In 2020, India had over 749 million internet users across the country, which grew from 494 million in 2018 (Statista 2021). The recent McKinsey report shows that the number of smartphone users, which was 5.4 per 100 people in 2014, has grown to 26.2 per 100 people by 2018 (Kaka et al. 2019).

YouTube and Facebook are the major digital avenues for content consumption across India as both have free content in regional languages. Several YouTube channels showcase regional and dubbed films, which are a major attraction to rural users. According to Noxinfluencer (2021), Goldmine telefilms is a YouTube channel with 57.4 million subscribers and more than 13 billion views until August 2021. It hosts more than 500 movies on its channel, with new additions almost every week. Furthermore, Marathi cinema became more urban in its stories, which created a disconnect with the rural audience. However, the Hindi dubbed Telugu cinema, mainly focused on action and comedy genres, is available on the Goldmine telefilms channel. The audience in rural Maharashtra is well received.

According to a report by KPMG (2019) on India's media and entertainment industry, the digital market in India is set to become the second-largest within the media and entertainment industry by 2020. The digital content industry grew by 43.4 per cent in the financial year 2018–19. The digital content consumers, which encompassed 528 million Indian residents in 2018, are expected to grow to more than 1 billion individuals by 2030. Until 2015, digital content creation and consumption were limited to specific metro city users as most of the content available was in the English language. Still, with the spread of fast internet connections in the rural hinterlands, the Marathi, Bengali, Tamil, and Telugu speaking user base has been rising in the last five years.

With the growth of over-the-top (OTT) platforms such as Netflix, Amazon Prime, Zee5, Sony LIV, and Eros Now, the films released in theatres are available to the consumers within a span of 6 to 8 weeks on their mobile devices. This reduced the attraction of travelling cinemas in rural Maharashtra and provided an avenue for creative talent in rural areas to produce their content in the form of short films, without depending on the film industries based in major cities like Mumbai and Pune.

To sustain travelling cinema, innovation and use of new technology will probably be very important. The reduction of the cost of the projector and its increased durability will help reduce the maintenance cost. The ease of deploying a digital projector will make it easier to organise the setup in less time. Augmented/virtual reality has already made a foray into India. In the future, travelling cinema owners can invest in providing a visual experience, which is impossible to have on a mobile device. In that case, it might bring back consumers to the tent.

12.9 Impact of COVID-19 pandemic

The entertainment industry also suffered a significant setback due to the COVID19 pandemic and the world economy. India wide lockdown was imposed at the end of March 2020, which brought all non-essential (i.e., other than health and public works sectors) movement to halt in the country. The single-screen theatres and multiplexes were ordered to be shut down in mid-March 2020, but they were allowed to start with 50 per cent capacity from November 2020 (Acharya 2020). Religious places and gatherings were not allowed to start again. Especially after Kumbh Mela held in the state of Uttarakhand was viewed as a super-spreader event leading to the second wave in India (Panday 2021), the rules and regulations were further put in place, and the second lockdown started from mid-April 2021.

Jatras, where travelling cinema shows were held, are part of religious gatherings; hence they could not operate since the COVID-19 pandemic began. Though it is too early to predict how much loss this had led to in terms of permanent closure of travelling cinemas, loss of employment, rising debt for travelling cinema owners, one can compare the condition with the Indian film industry. Hindi film industry, i.e. Bollywood, has suffered an estimated loss of 210 million from March to September 2020, only from a film exhibition point of view (Lalwani 2020). At the same time, other subsidiary revenue generation activities related to film screening may have suffered the worst (Krishan 2021). Looking at these conditions, the future of travelling cinema in a post-COVID world looks bleak. It does not have the finances or technology to continue its functioning in the same manner as the pre-COVID era.

12.10 Emerging alternatives and new initiatives

With advances in film projection technology, the costs of organising a film screening are falling. Digital projectors are better in picture quality and low maintenance than the old analogue projectors, which are bulky and difficult to operate. Considering this, a few of the agencies have launched their own privately run travelling cinema units.

Picture Time currently has 45 vans functioning in Maharashtra. Each van carries 18ft x 7ft in size portable screens, an air-conditioned inflatable tent, chairs, and surround-sound equipment. The fascination of watching the movie in an air-conditioned closed space, like a multiplex, is high among the aspirational rural populace.

Caravan Talkies, the most prominent digital distributor of films to multiplexes, owned by UFO, has created special vans carrying an LED video wall.

The van has an inbuilt sound system stationed at the venue of the film show. The setup does not require any dismantling after each show, and the vans have higher mobility over tent-type travelling cinemas.

Cinebaazar, an independent enterprise, started as a Master's in Business Administration course project, which was incubated into a business. Cinebaazar ties up with corporates to fund movie screenings in open spaces in rural areas. A week-long marketing exercise precedes the movie show, generally held on holiday or in the late evenings. A giant screen and sound system are erected in the village, where everyone gathers to see the movie for free. The enterprise generates revenue by showing advertisements and running marketing campaigns for the corporates in the rural areas.

Though the mode of operation is different for each of these initiatives, their primary intent is to reach India's vast untapped rural market. It is too early to determine if any of these initiatives will replace the traditional format of travelling cinema in the near future. It is important to note that these initiatives are developed by new-age entrepreneurs and not by an existing travelling cinema owner. They are filling up the vacuum created by the closure of travelling cinemas in rural areas.

12.11 Conclusions

Cinema, since its emergence, has always been a force to reckon with in the Indian cultural landscape. Travelling cinema has long been an important part of the Indian film industry and has contributed to enriching culture, lifestyle, and practices in rural areas. Travelling cinema had its heyday when the rural masses had limited sources of entertainment available to them. It furthered the art of cinema to the hinterlands of Maharashtra. It became a source of inspiration to many artists from rural backgrounds to have successful careers in the Marathi film industry. It braved the economic upheavals and yet managed to sustain itself. Travelling cinema illustrates that art can change the mode of delivery, but it tends to find a way to reach those who appreciate it.

New technologies have cut into the niche previously occupied by travelling cinema in India. Recently, new initiatives have sprung up, making innovative use of new technologies to reduce costs, tap into new sources of finance, and move into novel audio-visual entertainment formats. The advantages of travelling cinemas are that they can provide shared experiences and bring cutting-edge technologies to audiences in remote parts of the country. Travelling cinemas can also be used for cultural policy catering to rural or otherwise peripheral communities. The government may extend its support to the travelling cinema owners by exempting goods and service tax. It can also provide financial support by promoting government programmes and schemes, awareness about social issues and health practices as advertisements, utilising the reach of travelling cinema in remote rural areas. With the advent of digital technologies and internet services in rural areas, travelling cinemas can tie up with OTT platforms or media houses to show satellite releases of new movies on the same days it is available to the urban audience. In the last decade, upcoming start-ups like Picture Time, Caravan Talkies, and Cinebazaar have forayed into the travelling cinema space building new synergies with corporates, governments, and political parties to capture the vast rural market. Currently, it is in a phase of reinventing itself as a delivery mechanism more suitable to the needs of its consumers and content creators. The future looks bright for the travelling cinema if the foresight of the emerging start-ups is merged with the experience of the travelling cinema industry.

References

Acharya, P. (2020). Multiplexes, cinema halls open in Maharashtra after eight months. Available at: www.freepressjournal.in/mumbai/multiplexes-cinema-halls-open-in-maharashtra-after-eight-months (last accessed on 25 March 2022).

Adesanya, A. (1998). From film to video. In Haynes, J. (ed.), *Nigerian Video Films*, pp. 13–20. Jos: Nigerian Film Corporation.

Ben-Ghiat, R. (2003). The Italian colonial cinema: Agendas and audiences. *Modern Italy*, 8(1), 49–63. https://doi.org/10.1080/1353294032000074070 (last accessed on 25 March 2022).

Bhaumik, K. (2001). *The Emergence of the Bombay Film Industry, 1913–1936*. London: The University of Oxford.

Bird, J. H. (1949). *Cinema Parade: Fifty Years of Film Shows*. Birmingham, UK: Cornish Bros.

FICCI-EY (2019). *A Billion Screens of Opportunity*. Kolkata: Ernst & Young LLP.

FICCI-KPMG (2013). *The Power of a Billion: Realising the Indian Dream*. Mumbai: KPMG.

Hafeez, E., and Ara, A. (2016). History and evolution of the Indian film industry. *Journal of History and Social Sciences*, 7(2), 60–73. Available at: www.yourarticlelibrary.com/foods/history-and-evolution-of-indian-food/86788 (last accessed on 25 March 2022).

Hughes, S. (1981). Urban mobility and the history of cinema going in Chennai. *Urban Mobility and Cinema Going*, 39–48. Available at: https://eprints.soas.ac.uk/11998/1/Hughes_Urban_Mobility.pdf (last accessed on 25 March 2022).

Ingle, H. (2017). Early Marathi cinema: Prabhat Studios and social respectability. *Synoptique*, 5(2), 79–100.

Kaka, N., Madgavkar, A., Kshirsagar, A., Gupta, R., Manyika, J., Bahl, K., and Gupta, S. (2019). *Digital India: Technology to Transform a Connected Nation*, p. 36. India: McKinsey Global Institute.

Kamble, D. M. (2013). Growth and Prospects of Marathi Film Industry in Kolhapur, p. 60, Chapter-5. Doctoral Dissertation, Shivaji University, Kolhapur, India. Available at: http://hdl.handle.net/10603/147240 (last accessed on 25 March 2022).

Khan, F. (2016, 12 June). Documenting the dying tradition of travelling cinema in India. *The Economic Times*. Available at: https://economictimes.indiatimes.com/magazines/panache/documenting-the-dying-tradition-of-travelling-cinema-in-india/articleshow/52706744.cms (last accessed on 25 March 2022).

KPMG. (2019). India's Digital Future Mass of niches, p. 12. India: KPMG. Available at: https://assets.kpmg/content/dam/kpmg/in/pdf/2019/08/india-media-entertainment-report-2019.pdf (last accessed on 25 March 2022).

Krishan, M. (2021, 16 July). How India's COVID crisis has changed Bollywood. Available at: www.dw.com/en/how-indias-covid-crisis-has-changed-bollywood/a-58291931 (last accessed on 25 March 2022).

Lalwani, V. (2020). Exclusive! 5000 crore and counting! Bollywood faces heavy losses due to pandemic lockdown. Available at: https://timesofindia.indiatimes.com/entertainment/hindi/bollywood/news/figures-of-bollywoods-loss-till-date-due-to-covid-19-will-make-your-jaw-drop/articleshow/78101922.cms (last accessed on 25 March 2022).

Low, R., and Manvell, R. (1948). *The History of the British Film: 1896–1906*, p. 52. London, UK: Allen & Unwin.

Mahadevan, S. (2010). Traveling show-men, makeshift cinemas: The bioscopewallah and early cinema history in India. *BioScope: South Asian Screen Studies*, 1(1), 27–47. https://doi.org/10.1177/097492760900100106

Mujawar, I. (1969). *Maharashtra: Birthplace of Indian Film Industry*, p. 94. Pune, India: Chief Information Officer, Maharashtra Information Centre.

Nair, P. K. (1999). In the age of silence: Beginnings of cinema in India. *Screening the Past*. Available at: http://tlweb.latrobe.edu.au/humanities/screeningthepast/reruns/rr0499/PUdrr6.htm (last accessed on 25 March 2022).

Noxinfluencer (2021). Goldmines Telefilms YouTube stats & analytics dashboard. Available at: www.noxinfluencer.com/youtube/channel/UCyoXW-Dse7fURq30EWl_CUA (last accessed on 25 March 2022).

Olayiwola, A. (2011). Nollywood at the borders of history: Yoruba travelling theatre and video film development in Nigeria. *Journal of Pan African Studies*, 4(5), 183. Available at: www.jpanafrican.org/docs/vol4no5/4.5Nollywood.pdf (last accessed on 25 March 2022).

Panday, G. (2021, 10 May). India Covid: Kumbh Mela pilgrims turn into super-spreaders. Available at: www.bbc.com/news/world-asia-india-57005563 (last accessed on 25 March 2022).

Sharma, K. (2016, 13 May). Cinema travellers: Tracing the decline of tent cinema in India. *Hindustan Times*. Available at: www.hindustantimes.com/world-cinema/cinema-travellers-tracing-the-decline-of-tent-cinema-in-india/story-GsSoWpME45b4LwCpk8Ve6J.html (last accessed on 25 March 2022).

Statista (2021). The number of internet users in India from 2010 to 2020. Available at: www.statista.com/statistics/255146/number-of-internet-users-in-india/ (last accessed on 25 March 2022).

Toulmin, V. (2001). 'Local films for local people': Travelling show-men and the commissioning of local films in Great Britain, 1900–1902. *Film History*, 13(2), 118–137. Available at: www.jstor.org/stable/3815421 (last accessed on 25 March 2022).

Toulmin, V. (2010). Cuckoo in the nest: Edwardian itinerant exhibition practices and the transition to cinema in the United Kingdom from 1901 to 1906. *The Moving Image*, 10(1), 52–79.

13

MOLLYWOOD

The rise and fall of a subaltern cinema

Sanjukta Sattar, Abdul Shaban and Aleem Faizee

13.1 Introduction

Located on the Deccan plateau in western Maharashtra, Malegaon with a population of about 0.47 million (Census of India 2011) has been known for its textile industry for over a century. The textile industry is rooted in the caste occupation of Muslim weavers, the Ansaris. The town has been an epitome of the underdevelopment and hard work of its handloom or now power loom weavers (Shaban 2013). Notwithstanding the deprivations and underdevelopment, the town also emerged as an art and cultural centre of the subalterns.

Malegaon is known for its poets and playwrights. The town once also had a thriving film industry that spoofs Bollywood blockbusters, using limited resources and maximum creativity (Ansari and Handa 2011; Tiwary 2015). The subaltern film industry has produced remakes of the Bollywood films "contextualizing them to address local issues and to cater to local tastes" (Liang 2011: 54). The remakes of the Bollywood blockbusters like Sholay (1975) and Lagaan (2001) *Malegaon ke Sholay* and *Malegaon ki Lagaan*, respectively (Ansari and Handa 2011), brought the town in focus.

The films also portray local issues like price rises. With this infusion of local flavour, these films are more appealing to the indigenous population as they can relate to the issues depicted in the movies. The dialogues included words from the local dialect and is also delivered with *Khandeshi* (local Marathi dialect) accent. Intricate details of the daily lives and lifestyles of the local inhabitants are depicted in their films. In several remakes of Bollywood, Malegaon films have used innovations that are social and entertaining rather than technical. For instance, in the Malegaon remake of *Koi Mil Gaya*, the alien which is a character in this film recharges his energy by consuming *vada pav (a type of local burger)* and *chicken tikka*, two favourite dishes of the people of Malegaon, instead of sunlight as shown in the original movie. In the film, *Malegaon ke Sholay*, a Malegaonian version of Bollywood film *Sholay*, "cycles were used instead of horses and the train sequence was substituted with local buses" (Ansari and

DOI: 10.4324/9781003129370-17

Handa 2011). All these and much other innovativeness made the Malegaon film industry unique in its way.

"The innovativeness of the Malegaon films, for instance, lies as much in the remixing of narratives as it does in the ways in which low-cost infrastructure is recycled to make the films possible" (Liang 2011: 54). The film crew does not include a choreographer, costume designer, or make-up artist. The actors themselves take care of these requirements through self-improvisation of their dance steps, arranging their costumes or make-up. Shakeel Bharti who played the lead role in the remake of the Bollywood movie *Ghajni* managed to purchase a jacket similar to the one worn by the lead character in the original movie for INR 30. The movie was shot with a shoestring budget of INR 50,000 (about US$800). Generally, set props and accessories are all procured from second-hand shops. The film production is a joint effort as often the family members, relatives, and friends put their hands together to help the film crews, "the wife cooks for the film crew, the son assists in the camerawork and the daughter help in designing costumes" (Ansari and Handa 2011). The making of films in Malegaon has been more like a community project at times.

Over time the Malegaon film industry or 'Mollywood' evolved and grew to reach its pinnacle and then a sudden decline. The present chapter attempts to bring out the story of this evolutionary journey of subaltern movie terrain facilitating creative pursuits of local voices. The chapter uses the interviews of the persons who were/are engaged with the industry in any form at any point in time, and the information available from local newspapers, town's run websites, and YouTube channels. One of the authors of this chapter, Aleem Faizee, not only has grown up in the towns, seen the growth and decline of the Mollywood but has also been reporting about various issues of Malegaon in several newspapers and for the news site www.ummid.com. However, given the dearth of formal available sources of information on Mollywood, considerable information is based on the interviews of the persons related to the industry from September 2020 to February 2021. This is, therefore, largely, a story of the subalterns narrated by the subalterns (the people of the town) themselves. The rest of the chapter is divided into the following sections. Section 13.2 relates to the emergence of the cinema in the town while Section 13.3 discusses the role of early flagbearers. The first remakes of Bollywood cinemas, and more remakes and related stories are presented in sections 4 and 5, respectively. The travel from screen to TV channels is discussed in Section 13.6, while Section 13.7 discusses the national and international recognition of the cinema of the town. Techniques and innovations used in the Mollywood have been discussed in Section 13.8, while to encourage the cinema workers constitutions of awards by the Mollywood itself is related in Section 13.9. Section 13.10 discusses the decline of Mollywood cinema and the shift to YouTube. The last section presents some concluding thoughts.

13.2 Emergence of cinema

People in Malegaon have always been inclined to art and literature. Till the 1980s, the 24x7 work culture, which is now a norm, was not there. People worked only in the daytime, winding up all work before sunset. But they were not accustomed to going to bed early. Roaming about and sitting here and there till late in the night which one sees even today has been a routine for the people of Malegaon for decades.

To remain engaged and spend their time, they needed something. Religiously inclined and deeply bonded by Islamic cultures as they are, the residents refused to go for wine and alcohol – a routine practice in the neighbouring cities and towns. Against this backdrop they had only two options – either spend time with roadside chat groups or engage themselves in art and literature. The art and literature were chosen by a large section and to help them in this were libraries, public as well as private. Residents will approach these libraries and borrow books on fiction, religion, art, culture, and various other topics.

Among the local avid readers was Ghulam Mohammad Zaidi. Impressed by 'Kaali Duniya' (black world) and 'Neeli Duniya' (blue world) two adventure novels of Siraj Anwar of Delhi, Zaidi wrote his own story 'Qatil Khazana' (murderous treasure). Zaidi added related images and pictures in the story with the help of his elder brother Ghulam Sabir Siddiqui. 'Qatil Khazana' became a popular book and as mentioned by Siraj Dular, a Malegaon resident, "the book became especially popular among the children". Buoyed by the popularity of his storybook, Zaidi sent a copy to Siraj Anwar in Delhi. Siraj Anwar replied with an encouraging note. Since then, the interaction between both of them commences which continued through the exchange of letters. In one of his letters, Siraj Anwar invited Zaidi to Delhi. In Delhi, Zaidi had a chance to see the shooting of a documentary film Siraj Anwar was in the process of making. Zaidi spent quality time on a 'shooting set', and discussed the basics of filmmaking with Siraj Anwar. "Zaidi returned to Malegaon after a stay of more than a week in Delhi. But when he returned to Malegaon, he returned with a dream to make a film of his own", Siraj Dular recalls. The stage was now set for 'Qatil Khazana' in the form of a film, which came out in 1972, and so was the birth of Mollywood.

13.3 Early flagbearers

The early flag bearers of filmmaking in Malegaon were those acting in dramas and plays during school and college days. Advocate Zaheer and Siraj Dular were also selected for 'Qatil Khazana' solely because they had a proven track record of acting on school and college stages. Siraj Dular, while talking about the town's first film initiative, recollects various details many of which have never been documented. He recalls that Ghulam Mohammad Zaidi started working on the film in 1970 and released it on 10 November 1972, after enormous efforts of more than two years. He says, "the cost incurred on the making of the silent movie 'Qatil Khazana', the first film of Malegaon, was one thousand eight hundred and few rupees. If the expenses under the miscellaneous and expenditure heads are aggregated, the total cost of the film was close to INR 2,500 [approximately US$329; in 1972 the US$1 was equivalent to INR 7.59" (also see, Pritam 2021)]. Though the first film of Malegaon, which was premiered on 10 November 1972, ran for 20–22 days, it ended in a loss with a box office collection of only INR 1000. However, it paved the way for the future filmmakers of the town.

About 14 years later in 1986, Advocate Zaheer Ahmed, another lead actor of 'Qatil Khazaana' besides Siraj Dular, filmed 'Range Haath' on video camera. This film was a suspense thriller and was inspired by the Bollywood Hindi movie 'Bees Sal Baad' (Siddiqui 2011). This film was written, produced, and directed by Dr. Abu Bakr. The lead role in the film was played by Arshad Nazar, a prominent poet of the city. Some 39 years later, on 7 January 2011, the efforts of these pioneers were acknowledged and rewarded in a glittering award ceremony 'Salaam Malegaon', the local version of Bollywood's Filmfare Award. At the function, all the cast of 'Qatil Khazaana' were awarded. At the event, Ghulam Mohammad Ziadi was posthumously conferred with Malegaon's 'Dada Saheb Phalke Award' and was remembered as Malegaon ka Dada Phalke. (www.ummid.com/news/2011/January/09.01.2010/salaam_malegaon.htm).

Ghulam Mohammad Zaidi and his brother Ghulam Sabir Siddiqui, the first filmmakers of the town, due to financial losses in their maiden film, thereafter never gathered the courage to make another film again. However, Advocate Zaheer while focusing on his career as a lawyer, also tried his hand simultaneously as a photographer that earned him the credit of shooting "Range Haath", the town's second film and the first shot on a video camera.

Siraj Dular, a teacher by profession, remains one of the tallest actors of the town, playwright, and director. He did not act in any film after Qatil Khazana, but he established the 'Malegaon Art and Culture Association' comprising local film actors and drama artists. Under the banner of the association, Siraj Dular with fellow members like Asif Subhani and others wrote and staged a series of dramas and street plays or 'nukkad nataks'. The focus of these dramas was on social issues, like the one on Swine Flu which was staged in October and November 2009 and is still considered as the best play of Malegaon.

The series of plays, dramas, and 'Nukkad Nataks', which the Malegaon Art and Culture Association used to stage on different platforms and *chowks* (streets) of the town, encouraged Nasir Shaikh, a video parlour owner and a movie addict himself, to make films. Nasir Shaikh can be credited for his "pioneering role in Malegaon's tiny, low-budget but popular spoof-film industry known as Mollywood" (Gopal 2012). Siraj Dular and Advocate Zaheer fondly remember Nasir Sheikh's interest in art and culture especially in acting since his early childhood. "Nasir Sheikh would come not only to watch the dramas and plays we staged. But he would also sit and spend a lot of time as we practiced and rehearsed", says Siraj Dular. Advocate Zaheer fondly recollects:

> While shooting for 'Range Haath' at Jaju Wadi one day I saw a few boys of 8 to 9 years old sitting and watching while we shoot the film. The next day they were again there – sitting with the same determination, eagerness, and interest. We ignored them considering them as spectators. It was only later that Nasir confessed to me that one of them was he.

A short, bright, and shy boy with curly hairs, Nasir was just 9 then. Twenty years down the line he along with his friend Akram Khan became the pillar and identity of Mollywood.

Coming from humble family background, Nasir Shaikh with his brother was running a small video parlour (mini-theatre) on Qedwai Road in Malegaon. It was the time of videotape and cartridges. No projector no big screen. The films were screened on a small television set using a video player. People would sit on the ground to watch the films. Few chairs were there but they were reserved for VIPs. Nasir's video parlour was also most sought after for those interested in Hollywood English action and thriller movies which were not available in local theatres with big screens. Making available Hollywood films at that time was a daunting task. Hence a single title would run for weeks that the local film lovers would watch again and again. These Hollywood movies were a big source of inspiration, and the technical details were followed carefully by those who were interested in making videos. Nasir would closely watch the angle, cuts, and shots in these Hollywood films and then would apply them while shooting for local wedding and marriage functions. "Watching the same film again and again, actually 4–5 times a day for weeks, helped me in developing whatever instinct I have in me about film making", Nasir confides to one of the authors in a personal interview in October 2020.

13.4 The first remake

Some 500 meters from Nasir's video parlour was Milan Photo Studio. Established by Akram Khan's father Mehboob Khan in front of Municipal School No. 1. It was the first photo studio in the town. After Mehboob Khan died in 1985, Akram was the sole handler of Milan Photo Studio. Akram ran the studio till 1992 when he got a job offer from Saudi Arabia. He worked in Saudi Arabia as a 'photo lab operator' for five years and returned to Malegaon with a dream which he shared with his friend Nasir Shaikh. It was about the making of 'Malegaon ke Sholay', the first remake of a Bollywood film produced in the town by the local artists. Nasir Shaikh was the Director and Producer of 'Malegaon ke Sholay'. The script and dialogues were written by Akram Khan and Hamid Subhani, the younger brother of Asif Subhani who was one of the key members of the Malegaon Art and Culture Association. Interestingly, Nasir, Akram, and Hamid were lucky in finding the cast of their film who were 'lookalikes' of the original characters in Ramesh Sippy's 1975 Bollywood blockbuster movie 'Sholay'. Quiet appropriately for the film, they had 'Malegaon ka

Amitabh', 'Malegoan ka Dahrmendra', and of course also 'Gabbar', 'Thakur', 'Sambha', and 'Basanti', the immortal roles played respectively by ace stars Amjad Khan, Sanjeev Kumar, Mac Mohan, and Bollywood diva Hema Malini. Then came the historic day in 1999 when 'Malegaon ke Sholay' was premiered at Nasir's own video theatre. The theatre was packed to its capacity. And then there were only laughter, frequent squeals, and applauds, non-stop whistling and clapping, with a standing ovation at the end. It was a chilling winter night with the mercury dipping quite low, but the thrill resonating from the film made the environment warmer. Viewers found their own local youths acting like Bollywood heroes mesmerizing. But what impressed them the most was the innovations and improvisations used by the Malegaon film-makers and comedy scenes embedded with a local touch, and humorous dialogues in the local accent, probably making the spoof more popular than the original. A viewer shares:

> They came on bicycles instead of horses, used saw-tooth instead of swords. . . And the most interesting part of the film was our own youths were acting like Amitabh Bachhan, Dharmendra, and Sanjeev Kumar. It was all very interesting, forcing me to watch the film many times.

Unlike 'Qatil Khazana' which failed the box office, 'Malegaon ke Sholay' was a huge hit. The cost of making the film was a little over 50,000 Indian rupees but, the film fetched Nasir over 250,000.

13.5 More re-makes in quick succession

The success of 'Malegaon ke Sholay' encouraged Nasir, Akram, and their team to make more Bollywood remakes and spoofs. 'Malegaon Ki Shaan', 'Malegaon Ka Don', and 'Malegaon Ki Lagaan' followed within years and then there was no stopping for them. 'Malegaon Ke Karan Arjun', 'Malegaon Ka Ek Tha Tiger', 'Malegaon Ka Ghazani', 'Koi Hil Gaya', 'Malegaon Ka Rangeela', and the list is endless. In the meantime, encouraged by these hit spoofs, a few more teams started making their own films. Prominent among them were Al Amin Shaikh and Rafeeque Shaikh.

Like other heroes and villains of Malegaon film industry, Rafeeque Shaikh too was a power loom weaver coming from a poor family. Rafeeque Shaikh had mastered himself into mimicking Bollywood stars, including Shah Rukh Khan, with impeccable perfection. Initially he worked as mimicry artist. But after his successful role as Johnny Lever in 'Malegaon Ke Karan Arjun', he became popular as 'Rafeeque Johnny'. The re-make 'Malegaon Ke Karan Arjun' was produced and directed by Al Amin Shaikh – who later played the lead role in 'Malegaon Ka Chnitu', the silent comedy drama series that was screened on Sab TV from 2010 to 2014. It was Al Amin Shaikh and Rafeeque Shaikh who brought major changes in the Malegaon Film Industry permanently and forever.

13.6 The portrayal on national TVs

The popularity of Mollywood in the Khandesh region, in which Malegaon is located, grew over the years and the news about Mollywood would be regularly featured in local Urdu and vernacular newspapers. However, for the first time Mollywood hit the national TV in 2003 when a documentary film produced by Public Service Broadcasting Trust (PSBT), established in partnership with Prasar Bharati, India's National Public Broadcaster, was broadcasted on Doordarshan, India's national television.

Later, the year 2006 became pivotal for the Malegaon Film Industry as far as the media coverage is concerned. It was because of the deadly serial bomb blasts that had rocked the town on Friday 8 September 2006, killing some 32 persons and injuring over 300 persons. The incident had attracted the attention of all small and big media houses from India and abroad. Considering the gravity and location of the bomb blasts, in which the involvement of terrorists associated with right-wing Hindu extremist organizations was established for the first time (Ahuja 2017), journalists and TV crews with their OB vans remained stationed in the town for days. In their reports to cover aspects other than the blasts they also turned their focus on the Malegaon's film Industry. For weeks local heroes and their films were on national TV screens simultaneously with the detailed coverage of the September 2006 serial blasts.

After making the news in print and electronic media over the years at national level, the Malegaon film industry also hit the international headlines. The credit for this goes to Canadian Broadcasting Corporation (CBC) which had sent a five-member team led by Jacqueline Corkery to Malegaon in October 2008 as part of their project entitled as 'India Reborn'. The focus of the CBC project was economy, politics, food, agriculture, and entertainment in India, especially in rural parts of the country. The CBC included Malegaon and its film industry in the project. Jacqueline Corkery, who was covering the section on entertainment in the project, said:

> With no active support from the Government, the way the town is living up to the expectation is really amazing. Hours of power disruptions, more than a hundred years of power looms, poor weavers labouring hard for a miserable amount and still very humorous and jolly, caring damn about anything. It's all very fascinating.

She was amazed to find how despite the lack of technological savoir faire, the way these youngsters of Malegaon have produced so many films. (https://ummid.com/malegaon/malegaon%20film%20industry.htm)

The CBC's visit was an important event for Malegaon's cinema industry. Nasir Shaikh says:

> Till now we have concentrated only on providing some moments of laughter for the poor labours in Malegaon, who do not find any-

> thing in this town to freak-out after working extensively for the whole day . . . . . . and highlighting some local issues, their vision for film-making was limited. (https://ummid.com/malegaon/malegaon%20 film%20industry.htm)

Nasir added that only after being interviewed by the CBC team, various questions about motives behind making the films cropped up in their minds. Though the idea of adding useful social messages along with the comedy was there in the back of their mind from early stage, it materialized only after their interaction with the CBC team. Soon, the makers of the Bollywood spoofs and comedy re-makes got motivated to create a film to promote Polio vaccination in association with Malegaon Municipal Corporation. They further produced films like 'Malegaon ka Tana Bana' focusing on communal harmony, and 'Malegaon Ka Superman' as part of a mission to eradicate *Gutka* (tobacco product) consumption, which is rampant in the town, especially amongst the youngsters and has taken many lives.

Making films not only to provide some form of entertainment in the mundane lives of the poor labourers of Malegoan especially those working in the power looms but also creating awareness and spreading the messages about various socially relevant issues became the mission of the filmmakers.

13.7 Awards and recognition

The making of 'Malegaon Ka Superman' also proved pivotal for Malegaon's film industry in general and Nasir Shaikh in particular. Known as Nasir's most ambitious project, the film also caught the eyes of Bollywood bigwigs. The buzz about the film in Mumbai's film industry also reached director and cinematographer Faiza Ahmad Khan. And then what came into being was 'Supermen of Malegaon'. 'Supermen of Malegaon' records all details of the making of 'Malegaon Ka Superman' and revolves around Nasir Shaikh and his team. The most interesting part of the film, besides decades-old techniques used and innovations and improvisations adapted by the film producers and directors in Malegaon, was the apt portraying of 'flying man' which Nasir wanted to shoot. The shooting of 'Supermen of Malegaon' was held in parallel with the shooting of 'Malegaon Ka Superman'. Having seen the use of the green screen in one of those behind-the-scenes outtakes, Nasir realized he could use the process to make a special effects movie – specifically, to make Superman fly to Malegaon.

"This documentary follows the trials and tribulations of Nasir and his band of hobby filmmakers through their film's writing, planning, and its sometimes troubled shoot until it's completed", Faiza explained in an interview. Both the films got completed together. Faiza's 'Supermen of Malegaon' was released in cinemas on 29 June 2012, and received applause from national and international film critics. Before its release in 2012, the film was screened at Osian's Cinefan Film Festival, International Film Festival of India (IFFI) in November 2009 (www.ummid.com/news/November/20.11.2009/mollywood_at_iffi.htm), and was selected for a special screening in Berlin, Germany on December 4,

2011 (https://ummid.com/news/2011/December/01.12.2011/screening_of_malega_ka_superman_in_germany.htm). It received 15 national and international awards including the Jury Award for Best Documentary at Asiatica Film Mediale, Rome, the Jury Award for Best Documentary at Kara Film Festival, Pakistan, Best Debut Film at Film South Asia, Nepal, Best Editing, Documentary, and Director at the Asian Festival of First Films, Singapore, Best Editing at the Asian TV Awards, Singapore, Audience Choice Award for Documentary, Indian Film Festival of Los Angeles (IFFLA), Golden Camera Award for Best Documentary, US International Film and Video Festival, Gold Awards for Editing and Best Documentary and a Silver Award for Sound Design, Indian Documentary Producers Association, Best Documentary at Bollywood and Beyond, Stuttgart, Youth Choice Award at Vesoul Asian Film Festival and Special Mention at Best Film Festival, Romania.

While 'Supermen of Malegaon' ruled the show at various film festivals in India and abroad, and finally releasing in theatres on 29 June 2012, the release of 'Malegaon Ka Superman' hit the roadblocks one after the another. The lead actor Shafeeque Ahmed was himself addicted to *gutkha*. Yet, in his lead role as 'Malegaon Ka Superman', he campaigned against tobacco and *gutkha* consumption. During the shooting, he tried hard to overcome the bad habit but failed. Later in 2010, he was diagnosed with cancer. This was when he along with other people of the town was waiting for the release of the film. As the release of the film got delayed further, a special screening of the film was organized for ailing Shafeeque on 6 September 2011. Renowned film director from Bollywood, Anurag Kashyap, and producer Sunil Bora specially travelled from Mumbai to Malegaon for the special screening. "We wanted to give Shafeeque Ahmed a surprise *Eid* gift by organizing the special screening of the film in Malegaon", told Nasir. One day after watching the film along with Anurag Kashyap, Sunil Bora, and his fellow artists, Shafeeque succumbed to cancer on 7 September 2011 (https://ummid.com/news/2011/September/07.09.2011/malegaon_ka_superman_dead.htm).

13.8 Techniques and Innovations

Besides the sensibility with which the films were made by the filmmakers of Malegaon, the most impressive was the 'innovative techniques' local producers used to compensate for lack of financial and technical resources. Expensive cameras, delicate lighting arrangement, costly sound system, and using a crane for long shots were all beyond their reach. But what they had in plenty were the ideas and innovations to compensate for these shortcomings and overcome the hurdles arising due to limited funds and lack of awareness and access to the latest technologies. Hence moving train sequel was shot using a transport bus, and chasing Gabbar Singh's gang was shown riding on a bicycle instead of horses in 'Malegaon ke Sholay'. For 'Malegaon ki Shaan', they needed to show a moving table, they used a bullock cartwheel and two people to make the table move circularly. A bullock cart and bicycle also came in handy for them to use instead of a crane and trolley. While a bullock cart arm is used for long crane shots, bicycles are used for dolly and tracking shots.

Once the shooting of the film is over then starts the daunting task of film editing and dubbing. Unlink air-conditioned studios having all the latest equipment, here again, film producers in Malegaon had zilch. While Nasir would do 'in-video editing' from one VCR to another using two VCRs fixed on a small table in the first-floor balcony of his small 300 square metre home, Akram Khan had a similar setup in the courtyard of his house. The technique was not only difficult and time-consuming, but it also required synchronization, utmost perfection, and timing skill. The use of advanced techniques and tools was quite out of the reach of those who were making films. It took some time before they acquired the skills and knowledge of using advanced tools and techniques. Shahid Jamal, who was one of those who took interest in the technical aspects of filmmaking, was once gifted with a computer by his father Dr. Ibrahim who had migrated to the UK. Dr. Ibrahim sent a desktop computer through his friend in Mumbai for his children in Malegaon. But surprisingly "for weeks the whole set remained as it is in fully packed condition as we were inexperienced not only in computer operating but also in installing it", Shahid Jamaal recalled his initial helplessness. Shahid was also gifted still and video cameras from his father Dr. Ibrahim to pursue his hobby of photography. By the year 2000, the use of computers became prevalent among some of the residents of Malegaon but that was mainly used for keeping accounts and for typing purposes. None has tried out using computer applications for film and video editing.

It was after much trial and error that Shahid Jamal, as related by him, managed to somehow install the computer set and later learned how to use it. Soon he started trying editing of the images and videos he had shot using his cameras so far. But nothing worked out properly. He soon realized that "to use high-end computer applications is not child's play." He says:

> "I kept trying though without the needed result. One day when I was visiting the Bhangaar Bazaar, I saw a Compact Disk (CD) that had "Pinnacle Made Easy" imprinted over it".

The CD also had a picture of a camera and a film roll on its cover from which Shahid got an idea that it was related to photography and film editing. He was not yet aware if it was video editing software. It was only much later that he discovered that the CD was of the popular Pinnacle Video Editing Software Suite tutorials, which was more than what the filmmakers in Malegaon needed at that time.

After toiling for months on trials and hands-on, Shahid Jamal was finally ready for a demo session. He called Nasir, Akram Khan, and all 'big-wigs' of Malegaon cinema to show the wonders the computers can do to their films.

All of them were thrilled to no bounds. The first film that was edited and dubbed using the computers was 'Maut Ka Saaya' by Raju Sunny. Then it did not take long for Nasir and Akram to replace the VCRs on their table with the computer sets. The result was seen in 'Malegaon ka Don' and 'Munna'. 'Munna' was incidentally the first film with an original script and theme. Simultaneously, the journey of the Malegaon film industry that was started using an ordinary 16mm Movie camera and then a VHS camera, switched to 3CCD Digital Camera. Meanwhile, continuing his successful run Akram Khan decided to make the remake of the popular Kannada film "Rudra". Directed by Akram Khan, the lead role in the film was played by Mehmood Shaikh. With a budget of over INR 1 million, "Malegaon ka Rudra" is considered as one of the costliest films produced in Malegaon. This was the first film wherein cranes and trolleys were used instead of bullock carts and bicycles. In another first, a group dance was also included in the film for which female artists were hired from Dhule and Jalgaon whereas high-resolution 5CCD cameras were also used in the film for the first time. The cranes, trolleys, and 5CCD cameras were brought from Mumbai on rent. With all these introductions, the Malegaon film industry experienced major breakthroughs.

Another notable development was the filming and screening of 'Malegaon ka Chintu' a silent comedy series produced by Deepti Bhatnagar, which was directed by Nasir Shaikh, and the lead role 'Chintu' was played by Al Amin Shaikh alias Kittu alias Malegaon ka Chintu. The comedy series was screened on Sony SAB TV from August 2010 to November 2014 in three seasons. The first season was premiered on 6 August 2010, and concluded on 26 March 2011. The second season, named 'Chintu Ban Gaya Gentleman', was premiered on 15 December 2012 and concluded on 6 July 2013. It presents the eventful life of Chintu from the villages of Malegaon straight to exotic locales around the world. The third season 'Chintu aur Pintu' was premiered on 27 September 2014 and concluded on 30 November 2014. Since Nasir was directing the series and Al Amin was working as the lead role and the first season in itself was filmed in and around Malegaon, the entire members of the Malegaon Film Industry were in one way or another involved in the project. The series has a total of 75 episodes in three seasons and running over for more than four years had kept occupied and reserved local artists for the entire duration, giving them little time to produce their own films. After the success of Malegaon ka Chintu, Deepti Bhatnagar came out with another silent comedy series 'Rumm Pumm Po' in May 2015. Al Amin was also part of the cast. The series however could not impress viewers.

13.9 Malegaon Ka Filmfare Award

With their films receiving national and international acclaims, the local heroes of the town were now on the proverbial cloud nine. The best however still awaited them. That moment came on Friday, 7 January 2011 when a local NGO organized an award function titled 'Salaam Malegaon'. Salaam Malegaon was organized to felicitate the local heroes and pioneers of Mollywood – the Malegaon film industry. Owing to its success, and the enthusiasm and interest it had received, the award ceremony was later presented as the 'Malegaon Ka Filmfare Award'. And, for the local artists, it was a bigger ceremony than all their previous award events. "This is the unprecedented moment of my life. Recently, I had been awarded by various organisations in Delhi, Goa and other places. But getting an award in Malegaon and in such an impressive gathering is incomparable", expressed Nasir Shaikh, who was overwhelmed with much joy. Nasir's friend Akram Khan shared his opinion about what this award ceremony means to the people of Malegaon, "We are nothing in comparison with Hollywood and Bollywood. However, we are doing things in our innovative way. History will remember our efforts, though comparatively very small, in giving Malegaon a new identity" (https://ummid.com/news/2011/January/09.01.2010/salaam_malegaon.htm).

13.10 Decline of cinema, video parlours, and YouTube as saviour

There is no doubt that the last major series Malegaon ka Chintu brought fame, fans, money, and also riches to Nasir, Al Amin, and other local artists. However, it is also true that after 'Malegaon ka Chintu', different artists and groups associated with Mollywood got disintegrated. Post Malegaon ka Chintu, Nasir himself established a restaurant and is now spending most of his time running that. Mollywood lost its former zeal and enthusiasm and is struggling for its existence and sustenance.

As the local artists struggled to re-invent themselves after Deepti Bhatnagar packed up and bade Malegaon ka Chintu farewell, YouTube came as a saviour. The first to use YouTube space was Akram Khan. Akram Khan launched his YouTube Channel 'Khandesh Fun' in December 2016. The channel as of 31 May 2021 has an impressive 6.59 million subscribers. However, the man from Malegaon who is ruling the show on YouTube is not Akram but Rafeeque Shaikh – the local artist who became famous as 'Rafeeque Johnny' after his debut in 'Malegaon ke Karan Arjun' produced and directed by Al Amin Shaikh alias Malegaon ka Chintu. Rafeeque Johnny signed into YouTube in 2017 and launched a YouTube channel 'JKK Entertainment' in partnership with his friend Akbar Shaikh. The first video posted on JKK Entertainment was on 3 March 2017. The channel however very soon reached the coveted milestone of 10 million subscribers, which soon rose to 20 million, and now as of 31 May 2021, it has a whopping 27.6 million subscribers.

Besides its huge fan-following and subscribers, JKK Entertainment was also adjudged as Top Creator of the year 2020. It was also the top comedy channel for more than one and half years on 'Social Blade' website listing. What is common between Akram Khan's 'Khandesh Fun' and Rafeeque Shaikh's 'JKK Entertainment' is that they both rely heavily on Shafeeque Shaikh, famous as Shafeeq Chotu. Interestingly, it was Akram Khan who had launched Shafeeq Chotu in a series. Rafeeque Shaikh also came out with similar series with Shafeeq Chotu in lead role. But he soon left all his competitors, including Akram Khan, far behind, today being the co-owner of one of India's top YouTube comedy channels.

Besides immense fame and huge fan following, YouTube earned both Akram Khan and Rafeeque Shaikh money that the two had perhaps never imagined. But all this came with a heavy cost. For, whatever was remaining in Malegaon film industry after 'Malegaon ka Chintu' that too vanished and YouTube became their preferred platform to showcase the creative pursuits of the film/ actor fraternity of Malegaon.

Today artists of Malegaon are ruling the show on YouTube. But the innovation, humour, ideas, and out of the box methods and techniques for which the Malegaon film industry was famous are not to be seen in the present time. Mollywood as the film industry in on decline and its past fame and glory seems to be lost. The trajectory of growth and development of Mollywood, its rise and fall can be traced from Table 13.1. With a humble beginning based on its own stories made with a low budget using outdated tools and techniques, the industry moved ahead making Bollywood and even Hollywood spoofs with little budget and not so better equipment. During the third and fourth phases, respectively, the industry focused on making TV serials and short comedy films uploaded on YouTube in addition to some more remakes of Bollywood. The expenses for making films and videos for YouTube have increased phenominally. The industry except for one private channel did not get any support for its development and survival neither from government nor from any corporation.

Since 1972, Mollywood produced several entertaining movies (Table 13.2). However, the production of cinema has rapidly declined in the 2010s. There are several causes of the fall of Mollywood. One of the major causes of the decline is the rise of digital technologies. The availability of relatively cheaper rate internet and smartphones enabled the audience of the cinema to access other modes and channels of entertainment from YouTube to digital TVs. Earlier, they hardly had access to costly devices and the internet. A revolutionary

Table 13.1 Phases of Malegaon film industry

Phases	*Duration*	*Theme/Story*	*Budget*	*Camera used*
I	1972 to 1999	Own stories	2,000 to 10,000 INR	16mm movie camera/ VHS camera
II	2000 to 2010	Remakes of Bollywood films	10,000 to 20,000 INR	VHS and 3CCD cameras
III	2010 to 2014	TV serials	Produced by Sony's SAB TV	-
IV	2016 till now	Short comedy films for YouTube channels/ Remakes of Bollywood again	20,000 to 10 Lakh INR	3CCD and 5CCD cameras

Source: Compiled by authors

Table 13.2 Profile of Malegaon film industry

Film	*Year*	*Original film*	*Theme*	*Director*	*Actor*	*Expenditure (INR current prices)*	*Revenue earned (INR current prices)*
Qatil Khazana	1972	Own script	Suspense/ thriller	Ghulam Mohammad Zaidi	Advocate Zaheer and Siraj Dular	2,500	Less than 1,000
Range Haath	1987	Own script	Suspense	Hakeem Abu Bakr	Arshad Nazar	–	–
Desh Ki Pukar	–	–	–	Khursheed Siddiqui	–	4,400	–
Raat Ka Teesra Paher	–	–	–	Khursheed Siddiqui	Khursheed Siddiqui	4,500	–
Zara Zindagi	1995	Own script	Tragedy/ unemployment	Ateeque Sir	Ateeque Sir/ naeem akhtar/ haneef hamdani	40,000	40,000
Dehshatgard	1998	Own script	Crime	Nasir Shaikh	Siraj Dular	20,000	–
Gang War	1998	Own script	Crime	Nasir Shaikh	Saleem Jockey	18,000	–
Maut Ka Saudagar	1998	Own script	Crime	Ameen Fruitwala	Ameen Fruitwala	22,000	–
Aaj Ka Mugle Azam	1999	Own script	Comedy	Nasir Shaikh	Ateeque Sir/ haneef hamdani	25,000	–
Malegaon Ke Sholay	2000	Bollywood Movie Sholay	Remake (Comedy)	Nasir Shaikh	Shafeeque and others	50,000	250,000
Malegaon ki Shaan	2002	Bollywood Movie Shaan	Remake (Comedy)	Nasir Shaikh	Akram	–	–
Munna	2002	Own script		Nasir Shaikh	Akram	–	–
Malegaon Ka Don	2002	Bollywood Movie Don	Remake (Comedy)	Akram	Shafeeque, Akram	–	–
Malegaon Ka Karan Arjun	2002	Bollywood Movie Karan Arjun	Remake (Comedy)	Al Amin Shaikh	Al Amin Shaikh, Rafeeque Johnny	–	–
Malegaon ki Lagaan	–	Bollywood Movie Lagaan	Remake (Comedy)	Farogh Jafery	–	70,000	

Malegaon Ka Superman	2011	Hollywood movie Superman	Remake (Comedy)	Shaikh Nasir	–	–	–
Malegaon Ka Ghajni	2012	Bollywood Movie Ghajni	Remake (Comedy)	Shakeel Bharti	–	–	–
Malegaon Ka Rudra	2013	Remake of Kannada film Rudra	Remake (Comedy)	Akram Khan	Mehmood/Akram Khan	1000,000	–
Malegaon to Dubai	–		Remake (Comedy)	Muqeem Arshad	–	–	–
Koi Hil Gaya	–	Bollywood Movie Koi Mil Gaya	Remake (Comedy)	Akram Khan/ Mehmood	–	–	–
Malegaon Ka Tha Tiger	–	Bollywood Movie Ek Tha Tiger	Remake (Comedy)		Firoz Tarzan	450,000	286000
Malegaon ka Shera	2017	–	Remake (Comedy)	Md. Zubair	Md. Zubair, Pooja Chavan	–	–
Malegaon ki Rangeela	–	–	Remake (Comedy)	–	–	–	–
Malegaonwale Dulhaniya Le Jayenge	–	–	Remake (Comedy)	–	–	–	–
Malegaon Ka Mughal-e-Azam	–	–	Remake (Comedy)	–	–	–	–

Source: Compiled by authors

change with regards to ownership of mobile smartphones and personal computers, and this has been true to the country as a whole, has been seen in 2010s and this is the phase in which the cinema also declined in the town. The second major reason for the change has been the social and personal shocks that the two serial bomb blasts in the city in 2006 and 2008 generated. In the 2006 blast, 32 persons died and about 300 were injured, while the second bomb blast killed 6 persons and injured 100 persons. This changed the mood of a large number of Muslims to sombre. The orthodox religious groups started working with people to assuage the effect, which turned the people more conservative. As it is a Muslim majority town and as per some interpretations of Islam, dance, drama, music are considered un-Islamic. These resulted in a slow withdrawal of the people from cinema. It is also noteworthy that neither the state nor central government supported the cinema in the town. Today, we can say that the Mollywood success story of subaltern cinema has come to an end as hardly any new films are being made in the town, except those for short-comedies for YouTube. However, this is also true that mainstream cinema globally is also shifting to streaming channels like Netflix.

13.11 Conclusions

Malegaon, known for its textile industry, hard-working but poor power loom workers, has also been known in recent decades for its subaltern cinema. The town emerged as a centre for subaltern arts and culture with the Urdu language as its driving force. This gave rise to Mollywood which reached its pinnacle in the 2010s and has declined thereafter. The peculiarity of Mollywood has been that its heroes and villains and so other actors have not been from the world of the glamour but from the workers of the power looms, ordinary shops, and eateries. The majority of the cast and crew came from the Muslim community, mostly not well-off, mainly from amongst those who were daily wagers (Gupta 2012). The Mollywood growth filled the life of the town's people and especially workers with enormous dynamics and entertainments which local and contextual. It promoted a cosmopolitan culture with enormous possibilities of integration with the rest of the culture. It fostered ingenuity with limited resources. Mollywood has faced rapid decline because of many reasons and some of them include the rise of capital investment for digital technologies which enabled access to the audience of other modes of entertainment, the rise of religious conservatism, and lack of any support from other quarters. The decline of Mollywood is a great loss to the art and culture of the town, region, and the country as a whole. Despite the policy recommendation for the same (Shaban 2011), the state government especially working on the town's development also ignored it.

References

Ahuja, R. (2017, 18 April). Malegaon to Malegaon: The status of Hindu right-wing terror cases. *The Hindustan Times*. Available at: www.hindustantimes.com/india-news/malegaon-to-malegaon-the-status-of-hindu-right-wing-terror-cases/story-pcwOdnOOfriCII2chycQuN.html (last accessed on 25 March 2022).

Ansari, H., and Handa, N. (2011, 15 January). Malegaon 'ka' film industry. DNA Entertainment. Available at: www.dnaindia.com/entertainment/report-malegaon-ka-film-industry-1495032 (last accessed on 25 March 2022).

Census of India (2011). Primary census abstract. Available at: www.census2011.co.in/census/city/362-malegaon.html (last accessed on 25 March 2022).

Gopal, M. (2012, 15 July). Making it big in Mollywood, N arts & culture. Available at: www.thenationalnews.com/arts-culture/making-it-big-in-mollywood-1.360496 (last accessed on 25 March 2022).

Gupta, S. (2012, 29 June). Supermen of Malegaon. *The Indian Express*. Available at: http://archive.indianexpress.com/news/supermen-of-malegaon/968356/ (last accessed on 25 March 2022).

Liang, L. (2011). Piracy, creativity and infrastructure: Rethinking access to culture. Available at: https://docplayer.net/162801388-Piracy-creativit-j-and-infrastructure.html (last accessed on 25 March 2022).

Pritam, A. (2021). 1 USD to INR from 1947 till now, historical exchange rates explained. Available at: www.bookmyforex.com/blog/1-usd-inr-1947-till-now/ (last accessed on 25 March 2022).

Shaban, A. (2011). Multi-Sectoral Development Plan for Malegaon Town. Submitted to Maharashtra State Minorities Commission, Government of Maharashtra, Mumbai.

Shaban, A. (2013). The City of Terrors: Deprivation, segregation and communal conflicts in Malegaon. In Sharma, R. N. and Sandhu, R. S. (eds.), *Small Cities and Towns in Global Era: Emerging Changes and Perspectives*. Jaipur: Rawat Publications.

Siddiqui, S. (2011, 6 February). Green screen: Maleewood creates localised cinema. *The Sunday Gardian*. Available at: www.pressreader.com/india/the-sunday-guardian/20110206/282810712748740 (last accessed on 25 March 2022).

Tiwary, I. (2015). The discreet charm of local practices: Malegaon and the politics of locality. *Bioscope*, 6(1), 67–87.

Section V

ARTS AND CRAFTS

In India, a rich and diverse arts and crafts sector accounts for an extraordinarily large share of the workers engaged in CCI. Unique artisanal production and communities are an important part of the cultural and creative practices and traditions across the country. Every region has its own specific crafts, which reflect, sustain, and communicate wider intangible cultural heritage and diversity. What is more, some Indian regions have emerged as global hubs of arts and crafts production, which cater to customers throughout the subcontinent and international markets. The Government of India has identified several craft clusters in India and has devised a specific policy framework for their conservation and promotion. Chapter 14 discusses arts and crafts clusters as central elements in Indian cultural and development policy. As Chapter 15 documents, the gems and jewellery industry plays an important part in the economies of Gujarat and Rajasthan, and Jaipur has also emerged as a hub of gem and jewellery production by establishing effective access to the global and national market. The demand for crafts has created opportunities for several caste groups traditionally suffering from social marginalization, which entails opportunities for upward social mobility and for fostering social cohesion. Chapter 16 documents the Chamar artisanal leather works studios of Dharavi in Mumbai, which enabled many participating workers to harness traditional skills in the community and much improve their living conditions. However, many craftspeople in India are still subject to poverty and lack opportunities. The situation of the carpet weavers of Khairabad, discussed in Chapter 17, illustrates both the occasional success as well as the prevailing misery of traditional craftspeople of India. We hope this volume can promote the discussion on how to sustain initial improvements and build on them over the coming years.

DOI: 10.4324/9781003129370-18

14

HANDLOOM AND HANDICRAFT IN INDIA

Clusters and specializations

Sanjukta Sattar

14.1 Introduction

India is a land of diversity. This is also reflected in the large variety of handloom and handicrafts produced in the country which are the expression of the "traditional wisdom, cultural wealth, and secular ethos of our polity" (Government of India 2012a: 7). Each part of the country can be identified by its specialties in the types of handlooms and handicrafts, representing the cultural heritage and the community traditions, the indigenous skills, and knowledge which are passed down from one generation to the next many a times orally. The artisanal products are completely handmade or made with the help of hand tools and very rarely taking the help of mechanical means (UNESCO n.d.a). The raw material used by the artisans are mainly locally obtained which further adds to the products a very indigenous touch. Often the history (socio-cultural and economic) of that place has been found to be the contributing factor in the creation of a particular craft and weave.

> There are numerous expressions of traditional craftsmanship: tools; clothing and jewellery; costumes and props for festival and performing arts; storage containers, objects used for storage, transport and shelter; decorative art and ritual objects; musical instruments and household utensils, and toys, both for amusement and education. UNESCO (n.d.b)

"Many of these items or products may or may not have functional utility and can be used as a decorative item or gift" (EPCH n.d.). The products are also characterised by their varying period of usage as some are used only for a short duration, such as those created for using during religious rituals. Whereas there are other products like jewellery, utensils, which become "heirloom that are passed from generation to generation" (UNESCO n.d.a). Hawkings Jr. (2007)

DOI: 10.4324/9781003129370-19

categorises the typical crafts products "into 'handicraft' and 'traditional crafts'" (as cited in Rogerson 2010: 117) as certain products are crafted in particular regions since ages whereas there are other kinds of craft items which are outcomes of modern ideas, improvisations, and customisations in response to the contemporary requirements. Many of the "age-old handicrafts traditions have survived till date because of the inherent ability of the artisans to assimilate and respond to their changing ways of lives" (AIACA 2017: 3). This is a sector which is an important source of livelihoods for many. In India, it "provides low cost green livelihood opportunities to millions of families, supplementing incomes in seasons of agrarian distress, checking migration and preserving traditional economic relationship" (Government of India 2012a: 4).

Given the rich crafts tradition of India, this chapter explores its regional specialities based on its linkages with locally available resources, the traditional practices, and the trajectory of historical and economic development of the regions. The chapter uses the data available from various Government of India reports and Sixth Economic Census (2013–14), Ministry of Statistics and Program Implementation (MoSPI), Government of India, New Delhi. The chapter is divided into five sections. After this introductory section, the Section 14.2 discusses the growth and regional distribution of the handloom and handicraft industries, while in Section 14.3 promotion of special clusters and their specialities have been discussed. The next, Section 14.4, discusses the role and application of digital technologies in the preservation and development of handlooms and handicraft. The last section concludes the chapter.

14.2 Growth and regional distribution of handloom and handicraft

The handloom and handicraft sector in India experienced a downfall during the colonial rule as the British colonisers started importing machine-made products at a cheaper rate. It was only because of the earnest efforts, as part of the freedom struggle, made by national leaders like Mahatma Gandhi that the cottage industries of India were protected from destruction. Kamaladevi Chattopadhyay, who was inspired by Mahatma Gandhi's initiatives, took up the cudgel for the revival and development of handloom and handicrafts of India (Priya 2018; Dhamija 2016).

Today the handloom and handicraft sector in India is the second-largest generator of employment after agriculture (IBEF 2021). In 2017, this sector employed about 4.3 and 9.6 million people, respectively (Table 14.1), which included a large number of women and people belonging to the weaker sections of the society as mentioned by Minister of State for textile Ajay Tamta (Business Standard 2017). The handloom sector employment may remain static because of the mechanisation of weaving sector, but as forecasted by TARI (n.d.: 14), the employment in handicrafts may increase to about 13.46 million by 2022. Based on Sixth Economic Census data (2013–14), both in handloom and handicraft sectors majority of the people engaged are from rural areas (52.67%) and most of the handloom and handicraft units (59.63%) are located in rural setting. The production of handloom cloth during the year 2016–17 was 8.01 Billion sq. metres (TARI n.d.: 14), and the export of handloom products was of US$355.6 million and US$353.9 million in 2016–17 and 2017–18, respectively (TARI n.d.: 8). The total production of handicrafts including handmade carpets was of worth US$7.57 billion (Government of India n.d.a: 5) and exports of handicraft was of US$3.53 billion during 2019–20 (IBEF 2020). The share of textile and apparel (T&A) including handicrafts in India's total exports is quite significant at 11.8 % in 2019–20 (Government of India 2021: 1).

It is to be noted that what statistics mentioned by KPMG and other sources, mentioned earlier, do not match with the Economic Census, 2013–14 data (see Table 14.2). The total employment in handloom and handicraft sector as per the Economic Census 2013–14 were about 4.2 million while the total establishments were about 1.9 million. The possibility is that the aforementioned statistics by KPMG and other sources count all the peripheral industries employment as well which are not taken into account by the Economic Census, 2013–14.

Indian handloom and handicraft is known for its diverse and rich tradition of exquisite craftsmanship and wide array of articles and weaves indigenous to various parts of India. Some of the states significantly lead in this sector having larger share of handloom and handicraft units and also workers engaged in this sector. As per the Economic Census, 2013–14, West Bengal, Uttar Pradesh, and Odisha are the top three states where handloom and handicraft activities are dominantly present. West Bengal tops the list in terms of percentage share of Handicraft and Handloom workers, and is followed by Uttar Pradesh and Odisha, respectively (Table 14.2). Uttar Pradesh leads in the share of handloom and handicraft establishments, and West Bengal and Odisha follow Uttar Pradesh. Though Jammu and Kashmir, Madhya Pradesh, Telangana, Kerala, Bihar, Chhattisgarh, and the other North-Eastern states which are not occupying a position among the top ten states, in terms of share of Handloom and handicraft units and workers in this sector, are also known for their exquisite handloom and handicraft products which characterise those regions.

Table 14.1 Employment in the handloom and handicraft sector in India

Sectors	*Employment (in million)*			*Employment growth 2013–17 (in million)*	*Projected employment growth 2017–22 (in million)*
	2013	*2017*	*2022 (projected)*		
Handlooms	4.33	4.33	4.33	—	—
Handicrafts	7.32	9.60	13.46	2.28	3.86
Overall sectors	11.65	13.93	17.79	2.28	3.86

Source: KPMG n.d.: 6)

Table 14.2 Share (%) of top ten states in handloom and handicraft units and workers engaged therein, 2013–14

Rank	*States*	*Total handloom and handicraft workers*		*States*	*Total handloom and handicraft establishments*	
		Number (000)	*% to total workers in the sector*		*Number (000)*	*% to the total establishments in the sector*
1	West Bengal	330.1	17.62	Uttar Pradesh	769.6	18.30
2	Uttar Pradesh	310.0	16.55	West Bengal	746.2	17.75
3	Odisha	146.1	7.80	Odisha	305.5	7.27
4	Andhra Pradesh	141.3	7.54	Tamil Nadu	310.2	7.38
5	Tamil Nadu	127.4	6.80	Rajasthan	263.3	6.26
6	Rajasthan	124.0	6.62	Andhra Pradesh	254.0	6.04
7	Assam	911.0	4.86	Gujarat	245.8	5.85
8	Maharashtra	846.8	4.52	Maharashtra	215.3	5.12
9	Gujarat	679.4	3.63	Assam	189.9	4.52
10	Karnataka	628.7	3.36	Karnataka	149.4	3.55
India		4,204.8	–	India	1,873.6	–

Source: Based on data from Sixth Economic Census 2013–14 (MoSPI 2016).

The weavers and artisans from different parts of the country, lives in clusters producing similar types of products having equal prospects, and facing similar types of challenges, in specific geographic locations. In India, such clusters have existed since ages and stood out for their products at the national as well as international levels. These clusters, consisting of towns or contiguous groups of villages known for some specific products or a range of corresponding products that have been in existence for decades and centuries, epitomize the socio-economic heritage of the country (Singh 2010). For instance, traditional art of hand block printing is a speciality from Bagru a village located 30 km east of Jaipur city in Rajasthan practised by a "community of *Chhipas* or traditional crafts people who printed fabrics by hand" (Mahajan 2008). Unique design and luxuriant trellises produced using natural colours characterises this art. Another example is of Pipli applique work, a craft locally called *Chandua*, prepared by *Darjis* or tailor community belonging to Pipli village located about 24 km away from Bhubaneswar in the state of Orissa. These were originally used in the temples for daily rites and rituals, but presently this artwork used on wall hangings, decorative lampshades, umbrellas, bags, bedsheets, and various other products thus catering to the different types of consumer (Ghosh 2019; Ramaswamy 2011).

The diversity in the Indian handloom and handicrafts "is a result of the varied social, cultural, economic and religious interactions" (Government of

India n.d.a: 4) as well as influence of natural factors like topography and climate. Within India, people have migrated from one place to another because of environmental, social, political, and economic reasons, and this has resulted in the diversity and variations in their craft forms also. For example, "*Sungadi* of Madurai in the state of Tamil Nadu located in the southern part of India is a new expression of Bandhani textiles of Gujarat and Rajasthan" (Government of India n.d.a: 4), which are the states in north western part of India. Similarly, *Patola*, an exquisite weave from Gujarat is woven by the members of the Salvi caste originally from Karnataka and Maharashtra who moved to Gujarat in the 12th century.

The story of *Baluchari silk* is closely linked to the history of Bengal. *Baluchari silk sari* which is mainly worn by women across India and Bangladesh had its origin in Bengal in a small village on bank of river Bhagirathi, the distributary of river Ganga, called Baluchar in present Murshidabad district. In the 18th century, *Nawab* of Bengal Murshidquali Khan patronised the rich weaving tradition and brought the weavers and along with them this tradition of fine weaving, from Dhaka, the present capital of Bangladesh, to the Baluchar village in Murshidabad, West Bengal (Pawar 2014; Sarda 2017; Parinita 2021). The motifs woven depicted significant incidents and developments of that time, social practices and scenes from epics and mythology. But after a flood due to the change in the course of the river and subsequent submerging of the village, the *Baluchari* weavers and along with them the art of *Baluchari* weaving moved to Bishnupur village located in Bankura, West Bengal (Pawar 2014; Sarda 2017; Parinita 2021). Here the traditional industry of *Baluchari* weaving flourished but it started declining during the British rule due to political reasons and soon it became a dying art as most of the weavers were compelled to give up the profession (Pawar 2014). It was only in the first half of 20th century with the initiative of a famous artist Shubho Thakur that the rich tradition of *Baluchari* weaving was revived back (Pawar 2014; Parinita 2021). Similarly, the Bengal handloom sarees have created its own global identity and occupies a special status even in the era of contemporary fashion. The weave is known for its unique design and weaving patterns, colour combinations, with subtle variations in texture and pattern between *Dhania Khali, Tangail, Shantipuri* which are the variations of *Jamdani*, popularly known as *Dhakai Jamdani* as it has its roots in Dhaka in Bangladesh, though presently it is also woven in West Bengal in India. The "name *Jamdani* is of Persian origin and comes from the word *jam* meaning flower and *dani* meaning vase which is suggestive of the beautiful floral motifs on these sarees that are considered to be one of the finest variety of muslin that is handwoven from cotton, flourished under the patronage of the Mughals" (Chakrabarti 2016). However, the art faced a set back with colonisation by the British and decline of the Mughal rule in India. Post partition many weavers migrated from erstwhile East Pakistan (present Bangladesh) to West Bengal with which the art of *Jamdani weave flourished* in West Bengal in India (Chakrabarti 2016; Dutta 2018; Lyster n.d.).

Banarasi Silk Brocades which is a fine variant of silk has its origin in the city of Varanasi or Benaras in Uttar Pradesh. According to Ralph Flitch one of the early English traders and a chronicler who visited India during 1583 to 1586, Varanasi was known for its cotton textiles. Later on, it became a silk weaving hub when craftsmen migrated to the Indian subcontinent from Persia. "It is believed that local weavers learnt the skill of brocading from Iranian craftsmen who arrived in the wake of conquest by invaders from the region" (Balasubrahmanyan 2018: 4; also see Mohanty 1984). Among them some might have "settled in western and northern India as many weavers today describe themselves as descendants of these medieval immigrants" (Balasubrahmanyan 2018: para. 4). There are also other legends which suggests that this art of weaving *Banarasi* was introduced in Varanasi by Muslim silk weavers who migrated from Gujarat due to the occurrence of "famines, floods and fires in the region during medieval period between 14th and 16th centuries" (Balasubrahmanyan 2018: 3). Originally this variety was created exclusively for the royal family using real gold and silver threads, sometimes it took a year for completion. This fine weaving style with brocade and zari work reached its pinnacle during the Mughal era especially under the patronage of Emperor Akbar who was a great admirer of fine arts and craft (Nair 2016). Persian influenced patterns like florals, stylised leaves, *jhallar* or string of upright leaves and *jali* or *jaal* (net), characterised the Banarasi textiles. The Banarasi brocades we see today are "the product of a long history of cultural intermingling brought on by political conquests, trade and migration" (Balasubrahmanyan 2018: 3).

Lucknow, the capital of Uttar Pradesh located in the northern heartland of India, is famous for *Chikankari*, which is an ancient form of white floral embroidery, intricately worked with needle and raw thread. This art has been practised in Lucknow for almost two hundred years. The word *chikan* is probably derived from the Persian word 'chikin' or 'chikeen' which means a kind of embroidery fabric. According to Tyabji (2007: 11) "chikankari stems from white-on-white embroidery of Shiraz", a city of Iran, "and came to India as part of cultural baggage of Persian nobles at the Mughal court". Again, some researchers are of opinion that it is a Persian craft that has been brought to India by Noor Jehan, queen of Mughal Emperor Jahangir.

> Legend has it that it was Empress Noor Jehan, a noted aesthete and embroider, who, while making an Eid cap for her husband, the Emperor Jehangir, conceived the idea of using the fine white cotton mull for which Indian weavers were famous, as a base for her stitchery. (Tyabji 2007: 11)

This embroidery style was highly appreciated by the king and his nobles. The Mughals adored and patronized this art and "gave it its own distinctive character and design identity. Chikan was used for everything – from turbans and veils to *angarkhas*, *chogas* and palace interiors" (Tyabji 2007: 12). The embroidery was done on the finest *Dhakai Mulmuls* or *Muslins* which was produced and exported from Bengal. The cotton from which muslin was woven was cultivated in a region around Dhaka due to high humidity of that area. The cotton that was spun was extremely white in colour since the main rivers like Brahmaputra and the Ganges have bleaching properties. *Chikankari* comprises "44 different stitches out of which 22 variants of the six basic stitch techniques are known and practised even today" (Tyabji 2007: 17). With the end of the Mughal rule, the artisans and craftsmen who were patronised by the Mughals, moved to different parts of the country. Some of them "settled in West Bengal, as a result *Chikan* flourished in Calcutta, though it is no longer practiced there" (IndiaNetzone 2011). Other craftsmen of *Chikankari* moved to the Northern part of Awadh and got shelter in the royal courts of the descendants of Burhan ul Mulk, a Persian nobleman who was appointed as the governor of Awadh by the last Mughal King Bahadur Shah (Chakravarty 2003). Again there are other versions about the origin of *Chikankari* based on "evidence of embroidered muslin apparel in the paintings of Bagh (in Madhya Pradesh) and Ajanta caves (in Maharashtra) dating back to 9th century A.D." (Chand 2014: 3). Others trace back its origin to the time of King Harsha in the 7th Century A.D. who had a "liking for white muslin garments embroidered with patterns but no colour, no ornamentation, nothing spectacular to embellish it" (Manfredi 2017: 37). Even Greek ambassador Megasthenes during 3rd Century B.C. has written about the use of 'flowered muslin', which may had been reckoned as *chikan* by the Indians in the court of Chandragupta Maurya. But some also consider its recent origin inspired by Taj Mahal (Chand 2014: 4).

Kalamkari an exquisite 'pen art' from Andhra Pradesh is noted for its beautiful hand paintings on fabrics using natural vegetable dyes extracted from bark, flower, and roots of plants. Etymologically the word 'Kalamkari' has its origin in Persian words *kalam* meaning pen and *kari* meaning craftsmanship (Chandra 2015; Ghosh 2018; Srinivas n.d.). This form of art had received patronage from the Mughal rulers and reached its peak during the reign of Golkonda Sultanate of Hyderabad who called the skilled craftsmen practising this art as *kalamkars* and that's how this art got its name *kalamkari*. Originally a group of travelling singers, musicians, and painters called *chitrakattis* introduced this art in form of stage scenes and backdrops for the street plays they performed (Chandra 2015). The screens were painted on the spot depicting the episodes from Hindu mythology. Later to keep in with wider demand from other parts of the world the artisans came up with innovative patterns and ideas highly influenced by Persian motifs, scenes from Hindu mythology and religious symbols. This art has been presently popularised as block prints on sarees, dupattas, dress material, and home furnishing fabrics.

Madhubani painting (*also see* Chapter 8) is one of the distinct styles of painting from India which is practised in the Mithila region of Bihar in India and adjacent areas of Nepal which are traditionally done by women members of the family for generations. It has its uniqueness in the predominant use of bright coloured complex geometrical patterns for representing the ritual content for particular occasions related to festivals, religious rituals, social events, etc. The patterns are created with twigs, matchsticks, or even fingers using colours extracted from lampblack, clay, locally available flowers and creepers, powdered rice, turmeric, sandalwood, etc. (UMSAS 2022). There are three basic styles of *Madhubani* which varies with the caste or the social hierarchy of the painters (Ritu 2020; Szanton n.d.). The paintings created by the Brahmins who belongs to the highest rung of the caste hierarchy have vibrant colours and religious motifs of various gods. Probably to avoid the monotony due to lack of variety in the themes their focus was more on stylistic and intricate patterns in their paintings. The second type of paintings created by the *Kayasthas*, whose position in the social hierarchy is just next to the *Brahmins*, included motifs symbolizing procreation. The third style practised by the *Dusadhs*, who belonged to the lower rung of the social ladder, included common motifs of flora, fauna, and their daily life in their paintings depicted with secular motifs (f-pedia 2020). Their drawings appeared simpler having minimum ornamentation, less sophisticated with more emphasis on depth and volume. But presently they incorporate the motifs of their own mythologies in their paintings and use bright colours (UMSAS 2022).

These are some of the examples of the various craft traditions and weave types which bears the testimony of environmental, socio-cultural, economic, and political impacts. Patronage received from the ruling royal families and their followers and availability of the raw materials played vital role in the flourishing of most of the handloom and handicrafts, their survival, their translocation to newer places other than the place of origin, as well as in the decline.

14.3 Development and promotion of special clusters and their regional specialities

The handloom and handicraft sector has been an important source of employment generation and export, yet has been suffering due to the informal nature of functioning along with various other limitations like lack of education among the artisans, shortage of capital, poor exposure to new technologies, absence of market intelligence, and poor institutional frameworks. In order to overcome these constraints and for the development of handloom and handicraft sectors in the country, a number of schemes and programs have been initiated and implemented by Government of India (Table 14.3).

Government of India envisages to shape the handloom and handicraft sector into a "strong, competitive and vibrant sector" (Government of India 2012b: 3) that would lead to economic development, particularly, of rural areas. Programmatic interventions like cluster-based approach, conducting censuses and mapping the distribution of crafts and craftspersons within the country, working capital and credit availability to the weavers and artisans, ensuring availability of raw materials to individual weavers and artisans at reasonable prices,

Table 14.3 Existing schemes and programmes for development of the handloom and handicraft sector in India

A	**HANDLOOM SECTOR**
1.	**National Handloom Development Programme**
i)	Block Level Cluster
ii)	Handloom Marketing Assistance
iii)	Concessional credit/weavers Mudra Scheme
iv)	Handloom Census
v)	Bunkar Mitra
2.	**Handloom Weavers' Comprehensive Welfare Scheme**
3.	Yarn Supply Scheme
4.	Comprehensive Handloom Cluster Development Scheme
B.	**HANDICRAFT SECTOR**
1.	**National Handicraft Development Programme**
i)	Dastkar Shashtikaran Yojana under Ambedkar Hastshilp Vikas Yojana
ii)	Design and Technology Upgradation
iii)	Human Resource Development
iv)	Direct Benefit to Artisans
v)	Infrastructure and Technology Support
vi)	Research and Development
vii)	Marketing Support Services
2.	**Comprehensive Handicrafts Cluster Development Scheme**
i)	Mega Cluster
ii)	Special Projects under Integrated Development and Promotion of Handicrafts

Source: Government of India (2017).

launching health and life insurance schemes, distress relief, pension funds as a part of social security provisions to improve the quality of life of weavers and artisans, have been intended through the schemes like Amended Technology Upgradation Funds Scheme (ATUFS), PowerTex India Scheme, Scheme for Integrated Textile Parks, Samarth scheme for capacity building in Textile Sector, Silk Samagra – integrated silk development scheme, North Eastern Region Textile Promotion Scheme (NERTPS), etc. Special emphasis is being given to "cluster-based approach which is increasingly being recognized as one of the strategies for cost effective, inclusive, sustainable and integrated development of Micro, Small and Medium Enterprises (MSMEs)" (Government of India, n.d.b: 2). Considering this, Ministries of Central Government and the State Government have launched sector-specific cluster-based schemes which are part of umbrella schemes and programmes like National Handloom Development Programme (NHDP), National Handicrafts Development Programme, Comprehensive Handloom Cluster Development Scheme (CHCDS), and Comprehensive Handicrafts Cluster Development Scheme. The schemes are either Centrally Sponsored Schemes or are in partnerships with respective states.

14.3.1 Handloom clusters

The number of households engaged in handloom activities in India has risen from 2.78 million in 2009–10 to about 3.15 million households in 2019 (Government of India 2019a: 14). The increase in the number of households may be due to the successful implementation of various initiatives undertaken by the Government of India (Government of India 2019a: 14) since independence. These programmes and schemes aimed at identification and development of clusters, welfare of the weaver community, and also delivering financial assistance to the weavers. Some of these schemes we discuss briefly here.

The *Comprehensive Handloom Clusters Development Scheme* (CHCDS) is one such scheme which aims "to develop Mega Handloom Clusters located in easily identifiable geographical locations that specialise in specific products" (Government of India 2020: 1). Cluster is a concentration of units in a given location producing same or similar types of products with common opportunities and threats. A handloom cluster is a large concentration of handlooms producing fabrics. These handlooms could be "located in close proximity in two adjoining revenue sub-divisions or villages within an administrative district or across two (mostly adjoining) districts" (Government of India 2014: 4). These clusters identified by the Government are located in 7 states of India, namely Uttar Pradesh, Jharkhand, Assam, West Bengal, Bihar, Andhra Pradesh, and Tamil Nadu, which is having two mega clusters (Table 14.4). The main objectives of the schemes have been the integrated and holistic development of the respective clusters and improved competency.

There are also 31 Block Level Handloom Clusters which have been taken up during 2018–19 under CHDS for development benefiting 26,093 weavers. Largest number of handloom clusters sanctioned under *Integrated Handloom Cluster Development Scheme* (IHCDS), *Integrated Handlooms Development Scheme* (IHDS), *Comprehensive Handloom Clusters Development Scheme* (CHCDS), *Comprehensive Handlooms Development Scheme* (CHDS), *National Handloom Development programme* (NHDP), and *North Eastern Region Textile Promotion Scheme* (NERTPS) during 2006–07 to 2015–16 are found in Assam (158) followed by Manipur (128), Tamil Nadu (93), Meghalaya (84), Andhra Pradesh (78), Uttar Pradesh (62), Orissa (61), Jharkhand (57), Nagaland (54), Tripura (48), Arunachal Pradesh (44), and West Bengal (42).

NERTPS is a region-specific scheme. According to the Third Handloom Census 2010 (NCAER 2010: 27) out of 2.38 million looms across the country, 1.55 million are in North-eastern region. Similarly, out of 4.33 million persons engaged in weaving and allied activities at the national level 2.16 million are found in North-eastern region (NCAER 2010: 18).

Almost every state of India has an exclusive handloom product characterised by a distinct style. For example, *Brocade and Jamewar* from Benaras in Uttar Pradesh, *Chanderi* from Madhya Pradesh, *Bhagalpur silk* from Bihar, *Ikats, Gadwal, Vanapati, Nander, Venkatgiri* from Andhra Pradesh, *Karakal* sarees from Kerala, *Kancheepuram, Dharmavaram* from Tamil Nadu, *Jamdani, Tangail, Dhanekhali,*

Baluchari, Murshidabad Silk from West Bengal, *Sambalpuri* and *Bomkai* from Odisha, exceptional varieties of silks like *Eri, Muga, Paat*, delicate tribal weaves such as *Mirijim* on blankets, mattresses, and floor coverings, *Gamcha* (thin cotton towel) and *Mekhla-chaddar* (traditional Assamese dress) from Assam, *Phenek* and *Tongam* which are traditional designs weaved in Assam and Manipur, *Paithani* sarees from Paithan in Maharashtra, Patola silk sarees from Patan in Gujarat, are some examples of the rich variety of Indian Handloom sector. State-wise Uttar Pradesh has largest number of handloom clusters followed by Bihar and Madhya

Table 14.4 Handloom mega clusters under Comprehensive Handloom Clusters Development Scheme (CHCDS).

Sr. no	*Mega cluster*	*State*	*No. of looms*	*No. of weavers*	*Products*
1.	Varanasi	Uttar Pradesh	65,000	1,00,000	Sarees, Dress materials, Furnishing fabrics, Fashion accessories (Stole, Scarves, etc.)
2.	Godda	Jharkhand	27,000	4661	Sarees, dress material, Gamcha (towel), Panchi-suiting and dupatta, and furnishing
3.	Sivasagar	Assam	63,686	58,179	*Gamcha* (towel), *Mekhla-Chada*r and Muga *Riha (traditional dress worn by Assamese women)*, Sari, Shawl, Masali (handkerchief), Dhoti, Sula/Angarkha (Shirt), handbags
4.	Murshidabad	West Bengal	25,295	25,000	Sarees (fine quality & coarser variety), *Gamcha* (towel), dress material, fashion accessories (stole, scarves, etc.), furnishing fabric, dhotis and Lungis
5.	Virudhunagar	Tamil Nadu	23448	29050	Cotton sarees, art silk sarees, *lungis*, towels, grey *gada* (plain cotton grey fabric), bedsheets, etc.
6.	Prakasam and Guntur	Andhra Pradesh	43900	26958	*Jaquard* sarees, plain sarees, towels, dress materials, dress material, sheets, shirting fabric, plain fabric
7.	Trichy	Tamil Nadu	35517	47357	*Woraiyur* Cotton Sarees, Venkatagiri Cotton Sarees, *Chinnalapatti* art silk saree, *Variangaval* cotton dhotis, *Thatthaiangarpet* cotton dhotis, tie, and dye sarees, Tirubhuvanam silk sarees, and gada uniform cloth
8.	Bhagalpur	Bihar	5084	20000	*Tussar* silk saree, *Dupattas*, Stole, Suite pieces, bed linen, home furnishing items, Dress material, Stole, *Gamcha* (towel), *Lungi*, etc.

Source: Compiled by author from Handloom Cluster, Office of the Development Commissioner (Handlooms), Government of India. http://handlooms.nic.in/User_Panel/UserView.aspx?TypeID=2462

Pradesh. Table 14.4 shows the variety of products being produced in the eight mega clusters located in the seven states of India.

14.3.2 Handicraft clusters

For the development of the handicraft artisans, Government schemes like 'National Handicrafts Development Programme' (NHDP) and 'Comprehensive Handicrafts Cluster Development' (CHCD) have been implemented by the Government of India. To promote handicrafts and also mitigate the problems and challenges faced by this sector, various developmental activities initiated under the umbrella scheme NHDP which is implemented through seven schemes, included enrolment of artisans, formation of SHGs/ Federations/Societies imparting training to them, conducting workshops to develop new designs, assisting them in domestic marketing promoting exports, R&D, creating common infrastructure, providing credit facilities, and welfare schemes for the artisans (Government of India n.d.b). State-wise distribution of handicraft clusters showed that "37% of the clusters are located in the four states of which Uttar Pradesh tops the list with 282 clusters, followed by Orissa, West Bengal and Gujarat having 271, 245 and 199 clusters respectively" (Singh 2010: 28). Majority of the clusters produce products related to textile, followed by basketry and cane articles, woodwork, metalware, and earthenware. Some of the other products include carpets and durries, folk paintings, glass and stone ware, leatherwork, coconut shell and seashell craft, jewellery, toys and dolls, sholapith craft, papier mache, applique work, musical instruments, and various decorative items.

Among various schemes under NHDP for promotion and development of handicraft sector, Baba Saheb Ambedkar Hastshilp Vikas Yojana (BAHVY), which is a cluster development scheme, was launched in 2001–02 aiming to provide support to the handicraft artisans, which included basic inputs and infrastructure support as well as enabling the artisans to produce and tap the target markets and also compete globally. The recently sanctioned cluster projects covered under this scheme are spread over six regions covering 25 states (Tables 14.5a,b,c,d,e,f). Maximum number of freshly sanctioned handicraft clusters (65) as well as self-help groups (2465) under BAHVY scheme for the year 2016–17 is located in the North-Eastern Region. Cane and bamboo craft products are speciality of North-eastern region. Bamboo plants and canes of various species are found in abundance in the forests of the North-eastern part of India.

The Western Region has 54 sanctioned handicraft clusters and 1,575 self-help groups. This region is known for a beautiful blend of diverse variety of culture and tradition which is reflected in the handicrafts. Leather works, *Bidri* crafts (metal inlay work), paintings, cane and bamboo work, crochet embroideries, tie and dye crafts, bead works are some of the specialities of this region. One of the much-known creative speciality of this region is *Kolhapuri Chappal*,

Table 14.5a Craft clusters sanctioned under the Baba Saheb Ambedkar Hastshilp Vikas Yojana and their specialities in the north-eastern region, 2016–17

North-eastern region	*State*	*No. of clusters*	*No. of SHGs*	*Specialities*
1	Assam	27	1105	*Cane & Bamboo, water hyacinth craft, Wood craft, Hand embroidery, Jute work, Rabha Artistic textile, Karbi, Mising, Deori Artistic Tribal textiles, terracotta*
2	Manipur	26	1005	*Artistic textiles, tribal textiles hand embroidery, cane and bamboo craft, Natural Fibre, Jute craft, toys and dolls, dry flowers, cane and bamboo craft, Chumthang crafts, Wood carving, Stone carving, Nungbi Pottery Crafts*
3	Tripura	05	145	*Cane and Bamboo craft, Terracotta craft, Jute craft, Matting*
4	Mizoram	03	105	*Artistic Tribal Textiles, Hand Embroidery Crafts*
5	Arunachal Pradesh	02	70	*Artistic Tribal Textiles, Decorative items, Embroidery Crafts*
6	Nagaland	02	35	*Artistic Tribal Textiles, Embroidery Crafts*
Total		65	2465	–

Source: Compiled by author based on data from AHVY cluster sanctioned, 2016–17, www.handicrafts.nic.in/pdf/2016_17/Fresh_project_sanctioned_NER_2016_17.pdf

which is handcrafted footwear originally designed in Kolhapur, a town in the state of Maharashtra, which was also known by various other names like *Kapashi*, *Paytaan*, *Kachkadi*, *Bakkalnali*, and *Pukari* depending on the name of the villages where it was made. The origin of this art can be traced back to the 13th century and was initially designed and created by *saudagar* family of Maharashtra. These footwears are dyed with vegetable dyes, completely hand-stitched without using any nails, and decorated with golden cords. *Crochet* work is an integral part of Goan culture which is an outcome of the blend of Indo-Portuguese art. Another expression of the creative culture of this region is *Warli* paintings a form of tribal art from the North Sahaydri Range in the state of Maharashtra which is known to be one of the earliest forms of art in history. As the culture of the Warli tribe is nature based hence the elements of nature are mostly the focal themes in Warli paintings. The painting is characterised by use of intricate geometric patterns for depicting flowers, wedding rituals, hunting scenes, and the daily activities of the population traditionally done on a red ochre background with white paint. Another exquisite form of handicraft is the Bell Metal work or *Dokra* art which is an example of creative pursuit of the tribal population of the Raigarh and the Bastar districts of Chhattisgarh.

Table 14.5b Craft clusters sanctioned under the Baba Saheb Ambedkar Hastshilp Vikas Yojana and their specialities in the western region

Central region	*State*	*No. of clusters*	*No. of SHGs*	*Specialities*
1	Madhya Pradesh	24	405	*Jute craft, bamboo craft, bead work, Lac Bangle craft, artificial jewellery, hand embroidery and applique work, papier mache, zardozi, terracotta, dori craft, crochet work*
2	Gujarat	20	785	*Embroidery craft, Patch work, Bead work, Moti work, Tie& Dye, jewellery, bamboo craft and warli painting*
3	Chhattisgarh	05	190	*Cane & bamboo products, Terracotta, wood, metal craft, hand embroidery, Jute and Kaudi Shilp Crafts*
4	Maharashtra	04	160	*Tribal embroidery craft, zari patch work and bead work, warli paintings crochet work*
5	Goa	01	35	*Crochet embroidery*
Total		54	1575	–

Source: Compiled by author based on data of sanctioned list of clusters, 2016–17 www.handicrafts.nic.in/pdf/2016_17/Fresh_project_sanctioned_WR_2016_17.pdf

Table 14.5c Craft clusters sanctioned under the Baba Saheb Ambedkar Hastshilp Vikas Yojana and their specialities in the northern region

Northern region	*State*	*No. of clusters*	*No. of SHGs*	*Specialities*
1	Jammu and Kashmir	19	530	*Crewel, Sozni and Ari embroidery, Gabba embroidery craft, artistic textiles, papier mache*
2	Rajasthan	07	205	*Bandhej or Tie & Dye, hand embroidery, mirror craft and patch work, leather embroidery, leather craft, hand block printing, wood craft*
3	Punjab	04	117	*Hand embroidery and Tila Jutti, Phulkari craft*
4	Himachal Pradesh	02	60	*Artistic textile craft*
5	Haryana	02	55	*Pottery, hand embroidery, terracotta*
Total		34	967	

Source: Compiled by author based on data of sanctioned list of clusters, 2016–17, www.handicrafts.nic.in/pdf/2016_17/AHVY_NR_sanctioned_during_2016_17.pdf

Numbers of sanctioned clusters and self-help groups in northern region are 34 and 967, respectively, which are spread over the five states including Jammu and Kashmir, Rajasthan, Punjab, Himachal Pradesh, and Haryana. Northern region is a treasure house of a large variety of handicrafts and each

Table 14.5d Fresh craft clusters sanctioned under the Baba Saheb Ambedkar Hastshilp Vikas Yojana and their specialities in the central region

Central region	*State*	*No. of clusters*	*No. of SHGs*	*Specialities*
	Uttar Pradesh	30	1661	*Zari embroidery bead and patch work, zardozi, wood work, woollen craft, Red clay pottery, leather craft, moonj craft, Chikan embroidery, metal art ware, punja durry craft, applique work, stone craft, cane and bamboo craft*
	Uttarakhand	02	95	*Woollen fibre products, Hand embroidery, Metal craft*
Total		35	1756	–

Source: Compiled by author based on data of sanctioned list of cluster, 2016–17 www.handicrafts.nic.in/pdf/2016_17/Fresh_project_sanctioned_CR_2016_17.pdf

Table 14.5e Craft clusters sanctioned under the Baba Saheb Ambedkar Hastshilp Vikas Yojana and their specialities in the eastern region

Eastern region	*State*	*No. of clusters*	*No. of SHGs*	*Specialities*
1	Odisha	5	130	*Bamboo craft, Brass & Bell metal, stone carving craft*
2	Bihar	2	48	*Sujni and Crochet, Madhubani painting*
3	Jharkhand	2	40	*Bamboo work, terracotta*
Total		09	218	–

Source: Compiled by author based on data of sanctioned list of cluster, 2016–17. www.handicrafts.nic.in/pdf/2016_17/Fresh_project_sanctioned_ER_2016_17.pdf

Table 14.5f Craft clusters sanctioned under the Baba Saheb Ambedkar Hastshilp Vikas Yojana and their specialities in the southern region

Southern region	*State*	*No. of clusters*	*No. of SHGs*	*Specialities*
1	Karnataka	02	55	*Lambani mirror embroidery, wood inlay*
2	Andhra Pradesh	01	35	*Imitation Jewellery*
3	Kerala	01	35	*Pottery, Papier mache, screwpine articles*
4	Tamil Nadu	01	15	*Palm leaf products*
Total		05	140	

Source: Compiled by author based on data of sanctioned list of cluster, 2016–17. www.handicrafts.nic.in/pdf/2016_17/GIA_Project_sanctioned_SR_2016_17.pdf

of the states in this region has its own specialities. The Kashmiri carpets and shawls, papier mache articles, and Walnut wood products are well known for the splendid craftsmanship. The tie and dye or locally called *bandhej*, mirror craft, hand block printing wood craft, Rajasthani miniature paintings, Jaipuri quilts, blue pottery, jewellery with *meenakari* work are some of the exquisite variety of handicrafts from Rajasthan. *Tila Jutti* or leather footwear and hand embroidery products from Punjab, embroidered footwears called *Chamba Chappals*, silver and gold jewellery with antique look, coin necklaces, Kangra paintings, wood and stone crafts of Himachal Pradesh, pottery and durries from Haryana add to the variety of handicrafts that characterise the clusters in the northern region.

Central region has 35 sanctioned handicraft clusters and 1,756 self-groups. Uttarakhand is famous for exquisite woodwork, Tibetian carpets, copper ware, nettle fibre craft, lantana furniture basketry. The traditional artisans including *Tamtas* (copper smiths) are well-known for their hand-made utensils. Uttar Pradesh stands out for its wide variety of artistic wares from different parts of the state. Ceramic pottery, glass work, durries and Mirzapur carpets, metalware from Moradabad, marble carving and stone craft of Agra, cane furniture, terracotta and black pottery, hand block printing of Farrukhabad and Varanasi districts, leather work of Agra and Kanpur, stone jewellery, glass bangles of Firozabad *Chikankari of Lucknow*, *Zardozi* embroidery and *Brocade* from Banaras are some of the examples of the exclusive artistry of this region.

Eastern region has nine sanctioned clusters and 218 self-help groups. The handicraft products that characterise this region are based on local tradition and culture using naturally available resources like bamboo, clay, and metal. *Sujni* embroidery work which is a traditional craft originating from the Bhusura village in Bihar is a form of quilting originally made from old clothes like *sarees* and *dhotis*. This was originally practised by the Rajput women for preparing quilts for their newborns. Madhubani painting is very unique work of art which characterise this region. Stone carving and sculpting has been prevailing in Odisha since time immemorial and presently is recognised as one of the major handicrafts of this state. The brass and bell metal products of Odisha known for its utility as well as decorative value are created by artisans known as *Kansaris* who are from different parts of the state.

The southern region has five clusters and 140 self-help groups contributing to the variety of handicrafts special to this region. The art of *Lambani* mirror embroidery practised by the *Lambani* tribes in Sandur town of Karnataka was originally used for making their traditional attires. Now it is also used for creating products like bags, cushion covers, sarees, and home décor accessories. Geometric shapes are embroidered with contrasting-coloured threads and embellished with shells, coins, mirrors, and beads using 30 different types of stitches and 10 types of motifs to create a very colourful and shimmering effect in their traditional attires. The handcrafted articles from Kerala which are mainly prepared from locally obtained resources such as coconut shell, buffalo horns, wood, screw pine, cora grass, cane, bamboo banana, and other natural fibres are closely linked to the various rituals and festivals observed in the state. The replica of the face of a *kathakali* (traditional dance) dancer made of wood is a special craft item from this state. Each corner of the state has its own specialities like straw picture craft from Kollam district, wooden elephants from Thissur are to mention a few.

Embroidery work is a part of creative contribution of the handicraft clusters of almost all the regions. For example, *Crewel, Sozni*, and *Aari, Kashidakari* from Kashmir, *Phulkari* from Punjab, *Kantha* from West Bengal and Odisha, *Zardozi* and *Chikankari* from Uttar Pradesh, patchwork from Rajasthan, Mirror work from Gujarat and Rajasthan are some of the exquisite types of embroideries that can be traced in the different parts of India.

Under CHCD Scheme, Handicrafts Mega Clusters are being established at places where there is large concentration of craft and artisans. Mega clusters approach has been adopted for making further provisions and upgrading "the infrastructure and production chain at handicraft clusters which have remained unorganised and have failed to keep pace with modernization" (Government of India n.d.b). This approach aimed at employment generation through skill upgradation, development, and diversification of products and creation of market linkages. "Under CHCD scheme nine Mega Clusters have been sanctioned at Narsapur (Andhra Pradesh), Moradabad, Mirzapur-Bhadohi, Lucknow and Bareilly (Uttar Pradesh), Srinagar (Jammu & Kashmir), Jodhpur (Rajasthan) and Kutchh-Bhuj (Gujarat)" (Government of India 2019b).

14.4 Digital technologies and the handloom and handicraft sector

Use of digital technology can provide solutions to a number of problems faced by handloom and handicraft sectors, especially in terms of marketing of the products. A very recent initiative of online sale of handlooms and handicraft products is *Go Swadeshi Online* (meaning target digitally the domestic market) for supporting the weavers and artisans in the process of recovery from the loss incurred due to COVID-19 outbreak. Digital platforms can be used for spreading information, and promotion of the varieties of handloom and handicraft products and reaching the patrons and consumers globally. For the handloom and handicraft enterprises especially those "located in rural areas and with lesser resources, digital technologies can bring them visibility, market information, new customers and enable them to sell online" (Bisht 2016: 3). Information Communication Technology (ICT) can also give them access to information about new trends and designs, various government schemes, and also enable them to circulate the information and showcasing their products via websites and e-catalogues. For providing "direct marketing platform to the weavers/artisans, 21 leading ecommerce companies have been engaged for online marketing of handloom products" (Kaushik et al. n.d.: 28). Also to enable the weavers to directly place their orders for yarns and do online payments "National Handloom Development Corporation (NHDC) launched Enterprise Resource Planning (ERP) system and e-Dhaga mobile app in 2016" (Kaushik et al.

n.d.: 29). But digital technology can be a panacea only if the weavers and the artisans are digitally literate and having access to digital infrastructure. Hence this calls for the initiatives to familiarise and train the artisans and weavers to use ICT for getting better access to the market information and as well as publicising their products among the prospective consumers. Digital Loom Software like Digikala has been created by Microsoft which makes design work less time consuming, faster processing of handlooms, yet keeping the traditional heritage unspoilt. Digital Platforms can also effectively be used for documentation of the history of the origin, unique characteristics and regional distribution, as well as preservation of existing crafts through revival and popularisation of the dying arts by creating wider awareness, promotion, and generating interest about the products. Digital India initiative is one such programme that can help in revival of Indian traditional art and craft. The Government, NGOs, and Corporates in India have started taking the digital initiatives for marketing and design intervention in the handloom and craft sector; however, the initiatives are yet very limited in terms of the coverage of number of artisan. The lack of development of digital infrastructure, limited availability and access to technology, and illiteracy, including digital illiteracy, acts as a major barrier in digitalization of production and marketing processes in this sector.

14.5 Conclusions

India is a land of creativity and a treasure house of a large variety of handlooms and handicrafts. The richness of its tradition, variety of its culture, and excellence of its artisanship are well reflected through the handloom and handicrafts. The Indian craft tradition and the weave types which vary vividly bears the testimony of environmental, socio-cultural, historical, economic, and political implications. Locally available raw materials, traditional skills, cultural practices, socio-economic systems, and royal patronage led to the localisation of the handicrafts and handlooms of particular styles in particular regions leading to regional specialization. From the historical trajectory of the handloom and handicraft tradition of India, the impact of the Mughals, who were advocates of art and craft, is found to be conspicuously visible. The patronage received from the Mughals as well as other local rulers who were passionate about art and craft helped not only to nurture and conserve the rich tradition of handloom and handicrafts but also to revive some of the lost skills and creativity. After independence in 1947, much emphasis was given by the national government on the revival and development of the handloom and handicraft sector. The major problems plaguing this sector are low productivity due to unorganised production, less educated craftsmen, use of outdated methods of production, lack of raw materials and lack of requisite funding, information asymmetry, and poor market linkages. To address these issues, various schemes and programmes with special emphasis on cluster development have been taken up with the objectives of upgradation of infrastructure facilities, capacity building, increasing productivity and competitiveness, skill development and technology upgradation, employment generation, providing credit facilities, marketing linkages, and promotion of traditional products. Development of clusters located in various regions has been helping in preserving the regional creativity and heritage as well as the cultural diversity of the country expressed through variety of handloom and handicrafts of India.

References

AIACA (2017). National handicrafts policy report April 2017. Available at: www.aiacaonline.org/wp-content/uploads/2018/06/National-Handicrafts-Policy-Report_Full-version_Final.pdf (last accessed on 25 March 2022).

Balasubrahmanyan, S. (2018, 24 July). Woven embroidery: The brocades of Banaras. *Sahapedia*. Available at: www.sahapedia.org/woven-embroidery-the-brocades-of-banaras (last accessed on 25 March 2022).

Bisht, S. (2016). *Use of Information Communication Technologies (ICT) among Artisan Organisations in India, Survey Report*. New Delhi: Culture Sector, UNESCO. Available at: www.unesco.org/new/fileadmin/MULTIMEDIA/FIELD/New_Delhi/images/surveyreport.pdf (last accessed on 25 March 2022).

Business Standard (2017, 9 November). Indian textile & handicrafts industry is the largest employment generator after agri: Ajay Tamta. *Business Standard*. Available at: www.business-standard.com/article/news-cm/indian-textile-handicrafts-industry-is-the-largest-employment-generator-after-agri-ajay-tamta-117110900180_1.html (last accessed on 25 March 2022).

Chakrabarti, S. (2016, 23 November). The traditional art of Jamdani weaving: A glorious past and a shining future. *The Ethnic Soul*. Available at: www.craftsvilla.com/blog/traditional-art-of-weaving-jamdani-saree/#Motifs (last accessed on 25 March 2022).

Chakravarty, R. (2003). Chikan: A way of life. *EurIndia, N"de project:ALA/95/23–2003/77077*. Available at: http://eurindia.pc.unicatt.it/english/public_results/missions/Ruth%20Chakravarty.pdf (last accessed on 25 March 2022).

Chand, S. (2014, 21 June). Fab fabric adornments. *Deccan Herald*, DHNS. Available at: www.deccanherald.com/content/415085/fab-fabric-adornments.html (last accessed on 25 March 2022).

Chandra, S. (2015). Kalamkari, the art of painting with natural dyes. *Chitrolekha, Journal of Art and Design*, 5(2). Available at: https://chitrolekha.com/kalamkari/ (last accessed on 25 March 2022).

Dhamija, J. (2016, 23 June). Remembering Kamaladevi. *Garland*, World Craft Council, Australia. Available at: https://garlandmag.com/article/remembering-kamaladevi/ (last accessed on 25 March 2022).

Dutta, D. B. (2018). An in-depth study on Jamdani and Tangail weavers of Purba Bardhaman District, West Bengal, India. *Journal of Textile Engineering & Fashion Technology*, 4 (3), 263–270. doi:10.15406/jteft.2018.04.00150. Retrieved November 21, 2021.

EPCH (n.d.). *Background Note: Formulating a New Definition of Handicrafts*. Retrieved May 10, 2019, from www.epch.in/policies/Definition.pdf (last accessed on 25 March 2022).

f-pedia (2020, 20 February). Madhubani painting: Caste influence. *Folkartopedia, Connecting Culture & Communities*. Available at: www.folkartopedia.com/madhubani-painting-caste-influence/ (last accessed on 25 March 2022).

Ghosh, R. (2019). Pipli craftsmen adapt to modern needs for better prospects. *Village Square*. Available at: www.villagesquare.in/pipli-craftsmen-adapt-to-modern-needs-for-better-prospects/ (last accessed on 25 March 2022).

Ghosh, S. (2018). Retracting Kalamkari's journey: From classic to a contemporary textile art. *The Chitrolekha Journal of Art and Design*, 2(2), 4–28. Available at: www.chitrolekha.com/ns/v2n2/v2n201.pdf (last accessed on 25 March 2022).

Government of India (2012a). Report of the Steering Committee on Handlooms and Handicrafts Constituted for the Twelfth Five Year Plan (2012–2017). VSE Division, Planning Commission, New Delhi. Available at: http://handicrafts.nic.in/CmsUpload/22342016043422str_handloom0305.pdf (last accessed on 25 March 2022).

Government of India (2012b). "Report of the Working Group on Handlooms for the 12th Five Year Plan (2012–17). Planning Commission, New Delhi. Available at: https://niti.gov.in/planningcommission.gov.in/docs/aboutus/committee/wrkgrp12/wg_handloom1101.pdf (last accessed on 25 March 2022).

Government of India (2014). Cluster Development Project in NER: A Sub Scheme of North Eastern Region Textile Promotion Scheme (NERTPS). Office of the Development Commissioner for Handlooms, Ministry of Textiles, New Delhi. Available at: http://handlooms.nic.in/writereaddata/1233.pdf (last accessed on 25 March 2022).

Government of India (2017). Schemes for Development of Handloom and Handicraft Sectors. Ministry of Information & Broadcasting, New Delhi. Available at: http://inbministry.blogspot.com/2017/07/schemes-for-development-of-handloom-and.html (last accessed on 25 March 2022).

Government of India (2019a). *Fourth All India Handloom Census 2019–20*. New Delhi: Office of the Development Commissioner for Handlooms, Ministry of Textiles. Available at: from http://handlooms.nic.in/writereaddata/3736.pdf (last accessed on 25 March 2022).

Government of India (2019b). *Financial Assistance to Handicraft and Textile*. Press Information Bureau. Available at: https://pib.gov.in/PressReleasePage.aspx?PRID=1578541 (last accessed on 25 March 2022).

Government of India (2020). *Comprehensive Handloom Cluster Development Scheme (CHCDS)*. #Startupindia, Ministry of Textiles. Available at: www.startupindia.gov.in/content/sih/en/government-schemes/mega_cluster_scheme.html (last accessed on 25 March 2022).

Government of India (2021). Ministry of Textiles, Annual Report 2020–21. Available at: fromhttp://texmin.nic.in/sites/default/files/AR_Ministry_of_Textiles_%202020-21_Eng.pdf (last accessed on 25 March 2022).

Government of India (n.d.a). *Indian Handicrafts*. Office of Development Commissioner (Handicrafts), Ministry of Textiles, Government of India, New Delhi. Available at: http://handicrafts.nic.in/pdf/Perfect%20Destination%20Small%20Brochure%20for%20web.pdf (last accessed on 25 March 2022).

Government of India (n.d.b). Comprehensive Handicrafts Cluster Development Scheme (Chcds). http://texmin.nic.in/sites/default/files/11d_Guidelines_of_development_of_mega_cluster_scheme_Handicrafts_nmcc_cs_20090312.pdf (last accessed on 04 July 2022).

Hawkins Jr., R. W. (2007). *Enterprising Craft: South Africa: Alive with Possibility*. Pretoria: Government Printer.

IBEF (2020, November). Indian Handicrafts Industry & Exports. India Brand Equity Foundation. Available at: www.ibef.org/exports/handicrafts-industry-india.aspx (last accessed on 25 March 2022).

IBEF (2021, 31 March). India's handicraftcrafts: A sector gaining momentum. India Brand Equity Foundation. Available at: www.ibef.org/blogs/india-s-handicraft-crafts-a-sector-gaining-momentum (last accessed on 25 March 2022).

IndiaNetzone (2011, 2 November). History of Chikankari. Available at: www.indianetzone.com/56/history_chikankari.htm (last accessed on 25 March 2022).

Kaushik, K. V., Khanna, A., and Sah, S. (n.d.). *Indian handloom industry*. Position Paper, Thought Arbitrage Research institute (TARI), FICCI Ladies Organisation. Available at: www.ficciflo.com/wp-content/uploads/2019/03/Indian-Handloom-Industry-Final.pdf (last accessed on 25 March 2022).

KPMG (n.d.). *Human resources and skill requirements in the handlooms and handicrafts sector (2013–17, 2017–22)*, Vol. 13. Government of India, Ministry of Skill Development & Entrepreneurship & National Skill Development Corporation. Available at: https://nsdcindia.org/sites/default/files/Handlooms-Handicrafts.pdf (last accessed on 25 March 2022).

Lyster, S. T. (n.d.). The delights of Jamdani weaving. *The Textile Atlas*. Available at: www.thetextileatlas.com/craft-stories/jamdani-weaving (last accessed on 25 March 2022).

Mahajan, S. (2008). Contemporarisation of Bagru printing. *Fibre2Fashion.Com*. Available at: www.fibre2fashion.com/industry-article/3498/contemporarisation-of-bagru-printing (last accessed on 25 March 2022).

Manfredi, P. (2017). *Chikankari a Lucknawi Tradition*. New Delhi: Niyogi Books.

Mohanty, B. C. (1984). *Brocade Fabrics of India*, Vol. 1 & 2. Ahmedabad: Calico Museum of Textiles.

MoSPI (2016). All India Report of Sixth Economic Census. Government of India, New Delhi.

Nair, S. (2016, 21 September). Banaras and its impressive history in textile weaving. *Weaver Story*. Available at: www.weaverstory.com/blogs/news/banaras-and-its-impressive-history-in-textile-weaving (last accessed on 25 March 2022).

NCAER (2010). Third National Census of Handloom Weavers and Allied Workers 2010. Ministry of Textiles, Government of India, New Delhi. Available at: http://handlooms.nic.in/Writereaddata/Handloom%20report.pdf (last accessed on 25 March 2022).

Parinita (2021). Baluchari. *Parinita*. Available at: www.parinita.co.in/pages/baluchari (last accessed on 25 March 2022).

Pawar, Y. (2014, 30 November). Invoking the magic of a lost weave: A Baluchari sari exhibition in Mumbai. *DNA*. Available at: www.dnaindia.com/lifestyle/report-invoking-the-magic-of-a-lost-weave-a-baluchari-sari-exhibition-in-mumbai-2039502 (last accessed on 25 March 2022).

Priya, M. (2018, 8 March). Kamaladevi Chattopadhyay: The torchbearer of Indian crafts. *Sarangi*. Available at: www.sarangithestore.com/blogs/rustle-of-silk/kamaladevi-chattopadhyay-the-torchbearer-of-indian-crafts (last accessed on 25 March 2022).

Ramaswamy, C. (2011, 21 July). Pipli's live art heritage. *BL*. Retrieved November 20, 2021, from www.thehindubusinessline.com/news/variety/piplis-live-art-heritage/article23030658.ece (last accessed on 25 March 2022).

Ritu (2020, 18 June). Dalitbahujan women who broadened the Madhubani Canvas. *Forward Press*. Available at: www.forwardpress.in/2020/06/dalitbahujan-women-who-broadened-the-madhubani-canvas/#comments (last accessed on 25 March 2022).

Rogerson, C. (2010). The enterprise of craft: Constraint and policy challenges in South Africa. *Acta Academia*, 42(3), 115–144. Available at: http://journals.ufs.ac.za/index.php/aa/article/view/1259/1244 (last accessed on 25 March 2022).

Sarda, K. (2017, 17 July). Baluchari: Woven history. *Live History India*. Available at: www.livehistoryindia.com/story/forgotten-treasures/baluchari-woven-history/ (last accessed on 25 March 2022).

Singh, A. (2010). *Clusters in India, 2010*. New Delhi: Foundation for MSME Clusters (FMC).

Srinivas, P. (n.d.). Kalamkari paintings, the ancient art of India. *India the Destiny*. Available at: https://indiathedestiny.com/india-art-culture/art/kalamkari-paintings/ (last accessed on 25 March 2022).

Szanton, D. L. (n.d.). The politics of Mithila painting. Available at: https://orias.berkeley.edu/sites/default/files/the_politics_of_mithila_painting_2-2017.pdf (last accessed on 25 March 2022).

TARI (n.d.). *Indian handloom industry*. Position Paper, Thought Arbitrage Research Institute (TARI) for FICCI Ladies Organisation (FLO). Available at: www.ficciflo.com/wp-content/uploads/2019/03/Indian-Handloom-Industry-Final.pdf (last accessed on 25 March 2022).

Tyabji, L. (2007). Handcrafting a culture. *Seminar*. Available at: www.india-seminar.com/2007/575/575_laila_tyabji.htm (last accessed on 25 March 2022).

UMSAS (2022). Madhubani painting. Available at: https://umsas.org.in/madhubani-painting/ (last accessed on 25 March 2022).

UNESCO (n.d.a). Craft or Artisanal Product. Institute for Statistics. Available at: http://uis.unesco.org/en/glossary-term/craft-or-artisanal-products (last accessed on 25 March 2022).

UNESCO (n.d.b). Intangible Cultural Heritage: Traditional Craftsmanship. Available at: https://ich.unesco.org/en/traditional-craftsmanship-00057 (last accessed on 25 March 2022).

15

CULTURAL EMBEDDEDNESS OF GEMS AND JEWELLERY ENTREPRENEURS IN JAIPUR

Philippe Cadène

15.1 Introduction

This chapter examines the manufacture and sale of precious and semi-precious stones and jewellery, an economic activity rooted in the culture of Jaipur, a city located about 350 km south of Delhi. Jaipur is one of the major centres of gems and jewellery manufacturing in India (see Chapter 4). The city has also been known for its crafts and folk arts, and it also features as in this category of UNESCO's 'creative city network'. It has been the subject of numerous articles in media since the 1980s. Journalists have not only highlighted its magnificent monuments from a prestigious past but also the power of its jewellers, as well as its craftsmen and traders in semi-precious stones. They also quote the city's lively craft industries of colourful textiles, sculptures, and painted furniture. Formerly the capital of an eponymous kingdom, Jaipur is now the capital of the State of Rajasthan, an entity of the Indian federation grouping together several small kingdoms to which the British had granted a certain autonomy during the colonial period. Now with a population of more than three million and having grown extremely rapidly since the 1970s (Jawaid et al. 2017), the city has become a major tourist attraction in India and a place where quality craftsmanship in a variety of fields has developed. Home to a vibrant business community, the city has successfully modernised a gems and jewellery export industry developed in the late 19th century from the skills of local jewellers. The entire sector has thus opened up to the world market without destroying the business environment on which its development was based. On the contrary, this environment was considerably enlarged, diversified, and enriched throughout the 20th century and has been particularly strengthened over the last two or three decades with India's entry into the dynamics of globalisation (Rothermund 2008).

DOI: 10.4324/9781003129370-20

A remarkable anthropological survey was recently carried out on this theme in Jaipur, resulting in an interesting book that emphasises the role of merchant communities in the development of these activities (Babb 2013). Taking into account the historical dimension, which is fundamental for the dynamics studied, as well as the current changes linked to globalisation, this anthropological work appears essential for understanding this industry in Jaipur. In particular, it highlights the complexity of the business communities involved and attempts to describe the historical role of the Shvetambar merchant community, belonging to the Jain religious minority, in the development of these activities in Jaipur. There are also publications by Brian Brazeal (2012, 2017), also an anthropologist, which provides interesting information on the precious stone work and the communities involved. Studies on these activities have also been carried out on a more strictly on the economic or business level by various Indian professionals or academic institutions (Sharma and Sharma, 2014; Lucas et al. 2016; Devgun 2019). They show the importance of gems and jewellery activities in the urban economy, as well as its opening to export accompanied by industrialisation that led to profound changes both in terms of the actors involved and their organisations.

This chapter follows a qualitative methodology in analysing the cultural environment in which the production and sale of gems and jewellery have developed and are now deeply interwoven into the economic networks created by globalisation (Cadene and Vidal 1997). The collection of information was spread from 2009 to 2021, starting in the frame of a research project studying the globalisation of secondary metropolis in Asia (Cadene 2013). The interviews covered all the activities of the city and focused on the various actors involved. Meetings were also held with politicians, senior officials, and activists from various associations. The information used in the present chapter concerns the links between the development of gems and jewellery activities and the cultural framework that organises them. It aims to understand the links between various activities that make up this cultural environment and their evolution.

This latter approach draws its theoretical inspiration not only from the work of Karl Polanyi (1944) and Mark Granovetter (1985) on the embedding of economic factors in social systems but also from Allen J. Scott (2000) on the cultural economy of cities and Pier Luigi Sacco and Giorgo Tavano Blessi (2005) on cultural districts. The rest of the chapter is organised as follows. Section 15.2 discusses the development of stonecutting and goldsmithing in the city. Section 15.3 examines the embeddedness of the actors who organised these activities. Section 15.4 examines the links that unite them with the other actors of the economy in Jaipur and the extent to which these links are both maintained and modified by the changes accompanying Jaipur's integration into globalised networks. The last section concludes the chapter.

15.2 Gems and jewellery manufacturing and marketing: globalised activities linked to the history of the city

15.2.1 The construction of a world centre for emerald work

Jewellery was at the heart of the urban economy from the creation of Jaipur in 1727. Founded in the first half of the 18th century by Maharaja Sawai Jai Singh, the city wanted to show the prestige and power of royalty and to meet the needs of a developing economy. Abandoning the fortified city of Amber, perched on a hill, the sovereign established Jaipur 11 km further west, in a plain. The project was ambitious. The city was built in less than ten years according to a checkerboard plan established by Vidyadhar Bhattacharya, a prestigious architect of the period. Strict regulations unified the buildings and organised functional districts. The Maharaja accompanied his project with a policy aimed at attracting artists, scholars, merchants, and craftsmen. Regarding the latter, several bazaars were built, whose plots were offered free of charge to merchants from all over the north of the subcontinent, benefiting from tax concessions. Craftsmen's quarters were also established according to the same principles (Lane 2010; Khan and Kamal 2020). This policy bore fruit and Jaipur quickly became an important cultural and economic centre in the region (Bautès and Valette 2004).

The merchants and jewellery artisans who settled in the bazaar came from Amber, of course, but also from the large cities of the north of the subcontinent, such as Delhi, Agra, or Benares (Babb 2013). A specificity already existed in this activity due to the arrival in Amber, in the 16th century, of Sikh craftsmen from Lahore, an important city of the Mughal empire located in the part of the Punjab that is now in Pakistan. These craftsmen, followers of this minority religion in India, excelled in gold enamelling and specific jewellery work dominated by the red, green, and white colours associated with the empire to which the kingdom of Jaipur was then linked (Tillotson 2006). As with all activities, the production of jewellery was organised by merchants belonging to Hindu and Jain merchant communities established in the city. They distributed the various tasks to craftsmen working in families, who were members of communities specialised in the various aspects of this work, often Muslims. The Johari Bazaar district, southwest of the historic centre, was the preferred location for these activities and has retained this role. The anthropological work of Babb (2013), already cited, focusing on these merchant communities, shows how this activity was transformed from the end of the 19th century to specialise in cutting emeralds under the initiative of a member from the Khandelval Jain community, named Banjilal Tholia. The establishment of business relations with British and then French traders led Jaipur to become a centre for the trade and cutting of emeralds, the demand for which was growing worldwide at the time. The stones were extracted and acquired in Africa, worked in Jaipur and then sold to European traders. This activity made Jaipur rich for almost a century. It was in the hands of a new elite composed of members of merchant families specialising in the jewellery trade as well as newcomers to the business. Most, however, were Shvetambar Jains belonging to the Shrimal and Osval castes.

Changes occurred in this lucrative business after India's Independence in 1947 and the ensuing upheavals that followed. The city lost its royal capital status and became the capital of one of the Union states, while a large number of refugees arrived in Jaipur from Pakistan. The city expanded to accommodate the influx of people, while commercial activities increased. One university was established, bringing the city into the modern age. In the 1950s migration continued, sustaining population growth. The 1960s saw State-led industrial development, which resulted in the creation of a working-class among the city's population. The changes in urban society authorised to new players entering the emerald market, attracted by the wealth produced in this activity. The process began slowly in the 1960s but became more pronounced in the 1970's and specifically in the 1980s. The new players were members of merchant communities, generally Hindus, but sometimes Muslims as well. They came from other sectors of activity, such as textiles, and took advantage of the strong demand in the emerald market to launch this activity. These people got the necessary skills from the importance of this industry in the city and the business experience shared by all merchants. All they had to do was to obtain raw stones from international traders, find craftsmen to work on them, and then sell them to middlemen. Their entry into this growing market disrupted existing practices organised within a very closed environment, in which everyone respected each other's interests because they have dealt with each other for a long time (Brazeal 2012).

Transactions that were highly regulated by the milieu were increasingly speculative. Local traders went to international fairs and established offices in foreign cities that served as hubs for this market. Some of such cities were New York, Bangkok, and Hong Kong. Some of them also travelled to the places where the stones are mined to make purchases, mainly in Africa. In these places, these Jaipuri dealers often dealt with members of the Indian diaspora, who were very present in this global gemstone and diamond market, and who often belonged to their castes or to nearby trading communities. With family members now frequently living abroad and involved in the purchase of rough stones and the sale of worked products, Jaipuri traders got fully involved in this activity.

15.2.2 From emeralds to semi-precious gems and industrial goldsmithing

The 1980s were also the years when the Indian economy began to open to the world market, timidly at the beginning and more pronouncedly at the end of the decade. This heralded India's entry into the networks of globalisation with the arrival of technology and foreign capital, the increase in trade with the outside world, and the development of a middle class that began to consume sophisticated industrialised products.

In Jaipur, it was not until the mid-1990s that the atmosphere in the city changed. The transformation of the society was led by the development of the economy and its rapid integration into national and global networks. The links with the outside world, both with the major Indian cities and with some foreign countries, became increasingly strong and involved more and more activities. This process continued in the new millennium. The increase in domestic and foreign investment suddenly transformed Jaipur into a modern city. These were the private actors who led the initiative. Whether they were local or coming from other regions or abroad, these investors seized the opportunities opened up by the Indian government's liberal reforms and contributed to boosting the city's activities or creating new ones.

From the 1990s onwards, jewellery activities in Jaipur were no longer limited to buying, working, and selling emeralds. Very profound changes were taking place locally, linked to the global evolution of the sector. The quality of the stones work changed. Although Jaipur occupies an important place in the world in emerald cutting and polishing (Lucas 2016), this gemstone is losing its importance on the world market and is giving way to gems of lesser values. The change is all the more pronounced as an Indian market for semi-precious gems and mid-range jewellery is now developing driven by the expansion of the national middle classes (Shaban 2021). Jaipur's specialised circles are involved in the working of a hundred or so semi-precious stones of varying values, a hitherto marginal and somewhat despised activity. Tanzanite, a blue stone discovered only in 1967 near Kilimanjaro, which is becoming very fashionable in the North American market, is particularly valued. In addition, synthetic gems are becoming increasingly important, offering the possibility of entering the fancy jewellery market. These changes are taking place when the value of gems fluctuates according to the trends emerging from the Western fashion shows. Mechanisation is also developing for the cutting and polishing of these gems of lesser value in order to meet the demand of the international market for standardised colours and sizes.

In this context of globalisation of the activity, the essential phenomenon consists however in the passage from a specialised craft in the cutting and polishing of gems, organised by specific merchant communities, to a largely industrial manufacture intended for the Western markets, particularly North American and European countries. While in the early 1990s there were only four modern jewellery factories in Jaipur, there were more than 250 such factories by 2015, according to a report from the Gemological Institute of America. These experts note: "jewellery stores that once served the Maharajas, designer brands, retailers catering to the Bollywood crowd, and vertically integrated manufacturing/retailing companies all coexist and flourish in Jaipur" (Lucas et al. 2016). Mechanised mass production coexists with small craftsmen working with centuries-old techniques. Many of these entrepreneurs are investing or are planning to invest in computer-controlled cutting machines. However, these machines are primarily used to work the better-quality stones as a lot of these entrepreneurs also continue to employ the services of numerous small craftsmen located in the city or in the surrounding villages and with whom their families have been linked in some cases for several generations. This trend towards the development of a mechanised industry does not, therefore, lead to the destruction of the old production system based on small-scale manufacturers. It also leads to the strengthening of established relationships with a clientele of foreign merchants. The change in the marketing of products is, however, significant. On the one hand, more space is given to Western designers in the creation of products. On the other hand, niche products such as jewellery inspired by and those produced by tribal populations are being developed. Above all, the sale of jewellery is now being developed through television programmes aimed at middle-class Westernised families. Alongside handmade luxury jewellery, Jaipur is then developing a mass industrial production capable of constantly changing its products and passing within a few days from production to dispatch. This mass production is also carried out for the Indian market, which is growing steadily (Lucas et al. 2016). Exports are encouraged by the State through the establishment of Special Economic Zones (SEZ) where foreign investors are given facilities to set up businesses producing for the external market. Three SEZ house gems cutting and jewellery making companies in Jaipur, all managed by the Rajasthan State Industrial Development and Investment Corporation (Sharma and Sharma 2014). Nearly 50 of these enterprises are located in these areas, benefiting from easier custom clearances and access to shared facilities (Lucas et al. 2016).

Not only in such areas but at the scale of the entire city, this new importance given to jewellery is accompanied by a tendency for manufacturers to become independent of merchants, with some of them setting up industrial jewellery manufacturing companies or some craftsmen moving into the industrial stage. Although the members of the merchant communities retained their supremacy, the activity continued to be strengthened by the entry into the profession of many newcomers, members of diverse communities, who could intervene in the various tasks involved in the working and sale of gems and jewellery: workers, manufacturers, merchants, importers, exporters, and finally brokers. The latter, essential in Indian business, intervene in the exchange of gems to put the different partners in touch with each other and assure them of the fair value and the reliability in the transaction. They still play an important role despite the changes that the goldsmith's trade has undergone in Jaipur with the industrialisation going on in this sector.

15.3 The embeddedness into the Indian merchant communities' culture

The importance taken by semi-precious coloured stones and the development of the jewellery industry have been accompanied by the entry of diverse communities in this business. Now, there are present among the merchants some members of Brahmins and Kshatriyas communities, classified among the Hindu highest castes according to the Hindu *chaturvarna* (four orders) hierarchy. There are also some Muslims, coming from merchant or artisan groups, and some members of diverse Hindu communities classified as Sudras or low castes (Babb 2013). As in many other economic activities and many other Indian cities or towns, the traditional communities that used to control the business are now competing with newcomers and there is a mix in the social origins of the actors (Damodaran 2008). But the merchant communities that organised this business all along its history still lead the entire sector. These communities enjoy a high status in Indian society, just below Brahmins and Kshatriyas (Dumont 1980; Cadene and Durand-Dastes 1997; Sheth 1999). According to the rules of the caste system, they hold the legitimacy of trading activities and of lending money. In Jaipur, their seniority in the gems and jewellery activities allows them to maintain a strong influence in the conduct of business throughout the entire sector.

15.3.1 The specific identities of the jewellery merchant communities and their influence

Most of these merchant communities at the origin of the gems and jewellery business in Jaipur and forming along the 20th century the "emerald elite" as described by Lawrence Babb (2013) belong to the Osvals and Shrimals. In fewer numbers, there were also the Khandelval Jains. All of them were members of the Jain religious minority (Babb 2015). Their identities and practices significantly shape the cultural environment within which business is conducted across the entire sector.

Their influence is self-evident among the other members of the Hindu trading communities, Agravals, Maheshvaris, and Khandelval Vaishyas, who have long been a minority in these activities but have become increasingly numerous over the past 20 years. The field surveys conducted in Jaipur showed clear division between these different merchant communities. They are not attending the same places of worship and they are not included in the same business networks. But they all share similar cultural identities which are also very similar to that of the Jain merchants. These latter observe certainly more austere living practices and particularly assert for themselves non-violent behaviour in everyday life. But all these communities, Jains or Hindus, respect vegetarianism and value-independent business as well as financial success. They all place a premium on the reputation of families, based on their members' respect for community values and business probity. The trust that can be attributed to an individual is thus linked to the collective behaviour of the family group to which he or she belongs. Weddings, all arranged by families and carried out within each caste, are the moments when trust in the group is reaffirmed, which are essential for the smooth running of the business. These practices are manifested and even reinforced during the last 20 to 30 years (Babb 2013). Brian Brazeal (2017) explains that the great uncertainty in the gemstone market, and particularly in emeralds, linked to the difficulty of knowing the value of raw materials, contributed to a strong reference to probity, trust, and strengthening community ties. The development of activities has further reinforced these behaviours. Because of the uncertainty they entail, the changes in the sector do not alter the way business is done, regardless of the size of the companies, and especially the importance attached to the Community system. Economic strategies, while built by individuals, are established with reference to the family group and community ties.

The non-trading communities who have also been entering the gems and jewellery trade or establishing industries over the past 20 years are also influenced by the business communities that dominate the sector. The members involved are those who have long-term relationships with the business and are familiar with the practices of this specific environment. These newcomers may be Brahmins, more rarely Rajputs, established in the city, who also share high caste status according to Hindu values and who continue to interact with the different communities according to practices that do not differ fundamentally from those of the time of the ancient kingdom. Seizing the opportunities offered by the expansion of demand, they often intervene in exchange activities or act as intermediaries, facilitating transactions. The new entrants who are taking part in the changes in this economic sector may also be members of artisan communities that have been involved in gems and jewellery work for a long time and are taking advantage of opportunities brought about by market expansion and diversification to move into a new position. They are often members of the Bengali Muslims community or of the Soni community, both working as craftsmen in the sector. They benefit from the presence of their own communities to develop their business, but they operate in the same cultural world as the other groups.

All of these actors that built this complex economic environment are linked by relationships combining collaborative and competitive situations that make this sector of activity in Jaipur appear to be a vast industrial district (Pyke et al. 1990; Cadene and Holmstrom 1998). The production of gems and jewellery in the capital city of Rajasthan combines traders, producers of various status, and intermediaries, all of whom specialise in specific activities, but who, in combination, enable large production. They also manage together to establish and maintain norms that allow them to offer a sufficient and regular quality to enable them to position their products on the international markets. As in all industrial districts, these actors are part of a long history from which they inherit social and cultural practices that form the basis of their relationships.

A legacy lies in the various caste identities, the types of relationships and the hierarchies they imply. These particularly mark the economic hierarchies, but do not completely correspond to them. Nor do they prevent the changes mentioned from taking place. Another legacy is the way people relate to the groups they belong to. In Jaipur, as in India as a whole, individuals do not exist outside of their families and communities. This fact has a considerable influence on the functioning of economic activities and the management methods of companies. The place of individuals within their family or community is a key explanatory factor. Businesses, large or small, are above all family based. Strategies may be individual, but they are established with reference to the family group. Individual originality obviously exists, and increases as society opens up to the world, but there continues to be a strong sense of solidarity and belonging within families and communities, and also between communities in a given economic sector. But it can also provoke violent conflicts, ruptures within families as well as between communities, if the rules are not respected in the eyes of some. It also leads to strong social and cultural conservatism.

15.3.2 Strong social and cultural conservatism despite changes

Conservatism influences all the activities linked to jewellery by maintaining the privileged links woven for decades, if not longer, by the different communities that participate in it and, whatever their role in the activity, still holds a primary place in it. A few points can be made in this regard, which show that the important changes having taken place in the sector do not call into question the functioning of this social and economic system.

A particularly visible point is the predominantly male nature of all activities. From the purchase of the raw stones to the sale of the gems and jewellery through the various stages of production, only men are present at the various stages. Similarly, the presence of many child workers in the sector shows the weight of old forms of production. Although child labour has been banned from the industry, it remains important in the stone-cutting sector craftsmanship, where it represents around 10% of the workforce. Locally considered as a form of apprenticeship and associated with the poverty of families employed in industrial production, it now appears as a dark part of this activity, harmful as much by the school dropout it induces as by the diseases inherent in stone cutting and polishing (Tiwari et al. 2009).

Another point is the place and personality of intermediaries who play an essential role in all transactions since they ensure the links between the merchants and their clients. The weight of the members of the merchant castes is very important here. They also mediate negotiations on the quality of products and costs as well as the flow of money. Also in this activity, the Osval or Shrimal communities were predominant. Many of them are still present, but this work has now been opened up to others. However, these are often members of related communities. When this is not the case, they are members of local communities whose presence is both a sign and a factor of the growth of this economic sector in Jaipur. The growth of new intermediaries can be explained in terms of rise in demand and the multiplication of the number of people working in the sector that required more intermediaries to manage the situation. However, they largely work in close relations determined by caste and community networks which keeps the elements of trust between them intact.

An important point concerns technological and social innovations in production. In this area, the changes do not break either the old links between merchant and producer communities. It was seen previously that the transition to industry had not eliminated craft work and that industrialists, who are also merchants, still gave work to small artisans. A somewhat similar phenomenon occurs in the relationships within factories. Mechanisation transforms the craft industry just as it establishes new working arrangements. With the construction of industrial enterprises, there is also a new system of hierarchy between entrepreneurs and their employees that is being set up. The types of relationships between the various actors remains the same despite the changes. Although integration is taking place in the value chains with the transition to industry, the actors who used to dominate the sector remain, for many of them, at the top and a large part of the production is still done by craftsmen who can often be integrated into the dynamics of the companies.

The last point concerns change in the supply of precious metals and rough stones and the marketing of processed products. While the players are more numerous and varied than before, it is still a few have control of the foreign trade links that benefit most within the sector. Obviously, these are the ones with the most capital and the strongest networks. The changes that are taking place may alter the character of the players, but they do not change the principle of business.

15.4 Integration into a changing urban society

The strong cultural specificities of the merchant communities involved in jewellery activities in Jaipur thus appear, not as a factor of fragmentation within this economic sector, but on the contrary as a factor participating in its organisation. These communities have even shown themselves capable of integrating the important changes that the sector has undergone as it has entered globalisation. This resilience can be explained by their deep integration into local society and the relations they maintain with the various groups that structure it. Indeed, all the actors in the gemstone and jewellery economy participate fully in Jaipuri society and its culture.

15.4.1 The cultural weight of the Rajput nobility and its role in the development of a luxury hotel industry

The first to share common interests with the jewellery merchant communities were the members of the Rajput community. The Rajput community, considered a Kshatriya caste, is divided into different clans (Vergati 2000).

In Jaipur and its region, they formed the bulk of the nobility at the head of the kingdoms and lordships, or occupied the profession of arms. However, a large part of the Rajput community was only a peasantry with a martial culture. Since Independence, the Rajput nobility has lost its strict social status, but has mostly been able to maintain favourable economic positions by going into business. The community as a whole is engaged in various occupations.

In Jaipur, the development of international tourism has offered the noble families the opportunity to transform their palaces and luxurious mansions into hotels and to more or less control the tourism sector, especially high-end tourism (Cadene 2000). The initiative was launched by the Maharaja himself in the late 1950s by transforming the Rambagh Palace, one of the most prestigious residences of the Royalty, into a luxury hotel. But it was not until the 1980s that tourism development began and the offer multiplied with several palaces, but also with the *havelis*, the residences built by the Thakurs, the local lords, whom the king had invited to reside in Jaipur since the 18th century, thus creating a court (Khan and Kamal 2020). Many Rajputs, of more modest status, are also involved in tourism activities, either as small entrepreneurs, in transport for example, or as employees in the hotel business or in the various agencies dealing with tourists.

The relationship between the Rajput clans and the merchant communities has always been ambiguous, between distrust and collaboration. The two groups are distinguished by very different identities and sometimes antagonistic social practices. However, they are all immersed in a common culture, that of Rajasthani society and, more broadly, of Indian society. Concerning the merchant communities involved in the gems and jewellery business, the links are close because the Jaipuri nobility, together with those of the neighbouring kingdoms, were throughout the 18th and 19th centuries the main buyers of jewellery made in Jaipur (Babb 2013: 52). At the end of the 19th century, when the emerald cutting and trade activities developed, the opening up of Jaipur's economy was supported by the local nobility, who at that time began to travel to Europe. They accompanied the members of the merchant elite who, defying the caste rules forbidding distant travel, went there to meet their clients. This privileged relationship between the Rajput clans and the jewellery merchant communities continued throughout the 20th century and was extended towards the end of the century and the beginning of the new millennium with the development of the hotel sector in the city. The merchants obviously benefited from the influx of wealthy tourists to Jaipur, but also from the reputation that the luxury hotels brought to the city. They were invited to set up shops in the hotel common areas to sell their jewellery. They also do not hesitate to invest in the hotel business. It is a luxury economy that is being set up at a time when the country is opening up to globalisation and when a set of well-to-do social strata is emerging within Indian society as a result of the acceleration of growth since the 1990s.

15.4.2 Close links with communities in other economic sectors

The jewellery sector cannot be thought of in isolation from the city's other major activities. Again, the merchants in these various sectors have relationships of mistrust and cooperation. They generally belong to different communities, but their activities stem from a common history, dating back to the creation of the city. The same is true for the craftsmen, whose work may be different, but is in any case based on ancient know-how.

In addition to jewellery, textile production and trade are particularly important in Jaipur and contribute, like the hotel industry, to the city's standing in India and abroad. It is commonly known that textile artisans settled in Jaipur in the 19th century from small towns in Shekhawati, the region of Rajasthan north of Jaipur. However, a distinction must be made from the outset between two types of textile products. There are those which, in the history of the city, were intended for the rich families of the city, nobles and merchants, made of sophisticated embroidery. They are produced by highly skilled craftsmen and are sold through highly specialised merchants or intermediaries. For the past 30 years, they have been meeting the specific demands of the great Western and now also Indian fashion designers. Other textile products that have made Jaipur's reputation are of more modest origins. These are cotton fabrics printed with dots, circles and bands of yellow, green, red, and black colours that were and still are worn by village women. These latter products, which obviously concern most of the merchants or craftsmen in Jaipur, have undergone an evolution similar to that of jewellery. From the 1990s, the demand of the Western middle classes for handmade clothing exploded while in India a round of reforms led to developing textile exports (Roy 1998). In order to respond to the growth of the market, two changes took place in India's textile production areas. The first was the shift from dyeing and printing cotton to making ready-to-wear garments according to designs provided by Western customers and their designers. The second change was in the organisation of the activity, with the creation of industrial textile companies, some employing several hundred workers. In Jaipur, this shift has significant social consequences as explained here.

The merchants who controlled the bulk of the textile business were historically members of the specialised merchant castes established in the Bapu Bazaar district, from where they bought cotton fabrics in the south of the country through established community networks and gave orders to the craftsmen who worked for them. The latter were mainly members of the Chhipa community, specialising in dyeing and printing fabrics. This organisation was partly maintained, but the transition to the industry brought great upheaval. Some Chhipa master craftsmen took advantage of the arrival of foreign contractors to deal directly with them, freeing themselves from the traders. The scale of demand led to the construction of factories in the industrial zones, some of which were in the hands of former craftsmen. The textile merchants retained a large place in the city and also invested in the clothing industry, but they too took advantage of the opportunities offered by economic development. They are now positioning themselves, as already mentioned, in the jewellery business, the hotel business, and others. They are thus becoming competitors of the merchant communities formerly established in the jewellery sector, and even of the Rajput communities present in the hotel industry. However, their presence in these sectors allows for a broadening of demand that is beneficial to all. It is facilitated by the fact that these different groups of actors, despite their specificities, belong to a common culture, that is shared by the merchant castes. The same is true for the castes of artisans in the different sectors of activity, regardless of their religious affiliation.

The complexity of the business community network now exporting creative goods also includes actors from other activities. We should mention the modernisation and sale abroad of blue pottery combining Chinese and Persian traditions, made in Jaipur since the 19th century, the creation of papier-mâché and painted objects that are now famous in Western shops selling Indian products, miniatures that combine Hindu religious inspiration and Mughal romanticism, previously made on ivory, now made on substitute materials, sculptures of small objects made of various materials, glass bracelets, pens or even traditional furniture, adapted to Western uses. The manufacture or sale of such products initially made for Western customers enabled many entrepreneurs and traders to conduct sometimes flourishing businesses, often exporting, mainly to North America and Europe. It should also be noted that this range of handicrafts can now be found in many shops opened in Jaipur for all tourists visiting the city, foreigners and Indians alike. These activities do not represent a financial volume as important as textiles and ready-to-wear clothing, and their weight in Jaipur's economy is much lower than that of jewellery activities. However, like textiles, they participate in a system of relations between merchants and producers identical to that of the stone and jewellery sector, whose development they support through their presence in the city. They reinforce the values on which the functioning of productive and commercial activities within the urban environment is based. They also ensure an economic diversity which is indispensable in a period where globalisation brings strong uncertainties to the business market.

15.4.3 The development and connectedness of information technologies

The last activity that needs to be mentioned concerns IT. Its links with jewellery activities seem less obvious at first sight. However, the development of computer companies also appears to be based on the same cultural background on which the other activities discussed earlier are based, first and foremost those of stones and jewellery. All of them were born of the encouragement of the arts, sciences, trade, and crafts, provided by the royal power since the creation of the city. The city benefited early on from educational institutions created at the initiative of the palace. The oldest institution, the Maharaja's School, was established in 1844. Initially, the students belonged to the city's elite. But from the beginning of the 20th century, the number of young people who could attend higher education increased. The period of Independence led to the creation of the Maharani's college which offered girls a quality higher education, then to the creation of the University of Rajasthan with a huge campus in the south of the city. The Malviya National Institute of Technology created in 1963 provides a very good level of technological education. From the 1990s onwards, the number of private educational institutions increased rapidly, making Jaipur a city known for the quality of its education. The end of the 20th century was also the time when the first IT companies appeared in Jaipur.

The link between educational institutions and the development of computer companies is demonstrated by the accounts of the founders of the first companies. In the early stages of the development of these high-tech businesses, they were people from the city, mostly graduates of local institutes of technology. Some of them come from more reputable institutions, such as the Indian Institute of Technology in Delhi.

Some of these entrepreneurs, therefore, offer services to companies in other sectors of the city, which are increasingly using modern means of telecommunication. An important part of their clientele is the marketing of stones and jewellery. Towards the end of the 2000s, however, many of them started to work as subcontractors for foreign, often American, customers. This orientation is sometimes explained by the founders' experience of working abroad, and always by contacts with friends who have emigrated. Some explain that they have received funding from other sectors of the local economy, including of course jewellery entrepreneurs. The work offered is very varied. About half of these companies offer services such as the creation and management of websites, e-marketing, multimedia, delocalised services such as back office, or call centres. The other half develop software for various uses, for example for the management of large companies or for use in small offices or mobile telephony. Some of them were set up in Jaipur and offer their work to clients in Rajasthan or northern India, and sometimes abroad. Many have correspondents or even offices abroad, often in the United States, but also in Great Britain, the United Arab Emirates, and other Asian countries such as Singapore and Malaysia. The development of these local IT companies, but also the presence of qualified personnel on site, combined with the proximity of Delhi and the aid granted by the State of Rajasthan for the development of this sector, has contributed to attracting external investments. The IT sector in Jaipur is today marked by a mix of geographical origins. The social mix is also greater in this economic sector than in others. Nevertheless, the entrepreneurs are often members of communities close to those running businesses in other sectors and they appear to be a group bringing much needed modernity to the local economy.

15.5 Conclusions

From an ancient base, in which gemstone and jewellery merchants and artisans form a powerful group, economic activities in Jaipur are growing and diversifying. Nevertheless, they all remain marked by the city's particular urban culture, in which the Rajput nobility plays an important part, but also and above all in which the various merchant communities present in the city, as well as the communities of craftsmen who worked for them, held a major role. The Jaipuri society appears as a combination of industrial districts (Becattini 2004) organised on the same territory of the city and its surrounding areas, deeply rooted in a common culture that determines the goods they produce, the know-how used, and the methods of their organisation. At the heart of the urban economy, merchants and jewellery producers constitute an industrial district on their own and appear to be typical of this system. They constitute a group of families linked historically by relations of exploitation, domination, and also solidarity. At the top are the merchant families, in a hierarchical situation, some of them extremely rich and having strong links with a diaspora of gems and jewellery merchants. At the bottom are the day labourers, but also their children, who have been kept in poverty for decades. In the middle are the master craftsmen, who, since India's entry into the global dynamic, have sought to emancipate themselves by creating small businesses and controlling the entire local part of the value chain. Some are succeeding in doing so, by controlling the entire local value chain, from the acquisition of raw materials to the sale of finished products. Brokers are also playing an important role, as do today some stylists. It is certainly difficult to give precise data for activities related to stone cutting and polishing, and jewellery making in the city at the beginning of the 2020s. The cross-checking of several sources of information makes it possible to consider that the total number of people involved in this economic sector amounts to 200,000 in the city and around. All share a common culture. This culture is rooted in the collective values provided by the caste system, in its specific organisation within the Jaipuri society. It is also based on the values derived from the social organisation of the ancient kingdoms, which was recomposed at the time of colonisation and still exists more than 70 years after the creation of Independent India. The study also shows that, despite the changes, the jewellery district is consolidated by the presence within the city of other districts, including the ready-made garment district, whose actors, whether rich or poor, also share the common values of the local society. Caste affiliations, moreover, no longer play a role other than as a cultural reference for action. Thirty years of economic growth in India, which has seen the emergence of a vast middle class, have altered the economic hierarchies established by the caste system, which continues anyway to give the different communities in the city, as well as the newcomers, specific identities and to organise relationship inside and between almost all families and all communities.

In this context, it is easier to see how this complex relationship between economy and culture can lead to social and political tensions within the local society. The questioning of old situations through growth and openness to the world, as well as the maintenance of long-established positions, leads to a rise in intolerance as well as to the defence of a globalised world, regardless of the actors involved, their place in society, and their economic situation. Within the same families of gems and jewellery entrepreneurs and workers in Jaipur, there are now people who adhere to the theses of fundamentalist Hinduism and others who defend a society freed from the weight of the past. All of them, however, operate in the same cultural world from which they differentiate themselves.

References

Babb, L. A. (2013). *Emerald City: The Birth and Evolution of an Indian Gemstone Industry*. Albany: SUNY Press.

Babb, L. A. (2015). *Understanding Jainism*. Dunedin: Dunedin Academic Press.

Bautès, N., and Valette, E. (2004). Miniature painting, cultural economy and territorial dynamics in Rajasthan, India. In Power, D. and Scott, A. J. (eds.), *Cultural Industries and the Production of Culture*, pp. 208–223. London: Routledge.

Becattini, G. (2004). *Industrial Districts: A New Approach to Industrial Change*. Cheltenham: Edward Elgar Publishing.

Brazeal, B. (2012). Indian religions in the global emerald trade. *The Visual Anthropology Review*, 28(2), 120–132.

Brazeal, B. (2017). Austerity, luxury and uncertainty in the Indian emerald trade. *Journal of Material Culture*, 22(4), 437–452.

Cadene, P. (2000). Le développement du tourisme au Rajasthan. Usage ou abandon d'un patrimoine fragmenté. In Montaut, A. (ed.), *Le Rajasthan. Ses dieux, ses héros, son peuple. Hommage au Dr. N. Joshi*. Paris: Edition Langues'O.

Cadene, P. (2013). Mondialisation et hiérarchie urbaine en Inde: les métropoles secondaires. In Frank, M., Goldblum, C. and Taillard, C. (eds.), *Villes secondaires et métropolisation en Asie du Sud-Est*. Paris: Edition du CNRS-Alpha, Collection réseau Asie-Imasie.

Cadene, P., and Durand-Dastes, F. (1997). L'Inde de la caste, une terre d'exclusion? In Bailly, A. (ed.), *Terres d'exclusions, terres d'espérances*. Actes du Festival de Géographie de Saint-Dié 1996. Paris: Economica.

Cadene, P., and Holmstrom, M. (Eds.) (1998). *Decentralized Production in India Industrial Districts, Flexible Specialization and Employment*. New-Delhi: Sage Publications.

Cadene, P., and Vidal, D. (Eds.) (1997). *Webs of Trade: Entrepreneurship and Merchant Networks in Western India*. New-Delhi: Manohar.

Damodaran, H. (2008). *India's New Capitalists: Caste, Business and Industry in a Modern Nation*. Ranikhet: Permanent Black.

Devgun, R. (2019). *A Study on Emerging Problems of Exporters of Gems and Jewellery in Jaipur District, Rajasthan*. PhD Thesis, JECRC University, Jaipur.

Dumont, L. (1980). *Homo Hierarchicus: The Caste System and Its Implications*. Chicago: University of Chicago Press.

Granovetter, M. (1985). Economic action and social structure: The problem of embeddedness. *American Journal of Sociology*, 91(3), 481–510.

Jawaid, M. F., Sharma, M., Pipralia, S., and Kumar, A. (2017). City profile: Jaipur. *Cities*, 68, 63–81.

Khan, S. H., and Kamal, F. (2020). Jaipur: Journey from sand to city. *Ilkogretim Online: Elementary Education Online*, 19(4), 2791–2801. Available at: http://ilkogretim-online.org

Lane, K. (2010). *Colour of Paradise: The Emerald in the Age of Gunpowder Empires*. New Haven, CT: Yale University Press.

Lucas, A., Bhatt, N., Singhania, M., Sachdeva, K., Hsu, T., and Padua, P. (2016). Jaipur, India: The global gem and jewelry power of the Pink City. *Gems & Gemology*, 52(4), 332–367.

Polanyi, K. (1944). *The Great Transformation*. Boston, MA: Beacon Press.

Pyke, F., Becattini, G., and Sengenberger, W. (Eds.) (1990). *Industrial Districts and Inter-Firm Co-Operation in Italy*. Geneva: International Institute for Labour Studies.

Rothermund, D. (2008). *India: The Rise of an Asian Giant*. Yale: Yale University Press.

Roy, T. (1998). Economic reforms and textile industry in India. *Economic and Political Weekly*, 33(32), 2173–2182.

Sacco, P.L., and Tavano, B. G. (2005). Distretti culturali evoluti e valorizzazione del territorio. Pescara. *Global & Local Economic Review*, 8(1), 7–41.

Scott, A. J. (2000). *The Cultural Economy of Cities: Essays on the Geography of Image-Producing Industries*. Londres: Sage.

Shaban, A. (2021). Growth and determinants of the middle class in rural and urban India in the Post-Liberalisation Period. In Batabyal, A. A., Higano, Y. and Nijkamp, P. (eds.), *Rural-Urban Dichotomies and Spatial Development in Asia*, pp. 249–274. Singapore: Springer.

Sharma, P., and Sharma, R. (2014). Special economic zones in Rajasthan: A study of gems and jewellery segment in Jaipur. *ZENITH International Journal of Business Economics & Management Research*, 4(5), 24–35.

Sheth, D. L. (1999). Secularisation of caste and making of new middle class. *Economic and Political Weekly*, 34(34/35), 2502–2510.

Tillotson, G. (2006). *Jaipur Nama: Tales from the Pink City*. London: Penguin Books.

Tiwari, R. R., Saha, A., and Parikh, J. R. (2009). Respiratory morbidities among working children of gem polishing industries, India. *Toxicology and Industrial Health*, 25, 81–84.

Vergati, A. (2000). Clans Rajput, généalogies et identité dans l'ouest du Rajasthan. In Montaut, A. (ed.), *Le Rajasthan. Ses dieux, ses héros, son peuple. Hommage au Dr. N. Joshi*. Paris: Edition Langues'O.

16

LEVERAGING SKILLS INTO A CRAFT THROUGH SOCIAL ENTREPRENEURSHIP AND *JUGAAD* INNOVATION

The Chamar leatherworkers' studio in Dharavi, Mumbai

Meghamrita Chakraborty and Ellen Loots

16.1 Introduction

Emerging economies such as that of India typically face a scarcity of resources and volatility in the social environment, as well as a formal economy from which many individuals are excluded (Prabhu and Jain 2015). However, if cultural and creative industries can be engines for job creation, social empowerment and knowledge creation (UNCTAD 2010: xix; Shaban and Vermeylen 2015), they have vast potential in India because of its diverse social and cultural capital. Especially cities in India can act as a common and free space, in which people can let go of rigidities arising out of social structures; in cities, ideas can mix and people from different backgrounds can interact (Landry 2012). The metropolitan area of Mumbai has expanded over the years to accommodate the inflow of migrants and new activities, resulting in several clusters, for example Bhiwandi and Dharavi. The process of colonisation and the subsequent independence of the country had already fuelled the rise of such clusters. Several of them are categorised as slums; there is little recognition of the economic, industrial, and creative activity that has been sustained there for many generations. Despite the vibrant economic activity, the living conditions of the inhabitants are harsh.

Dharavi, touted as Asia's largest slum, is one of the most densely populated areas in Mumbai and located in the middle of India's financial capital. Dharavi is an 'entrepreneurial slum', in which more than 30% of the surface is under some form of commercial use (Iyer et al. 2011: 9). Historically a fishing village populated by the *Koli fisherman*, the place became a hub for leather manufacturing. Working with leather is something that only people of the lower Hindu castes

DOI: 10.4324/9781003129370-21

(also known as the scheduled castes) do, and is considered *impure* by the upper castes. The skills of leatherworkers are hardly ever recognised as valuable, and their lower-caste identity has always been used to perpetuate the discrimination prevalent within the Indian caste system. Apart from leather, Dharavi also houses workshops of pottery, textiles, rag picking, and recycling works; these, mostly informal, enterprises produce goods worth more than those produced by the special economic zones (SEZ) in India (Iyer et al. 2011). Dharavi's business activity and entrepreneurial nature make it imperative to see it as an 'industrial township rather than a residential area' (Iyer et al. 2011).

In recent years, there have been efforts to raise an awareness of the working conditions and to better the living conditions in Dharavi, with several non-governmental organisations (NGOs), independent field agencies, and self-help groups working in this direction.[1] The 'Chamar Studio' is an initiative by an entrepreneur who started to work with the leather craftsmen and cobblers of Dharavi, with the goal of designing and manufacturing bags. The name directly refers to the *Chamar*, a Hindu dalit caste traditionally working in the skinning of animals and the cobbling and tanning of leather. This venture is unique, because, instead of trying to dissociate from the traditional social stigmas of caste, the Chamar Studio aspires to bring the crafts and skills of the leatherworkers to the forefront, and to establish 'artistry' as their primary identity. In this paper, we create empirical evidence about how entrepreneurship can alleviate poverty and the precarious labour conditions of a societal group, with the Chamar Studio as a case.

Entrepreneurship in general and social entrepreneurship (SE) in particular often come in where government and institutions (including legal systems) fall short of creating viable living and working conditions for all citizens. Traditionally, SE has been studied in the US. Increasingly, SE scholars turn to novel contexts such as developing markets and study the new business models, organisational structures, and "strategies for brokering between very limited and disparate resources to create social value" (Seelos and Mair 2005: 244). In such contexts, for-profit and non-profit organisational activity are often combined (Dacin et al. 2011). Previous research has demonstrated that historical and contextual elements (including the lack of institutional arrangements) have a major impact on SE and the types of social innovations that come about in lagging economies (Prabhu and Jain 2015), with the examples of India (Duflo and Pande 2007; Banerjee et al. 2007) and neighbouring countries as Bangladesh (Mair et al. 2012).

We study the case of the Chamar Studio with a qualitative approach, which allows us to observe the activities of people in their natural setting and to question the social context in which phenomena occur. We conducted interviews with the founder, the workers, and two journalists who had written about the Chamar Studio. The first author had known Dharavi's leather shops and workshops for longer; she started building rapport with the founder and workers of the Chamar Studio since early 2019. In 2020, both authors visited the studio.

Only a few of the workers were comfortable in engaging in lengthy discussions. Therefore, data collection occurred in repeated visits to the studio, in which longer and shorter conversations would take place with the founder and/or the workers. Conversations were not recorded, but notes were made during and immediately after the visits. The coverage of the venture in social media, newspapers and magazines was examined and used as a means to triangulate findings.

The chapter is organised as follows: first, the industrial development of crafts in India is contextualised; second, the growth of Mumbai and Dharavi is described, with a focus on leatherwork; third, the Chamar Studio is described, after which, fourth, we introduce our key theoretical concepts, social entrepreneurship, and *jugaad*. Fifth, the nature of the social entrepreneurship of the Chamar Studio, as well as its innovative and *jugaad* approach, is explained. Finally, we conclude the chapter with major observations emerging from the study.

16.2 Crafts in Indian cities

Creative industries' researchers have argued that individuals, firms, and industries tend to cluster geographically, commonly in cities (e.g., Shaban and Sattar 2013; Chapain and De Propris 2009; Landry 2012). Numerous Western contemporary cities are considered to be creative places that encourage creative production. They allow culture and race to blend into creative ideas, and they give people the space to live out their ideas, aspirations, dreams, and conflicts (Landry 2012).

Many of India's metropolitan areas carry along a history of industrial production and migration. Historically, during the colonial rule, India's industries developed primarily in port cities and other strategic locations that facilitated trade and an easy distribution of goods (Saikia 2011). These include Bengal (the then capital of the East India Company), Bombay (Mumbai), Chennai, Surat, and Delhi. Railway and roadway networks assured the connections with the inner land with these cities. The infrastructure was adequate for bringing in raw materials from rural and surrounding areas for manufacturing and trade, and in distributing the final and imported products back to local markets (Saikia 2011). In the post-independent period, India has carried forward those colonial traditions, leading to the appeal of regions like Kolkata, Mumbai, and Chennai, which led to pulsating industrial activity and the influx of labour and raw materials (Saikia 2011).

This trend of industrialisation with pivotal roles for import as well as machine-made manufactured goods has been harmful to India's traditional crafts sectors and craftsmen. The decline in the need for workers in traditional non-farm activities between 1901 and 1951 strongly hit workers with limited social mobility opportunities, such as female workers (Reddy and Sarap 2017). However, the literature suggests that the traditional goods were not entirely supplanted by machine-made manufactured goods, and that the demand for traditional goods remained, helping the crafts sectors to survive even through the difficult colonial period (Reddy and Sarap 2017). Many artisans and workers migrated to urban areas with the hope to be able to sustain their work. Those massive migration processes in the 18th and early 19th century led to the emergence of several urban clusters, for example Bhiwandi, Malegaon and Dharavi in Mumbai, Surat in Gujarat, and Tirupur in Madras (now Chennai). Clusters developed in those areas where resources were available (Reddy and Sarap 2017). Craft activities are highly reliant on natural resources, such as the raw materials deriving from fauna and flora, as well as forests. Similarly, the climate is also a factor which affected the location processes; the warm and moist climate of Mumbai, for example, is essential for the spinning and weaving activities which have led to the growth of the cotton textile industry in the region. With cheap and skilled human capital abundant in well-connected locations such as ports and railway hubs, many crafts sectors blossomed in India's industrialised cities. Nonetheless, craft workers (of which there were, and still are, many) suffered low wages and low appreciation for their skills (Reddy and Sarap 2017).

Even though Indian Five Year Plans initially had a rather higher focus on the large and heavy industries, from the second plan onwards (1956–61) also crafts sectors have been included in the plans (Five Year Plans 1956). Nevertheless, policymakers have been "confounded over what to do in dealing with a traditional sector like crafts apart from suggesting that this could generate employment and income" (Reddy and Sarap 2017: 113). Such an institutional void paves the way for private initiatives to come up with solutions, as the Chamar Studio provides for leatherworkers.

16.3 The leather industry in India

Leather is one of the most widely traded commodities globally, steered by the demand by the fashion and footwear industry, as well as the furniture, interior design, and automotive industries. The leather industry in India accounts for approximately 13% of the world's leather production, good for jobs for 4.4 million people. India is the second-largest producer of footwear and leather garments in the world, and the second-largest exporter of leather garments. The leather industry in India has a long history.[2]

India's leather industry is strongly tied to the caste-based system. The society has been traditionally divided into a hierarchical caste system, based on birth and occupation (Sinha 1986). It is a form of social stratification in which people are born into a particular caste and in which social mobility is restricted. The four main castes are the *Brahmins* (the priests and teachers), the *Kshatriyas* (the rulers and warriors), the Vaishyas (the traders), and the Shudras who were supposed to serve the upper castes (Kamble 1983). Furthermore, the Dalits (like Chamar, Pasi Mahar, etc.), Chandalas and Adivasis are considered to be the impure ones, and were kept outside the purview of the caste system (Kamble 1983). According to Srinivas (1996), the concepts of 'purity' and 'pollution' are inherent to the caste system, leading to a number of 'untouchable communities' that until today have been excluded from other work than menial jobs, including cleaning and leather tanning activities. The caste-based oppression implies that members of the lower castes are denied access to resources. The religious sanctions inherent to the caste system have led to a practice that reserved several artisanal activities to the lower castes who have to serve the upper castes (Sinha 1986). Dalits like the leatherworkers (the Chamar) had the responsibility to serve the village and perform tasks deemed unhygienic by the upper castes (Sinha 1986), for example working with leather, which is a material derived from dead animals.

Furthermore, India's leather industry has traditionally been related to the 'self-sufficing Jajmani System', wherein leatherworkers in villages flayed, tanned, and made leather goods like shoes for their *'jajmans'* or patrons (Sinha 1986). The Jajmani System or this patron-client relationship originates in religion and is deeply entrenched within the societal structure. Because leather manufacturing was highly reliant upon the demand of the patrons as well as the army (Sinha 1986), as observed by Wiser (1936: 34–35),[3] "leatherworkers approximated the position of slaves of any of the menial castes of the village". A system of reciprocity was instituted by religious sanction: on the one hand, the Dalits (Shudras) were supposed to serve their Jajmans or patrons in every way; on the other hand, the patrons must foresee in life maintenance for their servants (Sinha 1986). If one of the patron's animals would die, it would become also the property of those working for him. The Dalits, particularly the Chamar, would then utilise the hide and sometimes even the flesh of the dead animal (Sinha 1986).

Before the Indian Rebellion of 1857, leather (also for the British army's equipment) was typically imported from England (Sinha 1986); this trade was historically in the hands of the Muslims because the Hindus considered it to be religiously impure (Sinha 1986). However, when this trade was disrupted, domestic leather procurement took over, leading to the opening of several private tanneries in Uttar Pradesh and other parts of the country. By 1899, the domestic trade of rawhide and skins from Madras had taken such a leap that prices of raw materials increased beyond what tanners in villages could pay (Sinha 1986; Gadgil 1971). This trend caused the breakdown of the Jajmani system and led to disputes over the rights of ownership over dead cattle. Many leatherworkers shifted towards agricultural work, or they moved to the urban tanning industry (Sinha 1986).

One location in which the leather industry took a giant leap is Dharavi in Mumbai. Initially, a creek inhabited by the indigenous fishermen community of 'Koli', the area dried up because of the expansion of Mumbai. The outbreak of the plague in 1869 caused the British government to expel the polluting and waste industries to this then distant creek region. Being unregulated land and mainly used as a rubbish dump, Dharavi attracted immigrant communities to settle and started to develop (KRVIA SPARC Report 2010). Among those communities were the Muslim leather tanners from Tamil Nadu, as well as potters from Saurashtra, and artisans and embroidery workers from Uttar Pradesh (KRVIA SPARC Report 2010). Attracting increasingly more immigrants, Dharavi became a site where the recycling of dumped goods created a livelihood for the majority of its inhabitants (Weinstein 2014). As such, in the second half of the 19th century, leather production by the Muslim immigrants started to become an established industry in Dharavi. Ever since, Dharavi kept attracting leatherworkers that escaped the penurious circumstances in the villages and hoped for a better livelihood in the Mumbai area (Weinstein 2014). In recent years, generations of leatherworkers have created their independent businesses of finished leather goods such as shoes or bags (KRVIA SPARC Report 2010).

In terms of health and safety, leatherworking is not optimal. The Factories Act of 1948 aims to formulate laws and policies governing occupational health and safety and sets rules regarding the hours of work, pay, health and safety of the workers. This act has categorised the leather industry as a 'hazardous industry' (Nihila 1993). Leather is toxic when it is being processed: tanning the leather requires the usage of heavy and sharp hand tools, contact with chemicals, and the inhalation of toxic gases (of which some combinations are lethal) during many hours a day (Nihila 1993). Furthermore, the working conditions frequently include working in cramped spaces with dim lights and poor ventilation (KRVIA SPARC Report 2010). Despite government regulations, most workers in the industry do so on an informal basis, without any registration. This impedes a clear monitoring process.

In recent years, the leather industry in India has been challenged. In 1996, pollution led to a city ban on tanning causing the leather industry to buy its hides from remote Deonar (KRVIA SPARC Report 2010). This meant that leatherworkers either had to shift towards the edge of the city or go through hassle in getting the raw material. Furthermore, a ban on cattle slaughter and tax reforms and drastic tax reforms like the introduction of Goods and Services tax, which cut down the profit in the leather trade, caused severe challenges to the leatherworkers ever since 2015. It is in this context that the Chamar Studio started off.

16.4 The Chamar Studio in Dharavi

Dharavi has been described as an entrepreneurial slum because of its self-sufficing nature (Iyer et al. 2011: 9). The Chamar Studio is one of the unique, entrepreneurial initiatives involving the leatherworkers of Dharavi. In-depth discussions with Sudheer Rajbhar, the founder, helped us understand the work of the Studio and the many ways in which the Studio influences the lives of its workers. Originally from Uttar Pradesh and growing up in the slums of Kandivali in Mumbai, Sudheer Rajbhar has seen society and its stereotypes. Himself belonging to the Bhar caste, categorised as the Other Backward Class (OBC) by the Indian Constitution, Sudheer is familiar with the derogatory tones referring to his and other low castes, and the prejudices and exclusion in the Indian society. After obtaining a degree in arts, Sudheer worked as an artist's assistant and exhibited his own work in celebrated exhibitions and festivals in Mumbai, for example the Kala Ghoda Art Festival. Drawing inspiration from his childhood in the slums, his work has generally been introspective, making use of collected leftover items as keepsakes. In 2015, Sudheer decided to start his own business that is on the intersection of an arts project and a social enterprise. He kick-started with a project that entailed the production of simple white cotton bags (or *thailas*) on which the word 'Chamar' was printed in different languages. By exhibiting these bags in a Mumbai-based curatorial art space (the Clark House Initiative), he sought to draw attention to the precarious labour conditions of the low-caste workers, and to see how people reacted to the word 'Chamar' in an artistic context.

Enthused by people's reactions, Sudheer decided to start a brand that would put in light the creativity and skills of the cobblers, leatherworkers, and other workers from the Dalit community: the 'Chamar Studio'. He had the sensitivity to recognise the cobblers and leatherworkers as artisans: they have the skills to manufacture and fashion leather, which, if adeptly applied, can be creative and productive at the same time. While 'Chamar' has commonly been used as a slur against the people belonging to the lower caste with whom people from other castes would disassociate, Sudheer, trying to break the stereotype, seeks to give positive attention to the skill associated with this notion, which is the skill of the leather artisans. Around that time (2015), numerous leatherworkers experienced difficulties in obtaining the raw material that sustains their livelihood because of the introduction of the cattle slaughter ban in India. Leather became scarce and thus expensive. In 2016, Sudheer started experimenting with an alternative to leather. He reckoned that (used) rubber could be the cheap, a more eco-friendly and less toxic alternative to leather, and suitable for bag production. Rubber does not lose its main qualities after being recycled; in the form of the glossy rubber sheets that are a component of rubber tyres, it was available at a local firm.

Together with a friend, who is a cobbler by profession and engaged with the municipality's waste management department, Sudheer started training the workers in waste segregation, hygiene practices, and stitching bags from the recyclable rubber sheets. The first batch of the Chamar Studio products was presented in a collection named 'Bombay Black' and entailed backpacks, satchels, handbags, and tote bags that carried traditional local names as 'Lady Batwa', 'Khisa', 'Jhola', and 'Bora'. Even if manufactured from a new material, the products have the typical zigzag suture that was used for the leather products. Priced between Rs. 600 and Rs. 6000 (the equivalent in US dollar is 8 to 85),[4] the bags are simple, minimalistic, and utilitarian, having the sheen of soft leather and a classy finish because of the black colour. Dharavi, the hub for informal leather work, became the centre of the Chamar Studio's operations thanks to the social entrepreneurship that Sudheer manifested.

16.5 Key concepts: social entrepreneurship and *jugaad*

Entrepreneurship is commonly associated with the presence of lucrative opportunities that are being discovered, evaluated, and exploited by imaginative individuals (Shane and Venkataraman 2000). In recent years, entrepreneurship scholars have started to empirically shift away from a dominant focus on high-growth, wealth-creating businesses and start-ups, to enterprises that address entrenched societal problems and catalyse social as well as economic value (Tobias et al. 2013; Seelos and Mair 2005). For example, with one-tenth of the world's population living in extreme poverty and poverty on the rise, still, in some countries,[5] entrepreneurs have been challenged to engage such a massive number of poor people. The entrepreneurship research field has identified at least two ways in which entrepreneurship does so: first, by firms (frequently within mature economies) that create a market in serving the needs of the poor while still making a return on their investment (e.g. Prabhu and Jain 2015; Prahalad and Hammond 2002); and second, by entrepreneurial solutions to alleviate poverty, or entrepreneurship as a means that can help individuals to 'break the cycle of poverty' (e.g., Bruton et al. 2013: 683). The Chamar Studio can be marked as a form of social entrepreneurship of the second type.

Regardless of its many competing definitions (Choi and Majumdar 2014), social entrepreneurship (SE) can be considered as an umbrella term for "the rapidly growing number of organisations that have created models for efficiently catering to basic human needs that existing markets and institutions have failed to satisfy" (Seelos and Mair 2005: 241). It combines "the resourcefulness of entrepreneurship with a mission to change society", not rarely in relation to the Sustainable Development Goals (Dacin et al. 2011; Seelos and Mair 2005). While the creation of social value has longer been considered as a by-product of the economic value that many entrepreneurs seek to create, in SE it is the other way around: social value takes centre stage, while economic value creation is mere needed to allow the business to achieve self-sufficiency (Dacin et al. 2011; Zahra et al. 2009; Mair and Marti 2006). SE commonly seeks to strike a balance between "doing good" and "doing well" (Prabhu and Jain 2015: 860). In order to survive, social entrepreneurs must find a poise (across a wide range of possible ratios) between their social motivation and a personal need to capture an economic return, or "part of the value in financial terms" (Seelos and Mair 2005: 244). Choi and Majumdar (2014: 364) have suggested to view SE as "a conglomerate of several sub-concepts" that "describe to a good extent the value achievement" (368) by SE, namely (1) social value creation, (2) the social entrepreneur, (3) the social entrepreneurship organisation, (4) market orientation, and (5) social innovation. It is ever more clear that many social entrepreneurs are inherently also innovators that develop new solutions. In India, for example, the phenomenon called 'Gandhian innovation' is based on the principles of sustainability and affordability: it relies on the premises that the Earth provides enough to satisfy everyone's need, and that innovations should benefit everyone (Prahalad and Mashelkar 2010).

The idea and concept of *jugaad* is widely prevalent in India and is used as a colloquial term in everyday contexts. Originally, the term symbolises any trick, connection, or combination that engenders the means to an end (Monier-Williams 2005). However, the literature also describes *jugaad* as 'creative improvisation' (Krishnan 2010), and as a 'concept, process, and product' all at the same time (Sekhsaria 2013). From the innovative use of household items to unique entrepreneurial ideas; *jugaad* is commonly used in daily conversations and work environments (Chaturvedi 2014). While, on the one hand, positively, it can refer to reconfiguring materials and finding solutions (Sekhsaria 2013), on the other hand, the concept can have a more negative connotation when referring to achieving something by undesirable means (Birtchnell 2011). However, in emerging markets such as India, Africa, or Brazil, *jugaad* often assists innovative entrepreneurs to working in 'resource-constrained settings', saving time and money, and providing affordable solutions to consumers (Rajdou and Prabhu 2013). These affordable 'constraint-based innovations' (Saraf 2009) frequently target the marginalised by addressing their basic requirement and needs (Prahalad 2009).

Prabhu and Jain (2015) have typified the mode of entrepreneurial innovation that is increasingly prevalent in India as *frugal, flexible,* and *inclusive*. Defined as "the art of overcoming harsh constraints by improvising an effective solution using limited resources", the *jugaad* approach to innovation can be found in different types of organisations, including social enterprises (Prabhu and Jain 2015: 847). Such a *jugaad* approach to entrepreneurial innovation is typically unconventional, yet context-friendly and bottom-up, with entrepreneurs making an "ingenious use of existing resources and technologies rather than pushing the technology frontier per se" (Prabhu and Jain 2015: 845; Chaturvedi 2014). In this manner, it is distinctive from the innovations in advanced economies that classically rely on research and development to deliver more benefits, at a higher cost, to a small niche of consumers (Prahalad 2012).

In the following sections, we will discuss the Chamar Studio along the key dimensions of SE (Choi and Majumdar 2014), and explain why Sudheer's innovative entrepreneurship can be considered *jugaad*, or: frugal, flexible, and inclusive.

16.6 Social entrepreneurship and *jugaad* innovation in the Chamar Studio

16.6.1 Social value creation

The social mission, or the creation of social value, is considered to be a prerequisite for SE (Choi and Majumdar 2014; Zahra et al. 2009; Seelos and Mair

2005). Even if the concept of social value is complex and ambiguous (Choi and Majumdar 2014), several aspects of the Chamar Studio are clearly socially motivated.

Firstly, Sudheer improves the economic lives and precarious working conditions of some of Dharavi's leatherworkers in a number of ways. He decided to find an alternative to the costly and toxic process of leather manufacturing and came up with the idea of using recyclable rubber tyres. Relying on the skills of the cobblers and leatherworkers, he was soon able to fashion bags out of the rubber sheets, which entails cutting parts of a readily available, recycled material, instead of the time-consuming and unhealthy preparatory processes of tanning and crusting leather. Also, Sudheer creates a working system that allows flexibility for the artisans. Most of them are engaged in some other form of daily work, and in their remaining labour time, they stitch the bags from out of their homes or workspaces, mostly in Dharavi and Santacruz East, or in the Chamar Studio workspace. As suggested by one of the workers (albeit not in these words), this flexibility improves their work-life balance.

Secondly, by relying on the typical cobbler's stitch or the zigzag suture pattern, Sudheer effectively deploys the skills that leatherworkers master in a creative process; at the same time, he creates challenging work and supports the workers in improving their skills. As the artisans become more apt with practice, they become able to complete more complex designs in a shorter time, which is satisfactory not only for the workers but also for the entrepreneur who sees a challenge in expanding product lines as well as the business.

Finally, by leveraging the traditional skill possessed by and associated with the Chamar community, and naming his studio/brand after them, Sudheer seeks to combat social class disparities and to create respect for the skill typically associated with a lower caste in India. Out of the conversations with the workers, it became clear that the idea of becoming more respected on the basis of their traditional work, appeared far-fetched. However, regularly working with the Chamar Studio has given them the hope to being able to pursue this further. Sudheer's intentions and efforts, thus, actively tap into social value creation and stretch further than those of many regular fashion designers or creative entrepreneurs.

16.6.2 The social entrepreneur

Social entrepreneurs are crucial in initiating social entrepreneurial activities: they are often innovators that envisage and realise social innovations and/or social change processes (Choi and Majumdar 2014). In the Indian context, social innovators have been found to "making ingenious use of existing resources and technologies, employing a mindset that combines improvisation with pragmatism and developing solutions for communities that have traditionally been underserved" (Prabhu and Jain 2015: 844; Ahlstrom 2010). In the case of Sudheer, as exposed in the previous sections, there is a clear interest in improving the economic lives of a lower caste community in India. In order to achieve this, he unambiguously relies on creative improvisation (cf. Amabile 1983) and an entrepreneurial mindset (McGrath and MacMillan 2000). As an artist, Sudheer is accustomed to create artworks and design objects with an aesthetic value, to which, with the Chamar Studio, he adds a functional and a social dimension. His entrepreneurial mindset is reflected in his proclivity, on the one hand, to advance his enterprise by including increasingly more workers (cf. infra), and, on the other hand, to work towards the usage of a novel bio-degradable organic raw material for a more sustainable approach to fashion.

16.6.3 The social entrepreneurship organisation

Different from membership organisations that focus on advocacy, or activist movements and other more punctual and loosely structured initiatives with a social objective, social entrepreneurship activities are commonly coordinated through an organisation that can possess various legal forms, and be located in several sectors, including the public sector (Stephan et al. 2016; Choi and Majumdar 2014; Mair and Marti 2006). In its ambition to roll out its social mission, the Chamar Studio is confronted with some coordination and strategic issues typical for a young entrepreneurial organisation that recognises the opportunities to expand. Yet, in order to develop a sustainable and viable business with a social mission in an environment such as India, it has been suggested that "a deep knowledge of the nature of the problem and the lifestyles and socio-cultural context of the communities or customers that one is dealing with" is needed to achieve a social venture's objective, as well as passion, commitment and local knowledges. These assets are more likely to spur social entrepreneurship compared with new technology or large amounts of capital (Prabhu and Jain 2015: 851).

The Chamar Studio makes the working and living conditions of its workers a main goal. Many poor people are in multiple occupations as a way of risk-spreading and of being capable to foresee in the daily needs of their families they must accommodate (Banerjee and Duflo 2007). This is not different for the cobblers and leatherworkers in Mumbai, who are often the breadwinners of a multi-generation household. The Chamar Studio wants to engage workers in such a way that it does not hamper their routines; yet, also, Sudheer developed an income-generating way in which workers can occupy "what would otherwise be wasted time" (Banerjee and Duflo 2007: 161). One of the primary associates and Sudheer's friend, Sachin, needs to support his own growing family. He has thus created a workspace in his own home from where he works and also trains/teaches other workers for the Studio.

On International Labour's Day in 2019, Sudheer launched a project which he labelled 'Blue Collar'. Blue collar jobs refer to the manual labour executed by the working classes for which no education is needed. Blue as a colour is for the Indian Dalit community symbolic for social justice and empowerment, associated with Dr. B.R. Ambedkar, a social reformer who had fought for Dalit's rights since before the independence of India. With the Blue Collar project, the organisation expands to a larger group of workers, namely the cobblers sitting in the local railway stations in Mumbai. While staying in the stations for days of 12 hours and more, many of these people only receive a few clients for shoe polishing or stitching. The Chamar Studio has arranged that also those cobblers can use the 'in between' time for creating rubber bags for which the material and training are provided by the organisation. According to Sudheer, this strategy leads to a more efficient use of the time and skills of workers, and to a greater visibility of the social enterprise, which adds to its social mission to improve workers' economic lives and create an awareness not only of the precarious situations, but equally so of possible solutions. Hence, a major challenge of the solutions to social problems as those that the Chamar Studio seeks to create is to scale up and eliminate poverty at a larger scale. While, typically, social ventures lack the resources to extend their solutions to larger contexts, and to generalise to other groups than the one initially targeted, the resources of the Chamar Studio are mainly the abundant human capital available, as well as waste materials. Small-scale models as the Chamar Studio could serve as an inspiration for other social entrepreneurs, who may benefit more from *scaling out* rather than *scaling up*, for example by training others who could take the applicable elements and tailor them to their own circumstances (Prabhu and Jain 2015).

16.6.4 Market orientation

Market orientation in SE can imply "commercial activities, which generate earned-income to ensure the sustainability of social entrepreneurial activities and self-sufficiency of the organization" as well as "commercial activities directly linked to the social mission to ensure the most effective and efficient distribution of social services and products" (Choi and Majumdar 2014: 368). The Chamar Studio mostly works on demand, based on orders received through their website and their social media channels. The selling proceeds are equally divided between the artist and the leatherworker. Social media as Instagram play an essential role in the marketing of the Chamar Studio products. Sudheer regularly places updates of the different Chamar Studio projects and media coverage, in order to interact with a potential clientele. One of his unique strategies has been to label the bags with traditional local names, ensuring a familiarity to a local clientele. At present, distribution at the international level has been very limited, which points at Sudheer's considerations of developing a gradual, sustainable project. Sudheer has chosen to portray the bags on an Instagram page with pictures of the artisans holding the bags in their daily workplaces or living spaces. The Chamar Studio insists that all its products are androgynous and not conforming to any gender norms. Everyone can use the bags according to their needs. In all of this, there is an effort to make potential customers realise that, despite the longstanding stereotypes, an occupation is more than work: it is a creative practice and the result of skilled craftsmanship, a tradition sustained throughout many generations of artisans. All in all, the market promotion by the Chamar Studio is frugal, comparable with that of other social enterprises that do not rely on large advertisement budgets but use the web, social media, and viral marketing tactics to spread the information about their products (cf. Prabhu and Jain 2015).

It is a delicate balance to seek for the attention needed to create a market of demand for the Chamar Studio bags, while safeguarding its social mission and avoiding the brand to become trending or a hype so typical in the fashion and design industries (Bhatti and Ventresca 2012). The Chamar Studio has been covered by local and international media, including lifestyle magazines such as Elle India, Livemint, Harper's Bazaar India, Scroll, The Hindu, and The Asian Age, to name a few. While such media attention can easily be considered as a recognition of the project, it can equally turn a product into a fad or fashion (Bhatti and Ventresca 2012) and lead to pressures onto the production capacity of the social enterprise. Also the fact that the Chamar Studio has begun supplying and showcasing its products in the stores of Le Mill, a multi-designer boutique in Mumbai, and in the Paper Boat Collective, which is a small lifestyle boutique in Goa, can be seen as a strategic move that adds to the viability of the business and labour security for the workers; at the same time, it detaches the bags from the environment where they were made, putting them on display in an environment of luxury goods, priced accordingly. The ways in which conspicuous consumption (acquiring luxury goods to display economic wealth) affects SE is far from understood, and particularly relevant when social entrepreneurs develop products that can be considered as artistic or design objects that only exist in limited batches.

16.6.5 Social innovation

Social innovation is commonly associated with SE, and the non-traditional, disruptive aspect of SE that sets it apart from regular service provision (Choi and Majumdar 2014). The innovative aspect comes natural when social entrepreneurs seek to find impactful solutions for social problems that occur in society. The typical Indian *jugaad* approach to innovation and entrepreneurship tends to be highly frugal, flexible, and inclusive (Prabhu and Jain 2015), what can undeniably be said about the Chamar Studio.

First, many Indian innovators are *frugal* in the sense that they make use of the scarce resources they have access to in an effective and economic way, and they are proficient at taking the cost out of the successive steps in an innovation process (from idea generation over development to the marketing of products or services) (Prabhu and Jain 2015; Prahalad 2012). Sudheer clearly does so by synergising an alternative, available raw material with the traditional skills of many workers who seek for additional revenues. Second, many Indian innovators are *flexible* thinkers and doers; they improvise and explore different options in an effectuation-like style (cf. Sarasvathy 2001) with the ability to adapt to volatile and changing circumstances (Prabhu and Jain 2015). The Chamar Studio has until today the features of a project-based enterprise, where subsequent projects with a similar objective lead to business growth. In this, Sudheer masters the approach of an artist, creatively conceiving projects and addressing opportunities that come forward. Third, innovators in India that are *inclusive* aim to develop goods and services for underserved communities and individuals that are constrained in their payment capacity. Including those excluded groups not only as customers, but as "members of an ecosystem producing and distributing these services, thereby augmenting their income and contributing to their development" (Prabhu and Jain 2015: 848), is precisely what the Chamar Studio accomplishes. With his social enterprise, Sudheer is an actor in a market-based economy who does not primarily seek for the development of a customer base of previously disqualified consumers, but he taps into a widely available human capital resource (skilled labour), and in doing so, he tries to include a poor community into the formal economy (cf. Bruton et al. 2013).

16.7 Discussion and conclusion

The Chamar Studio in Dharavi, Mumbai, is an example of an innovative social enterprise that, context-friendly, bottom-up, and by creative improvisation (Prabhu and Jain 2015), addresses social problems "through the use of local and cheap technologies combined with clever organizational and logistical arrangements" (Prabhu and Jain 2015: 848). We have exposed how it achieves its social mission through five components, namely social value creation, the social entrepreneur, the social entrepreneurship organisation, market orientation, and social innovation (Choi and Majumdar 2014). Likewise, we have illuminated how a *jugaad* approach, so typical for innovative entrepreneurship in India, characterises the Chamar Studio's activities.

Social enterprises often maintain peculiar models of value creation that can include economic, social, and cultural value (Seelos and Mair 2005), all in order to have an impact on society, be it at the local or global level. The typical social entrepreneur has been depicted as a social hero with 'entrepreneurial talent' (Seelos and Mair 2005: 244) who possesses, next to an altruistic motivation, also the determination to change society (ibid.). Many of the case studies in social entrepreneurship research have focused on the success stories of social entrepreneurs, who become heralded as archetypical examples, leading to a social entrepreneurial identity/stereotype and community (Dacin et al. 2011). In the case of Sudheer Rajbhar of the Chamar Studio, the Indian *jugaad* approach and his association with fashion and art add additional layers to his social entrepreneurial identity, seeking to blend functional, social, and aesthetic imperatives in a series of subsequent projects that fledge as an artistic portfolio. It does not surprise that a *jugaad* or frugal, flexible, and inclusive approach to entrepreneurial innovation reflects the business of Sudheer so effortlessly: *jugaad* requires a mindset and culture, and has a 'natural affinity' with creativity (Amabile 1983), as well as with an effectuation logic of business development (Prabhu and Jain 2015: 858; Sarasvathy 2001). While it has been suggested that *jugaad* can be applicable to other contexts than the Indian one, for example in relation to the recent maker movements in Western societies (Prabhu and Jain 2015), future research could scrutinise if artist-entrepreneurs are typically more frugal, flexible, and inclusive compared with other entrepreneurs. With our case study, we bring creativity into the equation and the SE literature.

Additionally, in contrast with SE-studies that consider how enterprises create a market in serving the needs of the poor (e.g., Prabhu and Jain 2015; Prahalad 2009), this case study considered how local resources in the form of the skills of the poor can be addressed in order to attenuate poverty. The study focused on workers rather than consumers. If this can be considered a contribution to extant SE-literature, it must be credited to Sudheer Rajbhar, whose vision is in line with that of thinkers such as Nobel prize-winner Muhammad Yunus, who believes that the poor have skills that remain under-utilised, and set up Grameen Bank in Bangladesh in order to accommodate for such a social failure.

One major challenge to social enterprises, including the Chamar Studio, is the growth challenge. Particularly in India: while many social enterprises have the motivation and commitment to act *jugaad*, they experience difficulties to scale up (Prabhu and Jain 2015). At the organisation level, scaling 'grassroots-generated innovations' (Prabhu and Jain 2015: 860) while striking a balance between doing good and doing well is a recurring challenge. Also at the aggregate or societal level, replicating and scaling the models of social enterprises to a level that really, severely, impacts society, remains tough (Seelos and Mair 2005). While scaling up may not always work out favourably, or not be an effective strategy for social enterprises, *scaling out* could be an alternative. However, the ways in which processes of scaling out are set in motion and become successful are to be investigated. The same holds true for the sustainability of social innovations within localised communities; while positive, social change needs entrepreneurial motivation, capacity, and opportunity (Stephan et al. 2016), the antecedents of SE's long-term effects (in context) are far from understood.

Acknowledgements

We acknowledge Sudheer Rajbhar and the workers in Chamar Studio. Data collection took place up to the first months of 2020; writing this chapter happened during the outbreak of the COVID-19 pandemic, which will imaginably have as disproportionate impact on the poor, through the loss of work and remittances, rising prices, and disruptions in education and health services,[6] also in India and, specifically, Dharavi.

Notes

1 Examples are Dharavi ART ROOM (www.facebook.com/dharaviartroom), the Society for Human and Environmental development's (S.H.E.D.: http://shedindia.org/), and the Society for Nutrition, Education and Health Action (SHENA: https://snehamumbai.org/). Last consulted on August 7th, 2020.

2 Sources: www.ibef.org/exports/leather-industry-india.aspx; www.investindia.gov.in/sector/leather; www.makeinindia.com/sector/leather; https://leatherindia.org/indian-leather-industry/. Last consulted August 7th, 2020.

3 Wiser (1936) quotes the Laws of Manu (Chapter I, Verses 87–91), p 34–5

4 To put the price of the products in perspective: the average monthly salary in a city like Mumbai was around US dollar 592 in 2019 (DEUTSCHE BANK RESEARCH, 16TH May 2019, 'Mapping the World's Prices 2019', www.dbresearch.com/PROD/RPS_EN-PROD/PROD0000000000494405/Mapping_the_world%27s_prices_2019.pdf)

5 https://openknowledge.worldbank.org/bitstream/handle/10986/30418/211330ov.pdf; last consulted August 7th, 2020.

6 www.worldbank.org/en/topic/poverty/overview, consulted August 7th, 2020.

References

Ahlstrom, D. (2010). Innovation and growth: How business contributes to society. *Academy of Management Perspectives*, 24(3), 11–24.

Amabile, T. M. (1983). The social psychology of creativity: A componential conceptualization. *Journal of Personality and Social Psychology*, 45(2), 357.

Banerjee, A. V., Cole, S., Duflo, E., and Linden, L. (2007). Remedying education: Evidence from two randomized experiments in India. *The Quarterly Journal of Economics*, 122(3), 1235–1264.

Banerjee, A. V., and Duflo, E. (2007). The economic lives of the poor. *Journal of Economic Perspectives*, 21(1), 141–168.

Bhatti, Y. A., and Ventresca, M. (2012). The emerging market for frugal innovation: Fad, fashion, or fit? Available at SSRN: https://ssrn.com/abstract=2005983

Birtchnell, T. (2011). Jugaad as systemic risk and disruptive innovation in India. *Contemporary South Asia*, 19(4), 357–372.

Bruton, G. D., Ketchen Jr., D. J., and Ireland, R. D. (2013). Entrepreneurship as a solution to poverty. *Journal of Business Venturing*, 28(6), 683–689.

Chapain, C., and De Propris, L. (2009). Drivers and processes of creative industries in cities and regions. *Creative Industries Journal*, 2(1), 9–18.

Chaturvedi, A. (2014). Jugaad. *International Journal of Management Issues and Research*, 3(2), 4–8.

Choi, N., and Majumdar, S. (2014). Social entrepreneurship as an essentially contested concept: Opening a new avenue for systematic future research. *Journal of Business Venturing*, 29(3), 363–376.

Dacin, M. T., Dacin, P. A., and Tracey, P. (2011). Social entrepreneurship: A critique and future directions. *Organization Science*, 22(5), 1203–1213.

Duflo, E., and Pande, R. (2007). Dams. *The Quarterly Journal of Economics*, 122(2), 601–646.

Factories Act (1948). Government of India Report. Ministry of Labour and Employment. Available at: https://labour.gov.in/sites/default/files/TheFactoriesAct1948.pdf (last accessed on 25 March 2022).

Five Year Plans (1956). Planning Commission. Government of India. Available at: https://niti.gov.in/planningcommission.gov.in/docs/plans/planrel/fiveyr/welcome.html (last accessed on 25 March 2022).

Gadgil, D. R. (1971). *The Industrial Evolution of India in Recent Times, 1860–1939*, 5th edition. Delhi: Oxford University Press.

Iyer, M., Macomber, J., and Arora, N. (2011). Dharavi: Developing Asia's largest slum (A). *Harvard Business School Case*, 710–004.

Kamble, N. D. (1983). *Deprived Castes and Their Struggle for Equality*. New Delhi: Ashish Publishing House.

Krishnan, R. T. (2010). *From Jugaad to Systematic Innovation: The Challenge for India*. Bangalore: Utpreraka Foundation.

KRVIA SPARC Report (2010). RE: Interpreting, imagining, developing Dharavi, Mumbai. Available at: https://knowyourcity.info/wp-content/uploads/2015/04/ReDharavi1.pdf (last accessed on 25 March 2022).

Landry, C. (2012). *The Creative City: A Toolkit for Urban Innovators*. London: Routledge. Available at: http://memoriadasolimpiadas.rb.gov.br/jspui/bitstream/123456789/496/1/IU063%20-%20Charles%20LANDRY%20-%20The%20criative%20city.pdf

Mair, J., and Marti, I. (2006). Social entrepreneurship research: A source of explanation, prediction, and delight. *Journal of World Business*, 41(1), 36–44.

Mair, J., Marti, I., and Ventresca, M. J. (2012). Building inclusive markets in rural Bangladesh: How intermediaries work institutional voids. *Academy of Management Journal*, 55(4), 819–850.

McGrath, R. G., and MacMillan, I. C. (2000). *The Entrepreneurial Mindset: Strategies for Continuously Creating Opportunity in an Age of Uncertainty*, Vol. 284. Boston, United States: Harvard Business Press.

Monier-Williams, M. (2005). *A Sanskrit-English Dictionary: Etymologically and Philologically Arranged with Special Reference to Cognate Indo-European Languages*. New Delhi: Motilal Banarsidass Publishing House.

Nihila, M. 1993. Development process and status of women: Tanning industry in Tamil Nadu. *Economic & Political Weekly*, 28(41), 2220–2228.

Prabhu, J., and Jain, S. (2015). Innovation and entrepreneurship in India: Understanding jugaad. *Asia Pacific Journal of Management*, 32(4), 843–868.

Prahalad, C. K. (2009). *The Fortune at the Bottom of the Pyramid*, Revised and updated 5th anniversary edition. New Delhi: Pearson Education, Inc.

Prahalad, C. K. (2012). Bottom of the pyramid as a source of breakthrough innovations. *Journal of Product Innovation Management*, 29(1), 6–12.

Prahalad, C. K., and Hammond, A. (2002). Serving the world's poor, profitably. *Harvard Business Review*, 80(9), 48–59.

Prahalad, C. K., and Mashelkar, R. A. (2010). Innovation's holy grail. *Harvard Business Review*, 88(7–8), 132–141.

Rajdou, N., and Prabhu, J. (2013). Frugal innovation: A new business paradigm, INSEAD knowledge. Available at: https://knowledge.insead.edu/innovation/frugal-innovation-a-new-business-paradigm-2375 (last accessed on 25 March 2022).

Reddy, N. D, and Sarap, K. (2017). *Rural Labour Mobility in Times of Structural Transformation: Dynamics and Perspectives from Asian Economies*. Singapore: Springer Singapore.

Saikia, D. (2011). The pattern of industrial location in India under liberalization: An analysis of the organized manufacturing industries. *International Research Journal of Management and Business Studies*, 1(7), 197–214.

Saraf, D. (2009). Indias indigenous genius: Jugaad. Available at: http://online.wsj.com/article/SB12474 5880685131765.html (last accessed on 25 March 2022).

Sarasvathy, S. D. (2001). Causation and effectuation: Toward a theoretical shift from economic inevitability to entrepreneurial contingency. *Academy of Management Review*, 26(2), 243–263.

Seelos, C., and Mair, J. (2005). Social entrepreneurship: Creating new business models to serve the poor. *Business Horizons*, 48(3), 241–246.

Sekhsaria, P. (2013). The making of an Indian STM & 'Technological Jugaad' as a Culture of Innovation. Available at: https://nanopdf.com/download/technological-jugaad-as-a-culture-of-innovation_pdf (last accessed on 25 March 2022).

Shaban, A., and Sattar, S. (2013). Industrial dispersal and clustering in India during Post-Reform Period and the role of small and medium towns. In Sharma, R. N. and Sandhu, R. S. (eds.), *Small Cities and Towns in Global Era: Emerging Challenges and Perspectives*, pp. 111–151. Jaipur: Rawat Publications.

Shaban, A., and Vermeylen, F. (2015). Trade in the creative sector comparing India with China, Brazil, and UK. *Economic & Political Weekly*, 50(20), 68–75.

Shane, S., and Venkataraman, S. (2000). The promise of entrepreneurship as a field of research. *Academy of Management Review*, 25(1), 217–226.

Sinha, S. (1986). Economics vs stigma: Socio-economic dynamics of rural leatherwork in UP. *Economic and Political Weekly*, 21(24), 1061–1067.

Srinivas, M. N. (1996). *Indian Society through Personal Writings*. New Delhi: Oxford University Press.

Stephan, U., Patterson, M., Kelly, C., and Mair, J. (2016). Organizations driving positive social change: A review and an integrative framework of change processes. *Journal of Management*, 42(5), 1250–1281.

Tobias, J. M., Mair, J., and Barbosa-Leiker, C. (2013). Toward a theory of transformative entrepreneuring: Poverty reduction and conflict resolution in Rwanda's entrepreneurial coffee sector. *Journal of Business Venturing*, 28(6), 728–742.

UNCTAD (2010). Creative economy report 2010. Available at: http:// unctad.org/en/Docs/ditctab20103_en.pdf (last accessed on 5 July 2022).

Weinstein, L. (2014). *The Durable Slum: Dharavi and the Right to Stay Put in Globalizing Mumbai*. Minneapolis: University of Minnesota Press.

Wiser, W. H. (1936). *The Hindu Jajmani System*. Lucknow: Lucknow Publishing House.

Zahra, S. A., Gedajlovic, E., Neubaum, D. O., and Shulman, J. M. (2009). A typology of social entrepreneurs: Motives, search processes and ethical challenges. *Journal of Business Venturing*, 24(5), 519–532.

17

CREATIVE WEAVING TOWN

The carpet industry of Khairabad

Rinku

17.1 Introduction

India is a culturally diverse country with every region having its peculiar art, craft, and music. From medieval times, the country has been globally known for its handloom and handicraft industries. According to the Indian Brand Equity Foundation (IBEF) (2021), the Indian handicraft industry is fragmented, with more than seven million regional artisans with an export value of USD 3.39 billion in the financial year 2019–20 (till February 2020). On the contrary handloom sector of India employs around 3.15 million workers and has an export value of USD 319.02 million in the financial year 2019–20 (Ministry of Textile 2020). In India, handloom and handicraft are small cottage-based industries spread in rural and urban centres. Artisans are engaged full time and (or) part-time in the craftwork (Vats 2014). The industry is fragmented and unorganised, with more than seven million regional artisans and more than 67,000 exporters promoting local art and craftsmanship in the domestic and global markets (Mitra et al. 2018).

The artisans possess unique skills rooting back to several generations, and now with market demand and technological enhancement, they are trying to make their living by converting it into a business. Digital technologies have come to their immense aid and helped them to commercialise their product. Some designers and craftspeople are inspired by the traditional handicraft and handloom techniques and infuse them with modern designs giving the products a new lease of life by enhancing their market demands (Evans 2005).

India's share in the international market for the craft is under 2%, while China stands at 30% (Agamuthu and Fauziah 2016). Small-scale industries can play a significant role in developing the economy, especially in India (Mitra et al. 2018). The Government of India identified creative clusters as essential for micro and small enterprises to grow strongly through mutual stimulation and leveraging common knowledge and markets. Typically, they benefit from

 DOI: 10.4324/9781003129370-22

lower taxes on handmade products. Creative clusters can create production efficiencies and provide a platform for artisans to access local and global markets (Bissel 2013; Evans 2005). The cultural sector is now considered essential for economic development, especially for South Asian countries (Shaban and Vermeylen 2015). The small craft firms within the sphere of creative industries occupy an important place, especially for those countries that are still in their industrialisation phase due to their significant contribution to the income and employment generation (Shafi et al. 2019).

Many creative artisanal clusters, specifically those engaged in carpet manufacturing, are spread across the geography of India. Uttar Pradesh has many such clusters, and some of these are Mirzapur, Varanasi, Bhadohi, Agra, and Khairabad. In this chapter, an attempt has been made to examine the size and growth of the carpet industry in Khairabad town of the Sitapur district of Uttar Pradesh.

Sitapur district is famous for the handmade carpets, called *dari or durry*, in the local language. Recently launched Uttar Pradesh Government's programme of One District One Product (ODOP) recognises Sitapur as a carpet making district. Khairabad was a part of the Awadh region, and it has been a weaver's town since the time of Mughals, who encouraged carpet making. Khairabad was an important trading centre for exporting rugs, bathmat, and durries, in India and abroad (Nevill 1905). The chapter engages with the sector of carpet production in the town, the creativity of the artisans, the design in carpet production, and its emerging export in different markets. A significant proportion of weaving activity is informal, and therefore getting accurate and reliable data on various aspects of the industry is difficult.

This study is based on the qualitative and ethnographic methods of data collection. More than 100 interviews were conducted with the entrepreneurs, weavers, government officials, journalists, and local political leaders. A review of local newspaper articles and available official documents was helpful to get an overview of the industry and ongoing policies and their implication at the local level. Ethnographic research and information gathered by observations became crucial to understanding the different structures and functioning of the industry and production process. Frequent visits to various villages helped me understand the social relations and networks and how subcontracting occurs in the industry.

The rest of the chapter is organised as follows. After this introduction section, Section 17.2 briefly examines the history of the carpet industry in India, while Section 17.3 discusses the export of Indian carpets. Section 17.4 examines the related policies in the state of Uttar Pradesh, where in Khairabad is situated. Section 17.5 presents an overview of carpet industry of Khairabad, and Section 17.6 examines the production and growth of carpets in Khairabad. Section 17.7 discusses the production relations and use of technology by entrepreneurs and producers. Section 17.8 deals with factors of production and location constraint of the carpet industry. This section also outlines the potential and existing use of digital technologies in the production and marketing of the products of the Khairabad carpet industry. The last, Section 17.9, concludes the chapter.

17.2 The carpet industry in India: a historical perspective

Carpet weaving is an age-old Indian tradition with the industry flourishing from the 16th century onwards. It is believed that the first Mughal emperor of India, Babar brought the carpet weavers from Persia to India to make carpets for him. Carpet weaving flourished during the reign of Akbar, the grandson of Babur. Akbar opened many carpets weaving centres in India, near his new capital city Agra. In these centres, carpet weavers from Persia made carpet for the palaces. Also, they taught the skills to others. That is why Agra and Bhadohi (near Agra) are still the most prominent carpet-making hub in India. In the beginning, the designs and patterns of carpets were Persian based, but after a while, a fusion of Indian designs and patterns emerged. In the earlier years of court carpet production, from 1580 to 1630 or so, the patterns of Indian carpets were heavily dependent upon Persian models (Walker 1997). During the reign of Mughal Emperor Shahjahan, Indian carpets reached to new heights; patterns were floral with geometric or calligraphic trims (Das et al. 2018). The new designs created a demand for Indian carpets in other parts of the world.

During the colonial rule in India, the condition of weavers was on the downfall because of a new tax system and high export duty introduced by the British government. Also, the introduction of English articles in India had thrown the weavers, carpenters, cotton dressers, black-smiths, shoemakers, etc., out of employment (Nanda 1974). The British neglected the public works and agriculture, which doomed millions of Indians to starvation by breaking up local industries, notably handweaving and hand spinning, which could not compete with British cotton fabrics flooding the Indian market (The Times of India 2007). Weavers of India were facing a shortage of raw material because most of the natural cotton produced in India was exported to England. This export shift happened due to the stoppage of raw cotton supply to England from America because of the American civil war. This civil war made Britishers export cotton from other colonies to England, and the massive export of cotton from India took place. In 1861 India contributed only 31 per cent of the total raw cotton imported into Great Britain; by 1862, the first full year of the war in America, India's contribution had leaped to 90 per cent of England's total raw cotton imports (Logan 1965: 40). This heavy export shot up raw cotton prices in the Indian market, and it was challenging for local weavers to buy the cotton from the market. The News of American Civil War gave opportunity to cotton merchants to increase the price of cotton, on 1 December 1861 cotton was selling at Rs. 18 and of 5 February 1862 it reached to Rs. 40 (Guha 1989). Weavers who managed to buy the raw cotton were unable to get the profit by selling the final product because the selling price of the product became much lower than before because of the imported cotton clothes from Britain (Harnetty 1971). On the contrary, high rates of export duty made it extremely difficult for the native weavers to export the finished product. During America's Civil War (1861–65), Britain bought India's crop, grown under regulation of imperial revenue and taxation, finished it into cheap textile using British technology, an oversold it the colony under the monopoly of its administration (Chatterjee 2018).

These conditions created a vicious cycle for the weavers and started alienating them from the weaving occupation. The weavers of coarse fabric had begun abandoning their trade by February 1862. A prominent merchant, Bansidhar reported that "the poorer classes of weavers have taken to working on the road and railways work for a living" (Guha 1989: 300). The advent of the East India Company and colonial rule in the early 19th century caused the collapse of the traditional crafts sector at the hands of machine-made goods (Reddy and Sarap 2017). Nationalists and intellectuals fought against the widespread de-industrialisation in India at the hands of cheap imported machine-made goods (Reddy and Sarap 2017). Especially in rural areas, the decline of employment in the handicrafts sector was more significant. The substantial drop in female employment; the handloom and handicraft sector heavily depend on their deft skill and work (Reddy and Sarap 2017). However, despite the difficult times, the significant way indigenous crafts continued to survive was the domestic demand for the goods (Reddy and Sarap, 2017).

17.3 Export of Indian carpets

Carpet Export Promotion Council (CEPC) (2019) points out that India has around 2500 carpet manufacturing units, about 200 are in the organised sector, and the remaining are in the small-scale industry. Today, India is the world's largest producer and exporter of handmade carpets in value and volume terms. Around 75% of carpets manufactured in India are exported (CEPC 2019). According to Mr Sanjay Kumar (CEPC executive director) (2019), Indian carpets are known worldwide for their excellent design, fascinating colours, and quality. "India's unique ability to adapt to any design, colour, quality and size as per the specifications of the carpet buyer has made it a household name in the international market".

The carpet export has shown positive growth from 1999–2000 to 2018–19, as shown in Figure 17.1. The 2008–09 and 2009–10 declined mainly due to the global recession (Sharma 2008; The Economic Times 2010). The data for the financial year 2019–20 is from March 2019 to November 2019. The United States and Germany are the two most prominent export destinations, accounting for 76% of the total export of carpet from India (CEPC 2019). The total global market size of both machine woven and handmade carpets and floor covering is about USD 35–40 billion per annum, and handmade rugs have a share of about USD 5 billion in them. India has a global market share

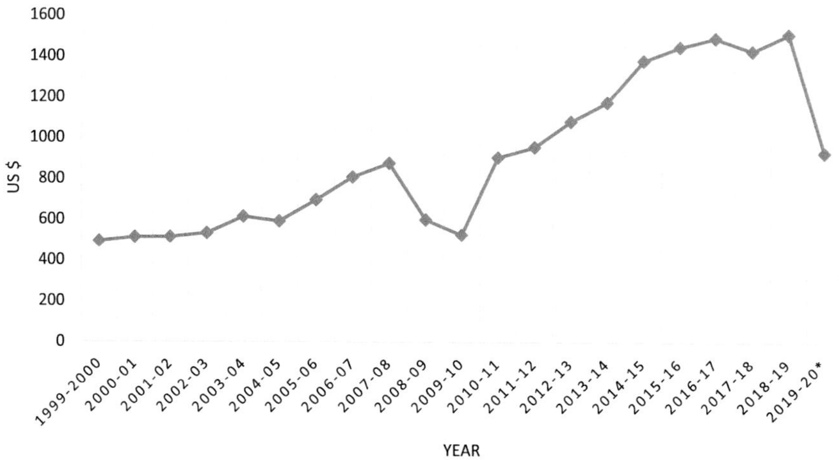

Figure 17.1 Annual export of carpet, rugs, druggets (including Namdhas) (in $ million)
Source: Based on data from Ministry of Textile (2020).

of approximately USD 1.6 billion, or about 35% in the handmade carpets and rugs category (CEPC 2019).

17.4 Policies and support for the handloom and handicraft sector in Uttar Pradesh

Since India's independence, the government has created several institutions, schemes, and welfare programmes for the handloom and handicraft crafts sector. Small towns and villages are the hubs of handloom and handicraft activities all over India. Most of the handloom and handicraft MSME's are based in Uttar Pradesh (CEPC). To promote the indigenous industries of handicrafts, processed foods, garments, and other traditional products manufactured by local, micro, small, and medium enterprises, MSME, Uttar Pradesh government has launched 'One District One Product' (ODOP) Scheme (ODOP 2019). ODOP is an initiative which is seen as a transformational step forward towards realising the true potential of a district, fuel economic growth and generate employment and rural entrepreneurship, taking us to the goal of Atma Nirbhar Bharat. Welcome page official website of ODOP (2019) mentioned that:

> The UP Government's One District-One Product Programme aims to encourage such indigenous and specialized products and crafts in UP that are found nowhere else – like the ancient and nutritious 'Kala Namak' rice, the rare and intriguing wheat-stalk craft, world-famous Chikankari and Zari-zardozi work on clothes, and the intricate and

stunning horn-bone work that uses the remains of dead animals rather than live ones, a nature-friendly replacement for ivory.

Under the ODOP Scheme, the State government of Uttar Pradesh has recognised every district for its indigenous and specialised products to provide encouragement, support, promote, and modernise the crafts and other specialised products to enhance their market reach (ODOP 2019). Now, ODOP has become the umbrella scheme in Uttar Pradesh for micro and small scale industries, under which previously existing schemes are clubbed.

There are several other schemes in operation for the promotion and development of the handicraft sector. The National Handicraft Development Programme (NHDP) implemented during 201–18 takes a holistic approach for promoting and developing the handicrafts sector under a single umbrella. Under the Ambedkar Hastshilp Vikas Yojna, the NHDP has several components like design and technology up-gradation, human resource development, direct benefit to artisans, infrastructure support, research and development, marketing and mobilisation of artisans. In India, carpet trade is managed by the Carpet Export Promotion Council (CEPC). CEPC focuses on providing benefits to carpet weavers and entrepreneurs, training, designing, health insurance, credit facility, international travel support, finding the buyer, and more.

Although, most artists/artisans and entrepreneurs do not get direct benefits due to the lack of the knowledge or formal document required to avail government programmes (Sindwani 2019). The other hurdles are poor implementation of policies, lack of inclusivity, and corruption in the process. On policy level, there has been no concerted and cohesive effort to address the challenges faced by the handloom and handicraft ecosystem, with most governmental offerings mired in bureaucracy and inefficiencies (Bissel 2013).

17.5 The carpet industry of Khairabad: an overview

Khairabad town is located about 80 km north of Lucknow (at National Highway 24), the capital city of state Uttar Pradesh. During the British period, it was under Oudh Province, and it was the centre for commerce and trade of agriculture produce and handmade cotton-based products (Nevill 1905). The town carpet making activity is a traditional skill performed mainly by the Muslim weaver community known as *Julahas or Ansaris.* Some other towns around Khairabad specialise in carpet making, which is *Laharpur* and *Biswan.* The carpets produced in Khairabad is both for selling in the domestic market and export.

Carpets from Khairabad are mainly cotton and woollen based, which are handwoven in pit loom. A pit loom is a traditional loom situated in the ground with a pit and peddles inside for weaving.[1] The carpet is handwoven, also known as flat weaved, different from tufted and knotted carpets/rugs. Khairabad carpet has a creative design and multiple combinations of colours which makes these carpets very aesthetic. It is said that skilled weavers observed the nature, things, and objects around them and created these designs and patterns of the carpet.

This process of innovations in methods and patterns continues. Carpets of Khairabad are exported to many Western countries through various channels. Due to a lack of information and technologies, most of the entrepreneurs from Khairabad are not directly engaged in the export of the carpets. Instead, carpets of Khairabad are bought by trades from Bhadohi, Agra, and Delhi and exported from there. Most commonly, contractors label Khairabad carpets as Bhadohi made carpets or Agra made carpets for the international buyers. And therefore, Khairabad lacks its name in the global market in this sector.

17.6 Production and growth of carpets in Khairabad

Khairabad industry is well known for its carpet production, and there is great potential for the growth of the carpet industry of Khairabad. There are around 50,000 pit-looms and more than 100,000 weavers in Khairabad (ODOP 2019). There are around 30 registered carpet manufacturing factories in Khairabad block, including 10 to 12 factories in Khairabad town. On the basis of field data estimate, in the year 2018–19, the average turnover of rugs factories in Khairabad town was approximately USD 80 million.

Quality manager of one of leading exporters of Khairabad block firm, David Massey, aged 29, says:

> Our firm is one of the leading exporters of carpet in Sitapur. We export to the USA, Germany and other European countries, Middle East and the UK. Our company's export volume is growing over the year. Our factory is located in a village, and we employ the whole village. Our focus is to provide jobs to women and youngsters, and our firm pays the highest wage compared to other firms in the district. Our factory has been engaged in carpet weaving activity for more than 25 years, and we have grown from a small firm to a registered exporter. Now we have two factories and three warehouses still our firm sublet the order to small contractors situated in rural areas of Khairabad.

However, significant weaving activity is local community-based and unorganised, not registered with government institutions and departments. Also, the demand-based production capacity of the registered factories is deficient since most of the factories have only 30 to 40 weavers.

Table 17.1 shows the estimated production of carpet in the Sitapur district. Since the production and export data is not available from government offices, the estimated data is taken from various sources including personal interviews of owners of factories and government officials. This estimated data is calculated based on the annual production of carpet in meters and the average selling

Table 17.1 Estimated production of carpet in Khairabad block and Sitapur district (including Khairabad) (in INR million)

Year	*Carpet production in Sitapur district*	*Carpet production in Khairabad block*
2015–16	3240	1660
2016–17	3296	1714
2017–18	3328	1740
2018–19	3400	1800
2019–20*	3000	1600
****AAGR%**	**1.62**	**2.74**
****CAGR%**	**1.21**	**2.04**

Source: Figure estimated by the author.

**Note 1:* Production data for the financial year 2019–20 is till January 2020

***Note 2:* For the calculation of Average Annual Growth Rate (AAGR) and Percentage Compound Annual Growth Rate (CAGR), Financial Year 2019–20 is not included since the whole financial year data is not available.

price of carpet per meter in the Sitapur district. Table 17.1 shows the last five years of carpet production data of Khairabad block, which ranges from 51.2% to 53.3% of the total carpet produced in the Sitapur district. Export of carpet from Khairabad block is around 90% of the total carpet produced in Khairabad block. Khairabad has excellent potential to increase the production and export of carpet in the national and international market and fulfil the existing carpet demand by increasing the production and supply of carpet. The carpet production in Khairabad has increased from INR 1660 million per annum in 2015–16 to about INR 1800 million in 2018–19. However, data of financial year 2019–20 is till month of January 2020.

The growth rate of the carpet industry over the last five years of Khairabad block and Sitapur (data including Khairabad block) show a dynamic pattern. The year 2019–20 is not included for the calculations since data of financial year 2019–20 is available till month of January 2020. The average annual growth rate (AAGR) of the production of carpets of Sitapur district has a positive trend of 1.62%. On the contrary, AAGR of Khairabad Block is 2.74%, which is higher than Sitapur district. Similarly, Compound Annual Growth Rate (CAGR) of Sitapur district is 1.21% and CAGR of Khairabad block is 2.04%.

17.7 Production relations and use of digital technologies

Historically, the weaver community of Khairabad started making carpets with cotton fabric and clothes in the pit looms from the time of Mughals in India. Khairabad was an important trading centre for exporting rugs, bathmat, and durries, in India and abroad (ODOP 2019). Most of the weaving work was traditionally done by the Ansaris, who are Muslim weaver community. Members of the Ansari community performed weaving activities from their house, setting up one or two pit looms. Over time, as demand for Khairabad carpets increased, few members of the Ansari community started their factories and became entrepreneurs and producers. These entrepreneurs receive production orders from big traders (most of the time) who are situated at Bhadohi (Uttar Pradesh), Surat (Gujarat), Delhi, and Jaipur (Rajasthan). These traders send the design and yarn to entrepreneurs to manufacture carpets. Most of the time, orders are large in quantity and entrepreneurs of Khairabad do not have large scale production capacity in their factories. In such a case, entrepreneurs sublet the work to contractors in rural areas of Khairabad, where work is done at the household level since there is an abundance of weavers.

Regarding the production order, one of the entrepreneurs, Shafeek Ahmad Ansari, aged 35, says:

> Carpet manufacturing is a family business. We have been doing this since the 1990s. Export was started by my uncle, Haji Jaleesh Ansari, in the year 2000. Khairabad carpet industry has excellent export potential, but we do not get government support and benefits. This situation leads us to export via contractors. We ship via and with the help of big traders who are situated in Jaipur, Delhi, and Gujarat. Sometimes we get big export orders from these traders as well with specific designs. Our production capacity is small, so we sublet the production work to house-based weavers in Khairabad and nearby villages.

The weavers who do not get any job have become daily wage labourers and agricultural labourers for their livelihoods. Weavers from rural areas do not have any bargaining power, and they are paid less than weavers from Khairabad town.

In Khairabad block there are seven entrepreneurs who are listed as exported under the government. It is interesting to see that for the past couple of years few of these entrepreneurs are using internet and social media plat forms for direct export and to eliminate the contractors (middle-man) from the exporting process. Earlier these exporters were dependent over contractors for purchase orders, design, raw material and samples. Also, these contractors use to take a significant part of the profit margin earned by the big entrepreneurs of Khairabad. Now, most of the designs and patterns have been sent by the international buying houses and traders via WhatsApp, Facebook, and other social media platforms. With the advent of social media and cheap internet facilities in India, international buying houses and traders send a carpet sample in image or pdf format which is to be produced. The weavers observe the designs of the online sent samples and create the design of the carpets for sample. Also, entrepreneurs of Khairabad town and skilled weavers do develop new designs and patterns with different types of materials. Now, these big entrepreneurs create new designs with the help of weavers and show it online to the international buyer. Hence, exchanging the new innovative carpet design sample has become a two-way process, where entrepreneurs also have liberty to create new designs and patterns and send it back to international buyer. This saves months of time for the buyer and entrepreneurs and production cycle is moving faster compared to earlier. Use of social media can bring higher volume production for Khairabad carpet industry.

The ability to adapt to any design, colour, quality, and size as per the carpet buyer's specifications makes it a household name in the international market (Hindustan Times 2019). This creativity of highly skilled weavers creates an opportunity for the entrepreneur to present the work in the local exhibitions visited by national and international buyers.

Most entrepreneurs and producers are not adequately educated to understand the benefits of registering the enterprise, which will allow them to avail the existing schemes. The registration process is complex and corruption in the process makes it difficult for petty entrepreneurs of Khairabad to register their enterprise under the government institution. On the contrary, the production is community and family based where informal setup is made for production. Most commonly these informal set constitute 10 to 20 pit looms in nearby area of Khairabad town and villages in Khairabad; where one person owns the land, another person has built the structure, the third person has taken the electricity connection, and all of them have arranged small amount of working capital. Although, for government all these things should belong to one person for registration. Most enterprises do not fulfil the norms given for registering factories, as some of them even do not have toilets or drinking water facilities.

This situation of informality in Khairabad carpet industry creates a dependency of petty entrepreneurs to get work from contractors and big entrepreneurs.

17.8 Factors of production and locational constraints

In traditional Indian societal structure, the caste, class, religious, and gender structures also determine the access to land, capital, raw material, production technologies, education, and market. Entrepreneurship and self-employment may signify an important aspect in this relation; the entrepreneurs have access and ownership over the physical factors of production like land and machinery. However, they have to depend on the labour of others (Massey 1995).

For entrepreneurs, specialised and technically trained workers can be an essential factor for spatial positioning or clustering in a specific region. However, the availability of cheap labour may also lead to the same. In both cases, the implication is that, since entrepreneurs depend on the work of others, it may determine their location choices for production. This labour dependency is an essential factor leading to the location of the carpet industry in and around Khairabad. Access to raw materials and capital is also a necessary factor in this structure. Access to raw material and capital becomes more relevant because in India caste, class, religion, and gender dictate access to land and capital. Entrepreneurs with traditional ownership over land and capital (mostly higher castes) may be better able to invest in production. Thus, even though they are dependent on cheap labour, the abundant labour supply in most rural areas would mean more bargaining power for the entrepreneurs. This bargaining power of entrepreneur increases in the regions where there is abundance of unskilled labour work. Unskilled labour is mostly the agricultural labourers who are employed during cropping season (for three to four months in a year) or under-employed. Entrepreneurs with second- or third-generation ownership over land and financial resources have perpetuated this structure further. They have spent substantial time accumulating the physical means of production on the one hand and creating a niche in the market on the other hand. The latter includes the social networks built with contractors, mediators, and cheap labourers. All these factors cumulatively impact locational decisions. Also, a particular section of the society has some level of monopoly over carpet production in Khairabad.

There is another category of entrepreneurs who do not have most of the resources compared to the entrepreneurs who have land, machinery, and capital for big-scale production. These are petty entrepreneurs of Khairabad who are small-scale producers who produce mainly for domestic buyers or contractors; these buyers and contractors sell their produce to the domestic and international markets and earn a significant profit. Petty entrepreneurs and small carpet producers are dependent on buyers and contractors to give carpet manufacturing orders with shape, size, colour, and design with raw material and some advance payment for the production process. This process creates a dependency on entrepreneurs and producers of carpet manufacturers of Khairabad over these buyers and (or) contractors. Also, this process of demand and supply hampers the creativity of the local weavers who abide to follow the instructions given by buyers and contractors. This dependency arises because of the unavailability of working capital to pay the day-to-day expenses and wages. A petty entrepreneur can design new carpets, but they do not have the working capital to run the factory.

However, these petty entrepreneurs also have social networks in villages, where another contractor has some land in the nearby village and a few looms. The abundance of labour-power in this area and the informal nature of work helps these contractors exploit the labour-power of the weavers. There are many contractors on which weavers of one to five villages have a dependency on their employment. These contractors are primarily direct or distant relatives, kins, or friends of entrepreneurs. Contractors get support and material (working capital and raw material) for production from entrepreneurs. So, these social networks also help create an economic network with reliability in the production process. Also, these networks provide a safety net between petty entrepreneurs and contractors, solving the problem of cash crunch and delayed payment in this kind of production process. In this type of production chain, small producers also become contractors or mediators who work for contractors or big producers in Bhadohi, Agra, Delhi, or Jaipur.

There are credit schemes available like ODOP, Mudra Loan Scheme, MSME Export promotion department schemes, etc., for the entrepreneurs and producers of carpet. Still, due to the informal nature of the enterprises, most entrepreneurs and producers cannot avail of loans and credit from the bank. To avail the benefit given by the government agencies, an enterprise needs to register with the government formally. Hence, the informal nature of the enterprise is one the leading causes of the inability to avail the credit facility by the entrepreneurs and producers of the carpet industry in Khairabad.

The primary raw material used for the handwoven carpet of Khairabad is cotton, which mostly comes from Panipat, wool from Jaipur, and jute, which is imported from Bangladesh. Wool, cotton, and mixed fabric (wool and cotton) are mainly used for export quality carpet making. The raw material cost varies from INR 40 to INR 400 per kilogram depending on the quality and type of raw material, excluding the price of dye. Registered factories of Khairabad buy raw materials directly from the market based on their production scale. On the contrary, petty producers and entrepreneurs get the raw material, shape, size, and design from contractors situated at different places. Khairabad does not have any depot for raw material storage to enable local producers and entrepreneurs' ready access. The raw material available in the local market is of cheap quality. It sells at a high rate, which gives a low-profit margin compared to the ordered work they get from contractors situated outside. However, the state government has approved a scheme for the raw material bank, design and sampling, selling, and exhibition of INR 22.50 million for the district (ODOP 2019).

Preparing raw material for carpet weaving goes through different stages: spinning the yarn, dyeing the yarn, opening, or reeling. The spinning of yarn starts with carding, which is the cleaning process of cotton or wool by hand. After carding, cotton or wool goes for spinning on traditional Charkha (spinning wheel), and the yarn is prepared. Prepared yarn is wrapped in big and loose lea, which goes for dyeing. After dyeing, yarn is kept for drying, and then dried yarn is tightly wrapped on a small piece of wood called reeling. Reels are used for final weaving on the pit loom by the weavers. Carding, dyeing, drying, and spinning at informal setup (by petty producers) is mainly done by the women and children within families. Petty producers do not hire anyone for carding, dyeing, drying, and reeling to minimise the cost of production and maximise profit margins. So, women and children of petty producer's families have to deal with the double burden, i.e. women have to do domestic work along with this work, and children compromise their education and playtime for carding, dyeing, drying, and reeling activity for which they are not paid.

There are 100,000 carpet weavers in the Sitapur district, and Khairabad hosts around half the carpet weavers (ODOP 2019). A weaver starts carpet weaving at the age of 16 and retires at sixty-five in Khairabad. Due to the informal nature of the industry, the majority of the weavers are not directly employed in any factory, and they get work based on demand. Most weaving is done at the household level, and there is no formal contract between employer and employee. This informality leads to no bargaining power for the artisans, and they get minimum wages for their work. A weaver is paid based on the size of the carpet or at per square feet or square meter carpet woven by them. Generally, the prices are as low as Rs 10 per square meter. Rs. 10 to Rs. 15 per meter square is paid for simple design, and if the design is intricate, then Rs. 35 to Rs. 40 per square meter is paid to the weaver. On average, a weaver earns Rs. 80 (Approx. Euro 1 per day) to Rs. 100 per day (Approx. 1.25 Euro per day at the current exchange rate). A weaver's work depends on the work order or demand. They often have employment for 2–3 days a week, and on other occasions, when demand is higher, they work all seven days a week. Weavers are not paid for their holiday since they work on informal contracts and piece basis.

A weaver who works in bigger units gets one day off in a week. Still, all the weavers cannot take off on the same day; they have to mutually decide the different days in a week to take off among themselves to maintain the appropriate workforce inside the factory. However, when there is more work, no off is given in that week. Just an hour off is given before lunchtime for the prayer since most of the weavers are Muslim. Weavers who work in factories get fixed wages monthly. In some factories, one day off in a week is included in weaver's wages, and if they are working without any weekly off for a holiday, they are paid 1.5 times or double their average daily wage.

Since there is no formal contract between the entrepreneur and weavers, there is no negotiation or bargain between weavers and entrepreneurs. Weavers work 10 hours a day in the factory and earn from Rs. 10,000 (approx. Euro 125 per month) per month to Rs. 12,000 per month (Euro 150 per month). A worker gets an hour for the lunch break and two tea breaks of 15 minutes each day.

The weaver working on piece basis from their homes, build more than one pit loom, the cost of building a pair of pit loom is about Rs. 15,000 to Rs. 20,000. In some cases, weavers do not have the capital to build the structure, so they borrow money from local lenders who charge a high-interest rate from 30% to 60%. This loan makes their life very difficult. They work hard with their family to repay the loan. Most weavers live in semi-pucca houses in their joint families.

In the Sitapur district, there are only seven registered exporters of carpet, and ten thousand people are employed in the carpet industry of Sitapur (ODOP 2019). Former chairman of Khairabad, Ateek Ahmad Ansari, said that the total export of carpet from Khairabad is around INR 100 crore in a year.[2]

Big and petty entrepreneurs of Sitapur and weavers and other workers related to the carpet industry of Khairabad are facing infrastructure challenges, lack of proper business knowledge, and unavailability of the market for the purchase of good quality raw material and selling their produce. The towns lack roads, railways, and warehouses to store the finished carpets and depot for raw material. One of the constraints for producers is the unavailability of a market for local producers. Handmade carpets are costly, which have less demand in the local market. Also, machine-made carpets which are cheaper than handmade carpets have shrunk the market share of the handmade carpets further. However, handmade carpets have demand and specific buyers in the national and international market to which they do not have adequate access.

To match the demand and supply of handmade carpets, entrepreneurs and petty entrepreneurs of Khairabad are using social media platforms. Now, buyers from domestic and international ask frequently for a new design, colour, and pattern developed using computer designing software. These designs are sent immediately via email or other social media platforms to the entrepreneurs. Entrepreneurs share these designs with weavers personally or via WhatsApp, Facebook, and Instagram and weaver of Khairabad use their creativity and skills to weave samples. These samples were again sent to buyers for the confirmation of the final weaving order. The introduction of social media platforms saves time, and details of order and type of products are completed within about four days. Earlier, the same procedure was done in 20 to 30 days, so social media is helpful for both entrepreneurs and buyers. Cheap internet and multimedia mobile phones have increased the access to social media platforms by entrepreneurs and weavers.

17.9 Conclusions

India is a culturally diverse country. The same is reflected in its arts and crafts as well. The handicraft industry in India is primarily known for its unique and traditional quality. Carpet weaving has a long history among the craft sector, flourishing from the 16th century onwards. Khairabad town hosts the conventional carpet weaving community or the Ansaris. Carpets of Khairabad are exported to many Western countries through various channels, and it is pretty popular as well. However, most of the carpets of Khairabad are shipped from Bhadohi, Agra, and Delhi because the entrepreneurs of Khairabad lack the education, networks, size of capital, and international business networks.

Today, India is the world's largest producer and exporter of handmade carpets and about 75% of carpets manufactured in India are exported. The carpet industry in India is primarily labour intensive. The factors of production and the resulting locational issues act as constraints to this industry. In traditional Indian societal structures, the caste and class structures also determine the access and availability of factors of production. Further, social networks built with contractors, mediators, and cheap labourers cumulatively impact the locational decisions.

There is also the group of '*petty entrepreneurs*', or small producers with limited access to resources. They produce primarily for domestic buyers and contractors. They are dependent on the contractors for orders which often affects the creativity of the artisans.

Since the work is unorganised, there is no contract between employers and artisans, which leads to exploitative working conditions and long work hours. Most entrepreneurs and producers are not adequately educated to understand the benefits of registering the enterprise, which will allow them to avail the existing government schemes. Moreover, the complexity and bureaucratic nature of the registration process makes it difficult for entrepreneurs to opt for formal registration.

The situation is mostly worse for women and children. Women and Children in their homes mostly do the task of dyeing, drying, and reeling. The unpaid work by women and children reduces the cost of production for the entrepreneurs. But this is counterproductive for the women and kids because they have to compromise on other productive activities like education. Their work thus goes almost unpaid. The use of social media and technology has aided artisans. Designs and patterns are now shared via social media. It is the skill of the artisans that only by looking at pictures they can replicate intricate designs.

Notes

1 Pit loom, stand loom, and frame loom are three kinds of looms predominantly used by handloom weavers. The pit loom is a loom situated on the ground / floor with a pit having two peddles set in the pit for the weaver to operate. Pit loom weaving is considered to be better weaving as the fabric woven retains the character of the fiber and fabric due to the proximity of the loom to the ground. The ground absorbs the tension and speed and makes the fabric more breathable (www.dacottonhandlooms.in/).

2 Ateek Ahmad Ansari is a former elected chairperson of Khairabad, and he is one of the seven carpet exporters of Sitapur district. He made this statement in a discussion in 2016.

References

Agamuthu, P., and Fauziah, S. H. (2016). Waste management and the circular economy in Asia. Available at: www.switch-asia.eu/site/assets/files/1208/switch-asia_briefing_no6_-_waste_management_-_screen_final.pdf (last accessed on 25 March 2022).

Bissel, W. (2013). Crafting a livelihood-building sustainability for Indian artisans. Available at: www.dasra.org/assets/uploads/resources/Crafting a Livelihood – Building Sustainability for Indian Artisans.pdf (accessed on 3 December 2021).

Carpet Export Promotion Council (2019). Available at: http://cepc.co.in/handmade-carpets (last accessed on 25 March 2022).

Chatterjee, A. K., (2018). How India fuelled slavery with the export of cotton. *The Hindu*. New Delhi. Available at: www.thehindu.com/society/how-india-procured-slavery-with-the-export-of-cotton/article25751881.ece (last accessed on 25 March 2022).

Das, N. B., Sharma, R. K., Pandey, A., and Narayanan, B. G. (2018). The existence of carpet industry in Bhadohi, India. *Trends in Textile Engineering & Fashion Technology*, 3, 323–332.

The Economic Times (2010). Carpet export slips 12 % in 2009–10. *The Economic Times*. Available at: https://economictimes.indiatimes.com/news/economy/foreign-trade/carpet-export-slips-12-in-2009-10/articleshow/5902789.cms?from=mdr (last accessed on 25 March 2022).

Evans, S. (2005). Creative clusters. *Urban Design Thinking*, 1–5. https://doi.org/10.5040/9781474228503.ch-028

Guha, S. (1989). The handloom industry of Central India: 1825–1950. *The Indian Economic & Social History Review*, 26(3), 297–318.

Harnetty, P. (1971). Cotton exports and Indian agriculture, 1861–1870. *The Economic History Review*, 24(3), 414–429.

Hindustan Times (2019). 38th India Carpet Expo-400 importers from 50 countries in Varanasi from today. *Hindustan Times, New Delhi*, 1–3. Available at: www.hindustantimes.com/varanasi/38th-india-carpet-expo-400-importers-from-50-countries-in-varanasi-from-today/story-szYAuGARbUGxrsCwdOcroJ.html (last accessed on 25 March 2022).

Indian Brand Equity Foundation (2021). Carpet industry and export destination. Available at: www.ibef.org/exports/carpet-industry-in-india.aspx (last accessed on 25 March 2022).

Logan, F. A. (1965). India's loss of the British cotton market after 1865. *The Journal of Southern History*, 31(1), 40–50.

Massey, D. (1995). *Spatial divisions of labour: Social structures and the geography of production.* London: Macmillan International Higher Education.

Ministry of Textile (2020). Fourth All India Handloom Census 2019–20. Office of the Development Commissioner for Handlooms, Government of India, New Delhi.

Mitra, A., Panja, A., and Prasad, R. (2018). The market for handicrafts. *Business Economics.* Available at: http://businesseconomics.in/market-handicrafts (last accessed on 25 March 2022).

Nanda, I. (1974). Asia: Imperialism and revolution in South Asia. *India Quarterly*, 30(1), 77–79.

Nevill, H. R. (1905). Sitapur: A gazetteer being volume XI of the district gazetteers of the United Provinces of Agra and Oudh. Available at: http://cslrepository.nvli.in/handle/123456789/2926 (last accessed on 25 March 2022).

ODOP (One District One Product) (2019). *Entrepreneurs*, Sitapur. Available at: http://odopup.in/en/article/sitapur (last accessed on 25 March 2022).

Reddy, D. N., and Sarap, K. (2017). *Rural labour mobility in times of structural transformation.* Singapore: Palgrave Macmillan.

Shaban, A., and Vermeylen, F. (2015). Trade in the creative sector: Comparing India with China, Brazil, and the UK. *Economic and Political Weekly*, 50(20), 68–75.

Shafi, M., Sarker, M. N. I., and Junrong, L. (2019). Social network of small creative firms and its effects on innovation in developing countries. *SAGE Open*, 9(4). https://doi.org/10.1177/2158244019898248

Sharma, R. (2008). Exports decline in October, to miss target for 2008–09. *Livemint*, 1–14. Available at: www.livemint.com/Politics/PqSEVJy6mQcuXtYSyx8OkM/Exports-decline-in-October-to-miss-target-for-200809.html (last accessed on 25 March 2022).

Sindwani, P. (2019). India's carpet industry which employs 2 million people and exports $ 1.8 billion every year has stagnated in the last five years. *Business Insider India.* Available at: www.businessinsider.in/policy/economy/news/indias-carpet-industry-which-employs-2-million-people-and-exports-1-8-billion-every-year-has-stagnated-in-the-last-five-years/articleshow/71550028.cms (last accessed on 25 March 2022).

The Times of India (2007, 16 May). Marx and 1857. Available at: https://timesofindia.indiatimes.com/edit-page/Marx-and1857/articleshow/2050352.cms (last accessed on 25 March 2022).

Vats, N. (2014). Indian handicrafts and globalization: A review. *IOSR Journal of Humanities and Social Science*, 19(1), 40–43.

Walker, D. S. (1997). *Flowers Underfoot: Indian Carpets of the Mughal era*. Metropolitan Museum of Art. Available at: www.metmuseum.org/art/metpublications/Flowers_Underfoot_Indian_Carpets_of_the_Mughal_Era

INDEX

For Product Safety Concerns and Information please contact our EU representative GPSR@taylorandfrancis.com Taylor & Francis Verlag GmbH, Kaufingerstraße 24, 80331 München, Germany